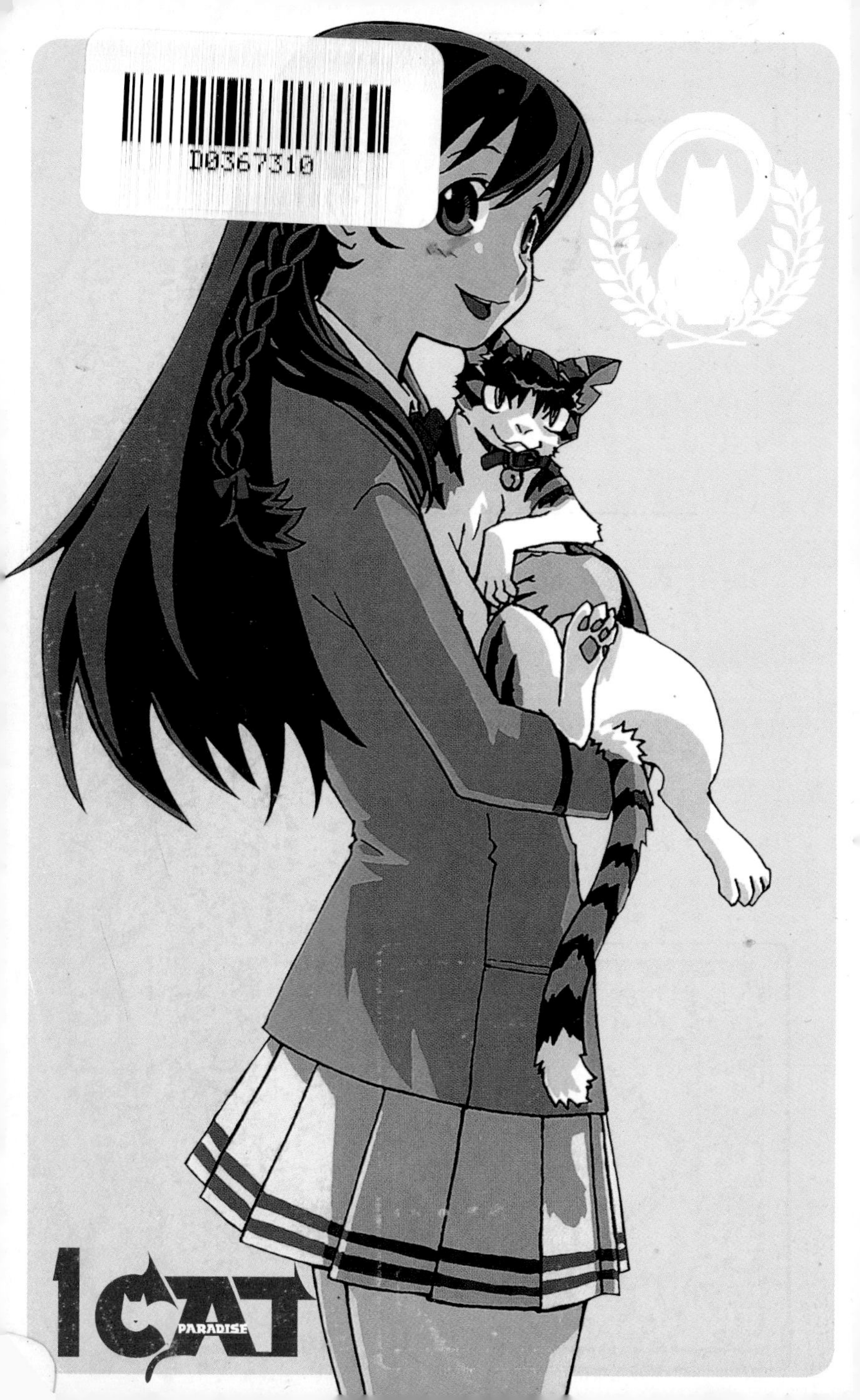
1
CAT
PARADISE

YUJI IWAHARA
CAT PARADISE

1

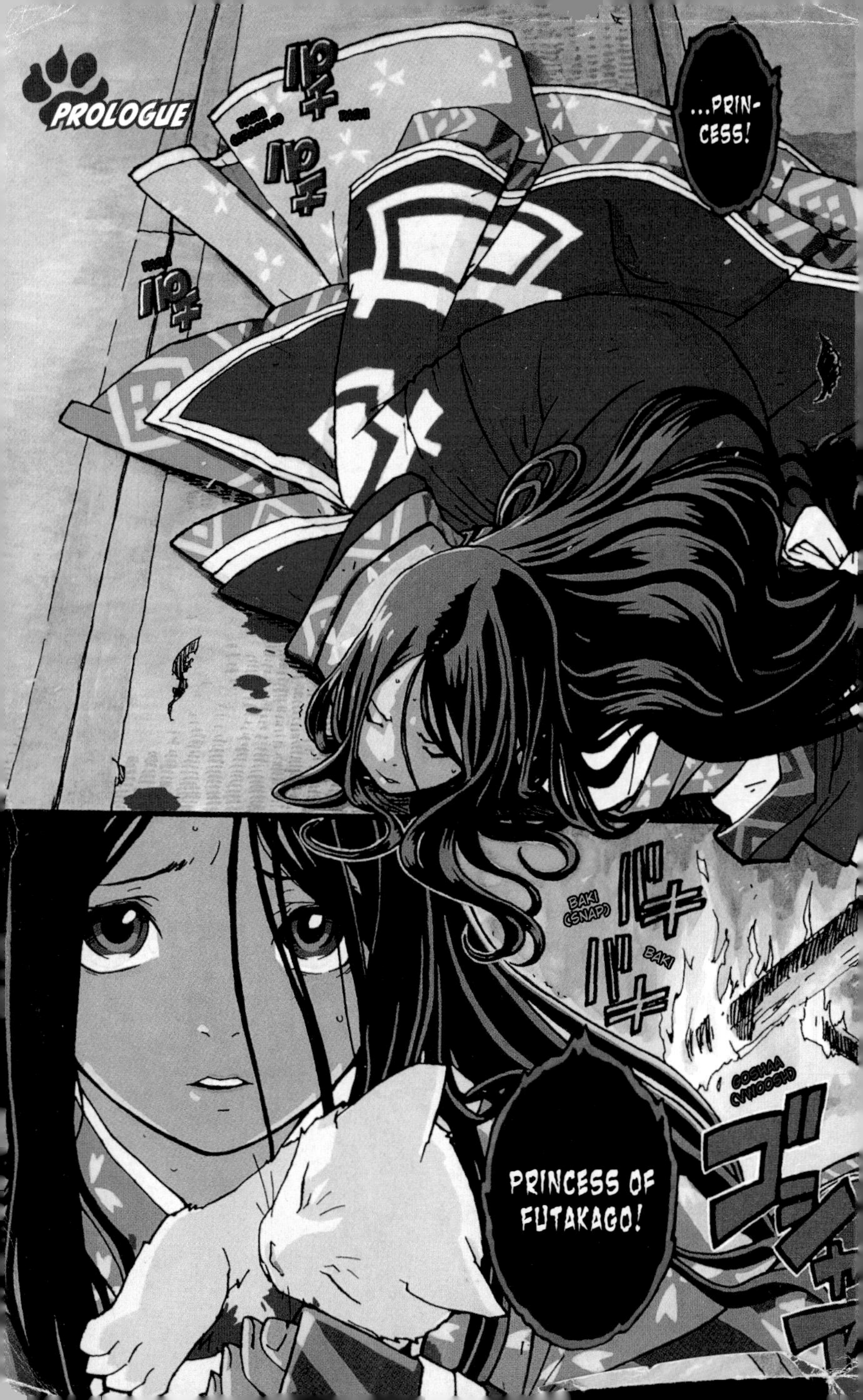
PROLOGUE
...PRIN-CESS!
BAKI (SNAP)
BAKI
GOSHAA (WHOOSH)
PRINCESS OF FUTAKAGO!

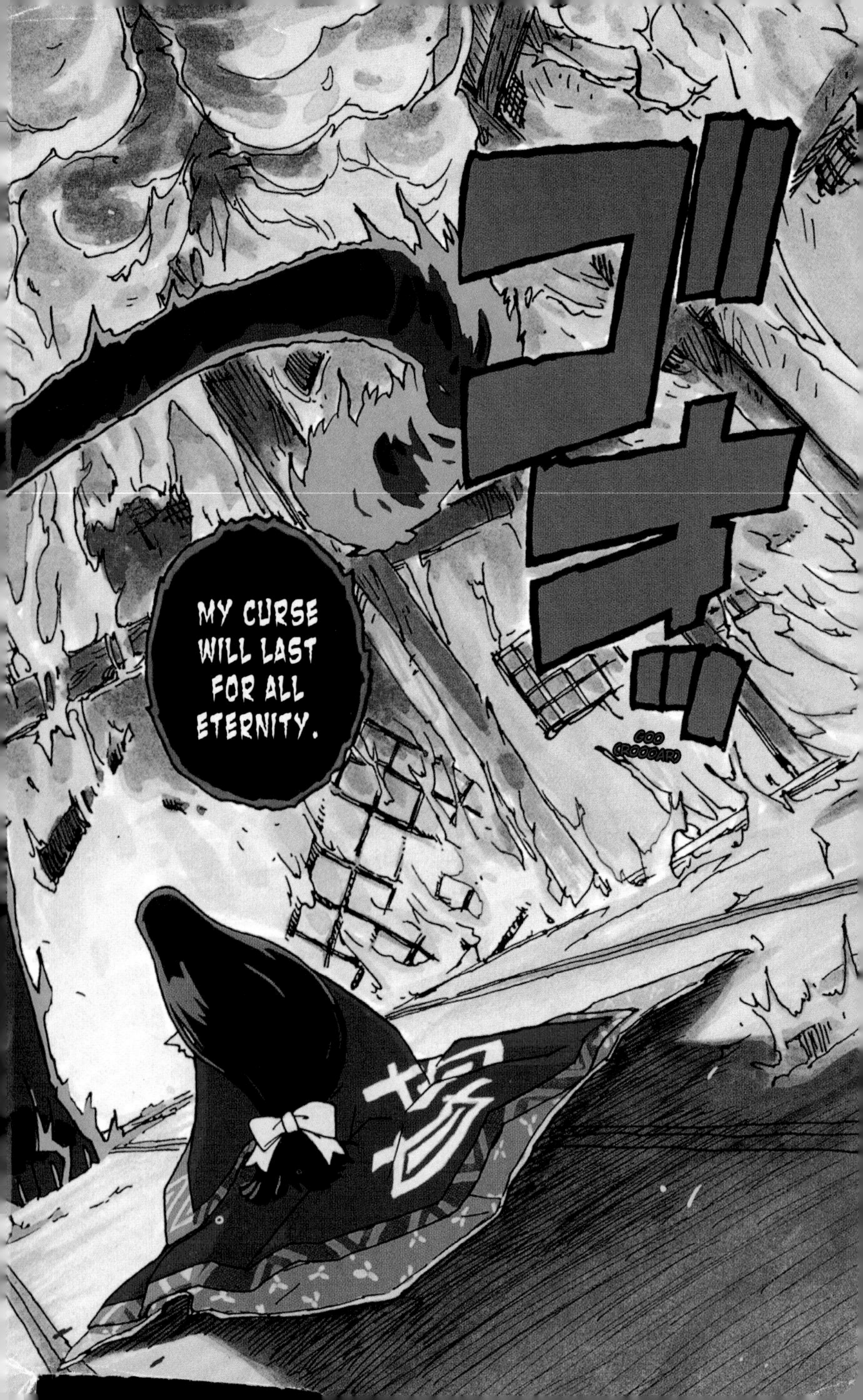
GOO (ROOOAR)
MY CURSE WILL LAST FOR ALL ETERNITY.

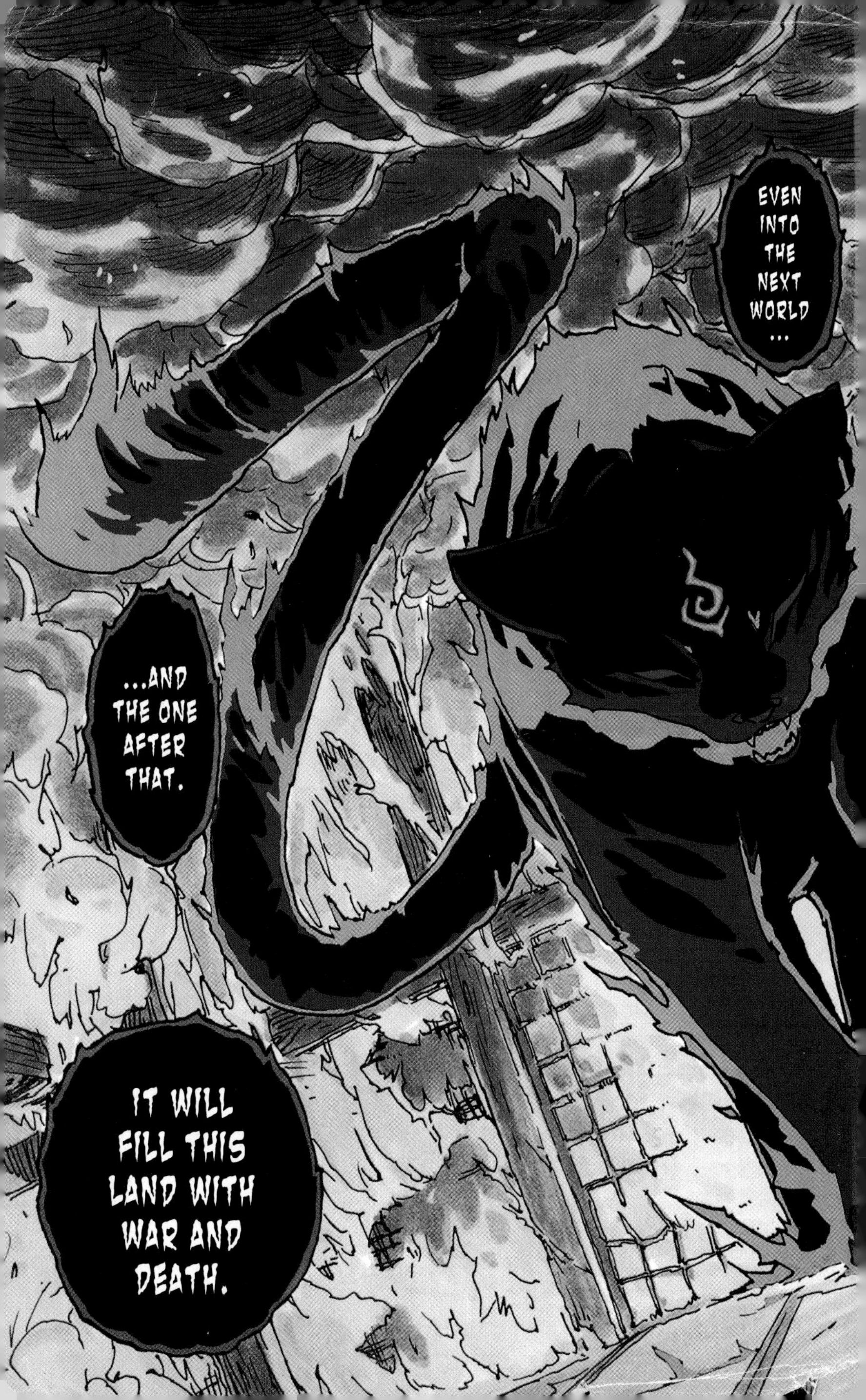
EVEN INTO THE NEXT WORLD...
...AND THE ONE AFTER THAT.
IT WILL FILL THIS LAND WITH WAR AND DEATH.

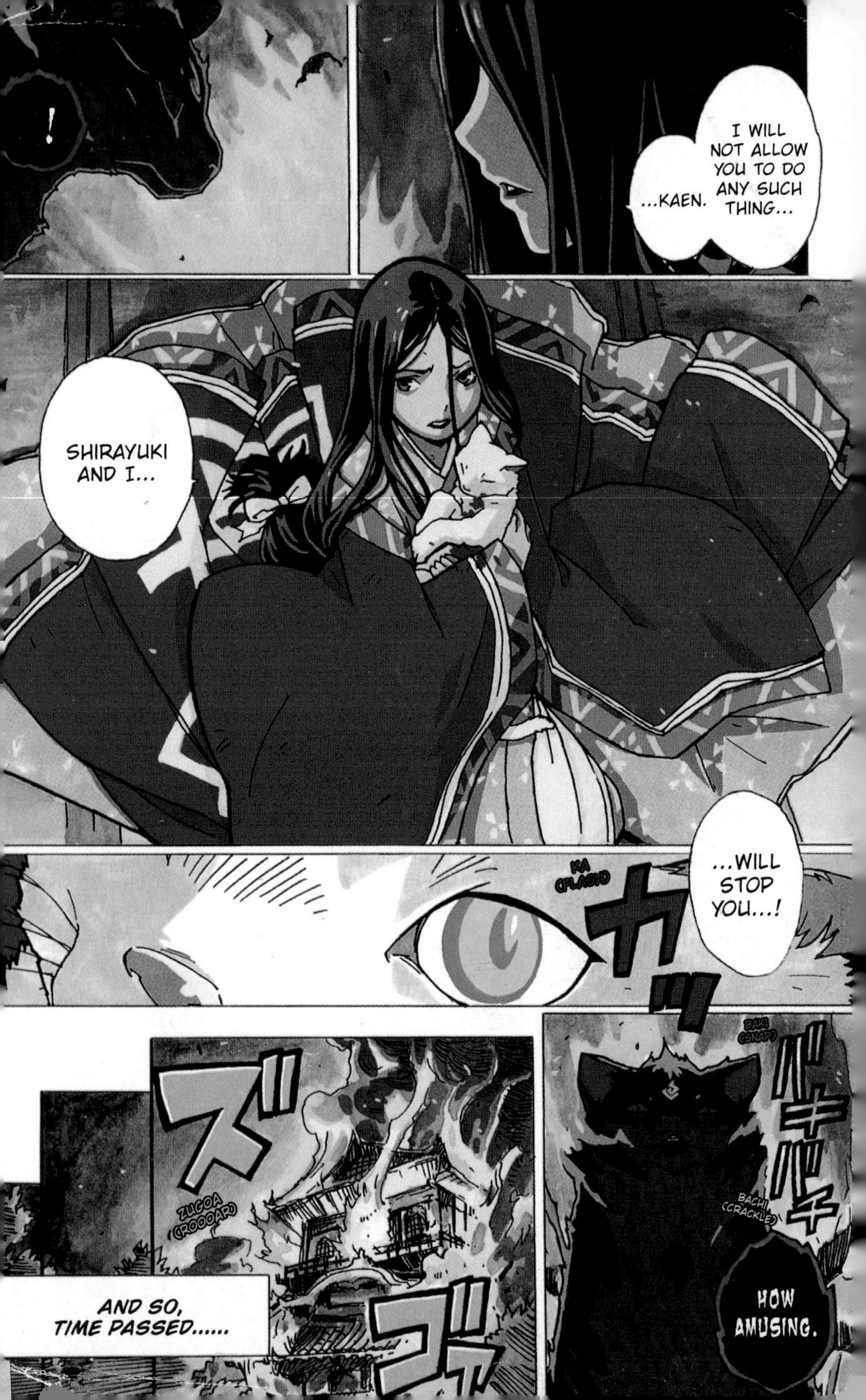
I WILL NOT ALLOW YOU TO DO ANY SUCH THING...
...KAEN.
!
SHIRAYUKI AND I...
...WILL STOP YOU...!
KA (FLASH)
BAKI (SNAP)
BACHI (CRACKLE)
HOW AMUSING.
ZUGOA (ROOOAR)
AND SO, TIME PASSED......

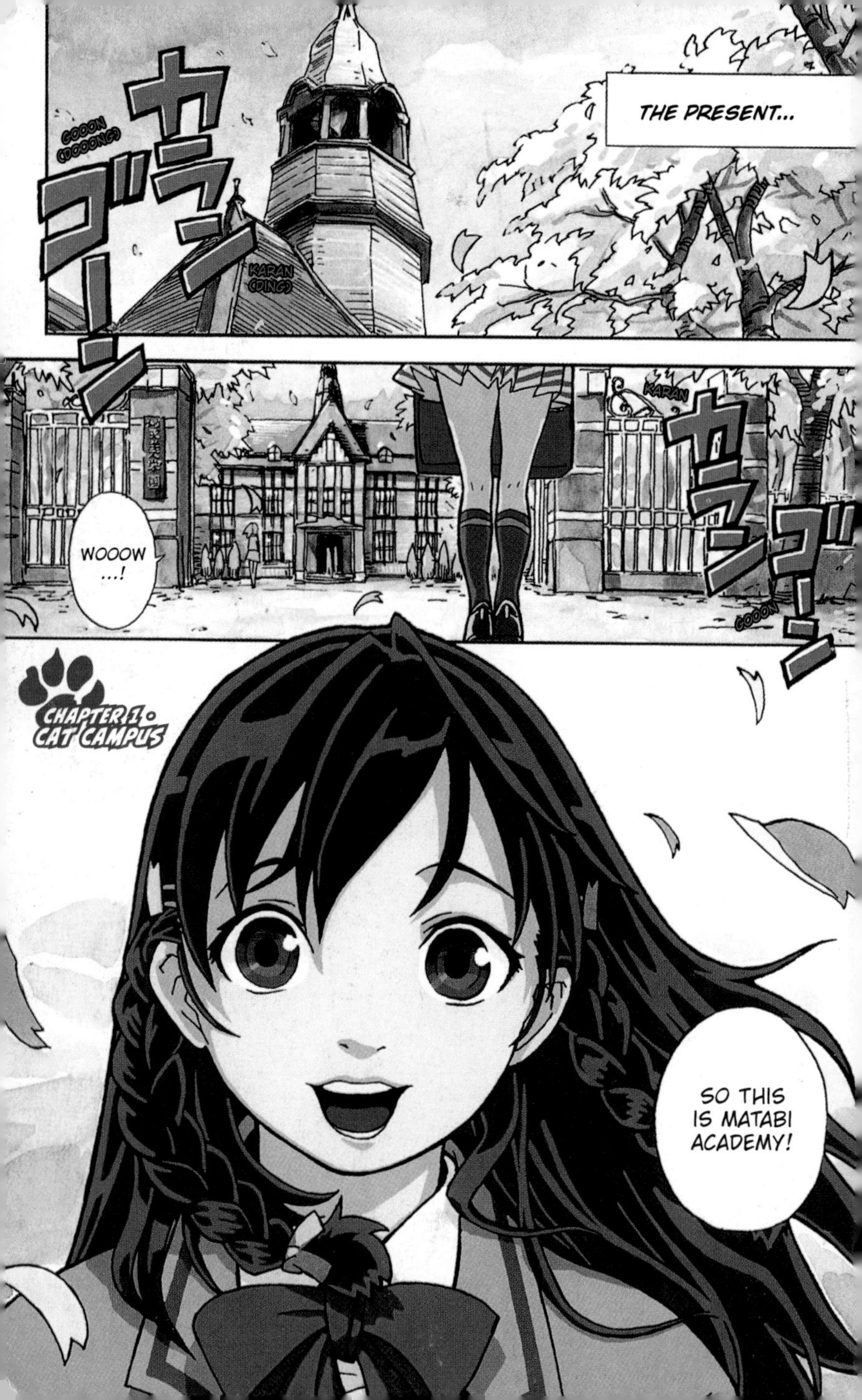
THE PRESENT...
KARAN (DING)
GOOON (DOOONG)
KARAN
GOOON
WOOOW ...!
CHAPTER 1. CAT CAMPUS
SO THIS IS MATABI ACADEMY!

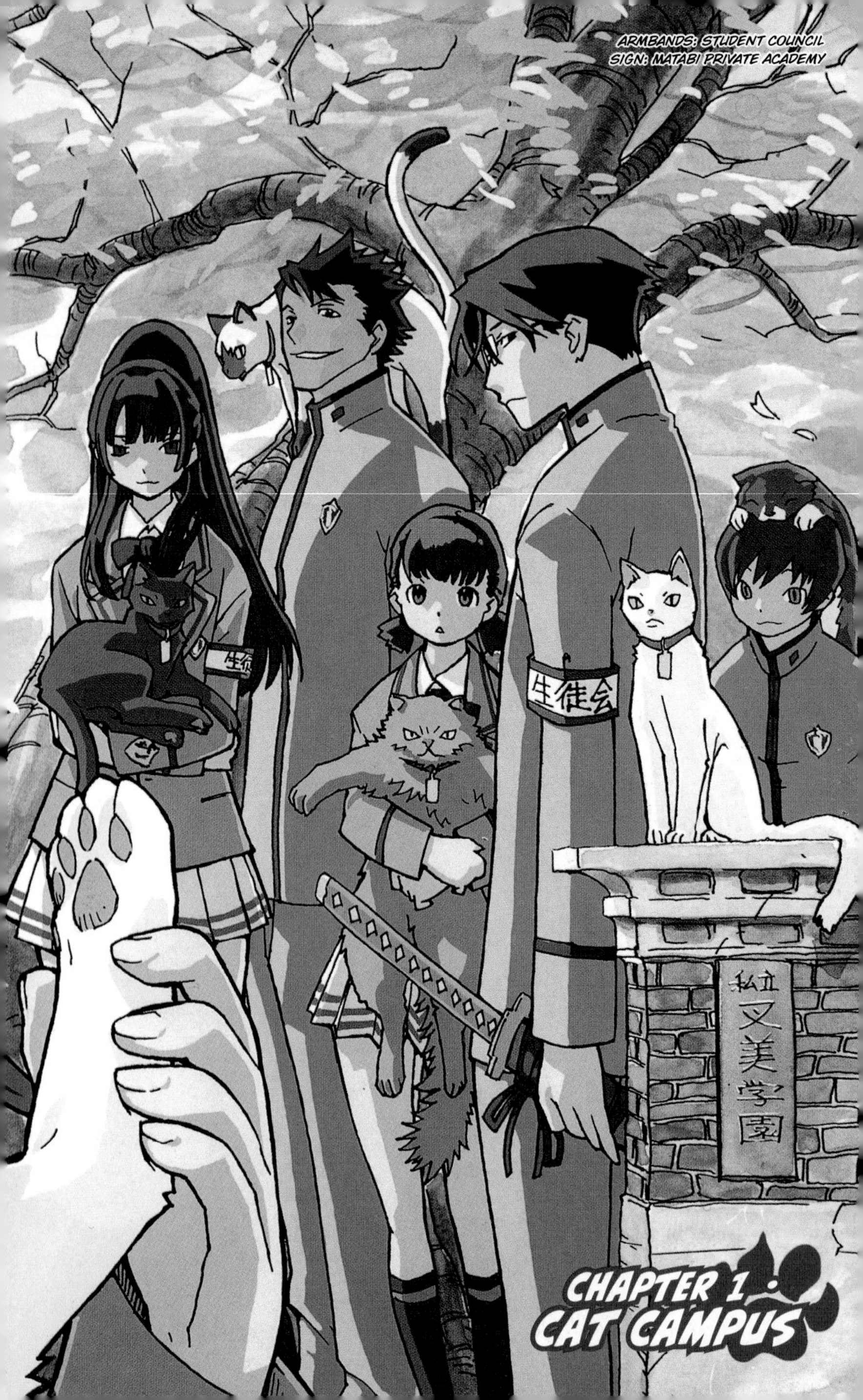
ARMBANDS: STUDENT COUNCIL
SIGN: MATABI PRIVATE ACADEMY
生徒会
私立
又美学園
CHAPTER 1 · CAT CAMPUS

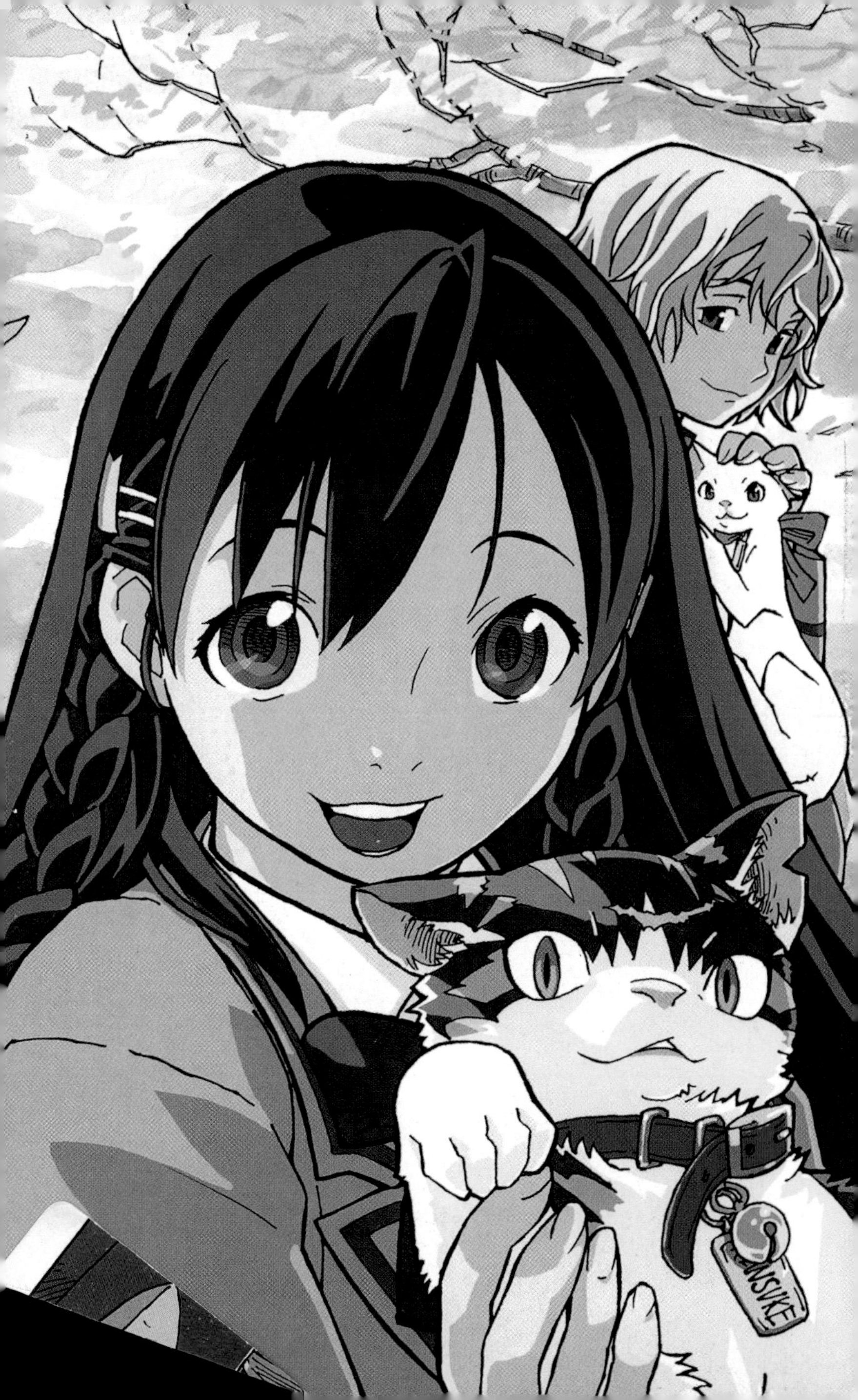

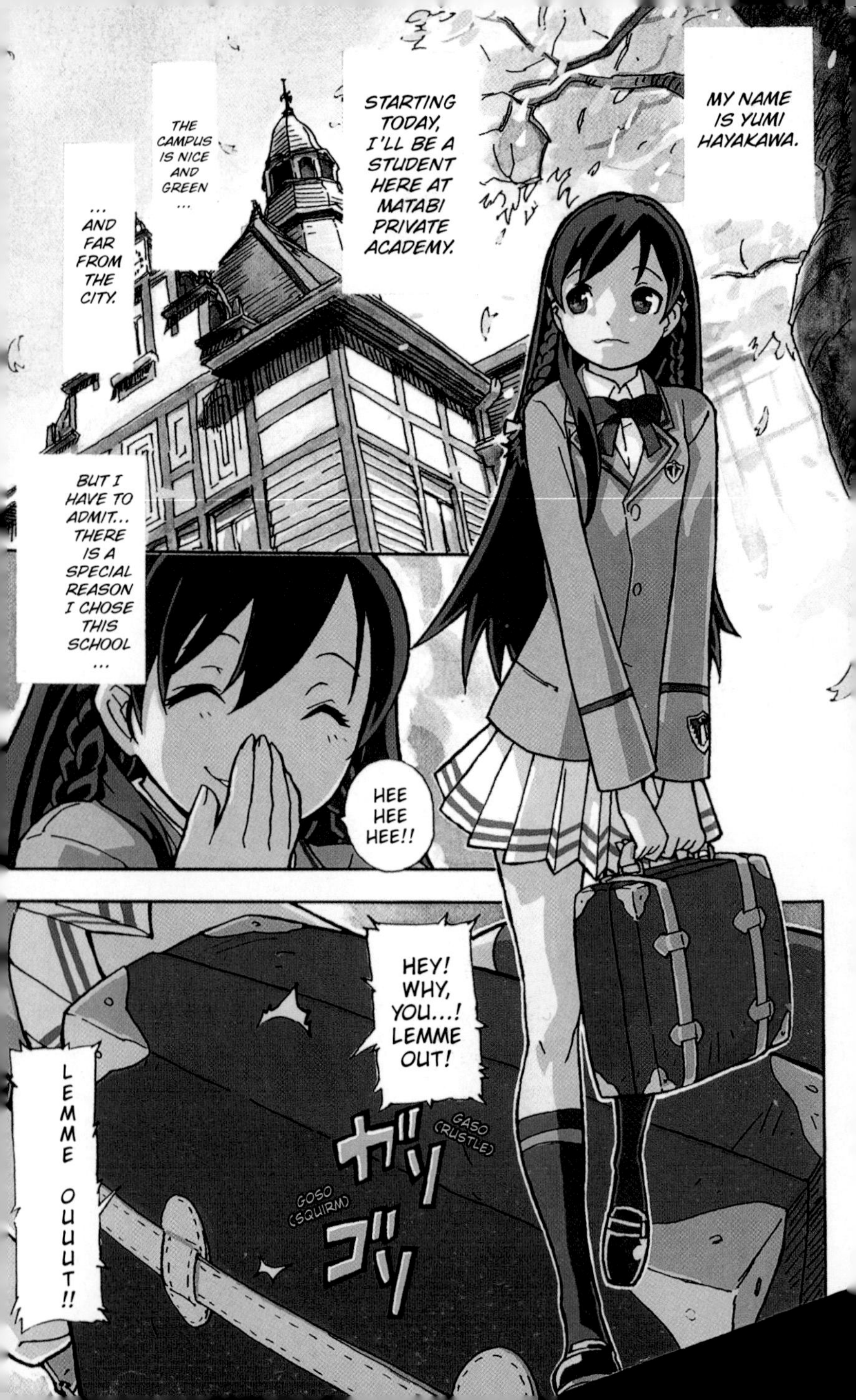
MY NAME IS YUMI HAYAKAWA.
STARTING TODAY, I'LL BE A STUDENT HERE AT MATABI PRIVATE ACADEMY.
THE CAMPUS IS NICE AND GREEN...
...AND FAR FROM THE CITY.
BUT I HAVE TO ADMIT... THERE IS A SPECIAL REASON I CHOSE THIS SCHOOL...
HEE HEE HEE!!
HEY! WHY, YOU...! LEMME OUT!
GASO (RUSTLE)
GOSO (SQUIRM)
LEMME OUUUT!!

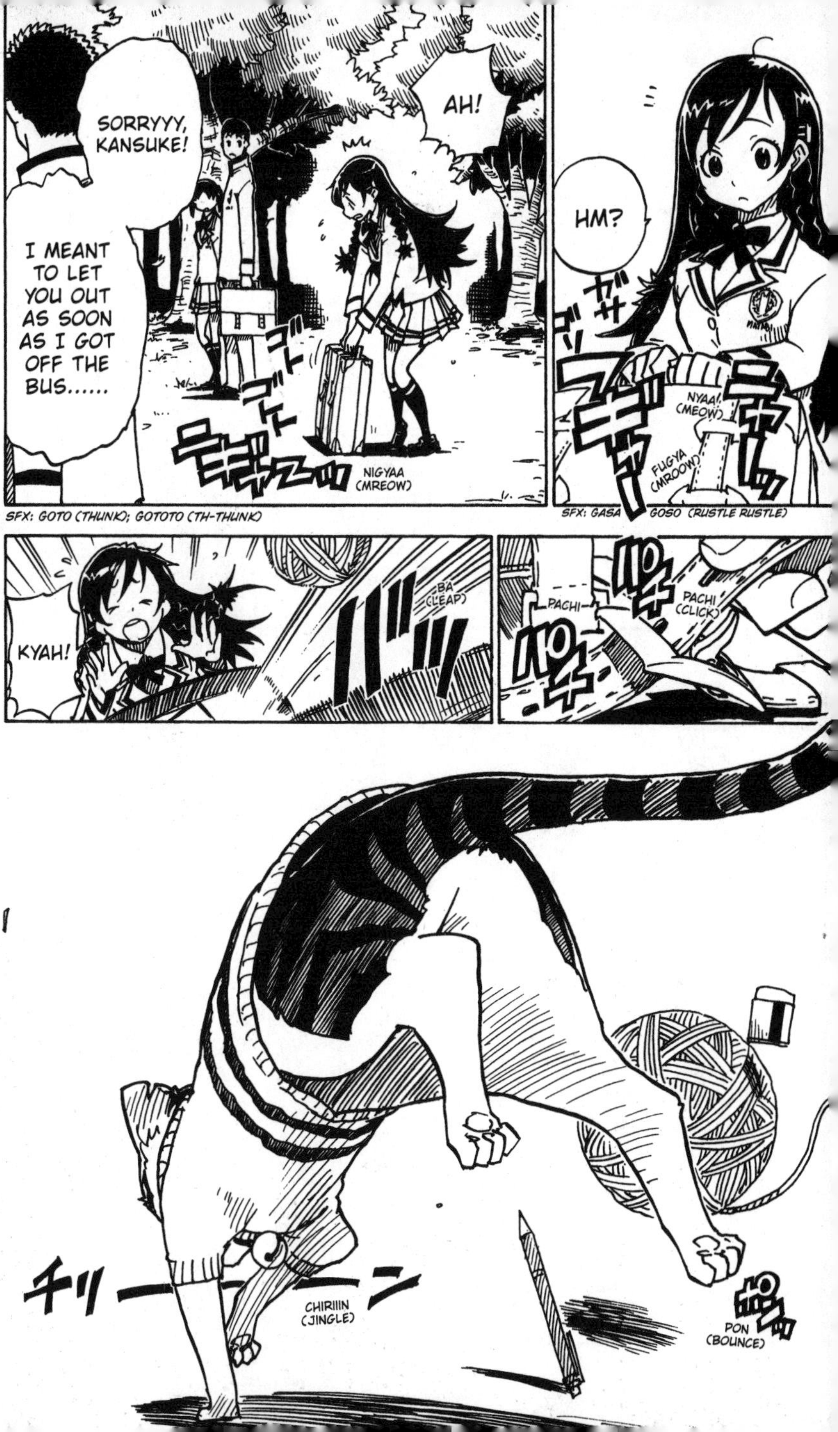
HM?
NYAA! (MEOW)
FUGYA (MROOW)
SFX: GASA GOSO (RUSTLE RUSTLE)
AH!
SORRYYY, KANSUKE!
I MEANT TO LET YOU OUT AS SOON AS I GOT OFF THE BUS......
NIGYAA (MREOW)
SFX: GOTO (THUNK); GOTOTO (TH-THUNK)
PACHI (CLICK)
PACHI
BA (LEAP)
KYAH!
PON (BOUNCE)
CHIRIIIN (JINGLE)

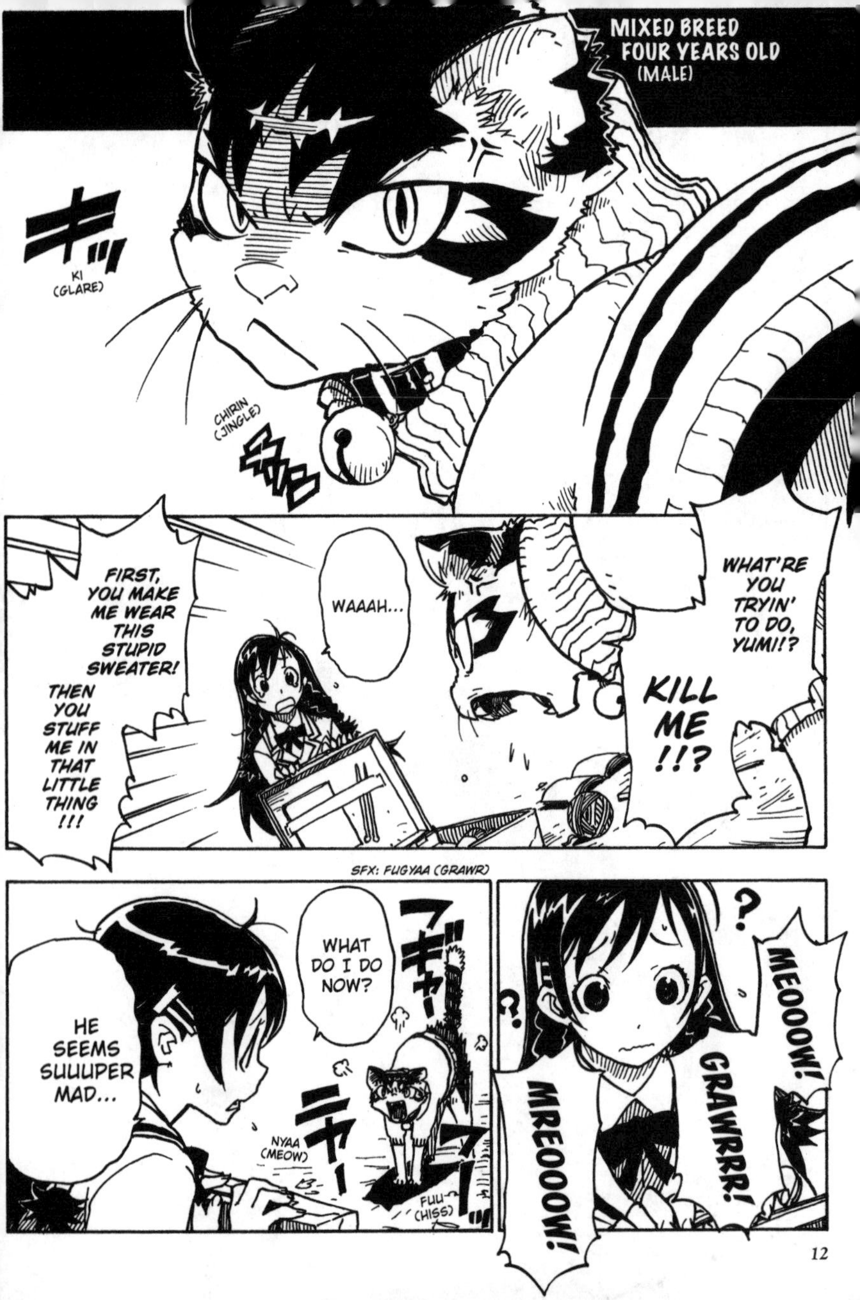
MIXED BREED
FOUR YEARS OLD
(MALE)
KI
(GLARE)
CHIRIN
(JINGLE)
WHAT'RE YOU TRYIN' TO DO, YUMI!?
KILL ME!!?
WAAAH...
FIRST, YOU MAKE ME WEAR THIS STUPID SWEATER!
THEN YOU STUFF ME IN THAT LITTLE THING!!!
SFX: FUGYAA (GRAWR)
MEOOOOW!
GRAWRRR!
MREOOOOW!
WHAT DO I DO NOW?
HE SEEMS SUUUPER MAD...
NYAA
(MEOW)
FUU
(HISS)

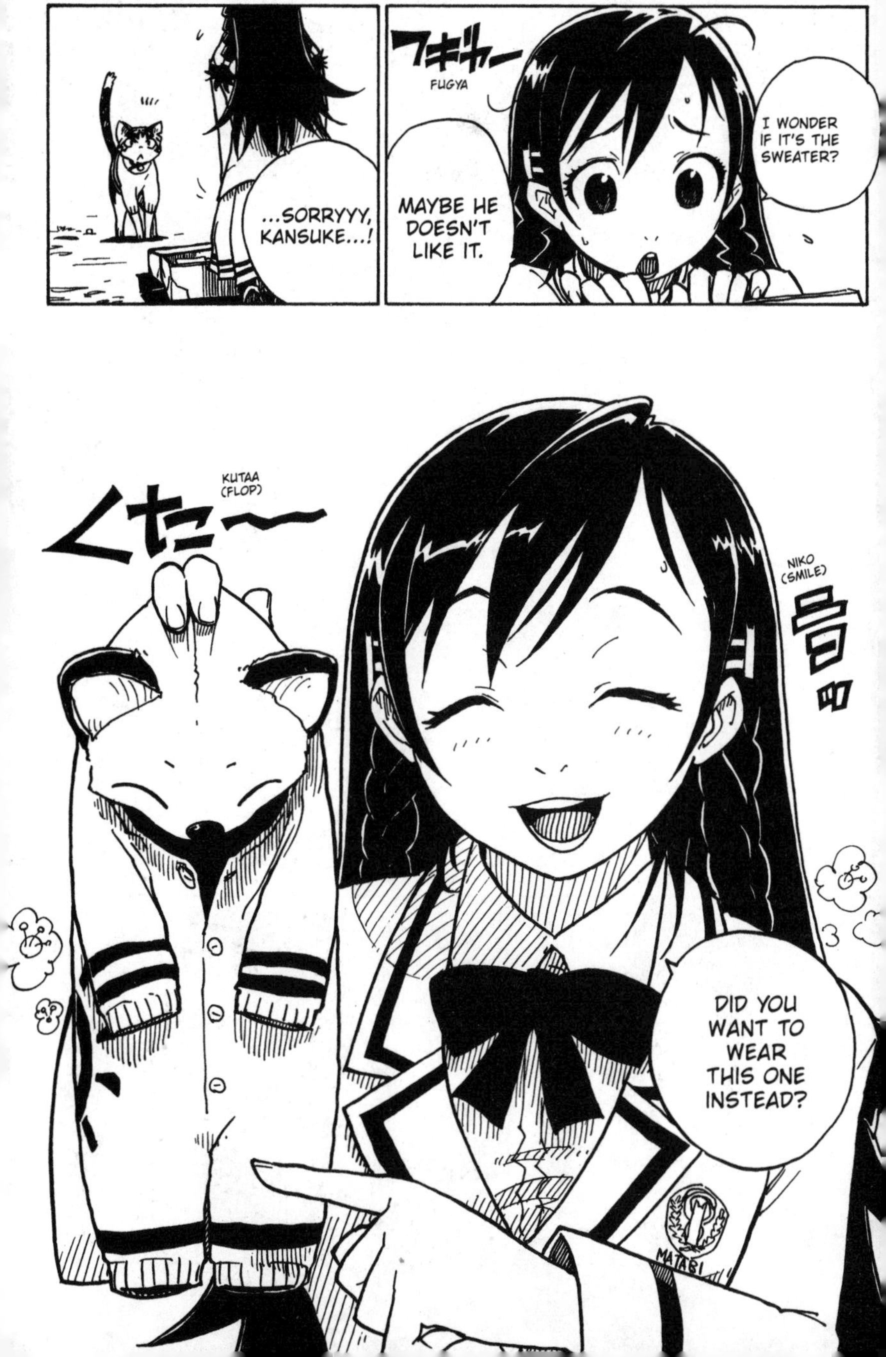

フギャー
FUGYA
I WONDER IF IT'S THE SWEATER?
MAYBE HE DOESN'T LIKE IT.
...SORRYYY, KANSUKE...!
NIKO (SMILE)
DID YOU WANT TO WEAR THIS ONE INSTEAD?
MATABI
KUTAA (FLOP)
くたー

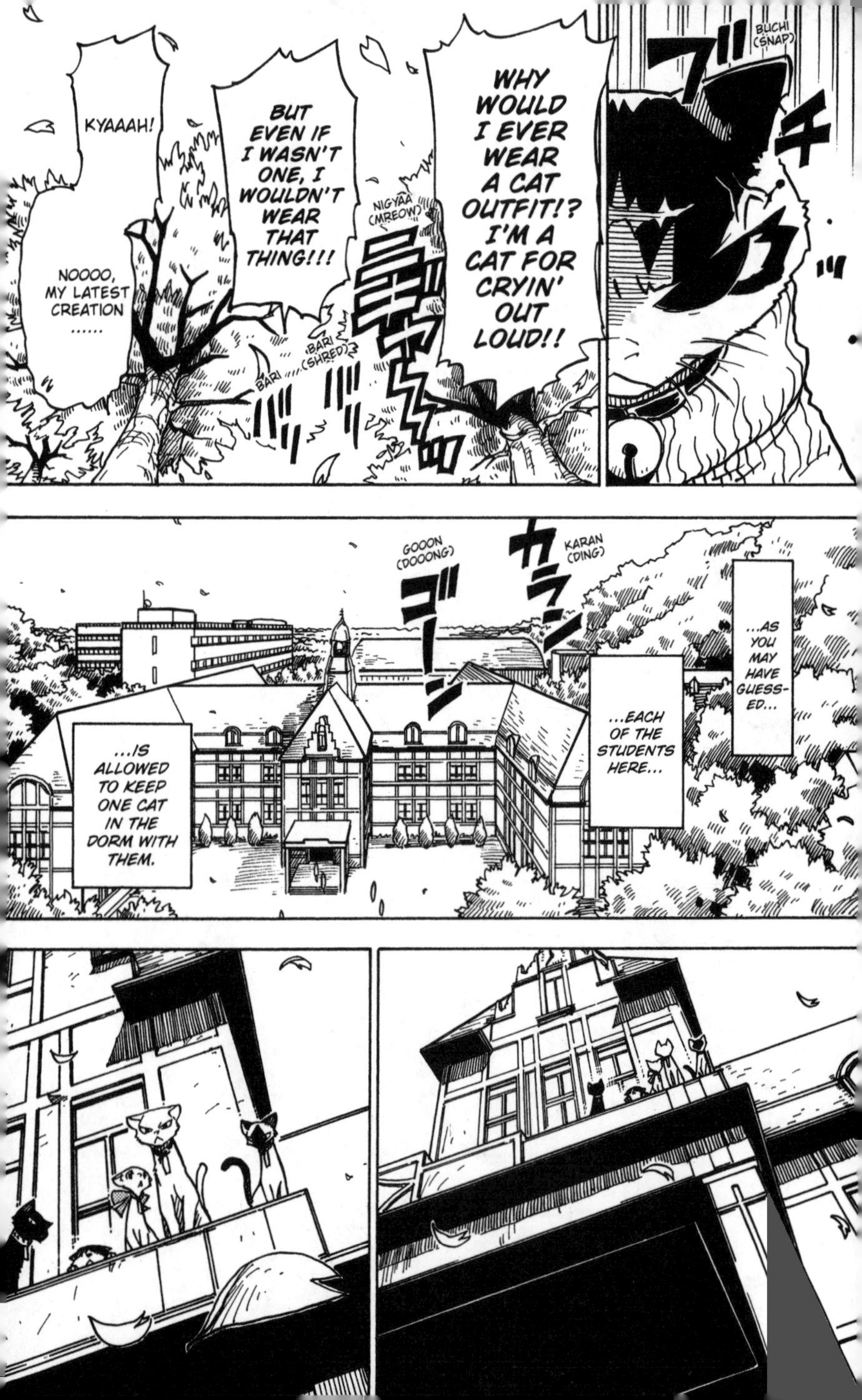
BUCHI (SNAP)
WHY WOULD I EVER WEAR A CAT OUTFIT!? I'M A CAT FOR CRYIN' OUT LOUD!!
NIGYAA (MREOW)
BUT EVEN IF I WASN'T ONE, I WOULDN'T WEAR THAT THING!!!
BARI BARI (SHRED)
KYAAAH!
NOOOO, MY LATEST CREATION ......
KARAN (DING)
GOOON (DOOONG)
...AS YOU MAY HAVE GUESSED...
...EACH OF THE STUDENTS HERE...
...IS ALLOWED TO KEEP ONE CAT IN THE DORM WITH THEM.

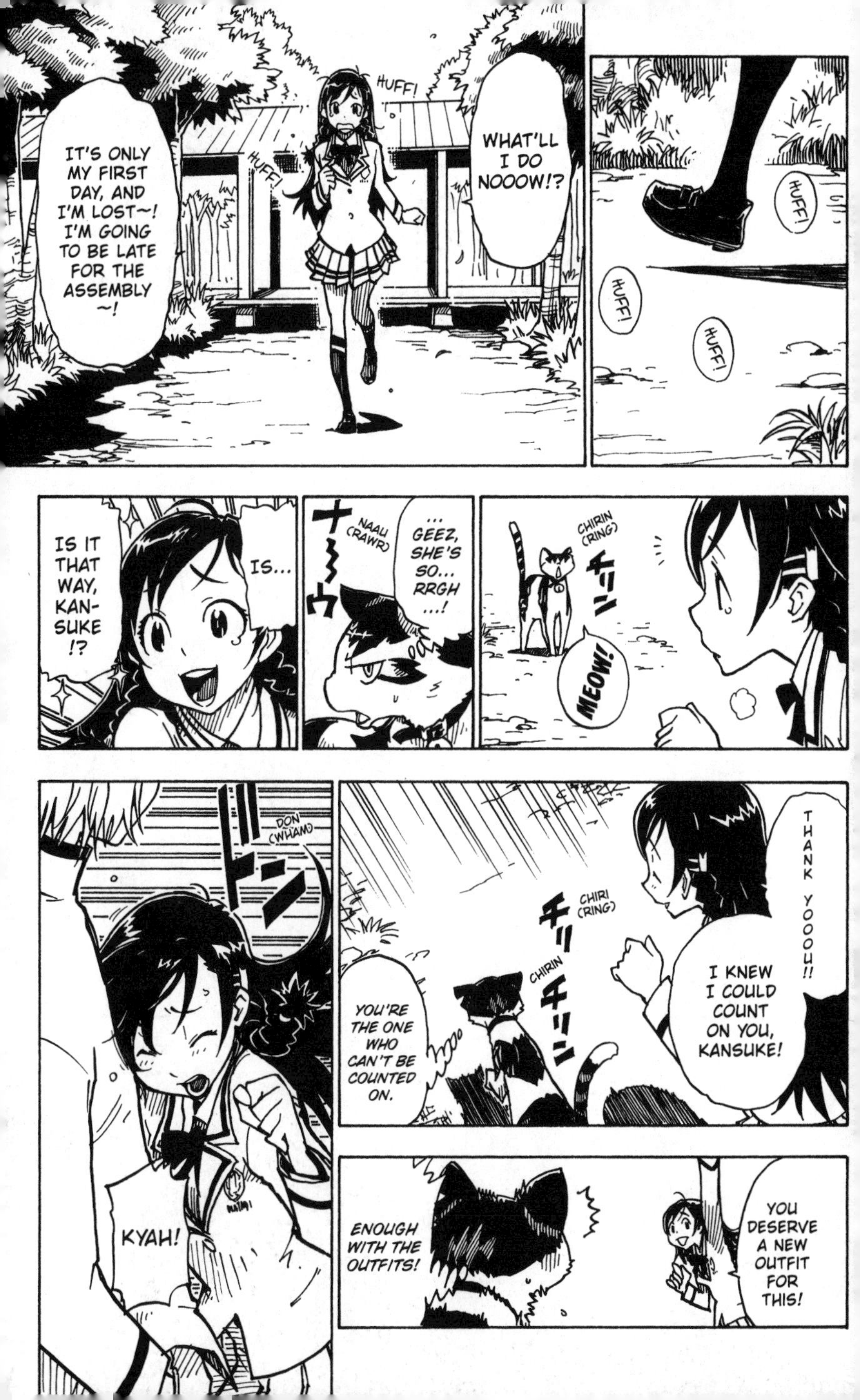
HUFF!
HUFF!
HUFF!
WHAT'LL I DO NOOOW!?
HUFF!
HUFF!
IT'S ONLY MY FIRST DAY, AND I'M LOST~! I'M GOING TO BE LATE FOR THE ASSEMBLY ~!
CHIRIN (RING)
チリン
MEOW!
NAAU (RAWR)
... GEEZ, SHE'S SO... RRGH ...!
IS...
IS IT THAT WAY, KANSUKE!?
THANK YOOOOU!!
I KNEW I COULD COUNT ON YOU, KANSUKE!
CHIRI (RING)
チリ
CHIRIN
チリン
YOU'RE THE ONE WHO CAN'T BE COUNTED ON.
YOU DESERVE A NEW OUTFIT FOR THIS!
ENOUGH WITH THE OUTFITS!
DON (WHAM)
ドン
KYAH!

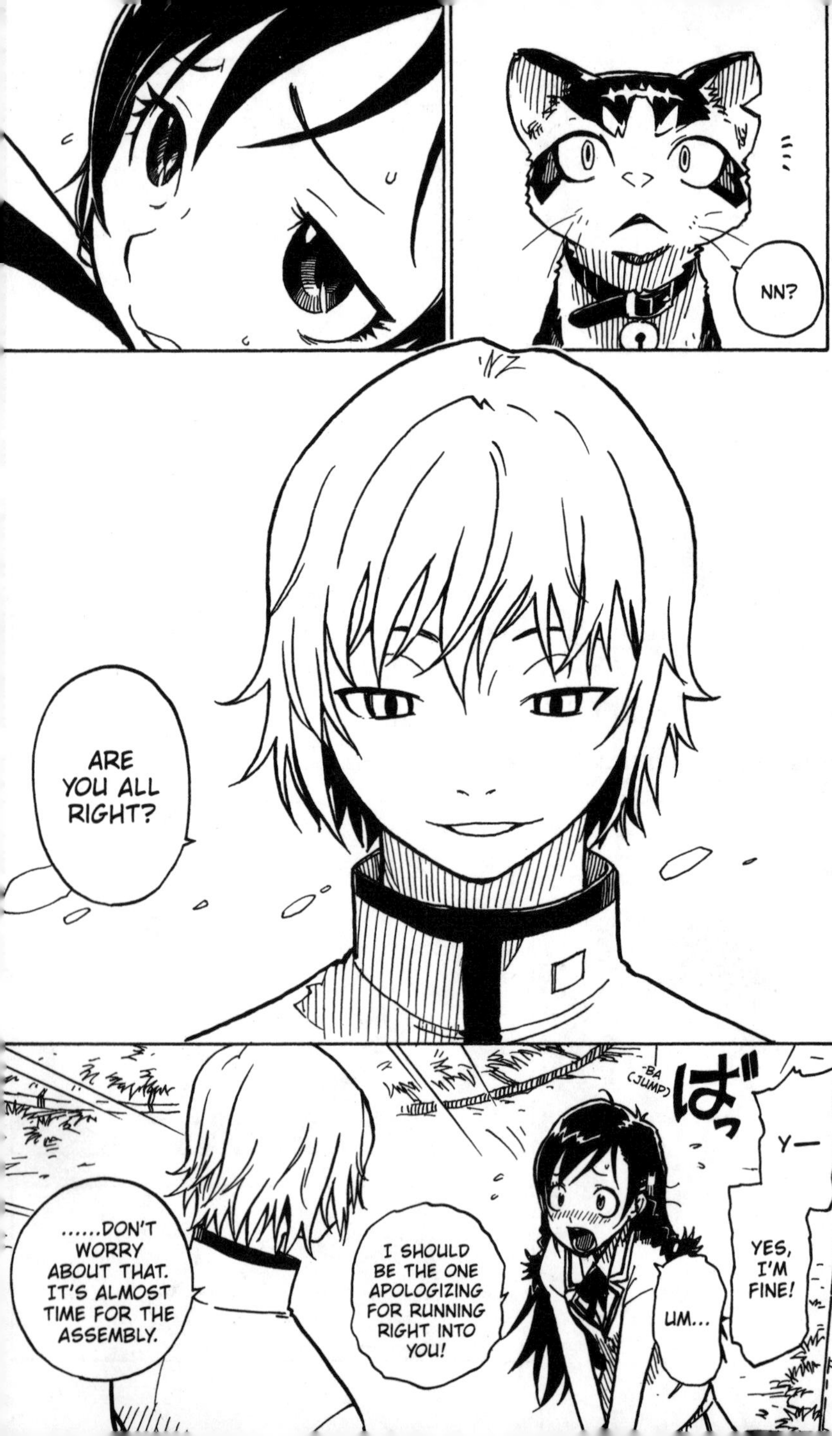
NN?
ARE YOU ALL RIGHT?
ばっ
-BA (JUMP)
Y—
YES, I'M FINE!
UM...
I SHOULD BE THE ONE APOLOGIZING FOR RUNNING RIGHT INTO YOU!
......DON'T WORRY ABOUT THAT. IT'S ALMOST TIME FOR THE ASSEMBLY.

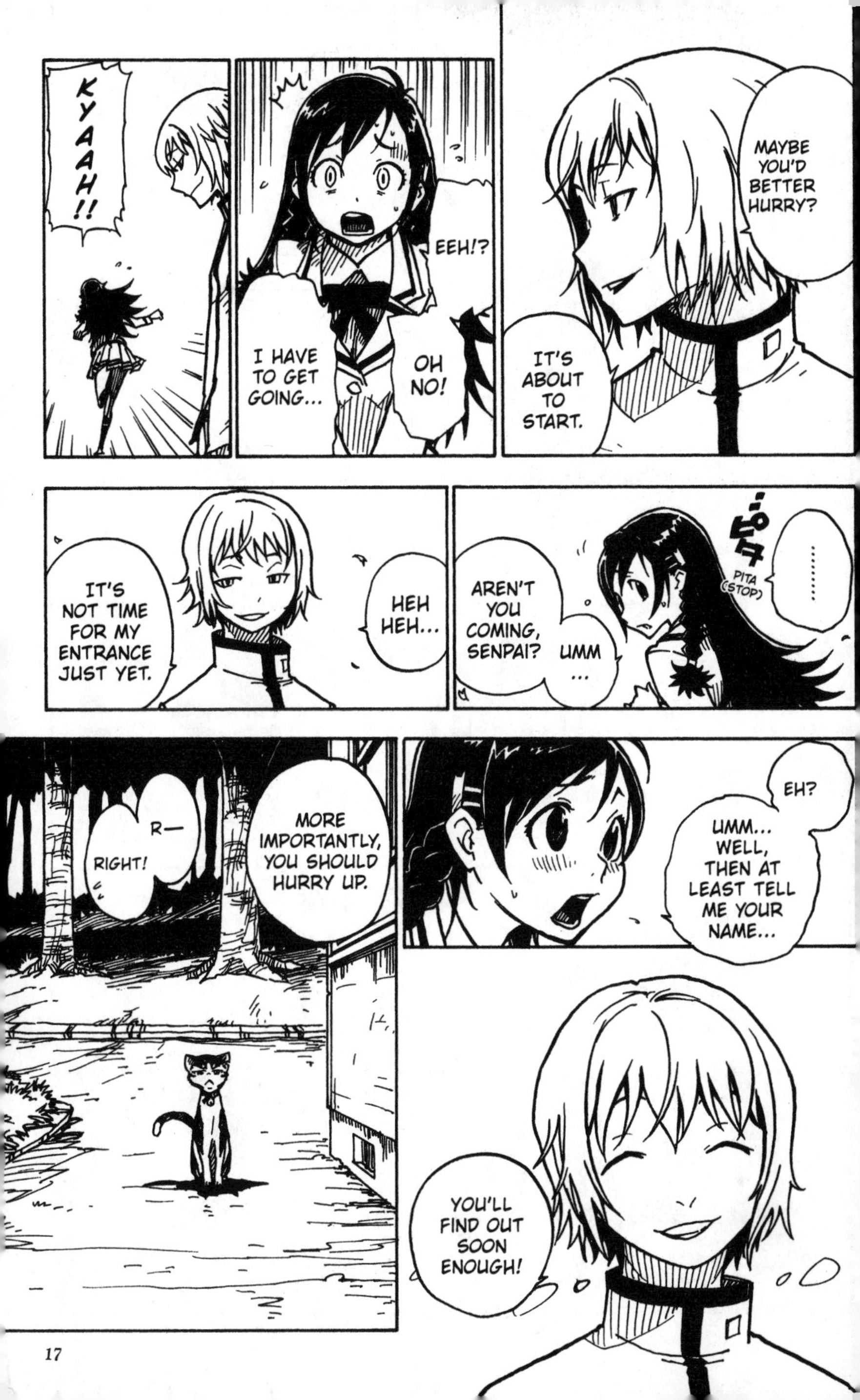
MAYBE YOU'D BETTER HURRY?
IT'S ABOUT TO START.
EEH!?
OH NO!
I HAVE TO GET GOING...
KYAAH!!
......
PITA (STOP)
AREN'T YOU COMING, SENPAI?
UMM ...
HEH HEH...
IT'S NOT TIME FOR MY ENTRANCE JUST YET.
EH?
UMM... WELL, THEN AT LEAST TELL ME YOUR NAME...
YOU'LL FIND OUT SOON ENOUGH!
MORE IMPORTANTLY, YOU SHOULD HURRY UP.
R— RIGHT!

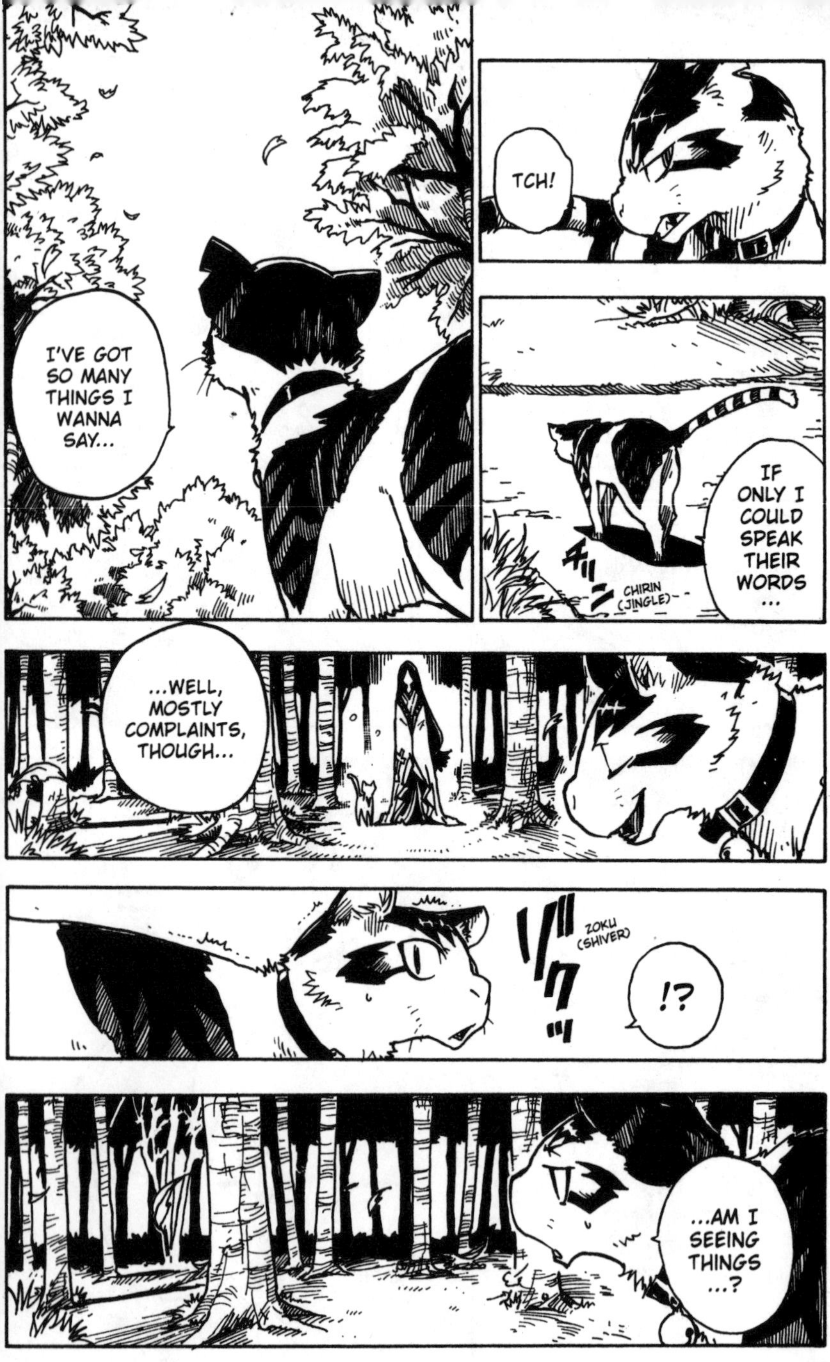
TCH!
IF ONLY I COULD SPEAK THEIR WORDS ...
CHIRIN (JINGLE)
I'VE GOT SO MANY THINGS I WANNA SAY...
...WELL, MOSTLY COMPLAINTS, THOUGH...
!?
ZOKU (SHIVER)
...AM I SEEING THINGS ...?

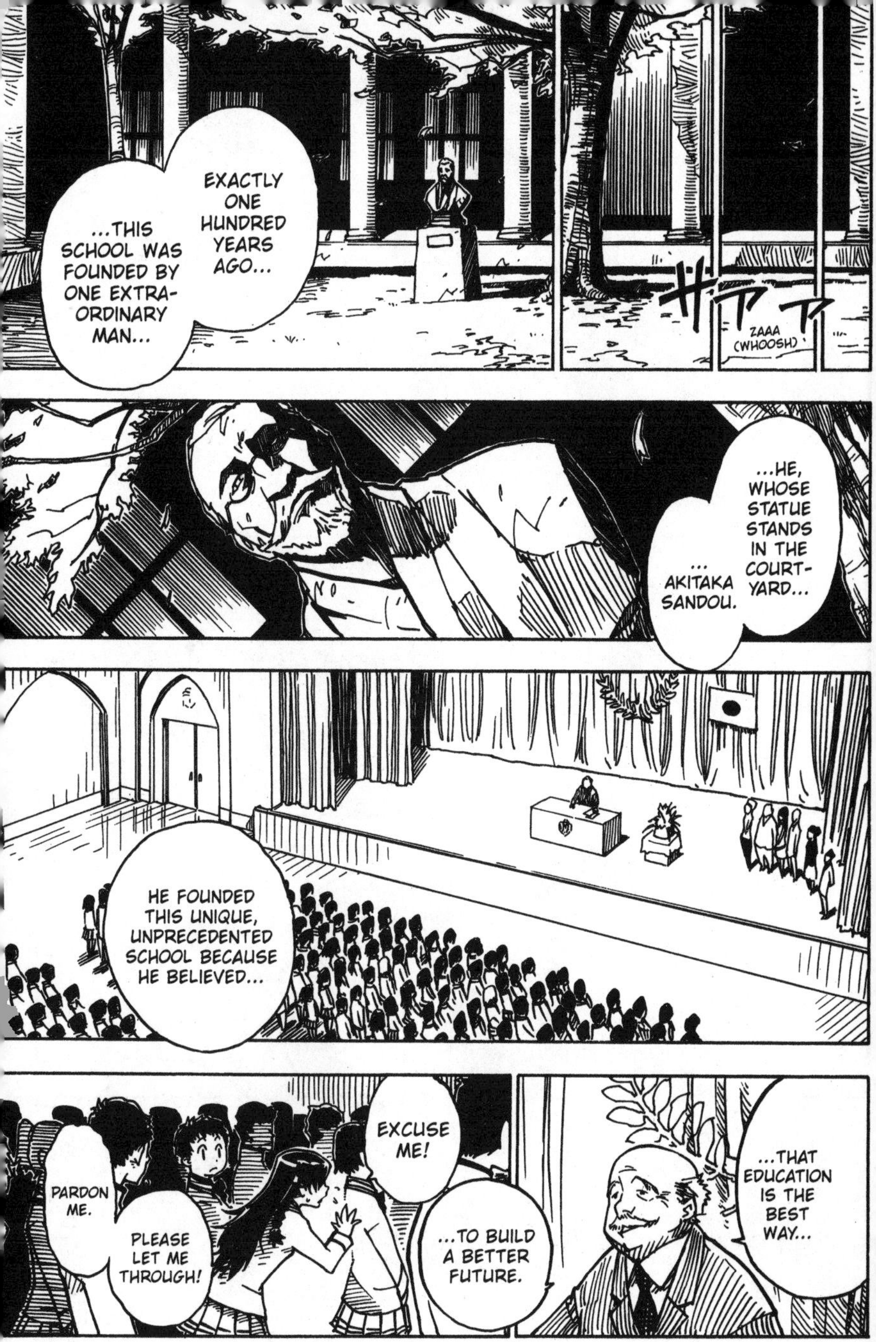
ザァァ
ZAAA (WHOOSH)
EXACTLY ONE HUNDRED YEARS AGO...
...THIS SCHOOL WAS FOUNDED BY ONE EXTRA-ORDINARY MAN...
...HE, WHOSE STATUE STANDS IN THE COURT-YARD...
...AKITAKA SANDOU.
HE FOUNDED THIS UNIQUE, UNPRECEDENTED SCHOOL BECAUSE HE BELIEVED...
...THAT EDUCATION IS THE BEST WAY...
EXCUSE ME!
...TO BUILD A BETTER FUTURE.
PARDON ME.
PLEASE LET ME THROUGH!

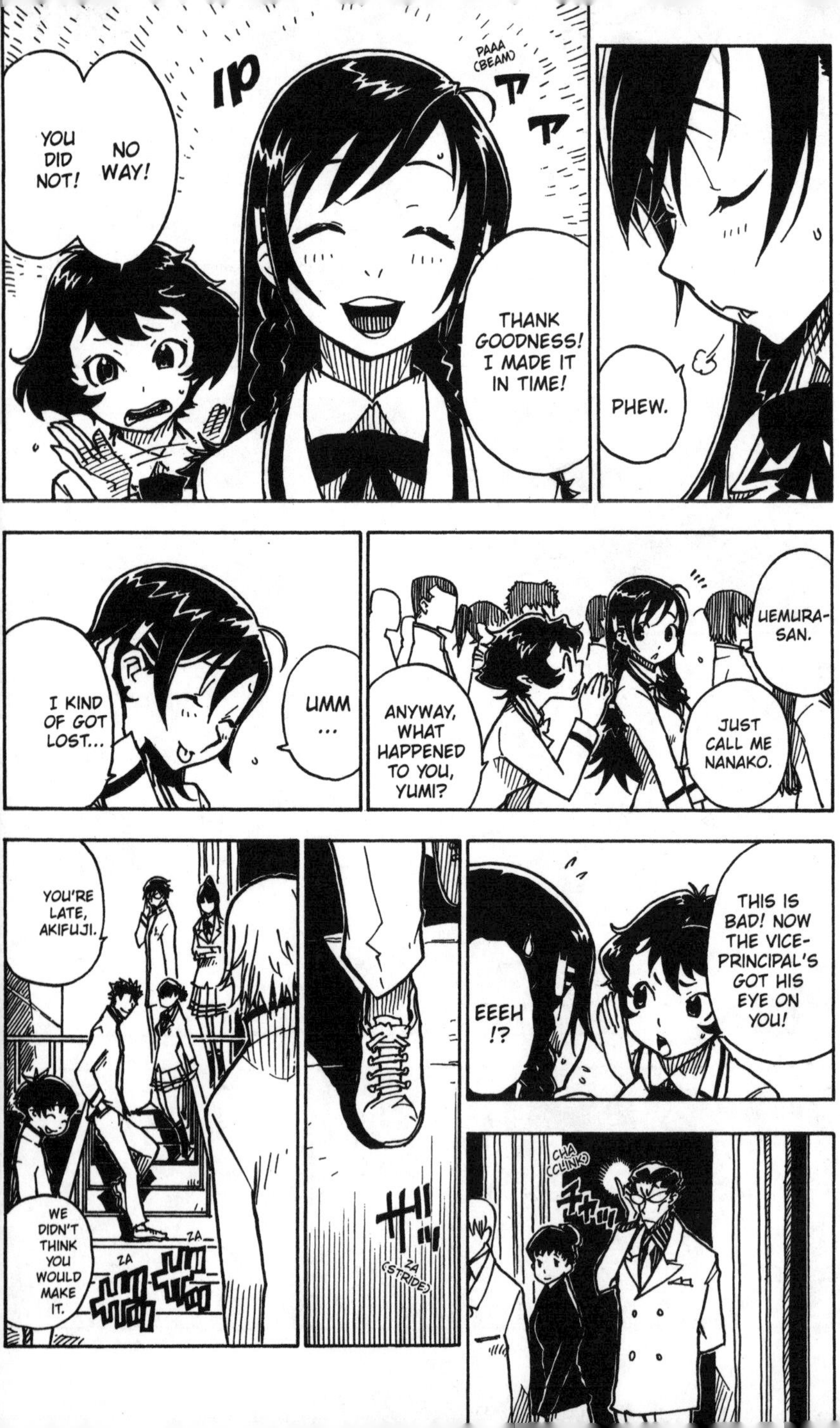
PHEW.
PAAA (BEAM)
THANK GOODNESS! I MADE IT IN TIME!
NO WAY!
YOU DID NOT!
UEMURA-SAN.
JUST CALL ME NANAKO.
ANYWAY, WHAT HAPPENED TO YOU, YUMI?
UMM ...
I KIND OF GOT LOST...
THIS IS BAD! NOW THE VICE-PRINCIPAL'S GOT HIS EYE ON YOU!
EEEH !?
CHA (CLINK)
ZA (STRIDE)
YOU'RE LATE, AKIFUJI.
ZA
ZA
WE DIDN'T THINK YOU WOULD MAKE IT.

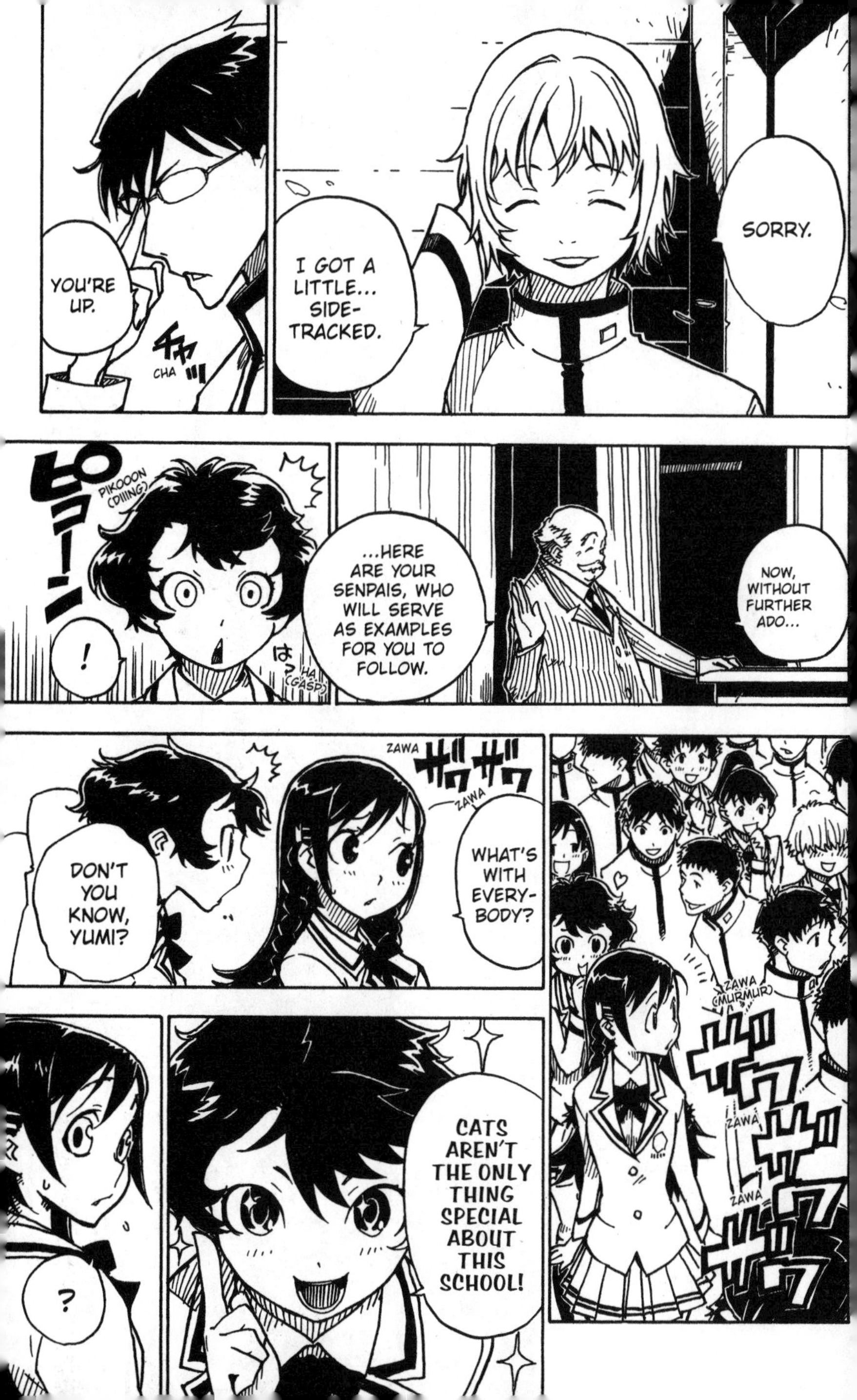
SORRY.
I GOT A LITTLE... SIDE-TRACKED.
YOU'RE UP.
チャ CHA
NOW, WITHOUT FURTHER ADO...
...HERE ARE YOUR SENPAIS, WHO WILL SERVE AS EXAMPLES FOR YOU TO FOLLOW.
は HA (GASP)
ピコーン PIKOOON (DIIING)
!
ZAWA (MURMUR)
ZAWA
ZAWA
ZAWA
ZAWA
WHAT'S WITH EVERYBODY?
DON'T YOU KNOW, YUMI?
CATS AREN'T THE ONLY THING SPECIAL ABOUT THIS SCHOOL!
?

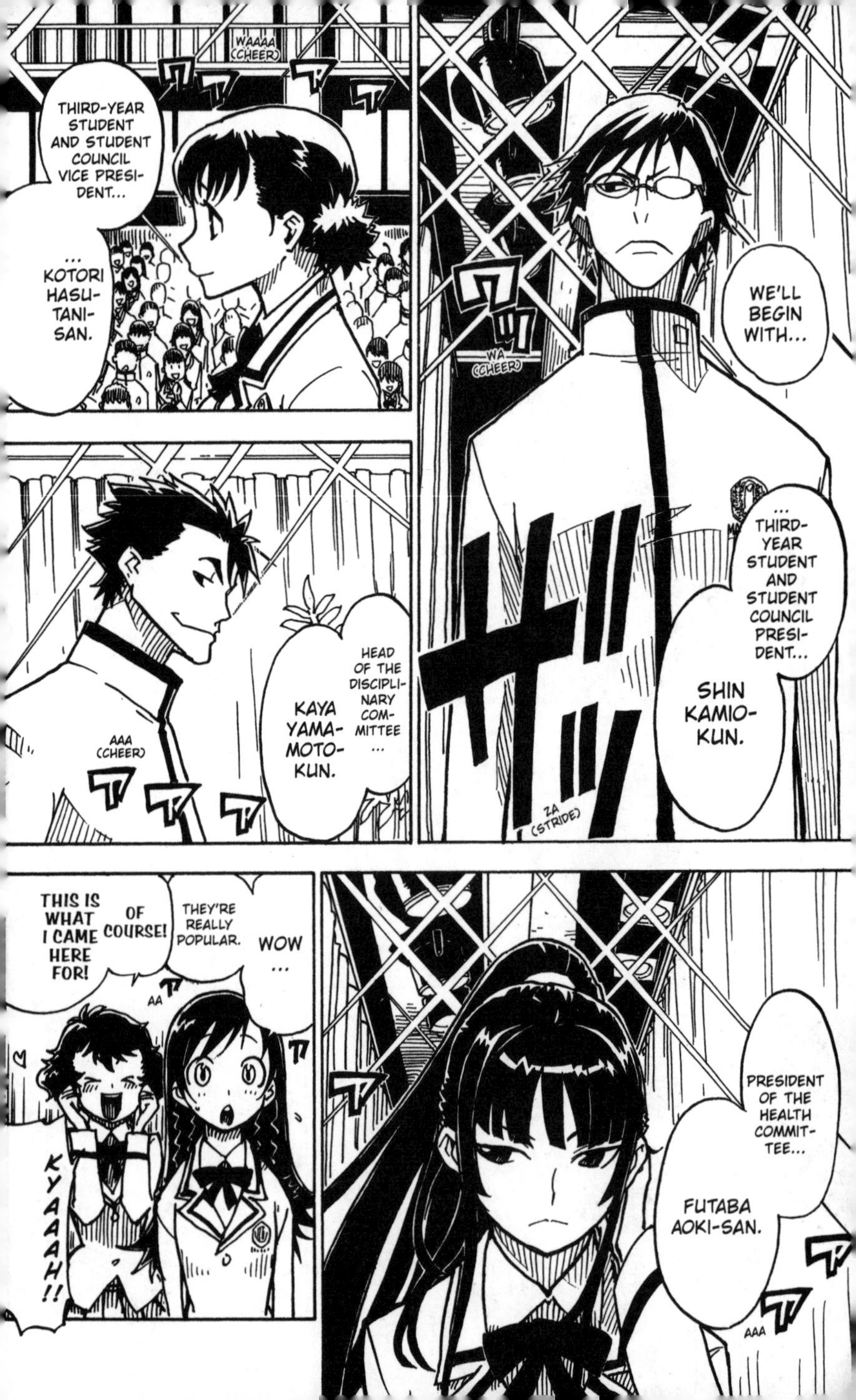
WE'LL BEGIN WITH...
WA (CHEER)
... THIRD-YEAR STUDENT AND STUDENT COUNCIL PRESIDENT...
SHIN KAMIO-KUN.
ZA (STRIDE)
WAAAA (CHEER)
THIRD-YEAR STUDENT AND STUDENT COUNCIL VICE PRESIDENT...
... KOTORI HASUTANI-SAN.
HEAD OF THE DISCIPLINARY COMMITTEE...
KAYA YAMAMOTO-KUN.
AAA (CHEER)
PRESIDENT OF THE HEALTH COMMITTEE...
FUTABA AOKI-SAN.
AAA
WOW...
THEY'RE REALLY POPULAR.
OF COURSE!
THIS IS WHAT I CAME HERE FOR!
AA
KYAAAAH!!

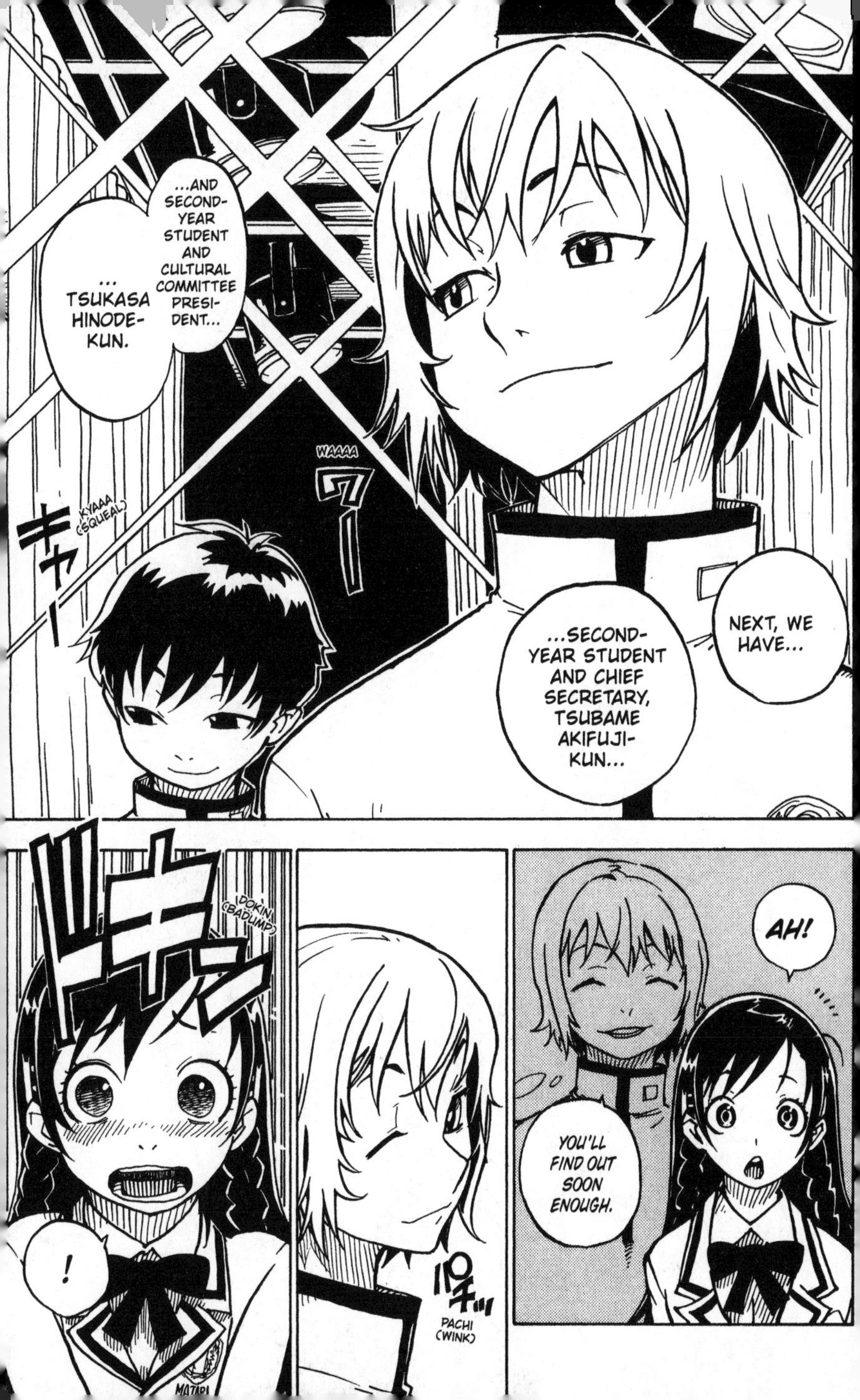
NEXT, WE HAVE...
...SECOND-YEAR STUDENT AND CHIEF SECRETARY, TSUBAME AKIFUJI-KUN...
...AND SECOND-YEAR STUDENT AND CULTURAL COMMITTEE PRESIDENT...
...TSUKASA HINODE-KUN.
WAAAA
KYAAA (SQUEAL)
AH!
YOU'LL FIND OUT SOON ENOUGH.
PACHI (WINK)
DOKIN (BADUMP)
!

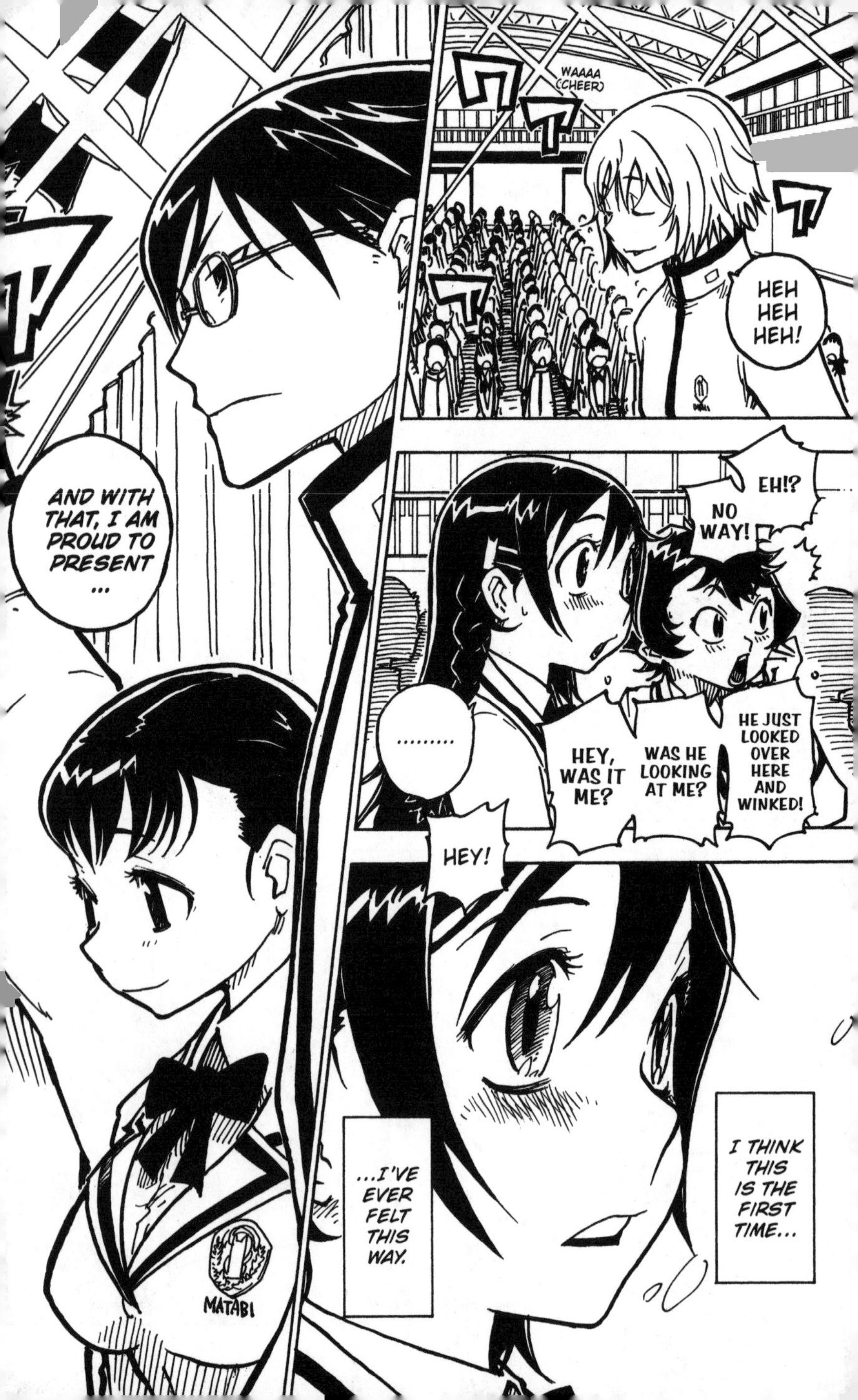
WAAAA (CHEER)
HEH HEH HEH!
EH!?
NO WAY!
....
HE JUST LOOKED OVER HERE AND WINKED!
WAS HE LOOKING AT ME?
HEY, WAS IT ME?
HEY!
I THINK THIS IS THE FIRST TIME...
...I'VE EVER FELT THIS WAY.
AND WITH THAT, I AM PROUD TO PRESENT ...
MATABI

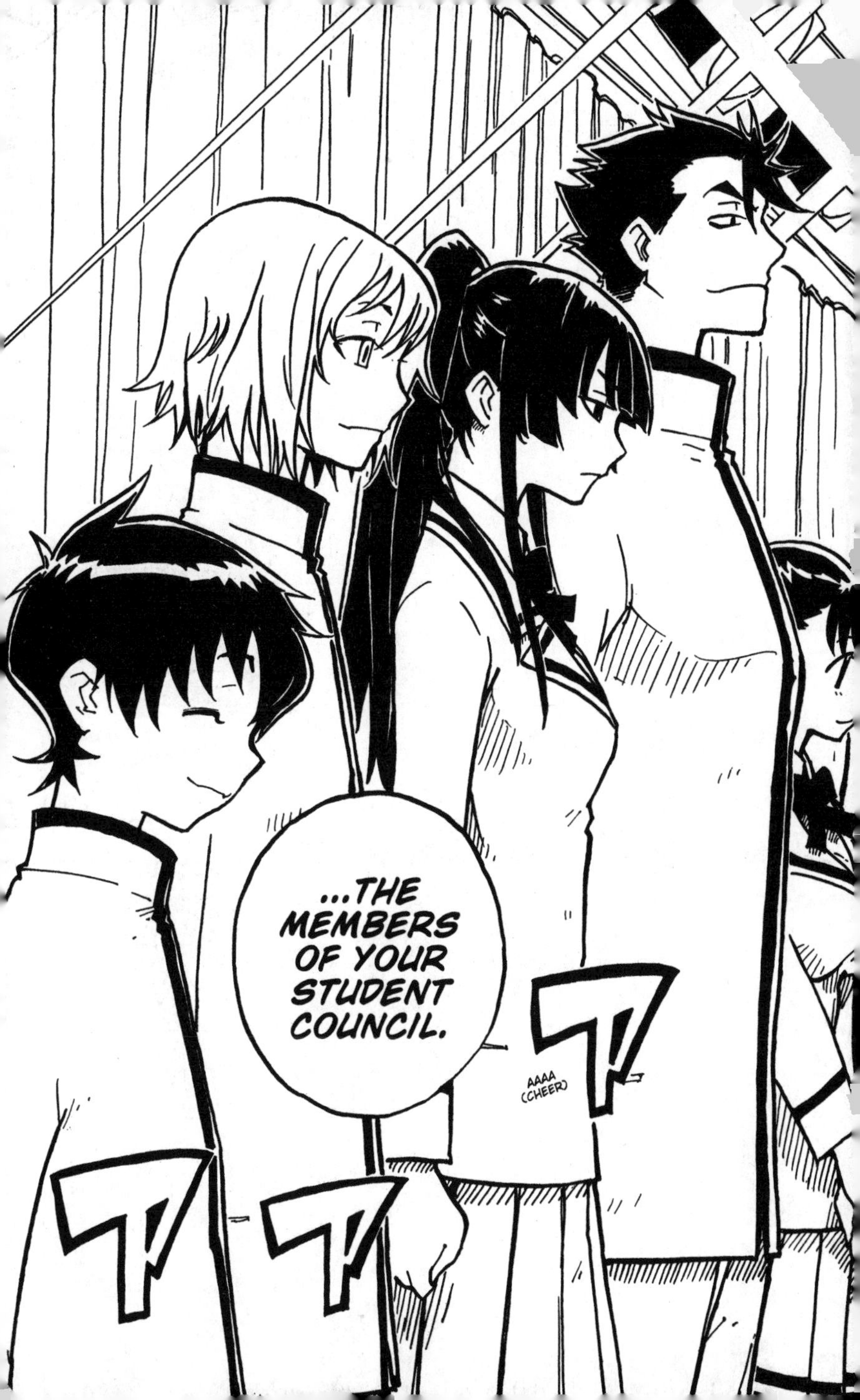
AAAA (CHEER)
...THE MEMBERS OF YOUR STUDENT COUNCIL.

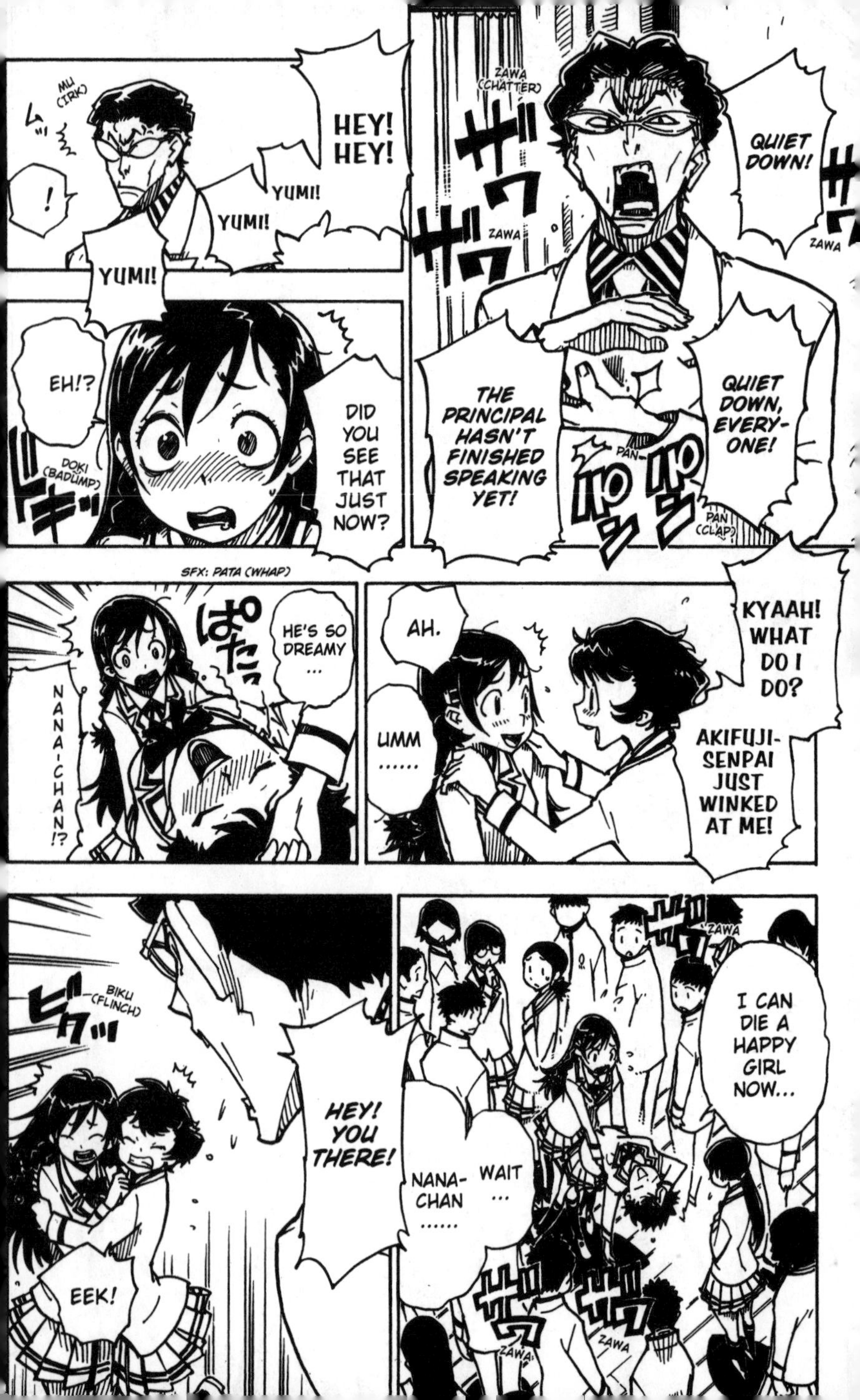
ZAWA (CHATTER)
QUIET DOWN!
ZAWA
ZAWA
QUIET DOWN, EVERY-ONE!
THE PRINCIPAL HASN'T FINISHED SPEAKING YET!
PAN-
PAN (CLAP)
HEY! HEY!
YUMI!
YUMI!
YUMI!
MU (IRK)
!
DID YOU SEE THAT JUST NOW?
EH!?
DOKI (BADUMP)
SFX: PATA (WHAP)
KYAAH! WHAT DO I DO?
AKIFUJI-SENPAI JUST WINKED AT ME!
AH.
UMM ......
HE'S SO DREAMY ...
NANA-CHAN!?
ZAWA
I CAN DIE A HAPPY GIRL NOW...
WAIT ...
NANA-CHAN ......
ZAWA
ZAWA
HEY! YOU THERE!
BIKU (FLINCH)
EEK!

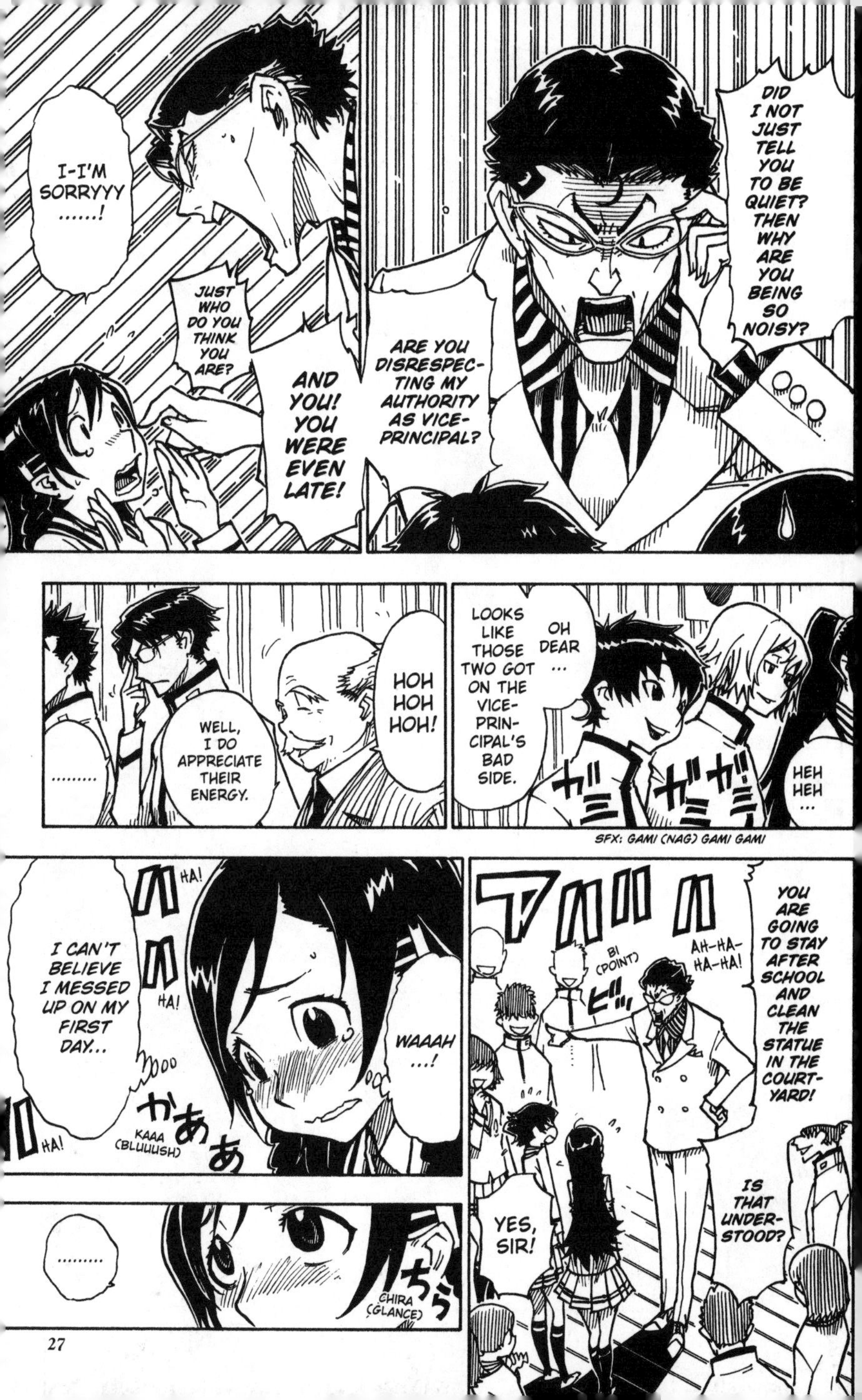
DID I NOT JUST TELL YOU TO BE QUIET? THEN WHY ARE YOU BEING SO NOISY?
ARE YOU DISRESPECTING MY AUTHORITY AS VICE-PRINCIPAL?
AND YOU! YOU WERE EVEN LATE!
JUST WHO DO YOU THINK YOU ARE?
I-I'M SORRYYY ......!
HEH HEH ...
OH DEAR ...
LOOKS LIKE THOSE TWO GOT ON THE VICE-PRINCIPAL'S BAD SIDE.
HOH HOH HOH!
WELL, I DO APPRECIATE THEIR ENERGY.
....
SFX: GAMI (NAG) GAMI GAMI
YOU ARE GOING TO STAY AFTER SCHOOL AND CLEAN THE STATUE IN THE COURTYARD!
AH-HA-HA-HA!
BI (POINT)
IS THAT UNDERSTOOD?
YES, SIR!
WAAAH ...!
HA!
HA!
I CAN'T BELIEVE I MESSED UP ON MY FIRST DAY...
HA!
KAAA (BLUUUSH)
CHIRA (GLANCE)
....

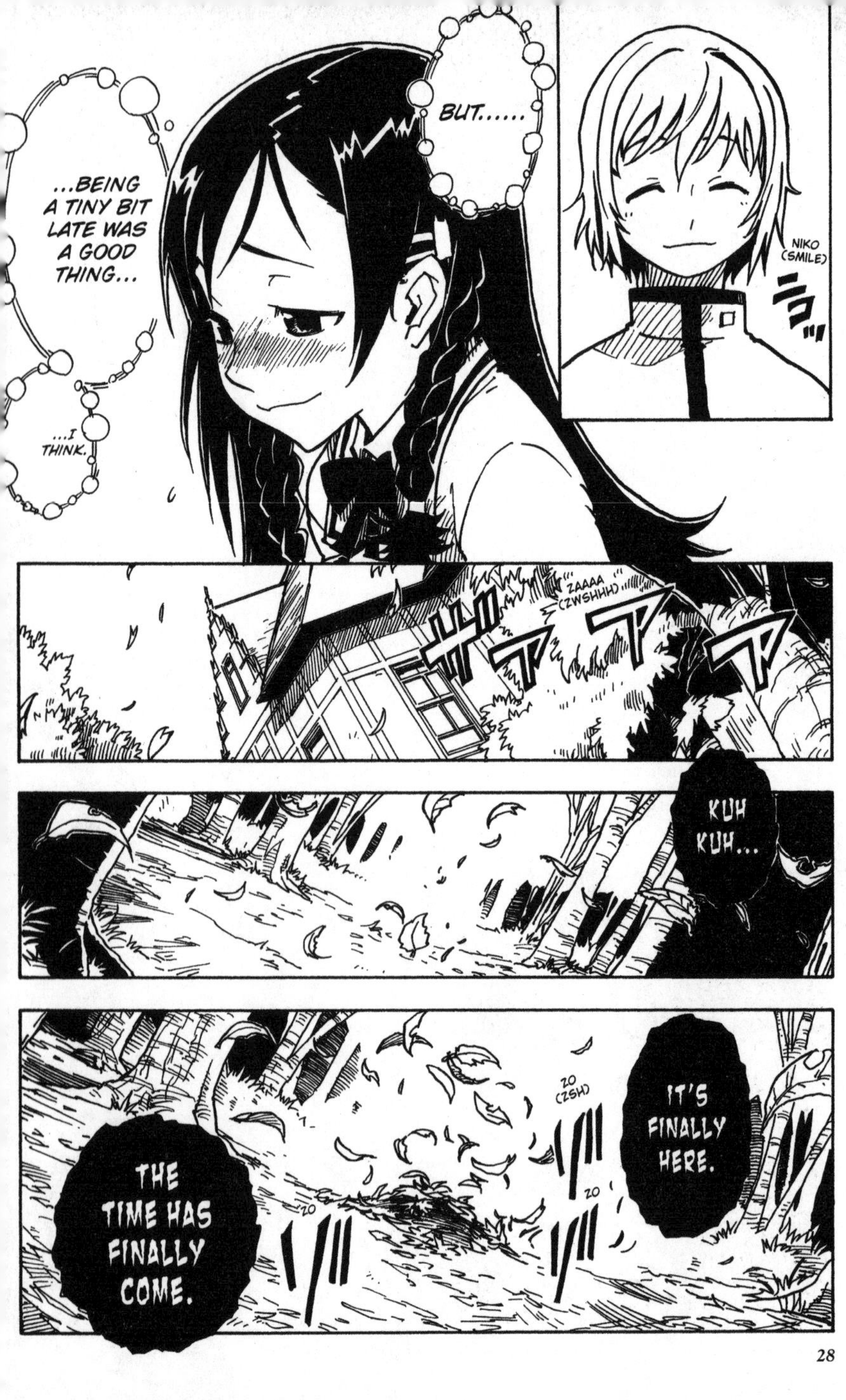
NIKO (SMILE)
BUT......
...BEING A TINY BIT LATE WAS A GOOD THING...
...I THINK.
ZAAAA (ZWSHHH)
KUH KUH...
ZO (ZSH)
IT'S FINALLY HERE.
ZO
ZO
THE TIME HAS FINALLY COME.

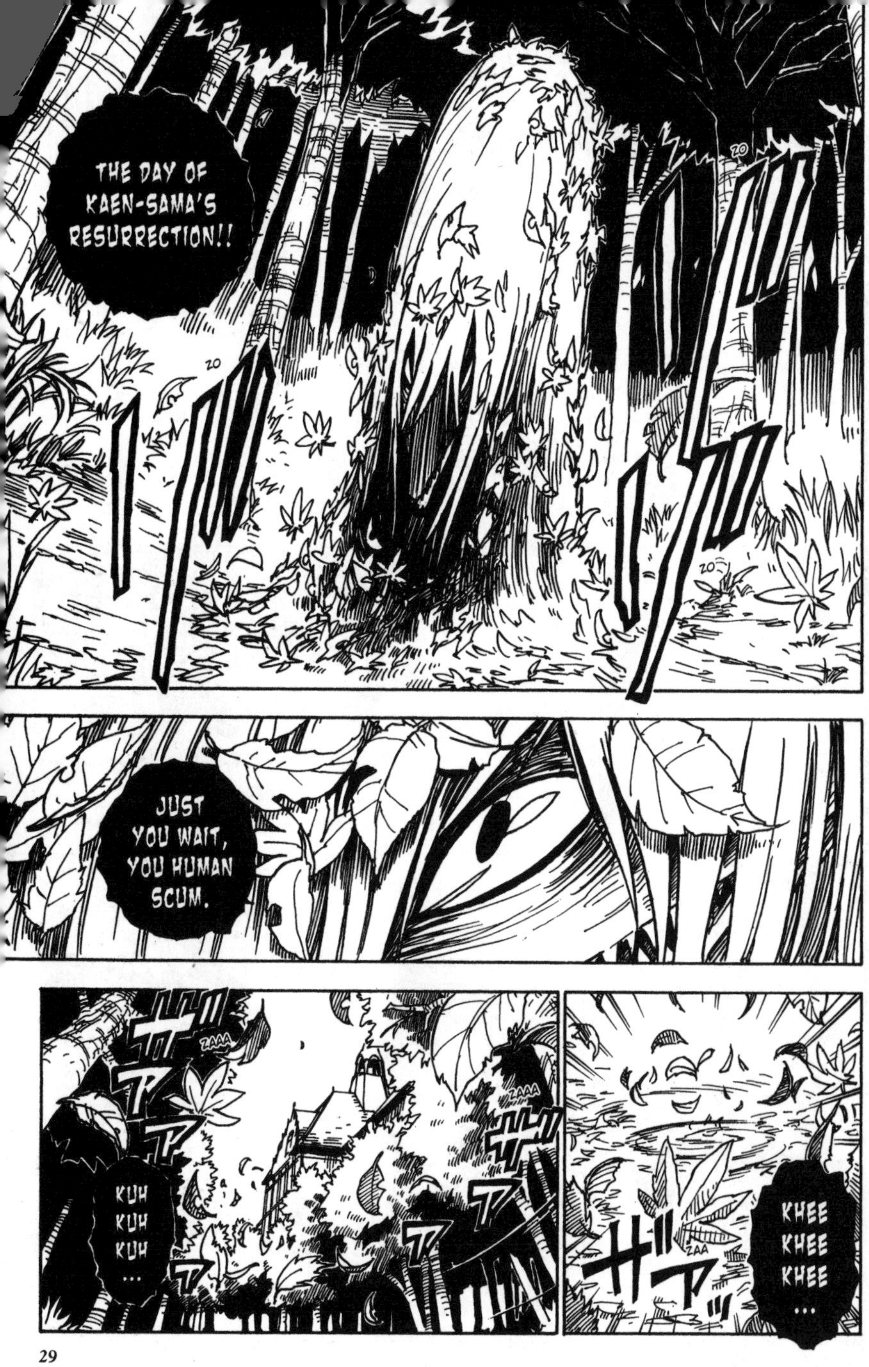
ZO
THE DAY OF KAEN-SAMA'S RESURRECTION!!
ZO
ZO
JUST YOU WAIT, YOU HUMAN SCUM.
ZAA
KHEE KHEE KHEE ...
ZAAA
ZAAA
KUH KUH KUH ...

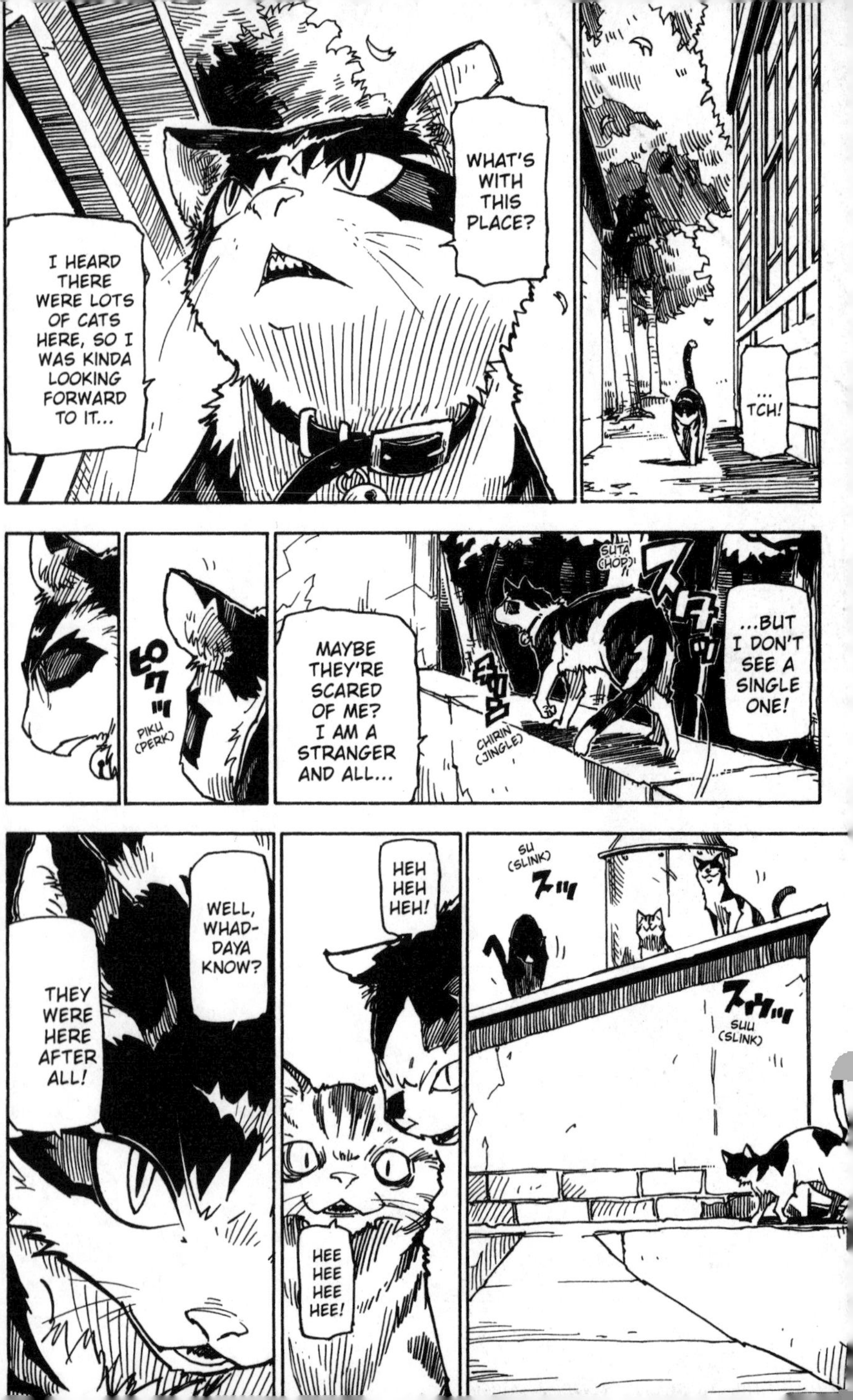
...TCH!
WHAT'S WITH THIS PLACE?
I HEARD THERE WERE LOTS OF CATS HERE, SO I WAS KINDA LOOKING FORWARD TO IT...
SUTA (HOP)
...BUT I DON'T SEE A SINGLE ONE!
CHIRIN (JINGLE)
MAYBE THEY'RE SCARED OF ME? I AM A STRANGER AND ALL...
PIKU (PERK)
SU (SLINK)
SUU (SLINK)
HEH HEH HEH!
HEE HEE HEE HEE!
WELL, WHADDAYA KNOW?
THEY WERE HERE AFTER ALL!

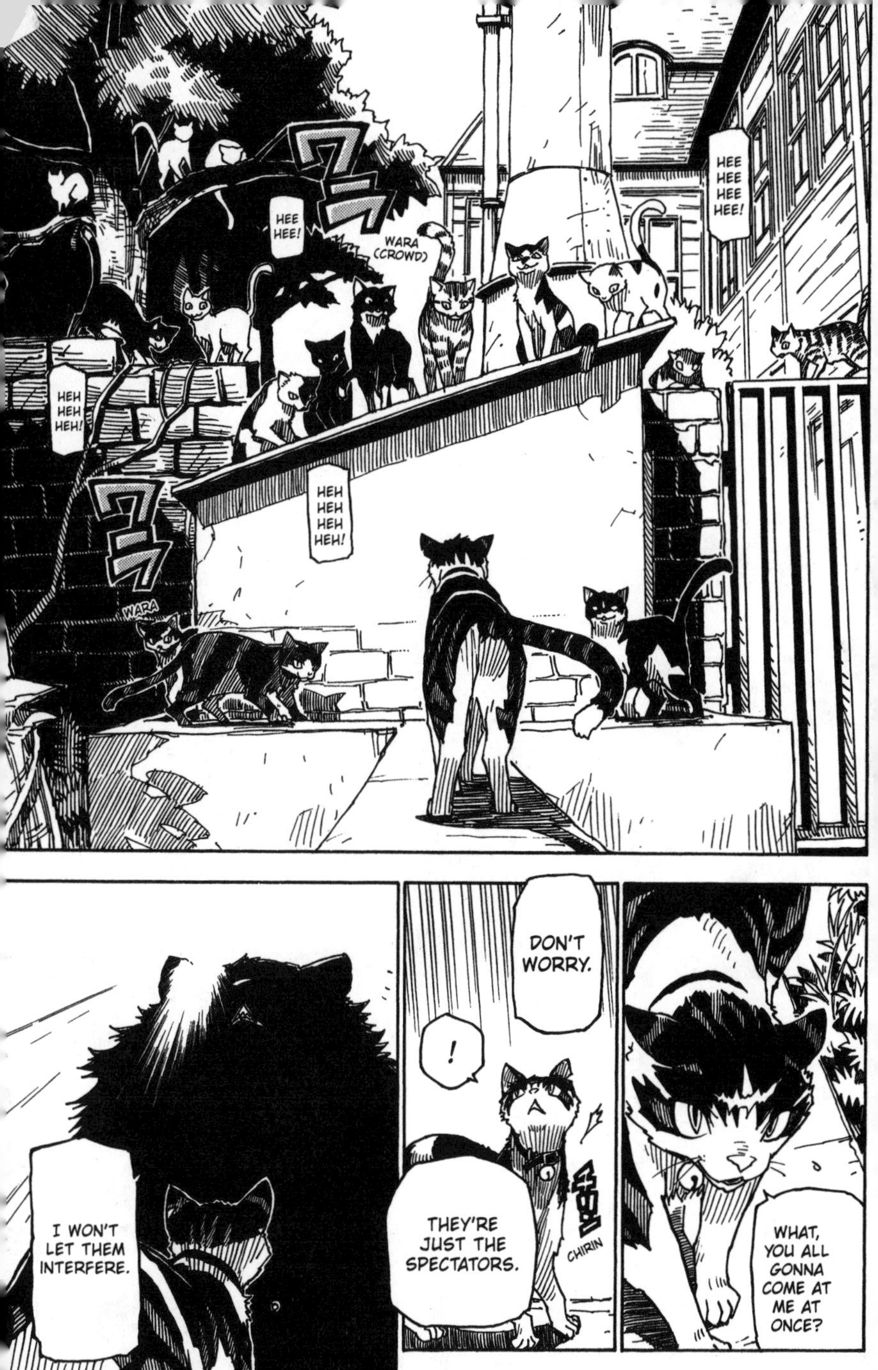
HEE HEE HEE HEE!
WARA (CROWD)
HEE HEE!
HEH HEH HEH!
HEH HEH HEH HEH!
WARA
WHAT, YOU ALL GONNA COME AT ME AT ONCE?
DON'T WORRY.
!
CHIRIN
THEY'RE JUST THE SPECTATORS.
I WON'T LET THEM INTERFERE.

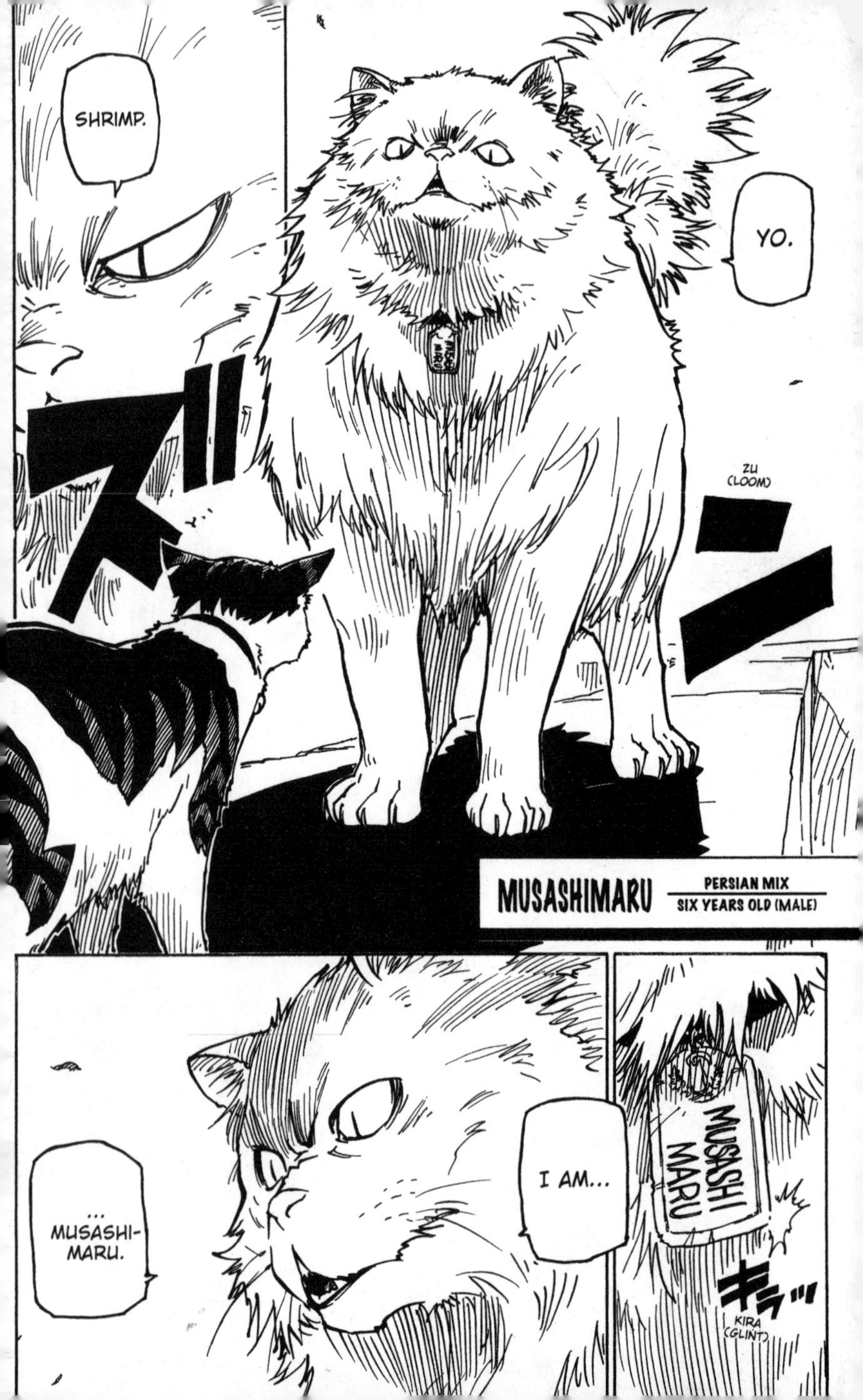
YO.
ZU
(LOOM)
MUSASHIMARU
PERSIAN MIX
SIX YEARS OLD (MALE)
SHRIMP.
MUSASHI MARU
KIRA
(GLINT)
I AM...
... MUSASHI-MARU.

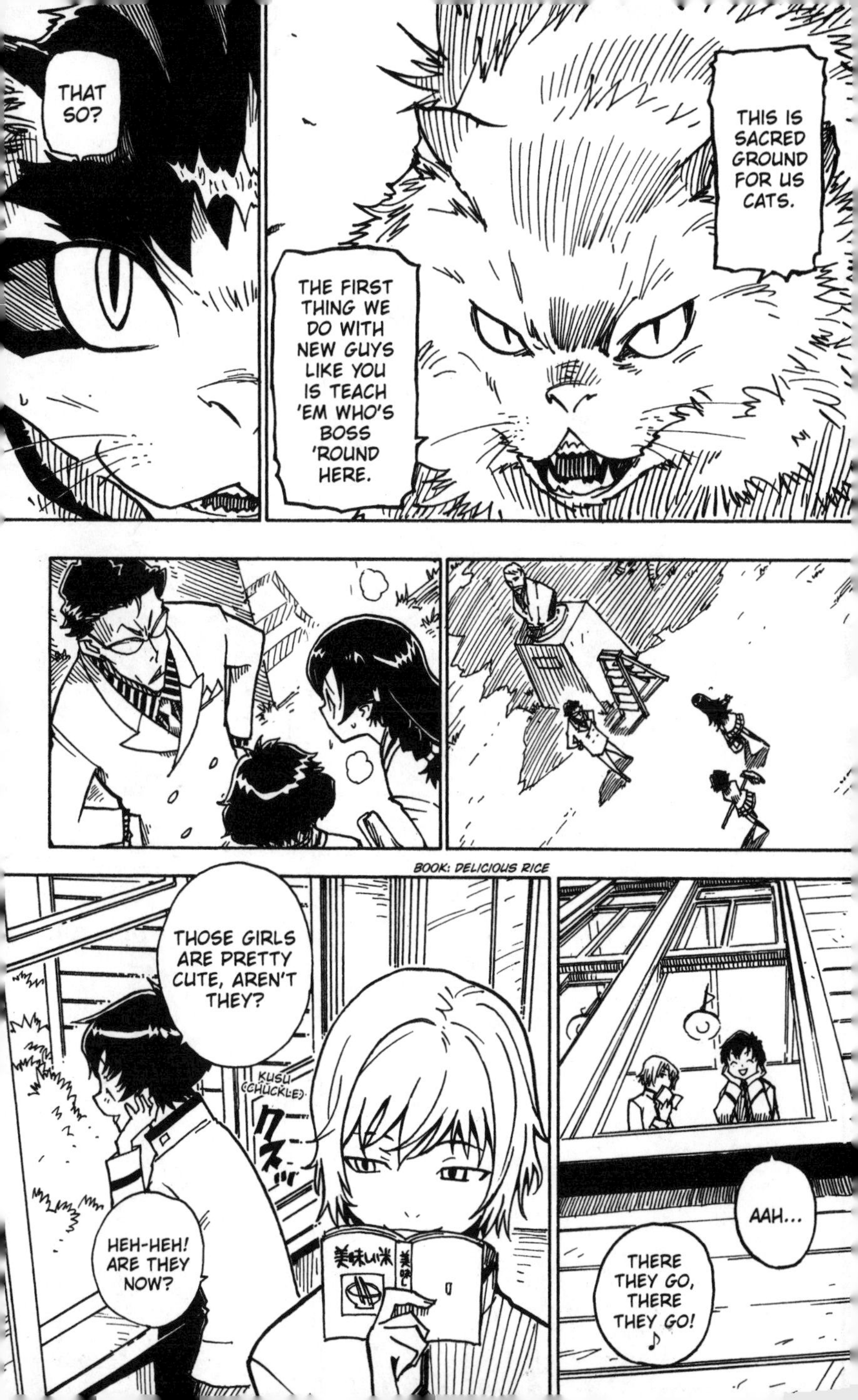
THIS IS SACRED GROUND FOR US CATS.
THE FIRST THING WE DO WITH NEW GUYS LIKE YOU IS TEACH 'EM WHO'S BOSS 'ROUND HERE.
THAT SO?
BOOK: DELICIOUS RICE
AAH...
THERE THEY GO, THERE THEY GO! ♪
THOSE GIRLS ARE PRETTY CUTE, AREN'T THEY?
KUSU (CHUCKLE)
HEH-HEH! ARE THEY NOW?
美味しい米

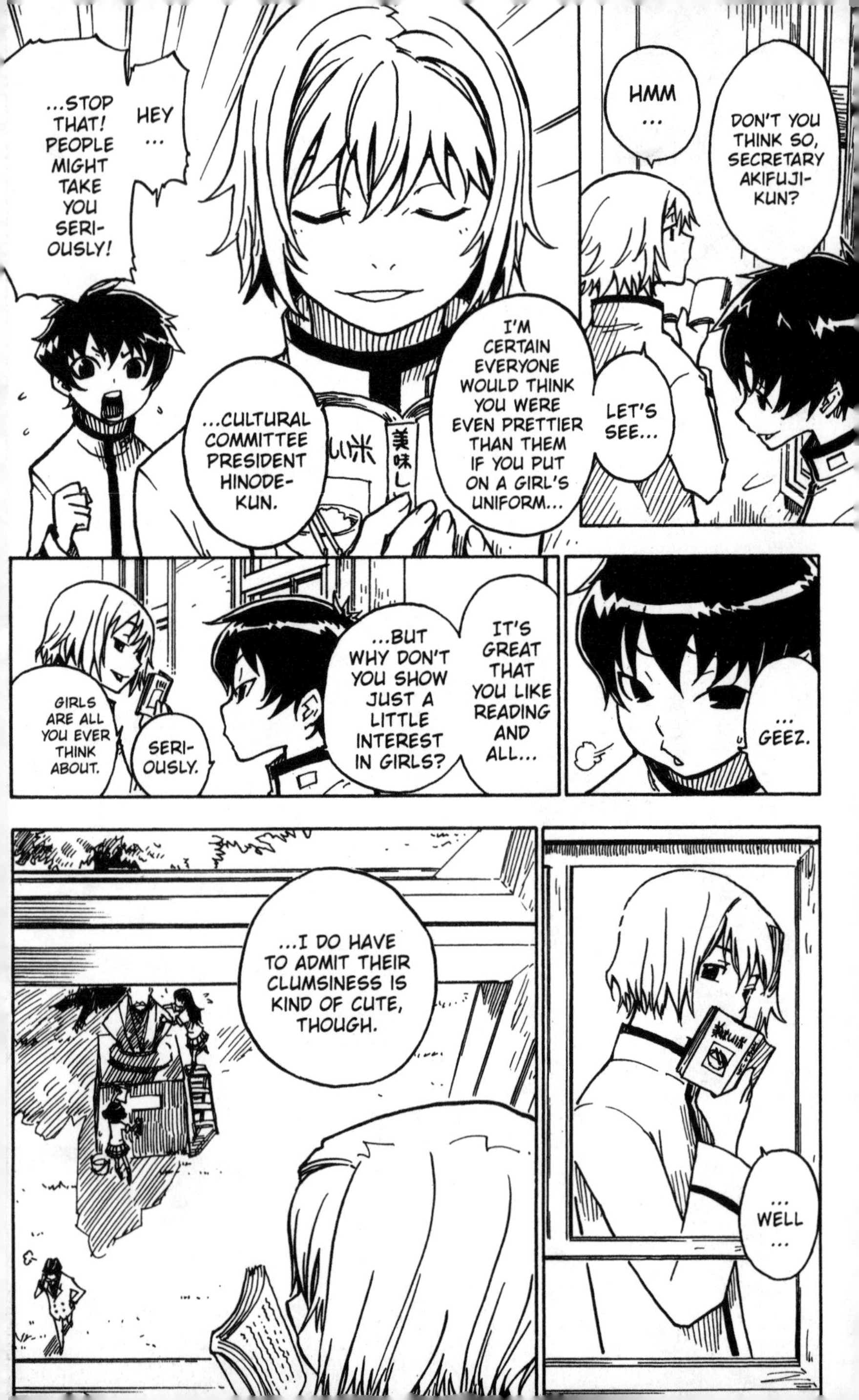
HMM ...
DON'T YOU THINK SO, SECRETARY AKIFUJI-KUN?
LET'S SEE...
I'M CERTAIN EVERYONE WOULD THINK YOU WERE EVEN PRETTIER THAN THEM IF YOU PUT ON A GIRL'S UNIFORM...
...CULTURAL COMMITTEE PRESIDENT HINODE-KUN.
HEY ...
...STOP THAT! PEOPLE MIGHT TAKE YOU SERI-OUSLY!
... GEEZ.
IT'S GREAT THAT YOU LIKE READING AND ALL...
...BUT WHY DON'T YOU SHOW JUST A LITTLE INTEREST IN GIRLS?
SERI-OUSLY.
GIRLS ARE ALL YOU EVER THINK ABOUT.
... WELL ...
...I DO HAVE TO ADMIT THEIR CLUMSINESS IS KIND OF CUTE, THOUGH.

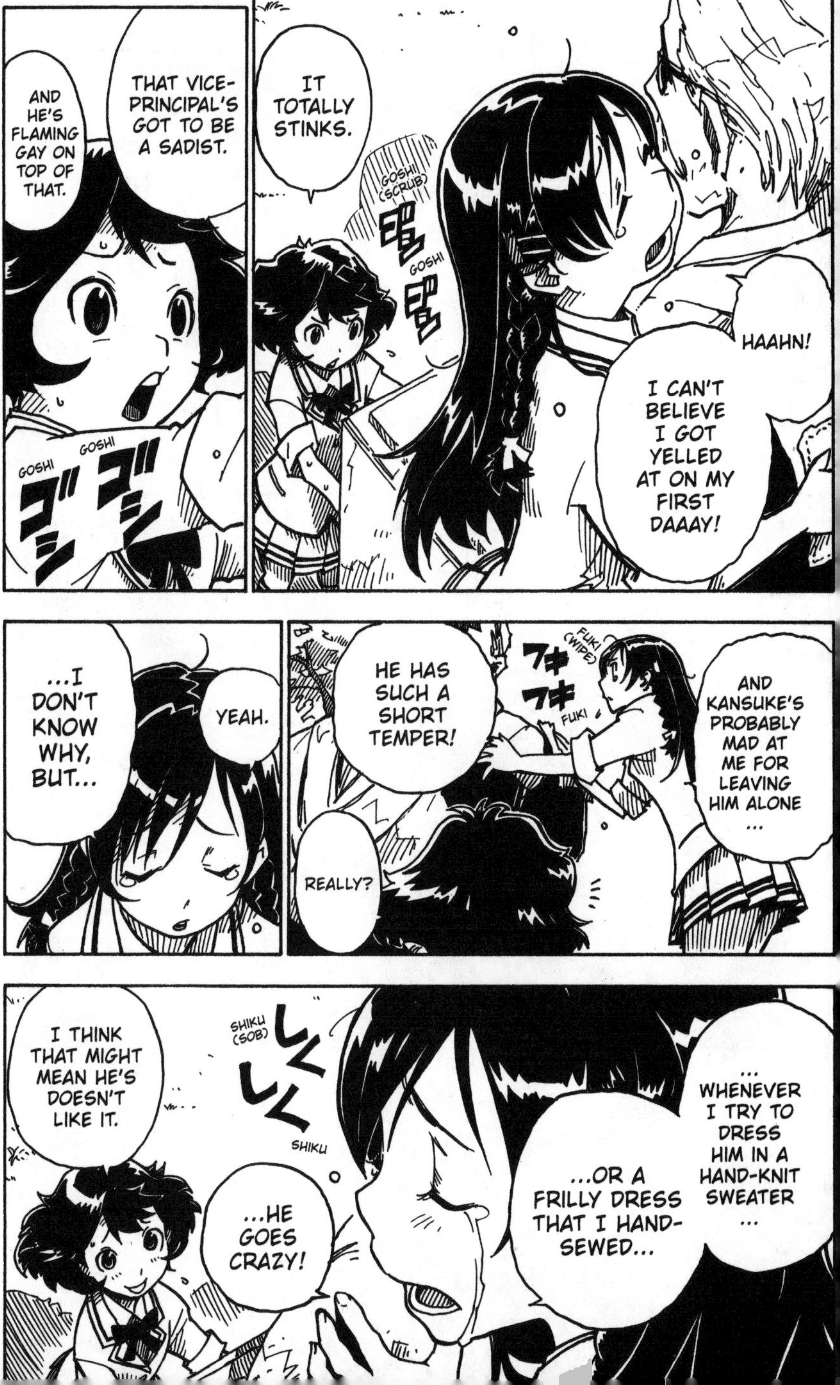
HAAHN!
I CAN'T BELIEVE I GOT YELLED AT ON MY FIRST DAAAY!
GOSHI (SCRUB)
GOSHI
IT TOTALLY STINKS.
THAT VICE-PRINCIPAL'S GOT TO BE A SADIST.
AND HE'S FLAMING GAY ON TOP OF THAT.
GOSHI
GOSHI
AND KANSUKE'S PROBABLY MAD AT ME FOR LEAVING HIM ALONE ...
FUKI (WIPE)
FUKI
HE HAS SUCH A SHORT TEMPER!
REALLY?
YEAH.
...I DON'T KNOW WHY, BUT...
... WHENEVER I TRY TO DRESS HIM IN A HAND-KNIT SWEATER ...
...OR A FRILLY DRESS THAT I HAND-SEWED...
SHIKU (SOB)
SHIKU
...HE GOES CRAZY!
I THINK THAT MIGHT MEAN HE'S DOESN'T LIKE IT.

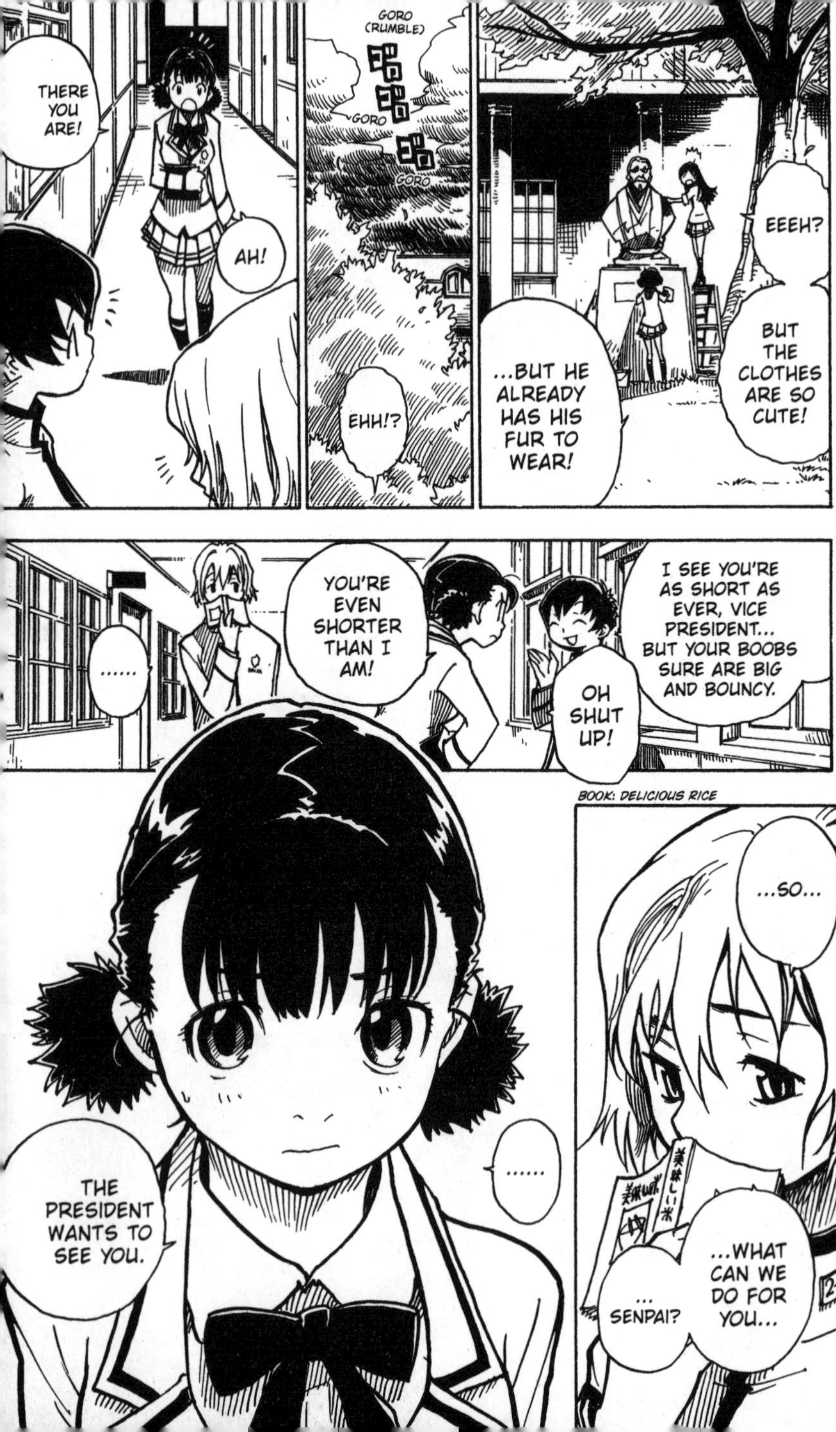
EEEH?
BUT THE CLOTHES ARE SO CUTE!
...BUT HE ALREADY HAS HIS FUR TO WEAR!
GORO (RUMBLE)
GORO
GORO
EHH!?
THERE YOU ARE!
AH!
I SEE YOU'RE AS SHORT AS EVER, VICE PRESIDENT... BUT YOUR BOOBS SURE ARE BIG AND BOUNCY.
OH SHUT UP!
YOU'RE EVEN SHORTER THAN I AM!
......
BOOK: DELICIOUS RICE
美味しい米
...SO...
...WHAT CAN WE DO FOR YOU...
... SENPAI?
2-B
......
THE PRESIDENT WANTS TO SEE YOU.

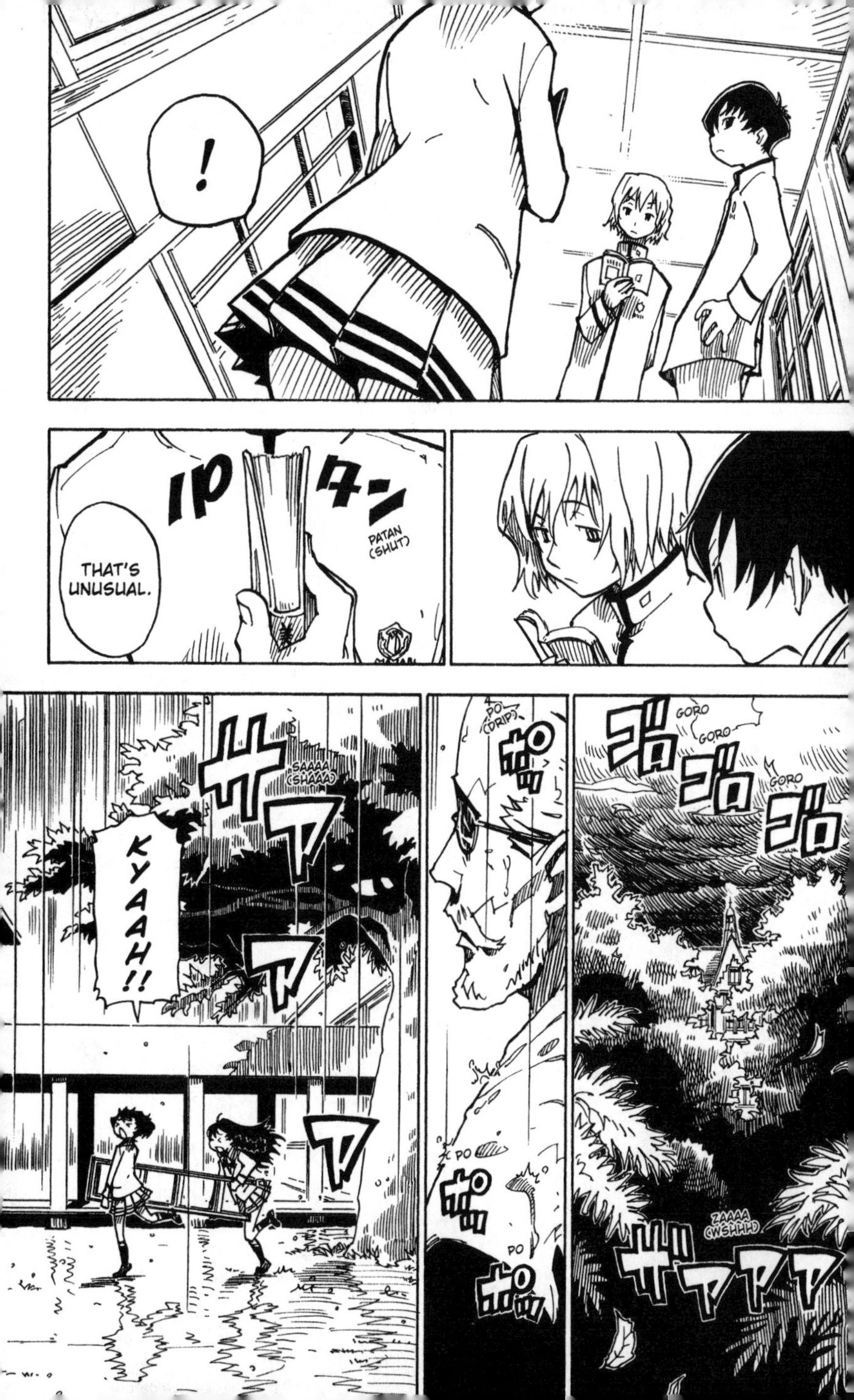
!
PATAN (SHUT)
THAT'S UNUSUAL.
GORO
GORO
GORO
ZAAAA (WSHHH)
PO (DRIP)
PO
PO
SAAAA (SHAAA)
KYAAAH!!

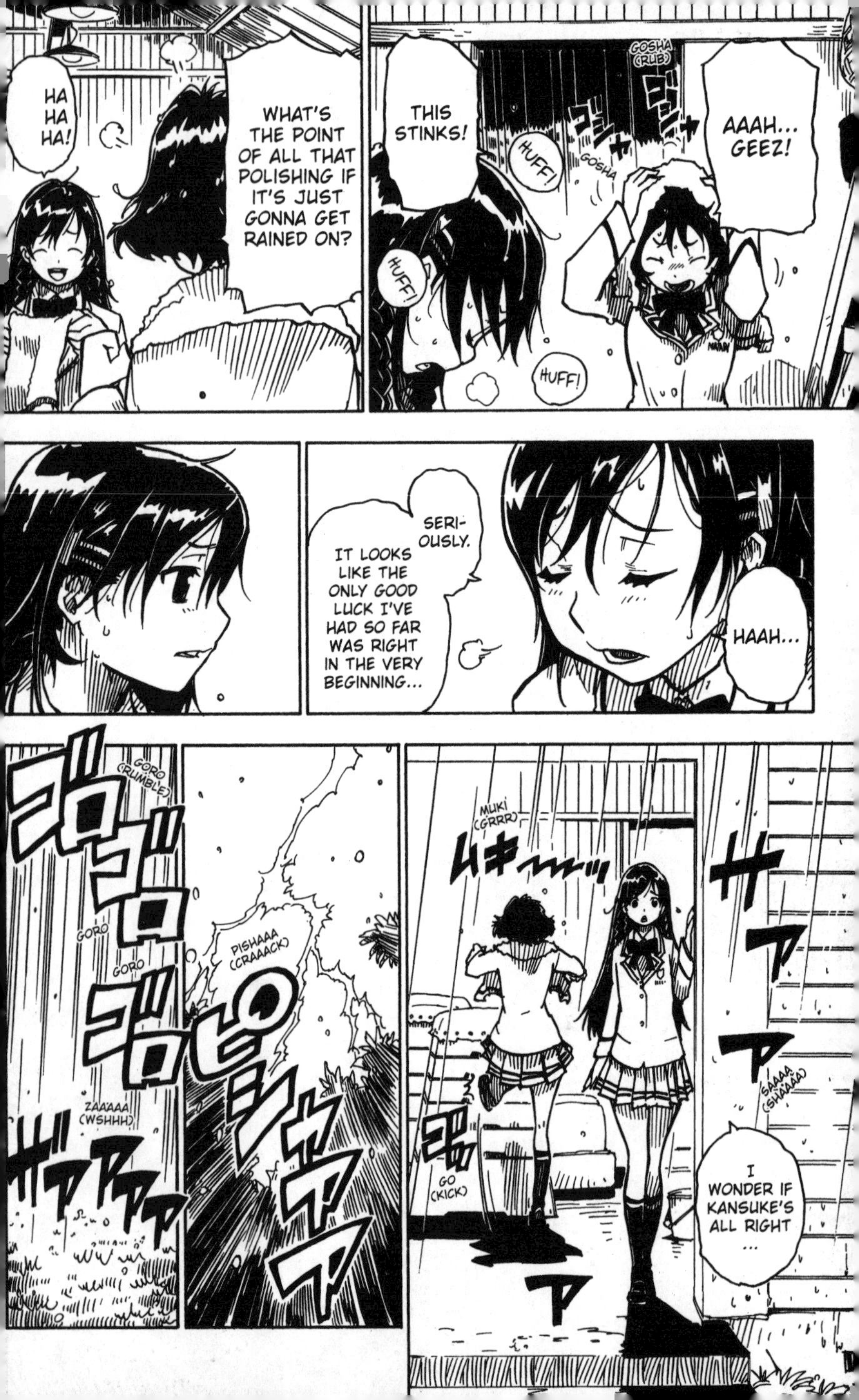
GOSHA (RUB)
GOSHA
AAAH... GEEZ!
THIS STINKS!
HUFF!
HUFF!
HUFF!
WHAT'S THE POINT OF ALL THAT POLISHING IF IT'S JUST GONNA GET RAINED ON?
HA HA HA!
HAAH...
SERI-OUSLY.
IT LOOKS LIKE THE ONLY GOOD LUCK I'VE HAD SO FAR WAS RIGHT IN THE VERY BEGINNING...
SAAAA (SHAAAA)
I WONDER IF KANSUKE'S ALL RIGHT...
MUKI (GRRR)
GO (KICK)
GORO (RUMBLE)
GORO
GORO
PISHAAA (CRAAACK)
ZAAAAA (WSHHH)

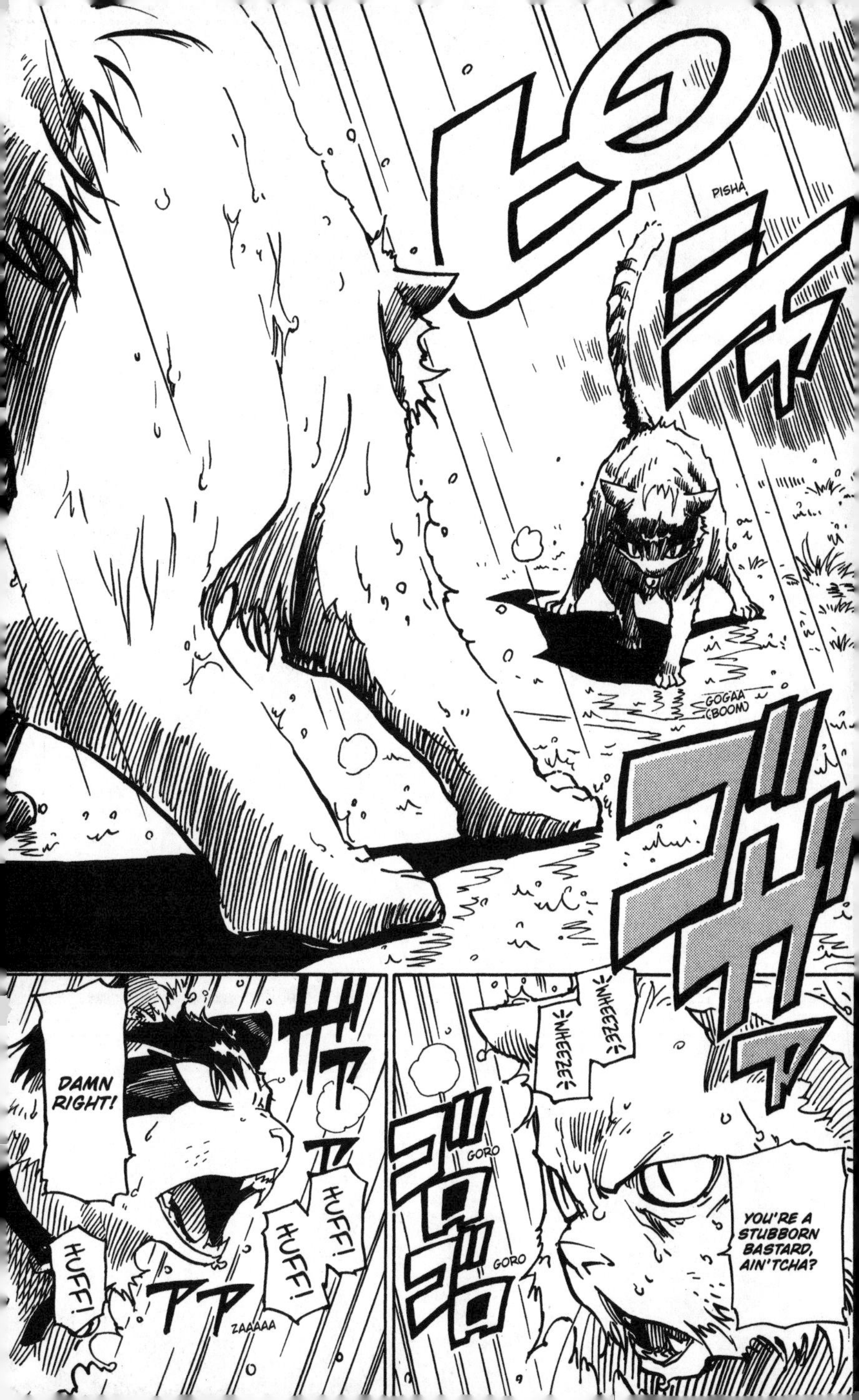

PISHA
GOGAA (BOOM)
WHEEZE
WHEEZE
GORO
YOU'RE A STUBBORN BASTARD, AIN'TCHA?
GORO
HUFF!
HUFF!
DAMN RIGHT!
HUFF!
ZAAAAA

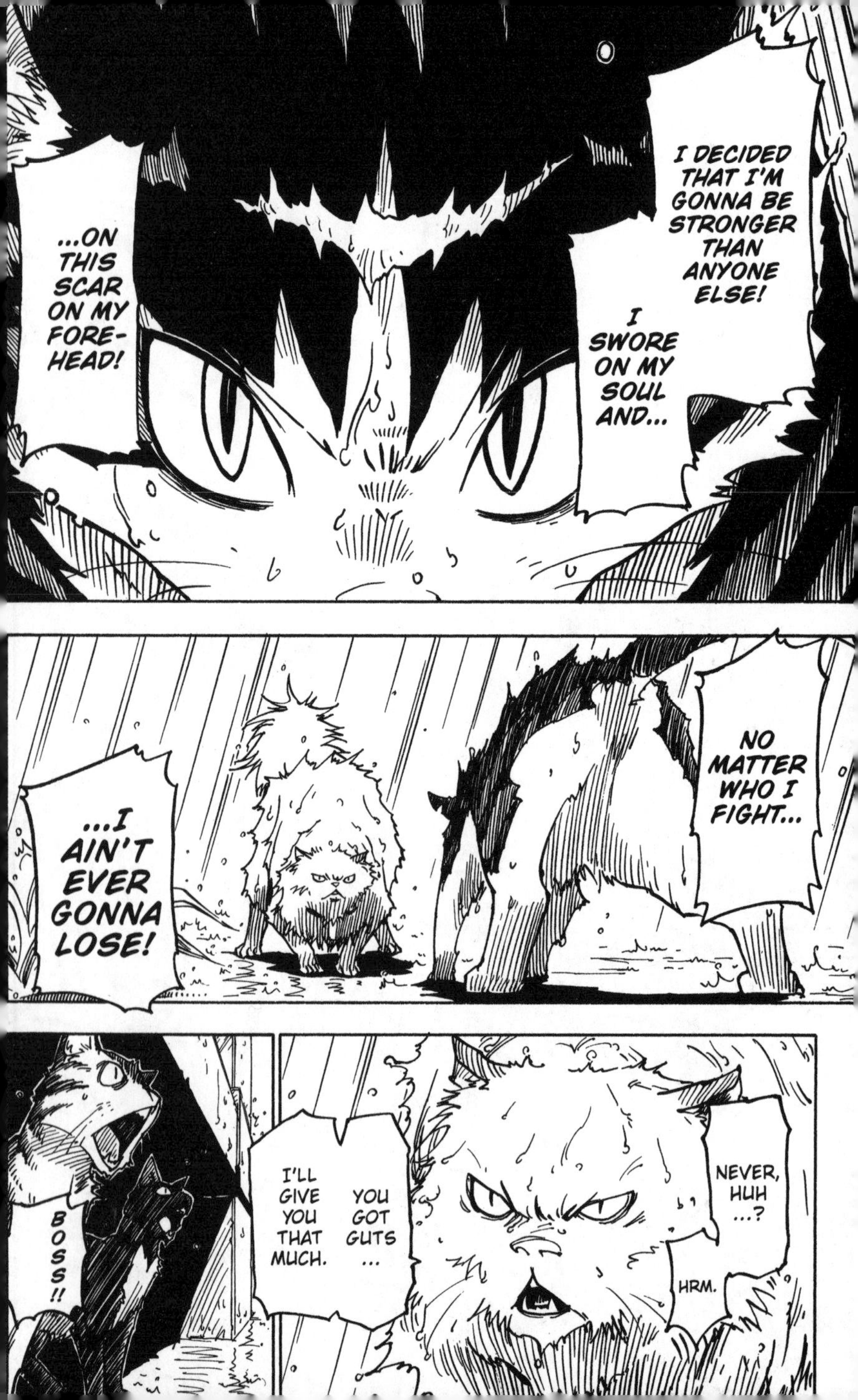
I DECIDED THAT I'M GONNA BE STRONGER THAN ANYONE ELSE!
I SWORE ON MY SOUL AND...
...ON THIS SCAR ON MY FORE-HEAD!
NO MATTER WHO I FIGHT...
...I AIN'T EVER GONNA LOSE!
NEVER, HUH ...?
HRM.
YOU GOT GUTS ...
I'LL GIVE YOU THAT MUCH.
BOSS!!

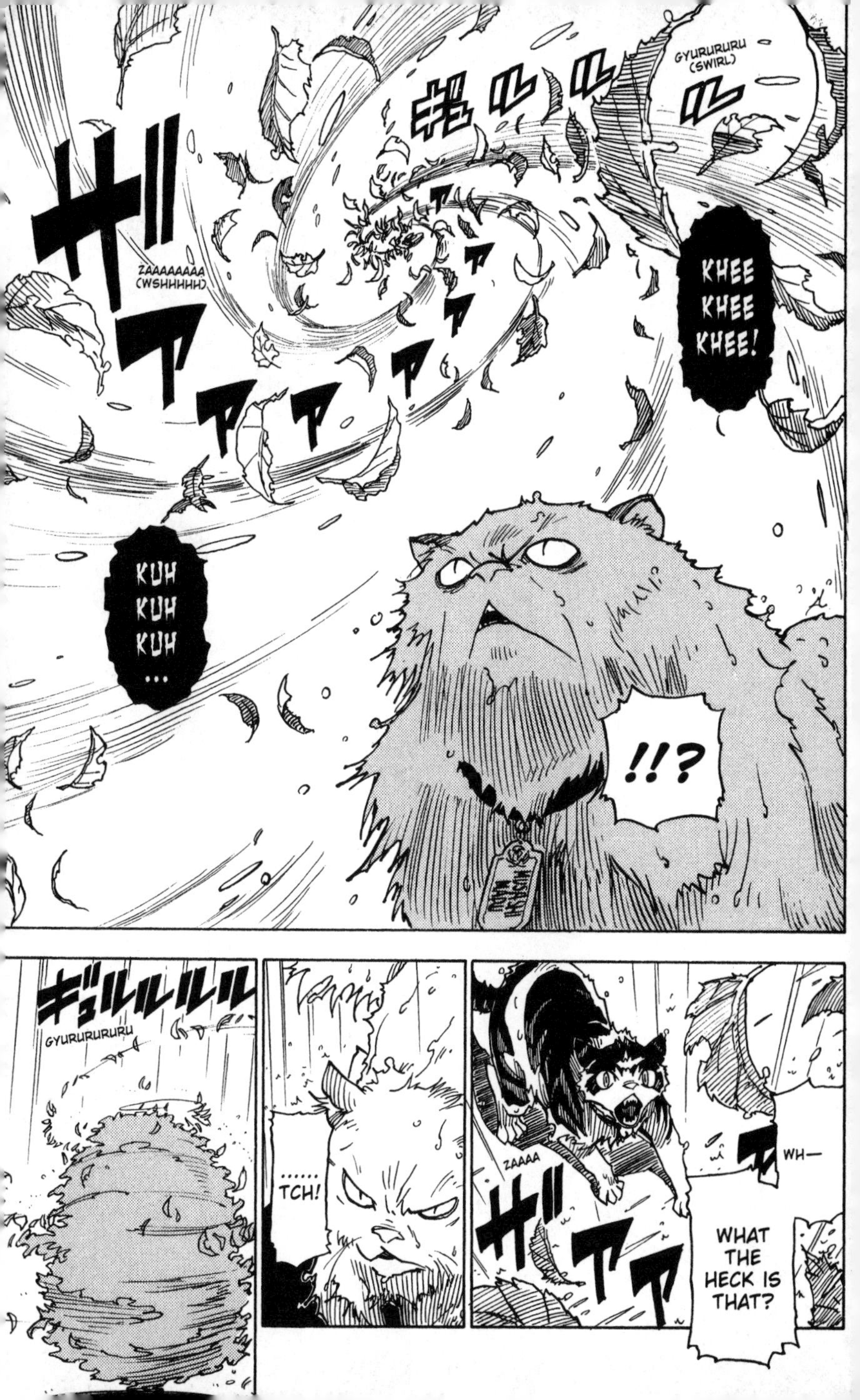
GYURURURU (SWIRL)
KHEE KHEE KHEE!
ZAAAAAAAA (WSHHHHH)
!!?
KUH KUH KUH ...
WH—
ZAAAA
WHAT THE HECK IS THAT?
...... TCH!
GYURURURURU

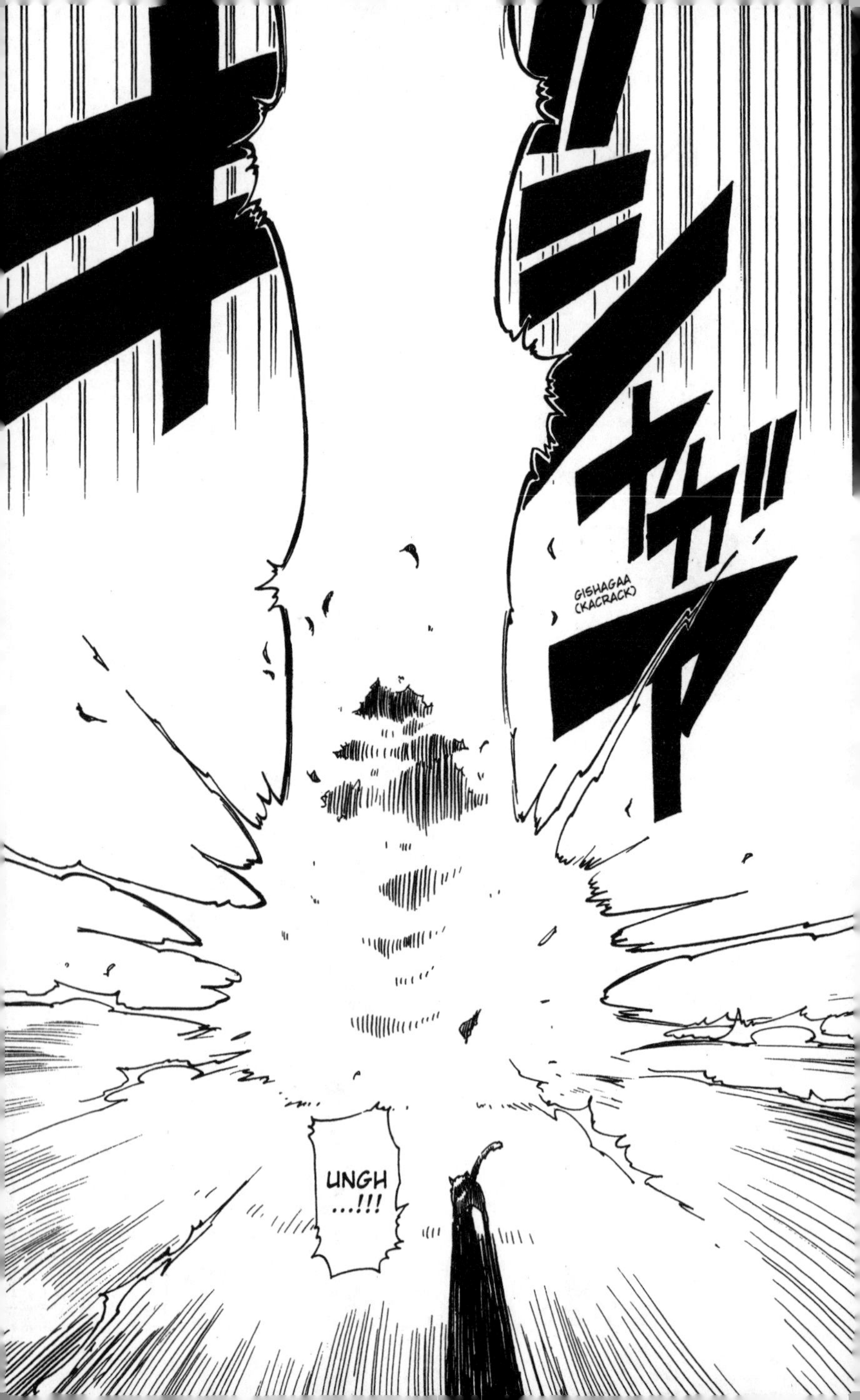
GISHAGAA (KACRACK)
UNGH ...!!!

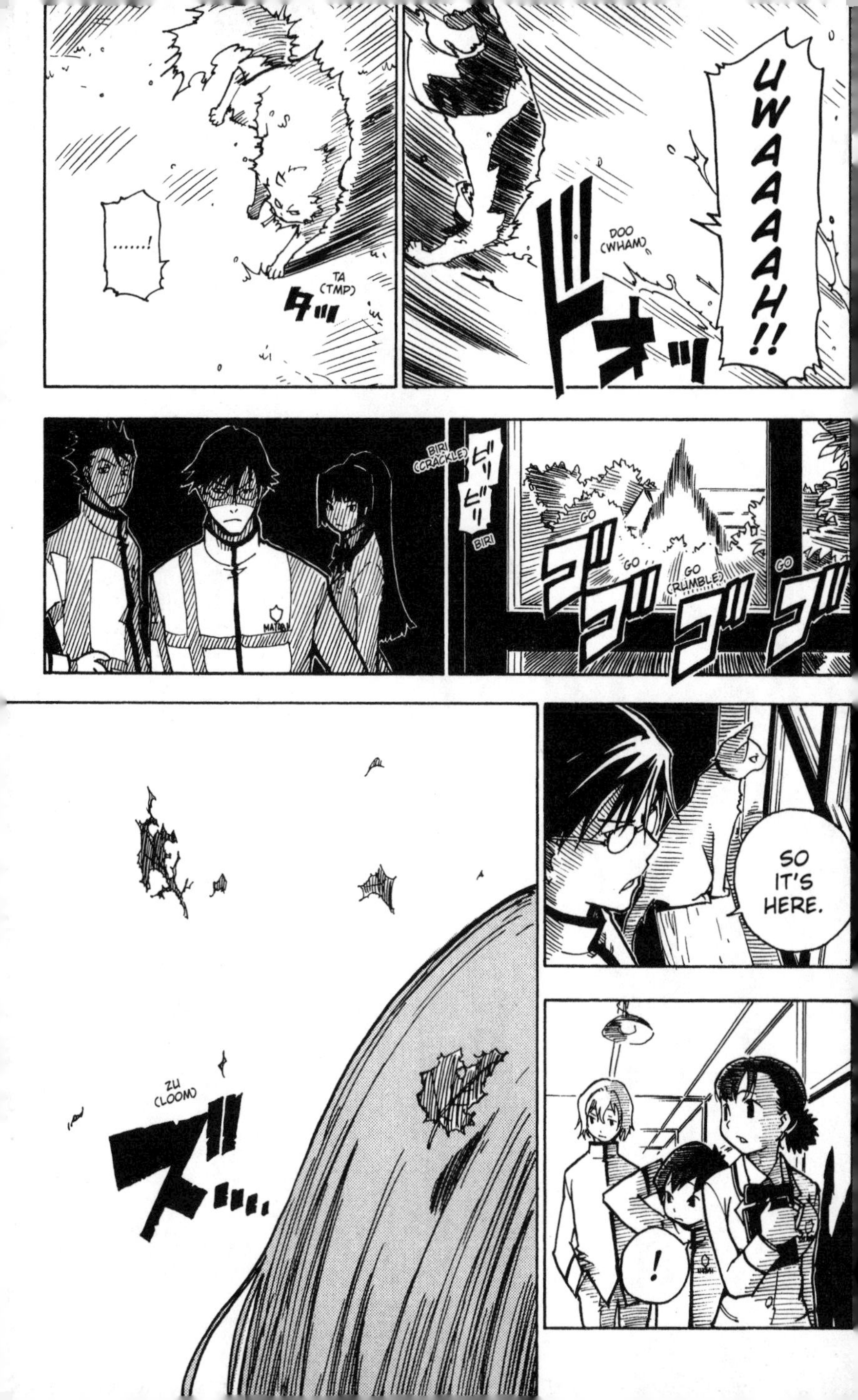
UWAAAAAH!!
DOO (WHAM)
TA (TMP)
......!
GO GO GO (RUMBLE) GO
BIRI (CRACKLE) BIRI
SO IT'S HERE.
!
ZU (LOOM)

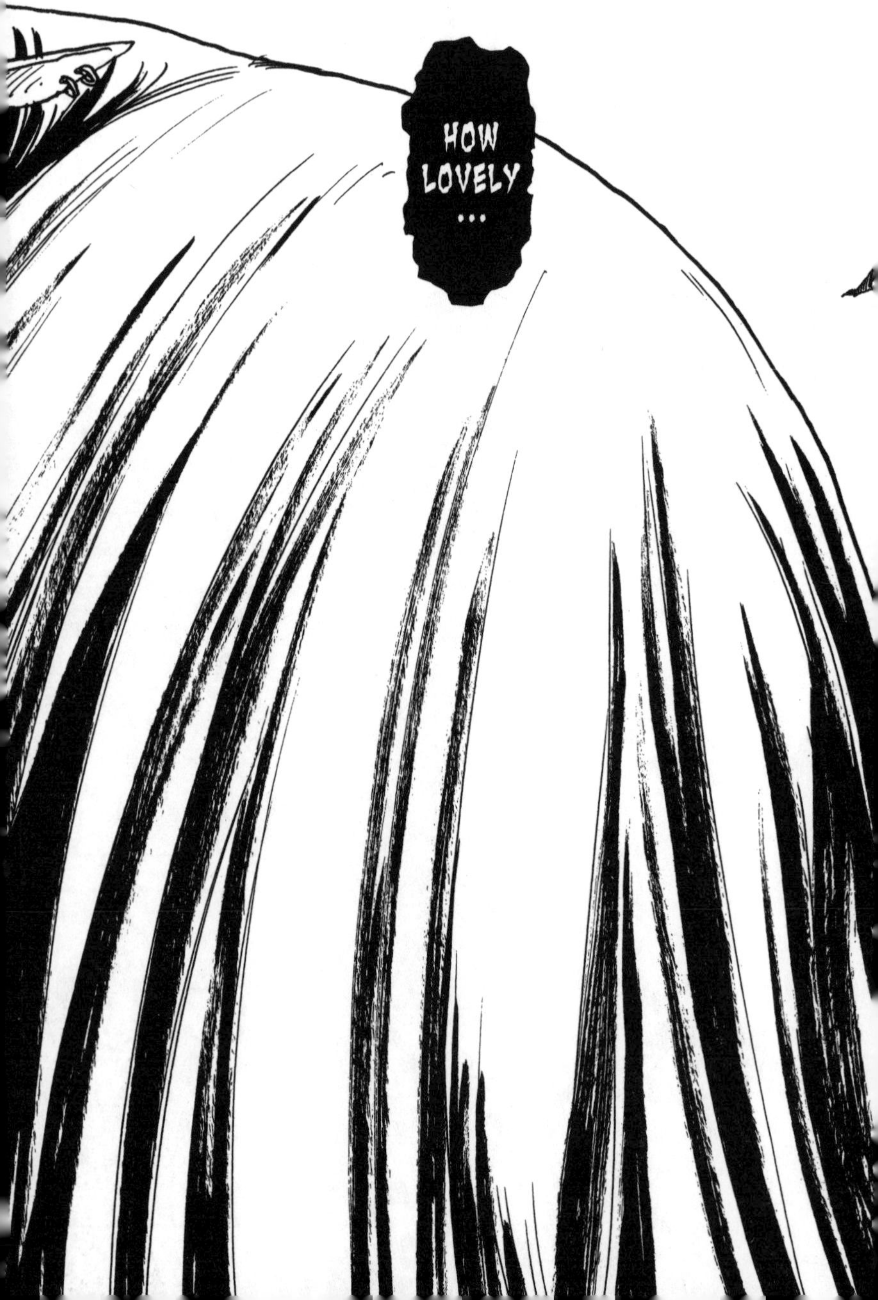
HOW LOVELY ...

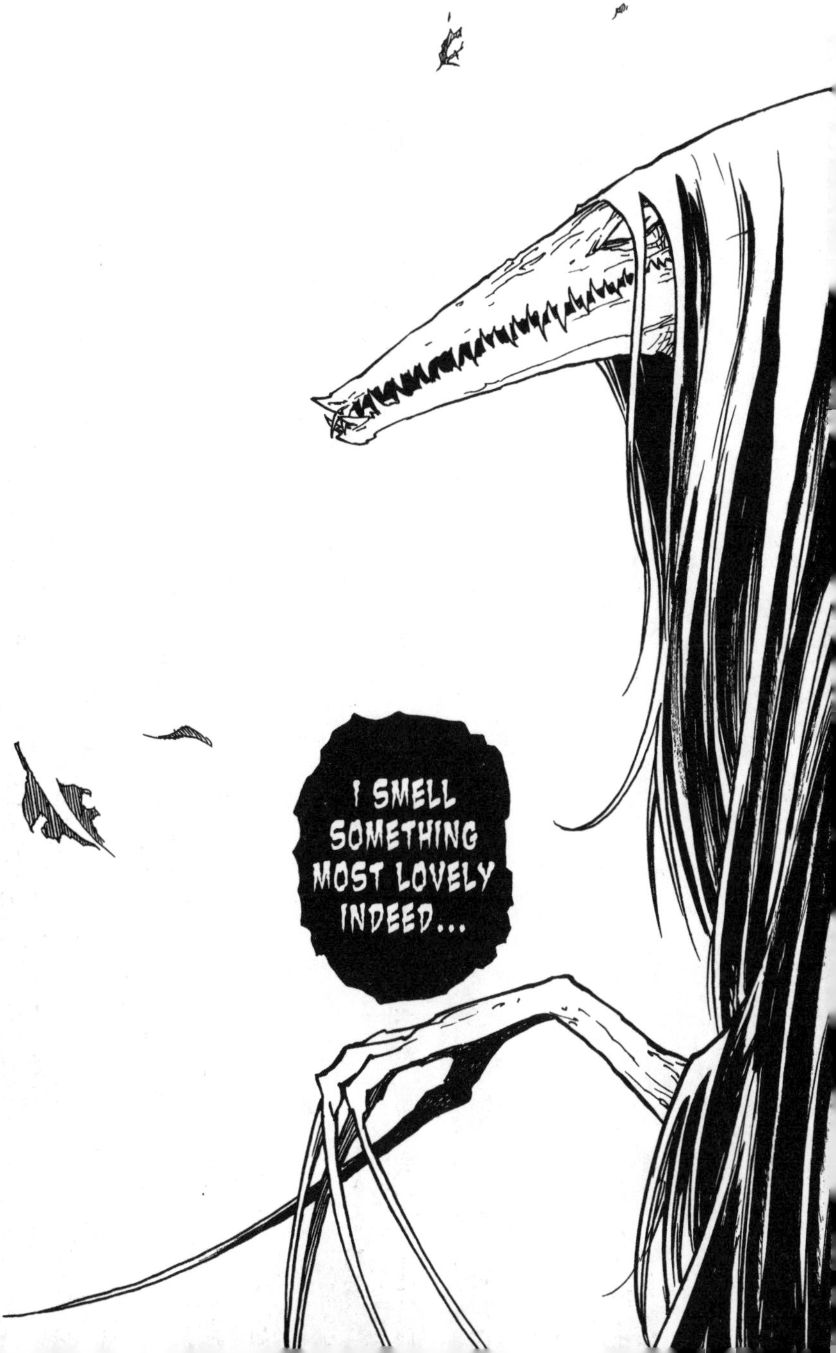
I SMELL SOMETHING MOST LOVELY INDEED...

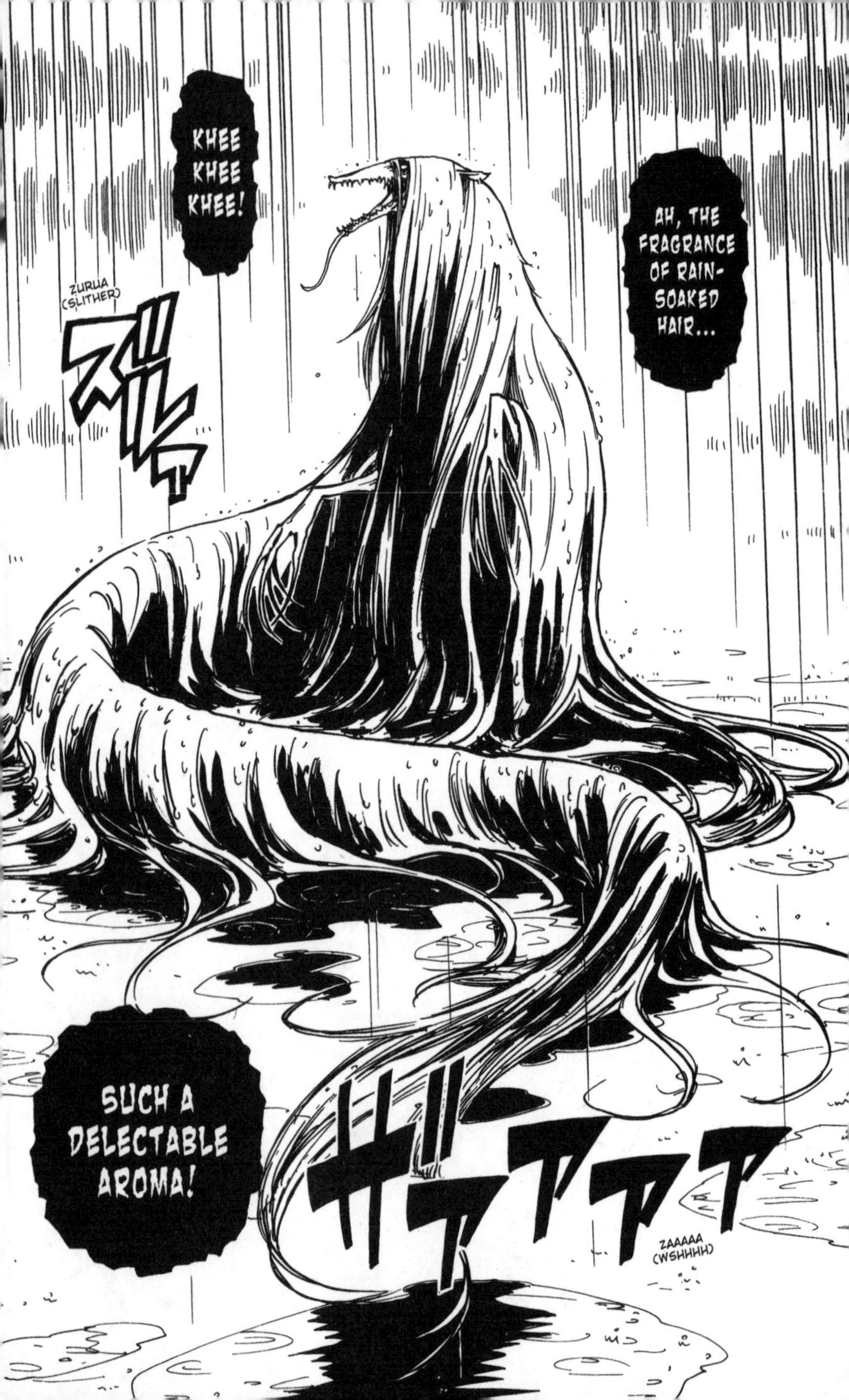
AH, THE FRAGRANCE OF RAIN-SOAKED HAIR...
KHEE KHEE KHEE!
ZURUA (SLITHER)
ZAAAAA (WSHHHH)
SUCH A DELECTABLE AROMA!

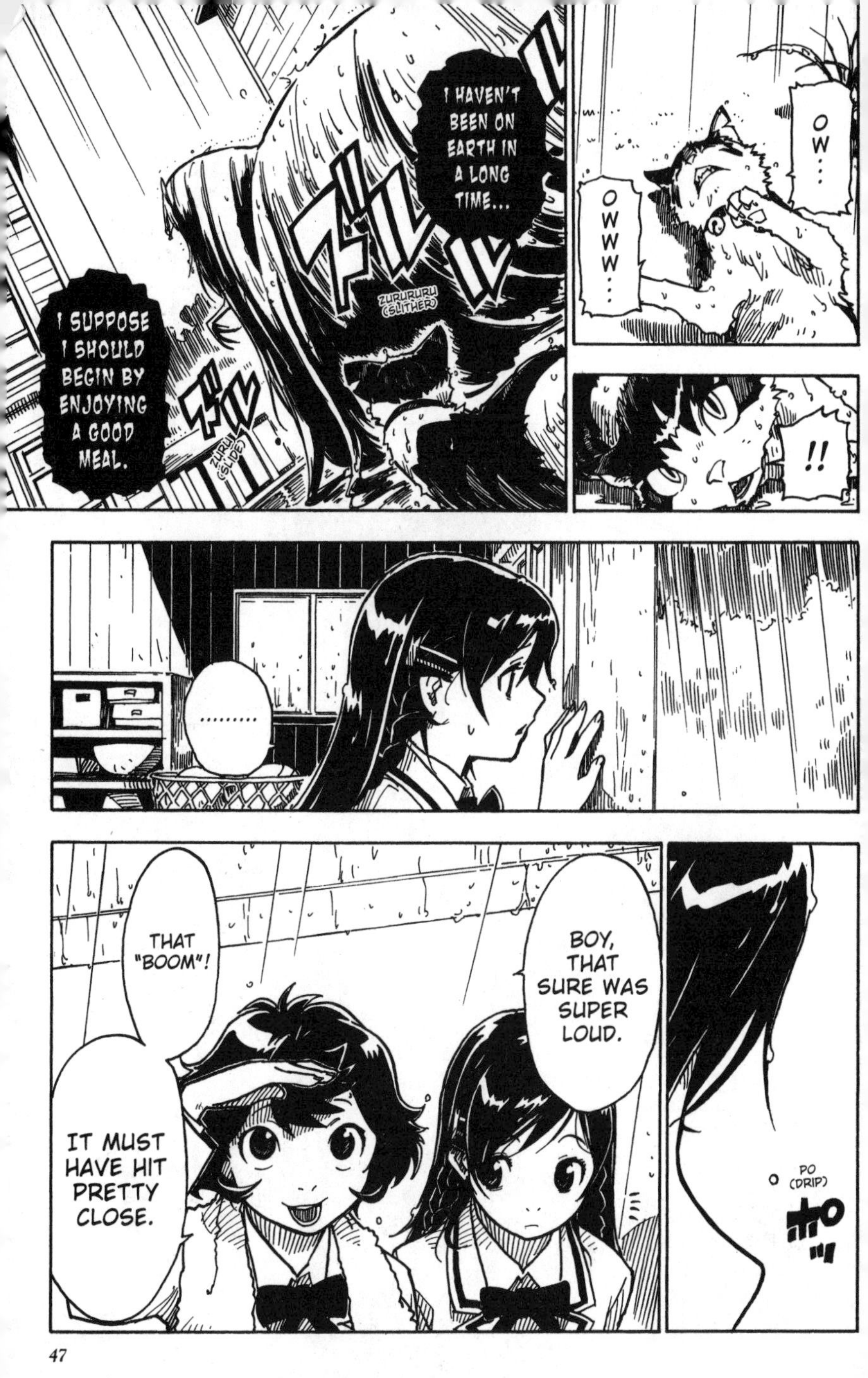
OW...
OWWW...
!!
I HAVEN'T BEEN ON EARTH IN A LONG TIME...
ZURURURU (SLITHER)
ZURU (SLIDE)
I SUPPOSE I SHOULD BEGIN BY ENJOYING A GOOD MEAL.
....
PO (DRIP)
BOY, THAT SURE WAS SUPER LOUD.
THAT "BOOM"!
IT MUST HAVE HIT PRETTY CLOSE.

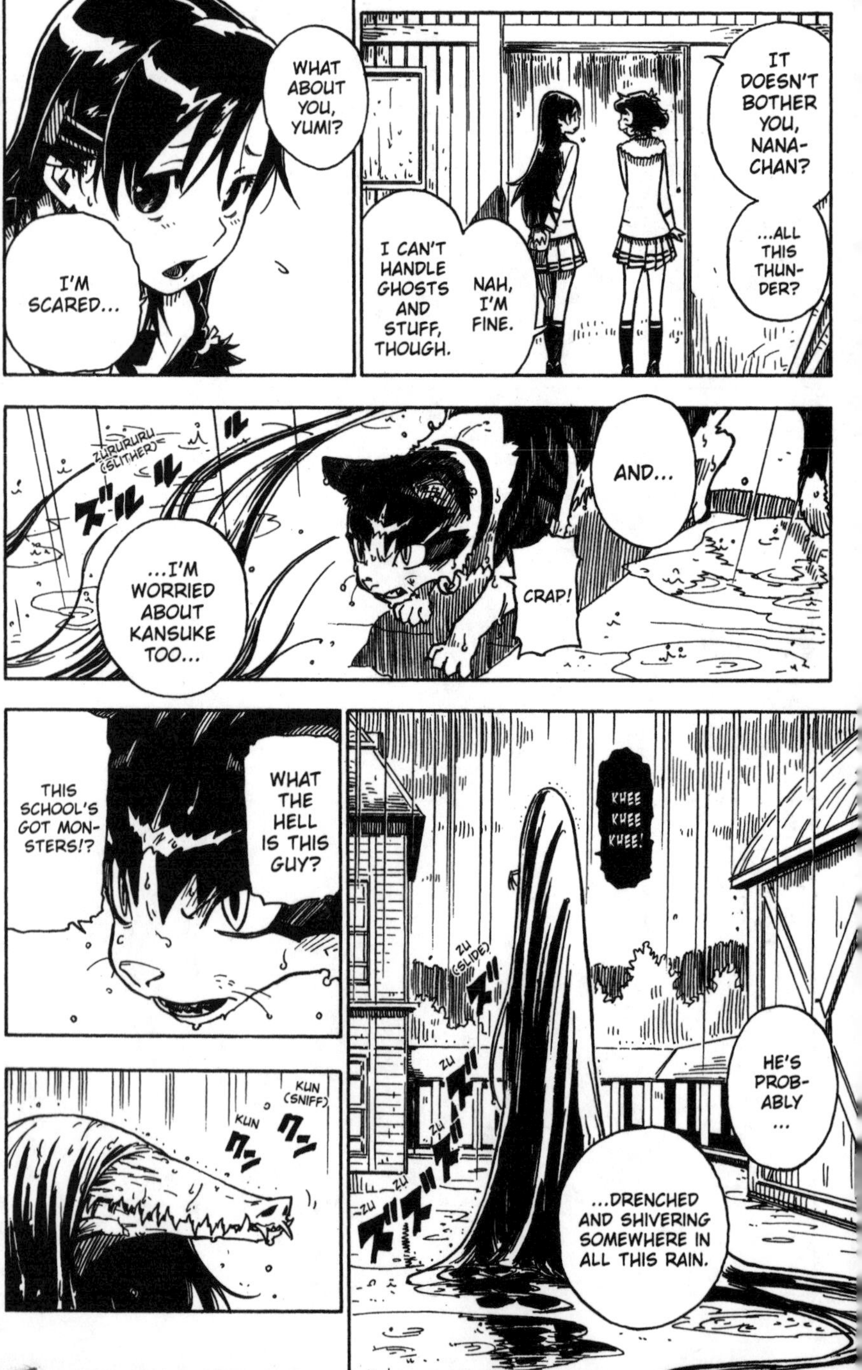
IT DOESN'T BOTHER YOU, NANA-CHAN?
...ALL THIS THUNDER?
NAH, I'M FINE.
I CAN'T HANDLE GHOSTS AND STUFF, THOUGH.
WHAT ABOUT YOU, YUMI?
I'M SCARED...
AND...
CRAP!
ZURURURU (SLITHER)
...I'M WORRIED ABOUT KANSUKE TOO...
KHEE KHEE KHEE!
ZU (SLIDE)
ZU
ZU
ZU
ZU
HE'S PROBABLY...
...DRENCHED AND SHIVERING SOMEWHERE IN ALL THIS RAIN.
WHAT THE HELL IS THIS GUY?
THIS SCHOOL'S GOT MON-STERS!?
KUN (SNIFF)
KUN

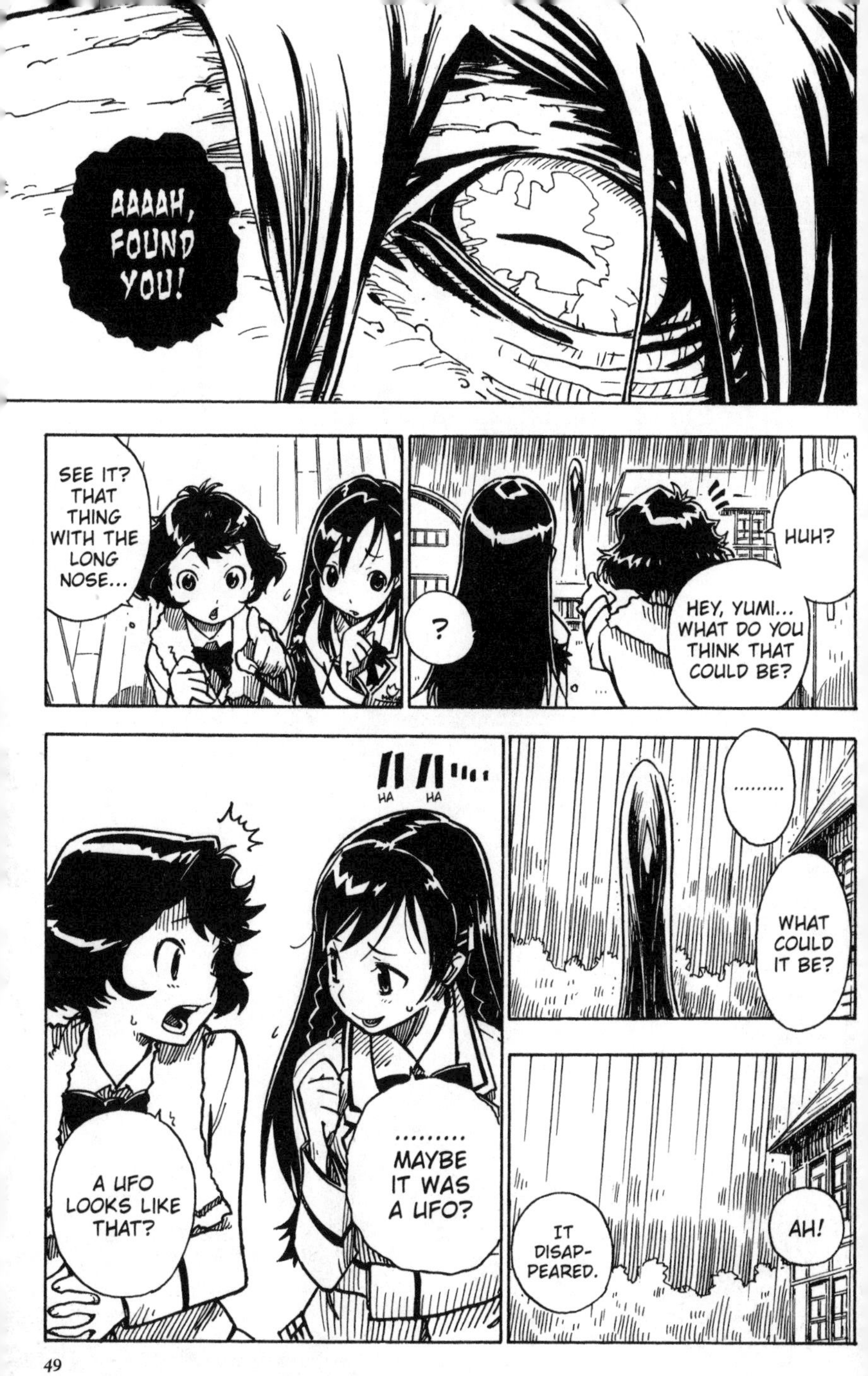
AAAAH, FOUND YOU!
HUH?
HEY, YUMI... WHAT DO YOU THINK THAT COULD BE?
?
SEE IT? THAT THING WITH THE LONG NOSE...
....
WHAT COULD IT BE?
AH!
IT DISAPPEARED.
HA HA
.... MAYBE IT WAS A UFO?
A UFO LOOKS LIKE THAT?

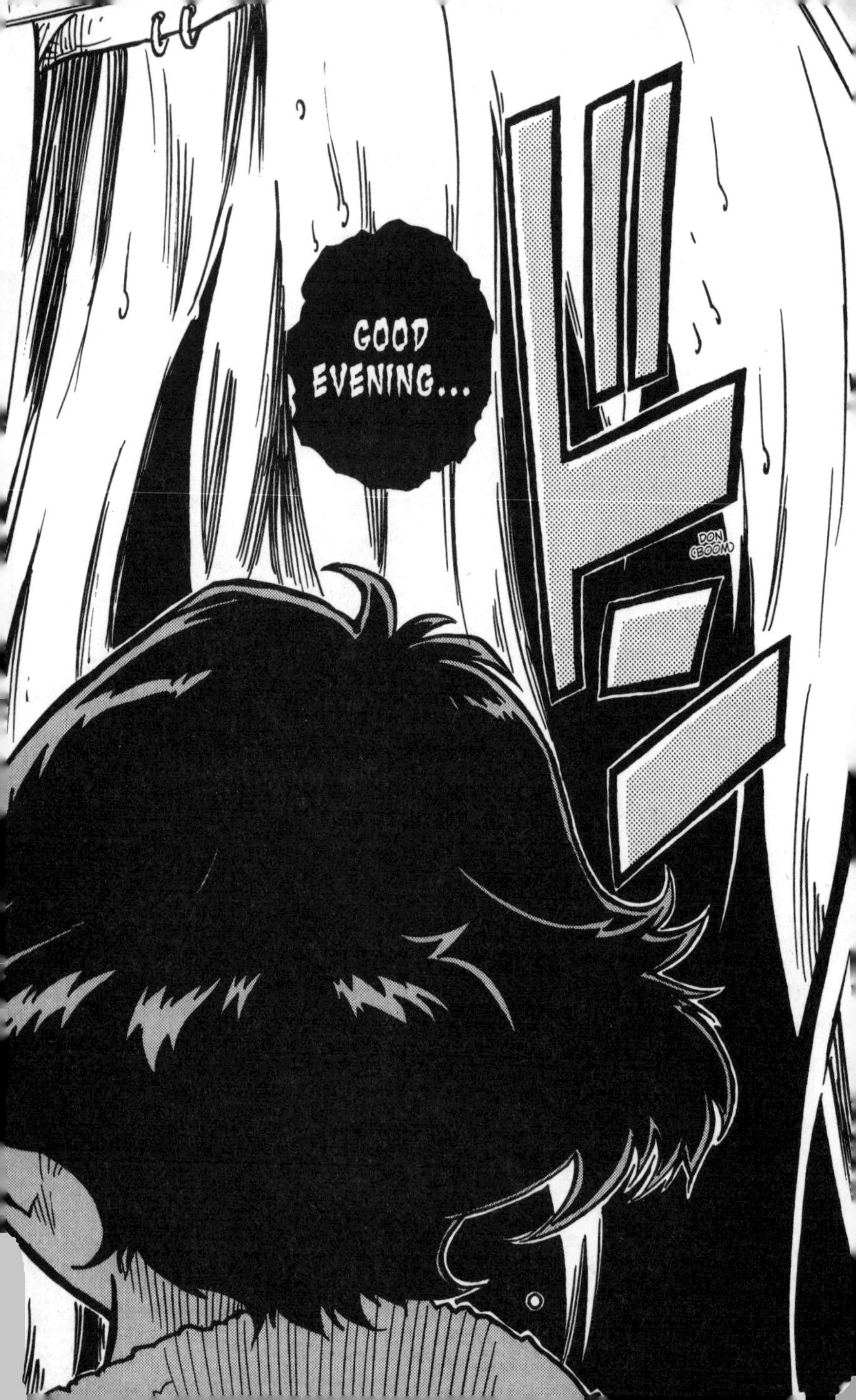
GOOD EVENING...
DON (BOOM)

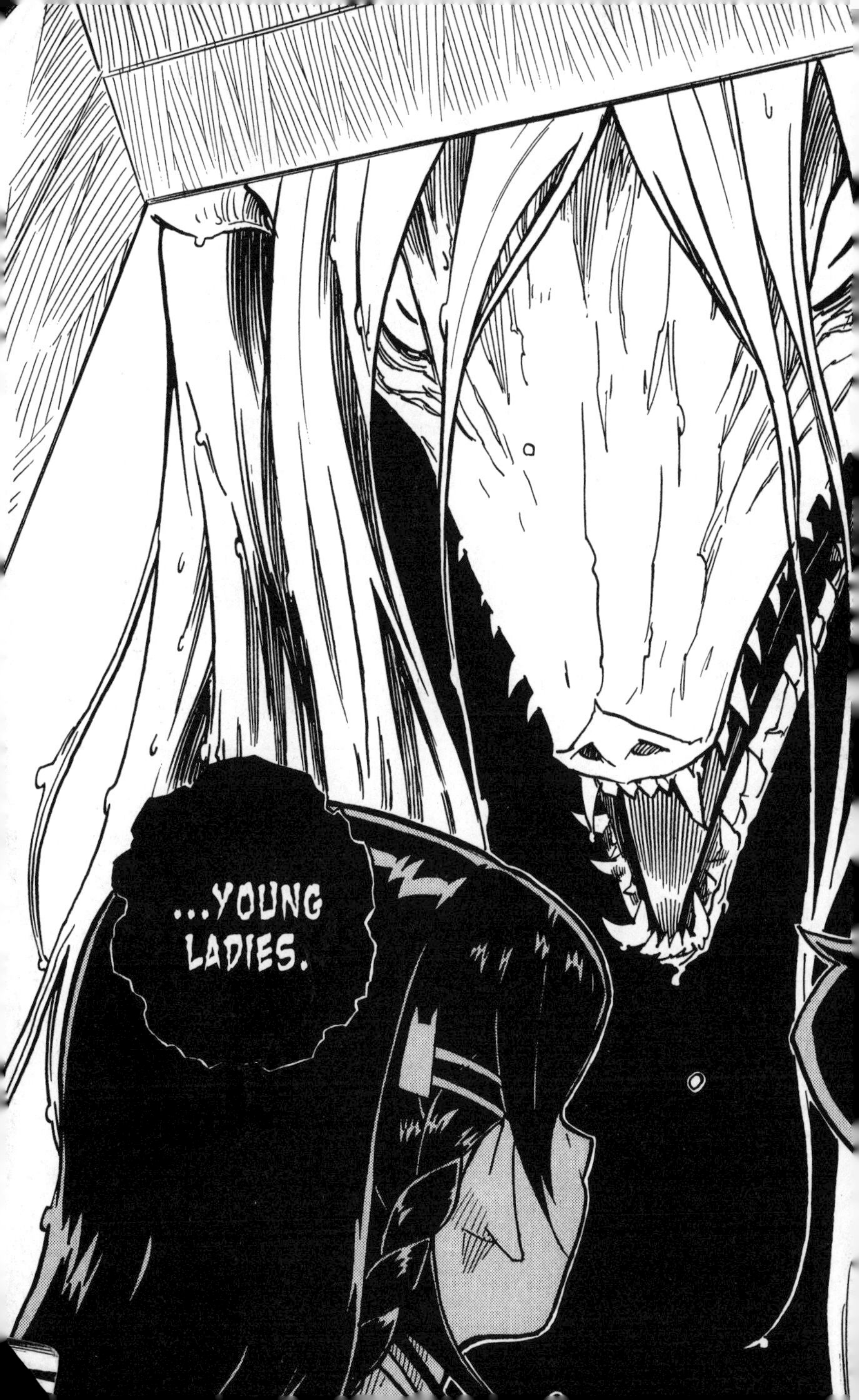
...YOUNG LADIES.

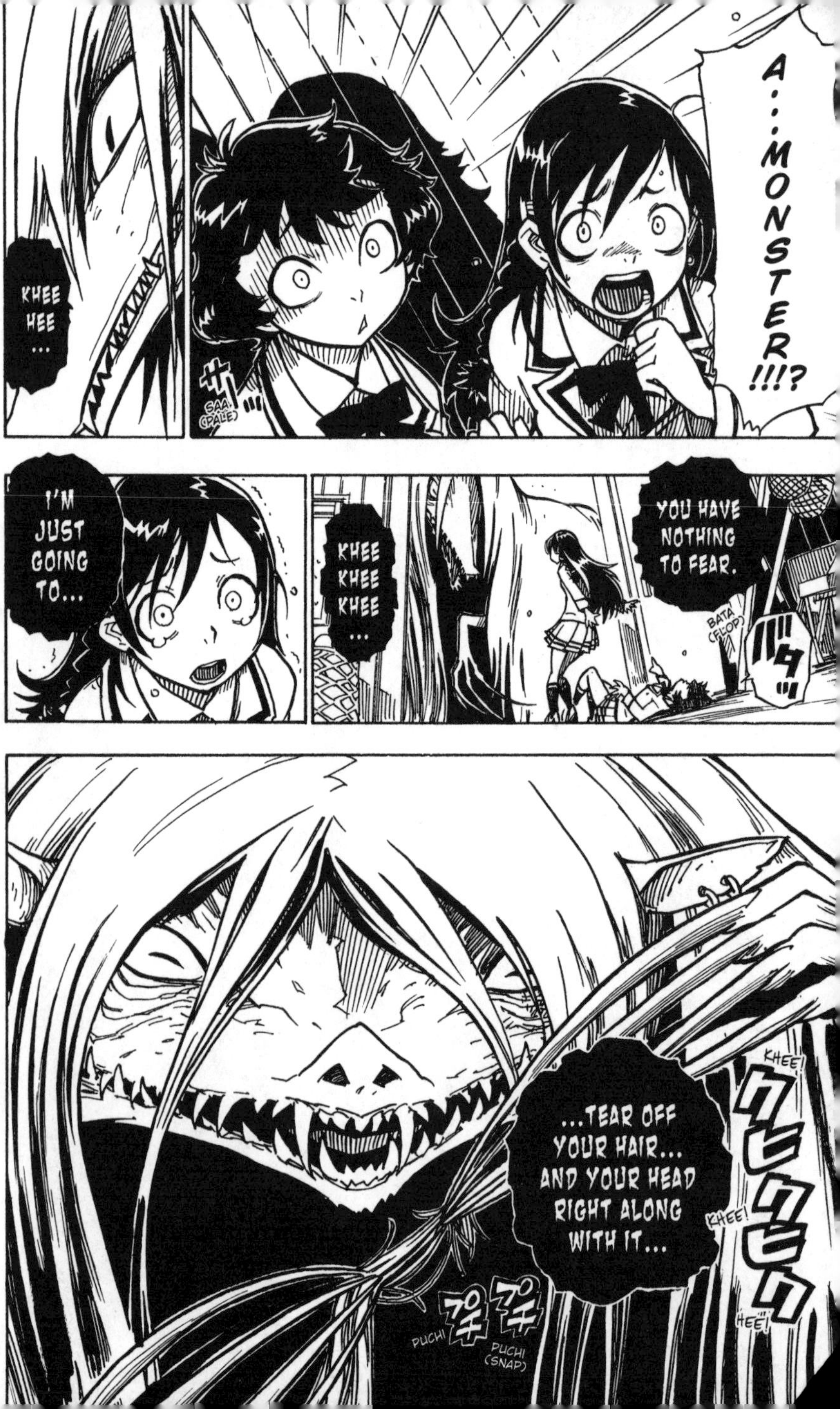

A...MONSTER!!!?
SAA (PALE)
KHEE HEE ...
YOU HAVE NOTHING TO FEAR.
BATA (FLOP)
KHEE KHEE KHEE ...
I'M JUST GOING TO...
KHEE! KHEE! HEE!
...TEAR OFF YOUR HAIR... AND YOUR HEAD RIGHT ALONG WITH IT...
PUCHI PUCHI (SNAP)

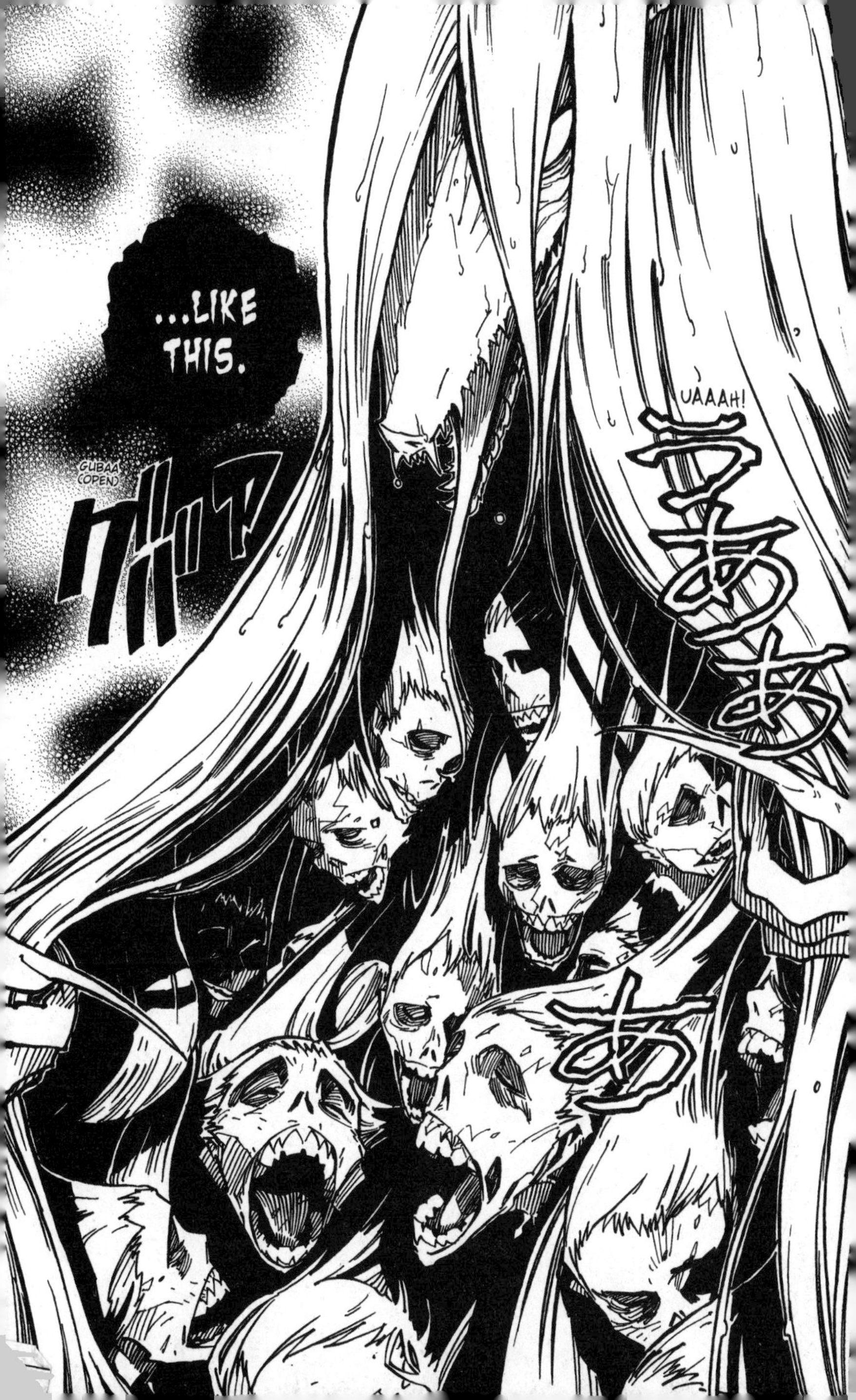
...LIKE THIS.
UAAAH!
うあああ
あ
GUBAA (OPEN)
グバァ

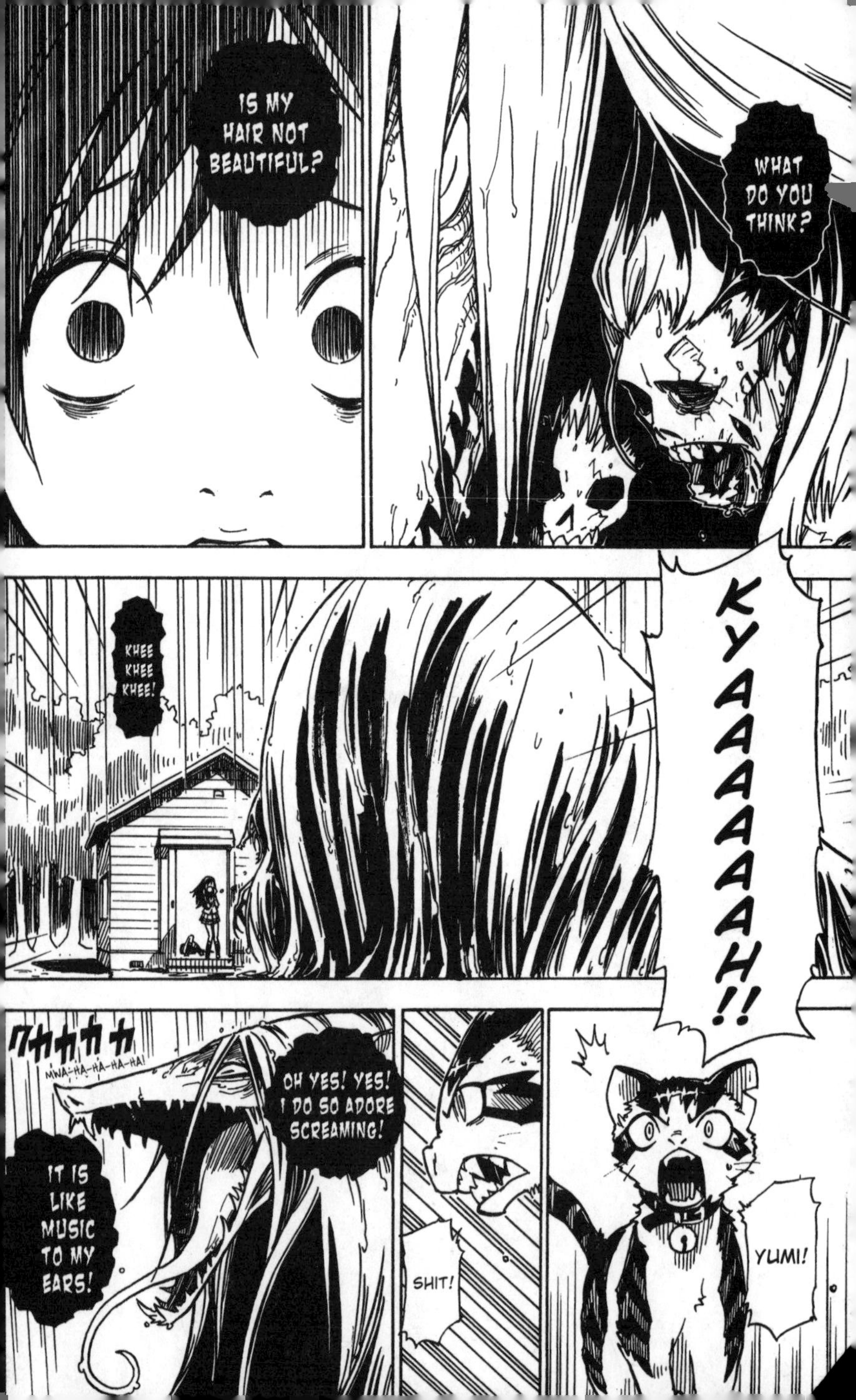
WHAT DO YOU THINK?
IS MY HAIR NOT BEAUTIFUL?
KYAAAAAAAH!!
KHEE KHEE KHEE!
YUMI!
SHIT!
クカカカカ
MWA-HA-HA-HA-HA!
OH YES! YES! I DO SO ADORE SCREAMING!
IT IS LIKE MUSIC TO MY EARS!

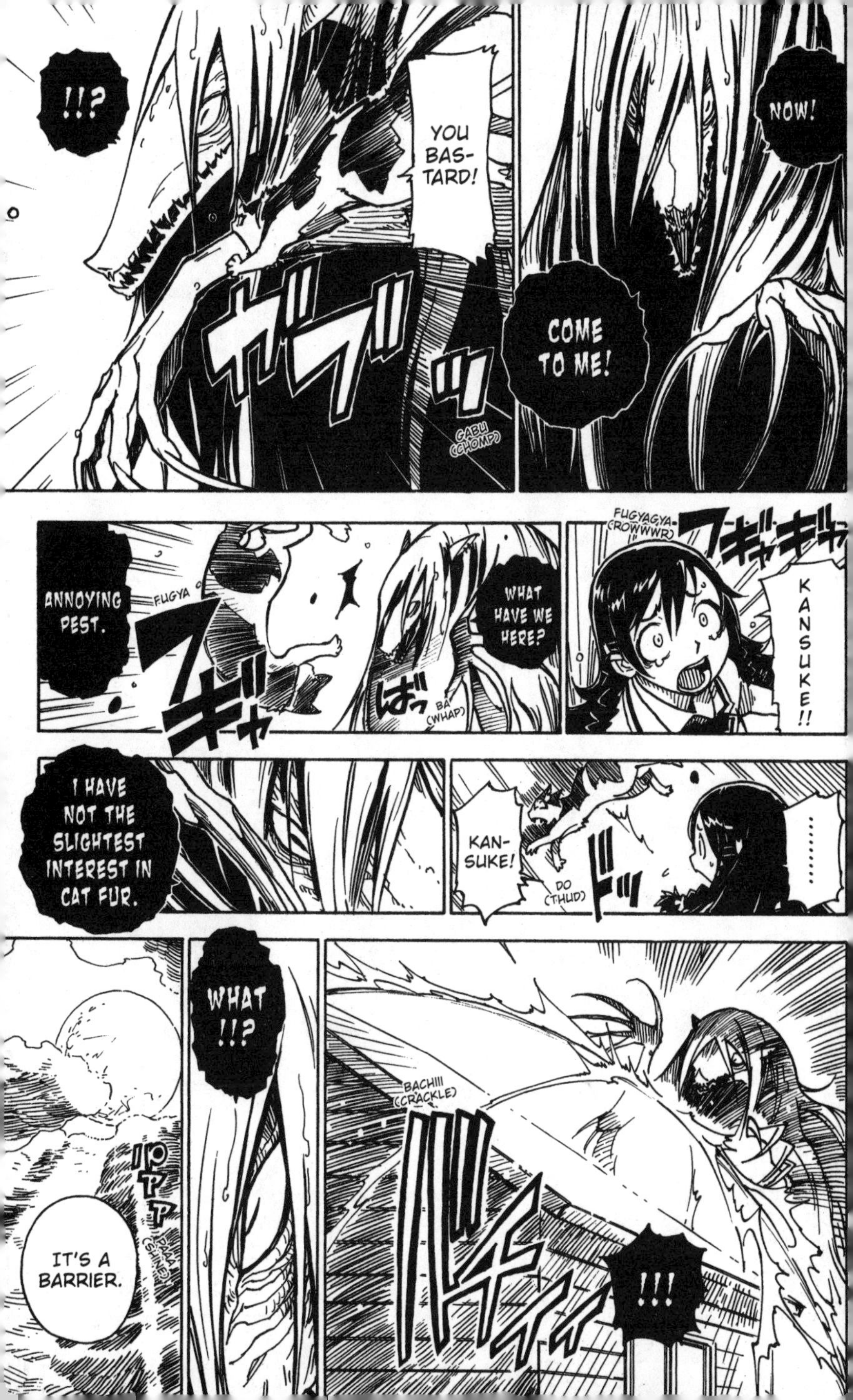
NOW!
COME TO ME!
YOU BAS-TARD!
!!?
GABU (CHOMP)
FUGYAGYA (ROWWWR)
KANSUKE!!
WHAT HAVE WE HERE?
ANNOYING PEST.
FUGYA
BA (WHAP)
....
KAN-SUKE!
DO (THUD)
I HAVE NOT THE SLIGHTEST INTEREST IN CAT FUR.
BACHIII (CRACKLE)
!!!
WHAT !!?
PAAA (SHINE)
IT'S A BARRIER.

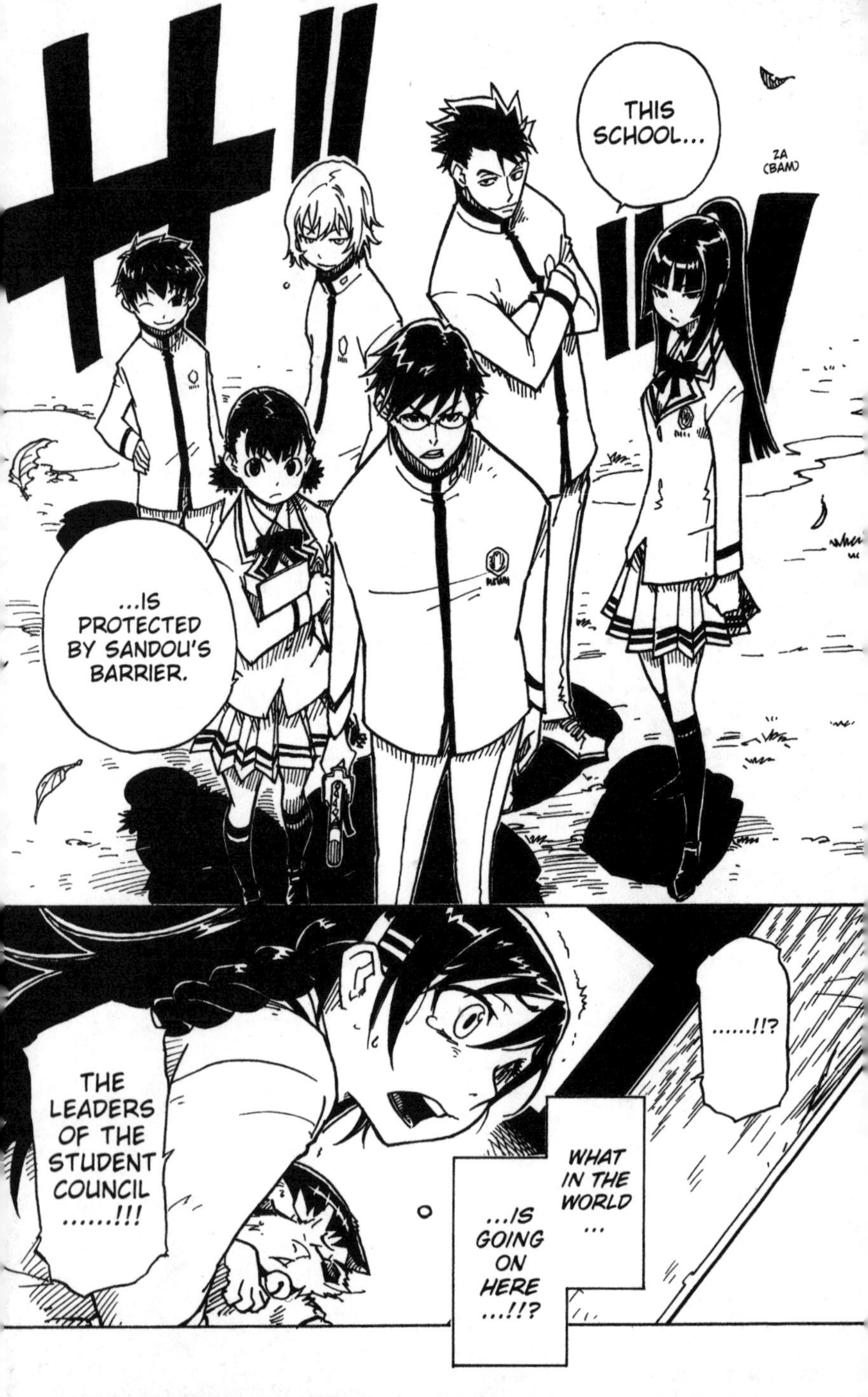
ZA (BAM)
THIS SCHOOL...
...IS PROTECTED BY SANDOU'S BARRIER.
......!!?
WHAT IN THE WORLD ...
...IS GOING ON HERE ...!!?
THE LEADERS OF THE STUDENT COUNCIL ......!!!

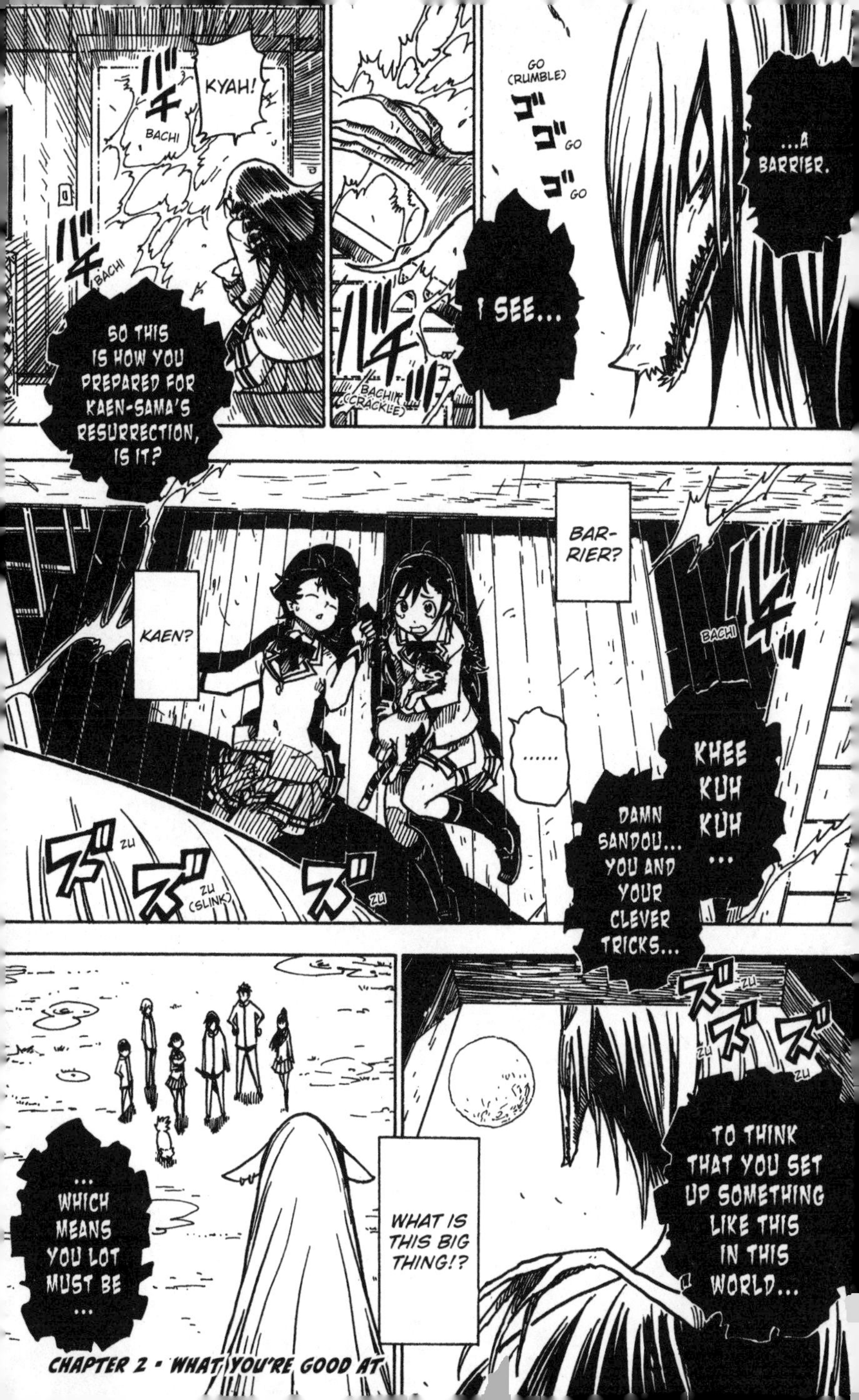
...A BARRIER.
GO (RUMBLE)
ゴゴゴ GO GO
I SEE...
バチ BACHI (CRACKLE)
KYAH!
バチ BACHI
バチ BACHI
SO THIS IS HOW YOU PREPARED FOR KAEN-SAMA'S RESURRECTION, IS IT?
BAR-RIER?
バチ BACHI
KAEN?
......
KHEE KUH KUH...
DAMN SANDOU... YOU AND YOUR CLEVER TRICKS...
ズ ZU
ズ ZU (SLINK)
ズ ZU
ズ ZU
ズ ZU
ズ ZU
TO THINK THAT YOU SET UP SOMETHING LIKE THIS IN THIS WORLD...
WHAT IS THIS BIG THING!?
...WHICH MEANS YOU LOT MUST BE...

CHAPTER 2 • WHAT YOU'RE GOOD AT

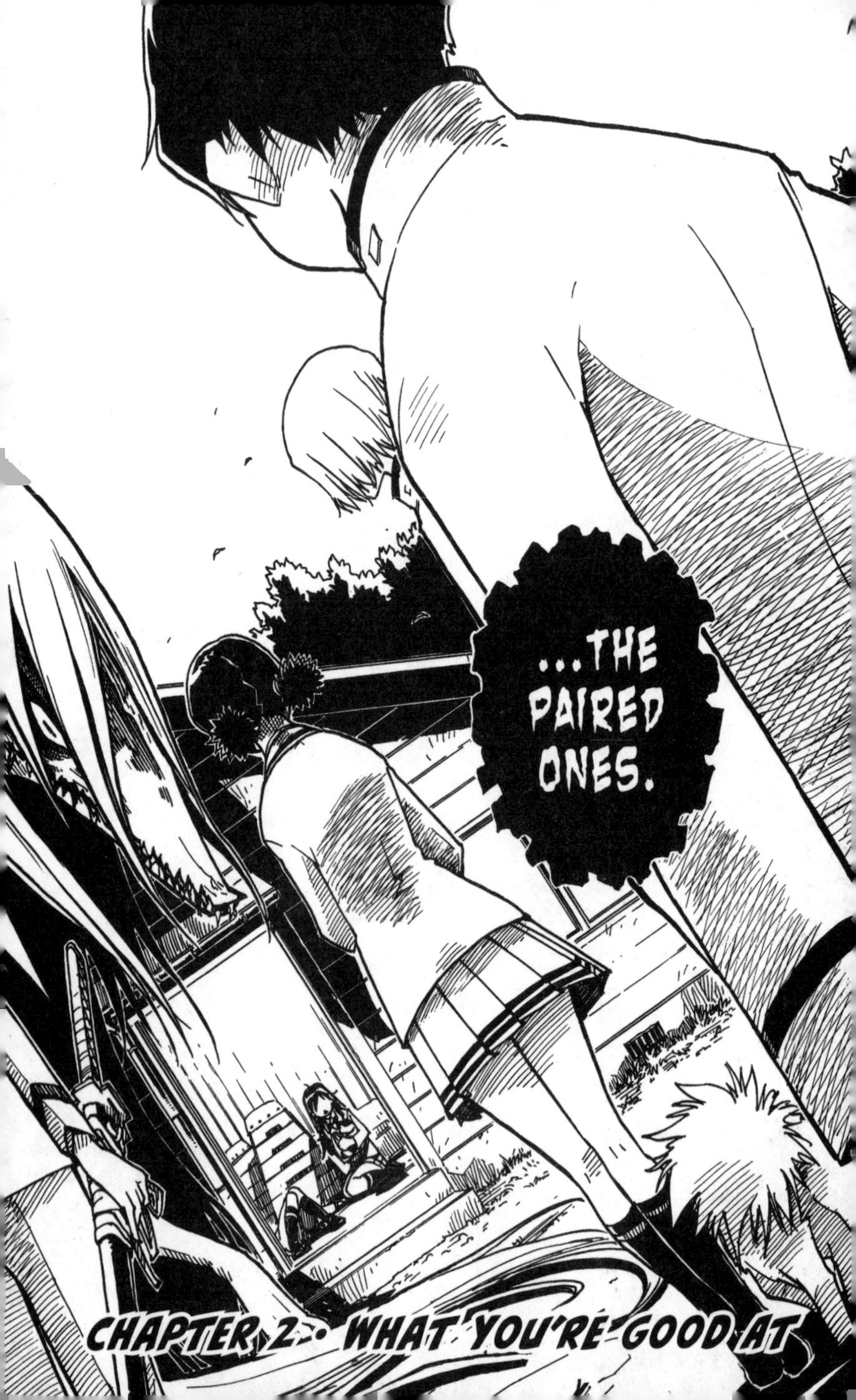
...THE PAIRED ONES.
CHAPTER 2 • WHAT YOU'RE GOOD AT

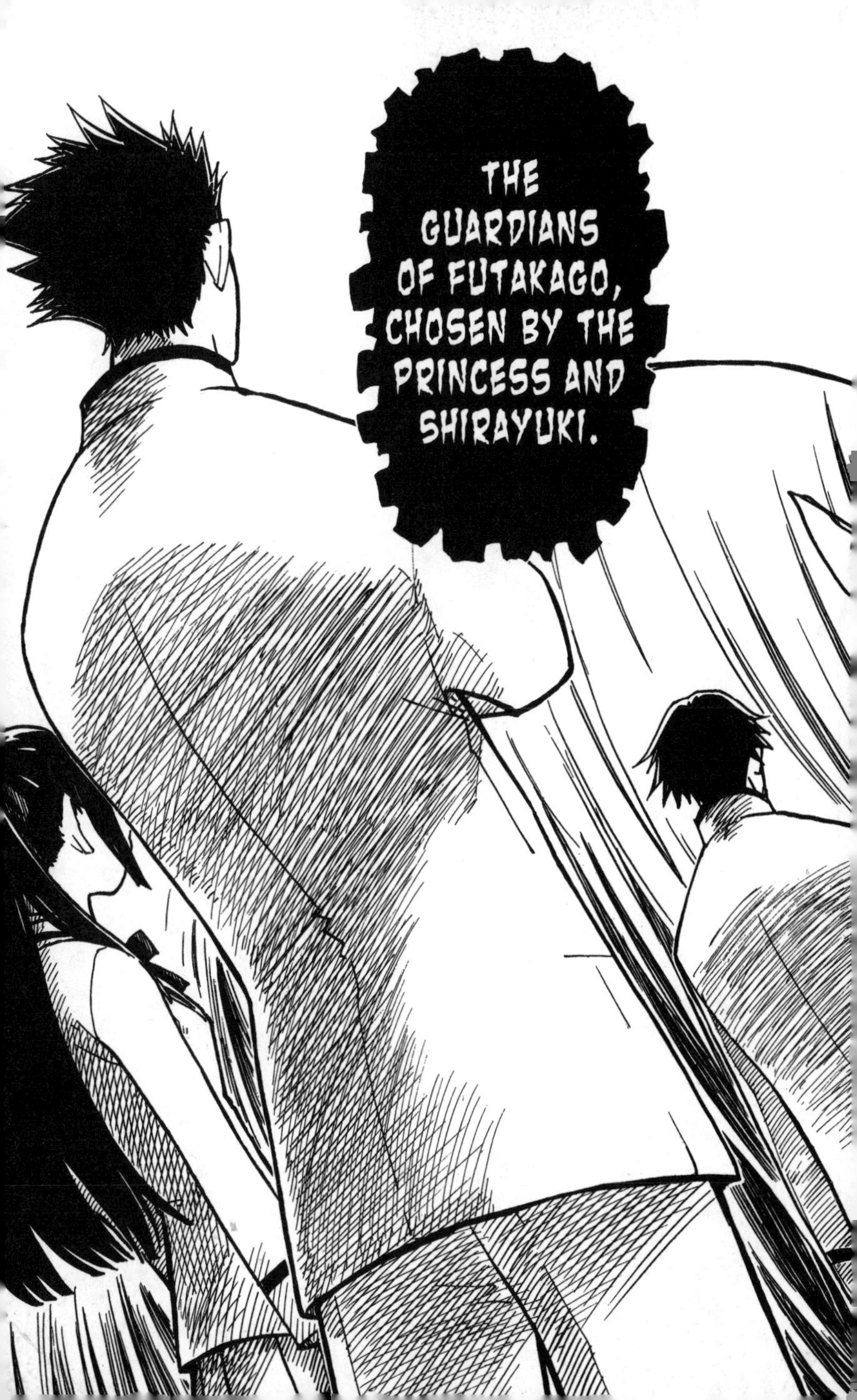
THE GUARDIANS OF FUTAKAGO, CHOSEN BY THE PRINCESS AND SHIRAYUKI.

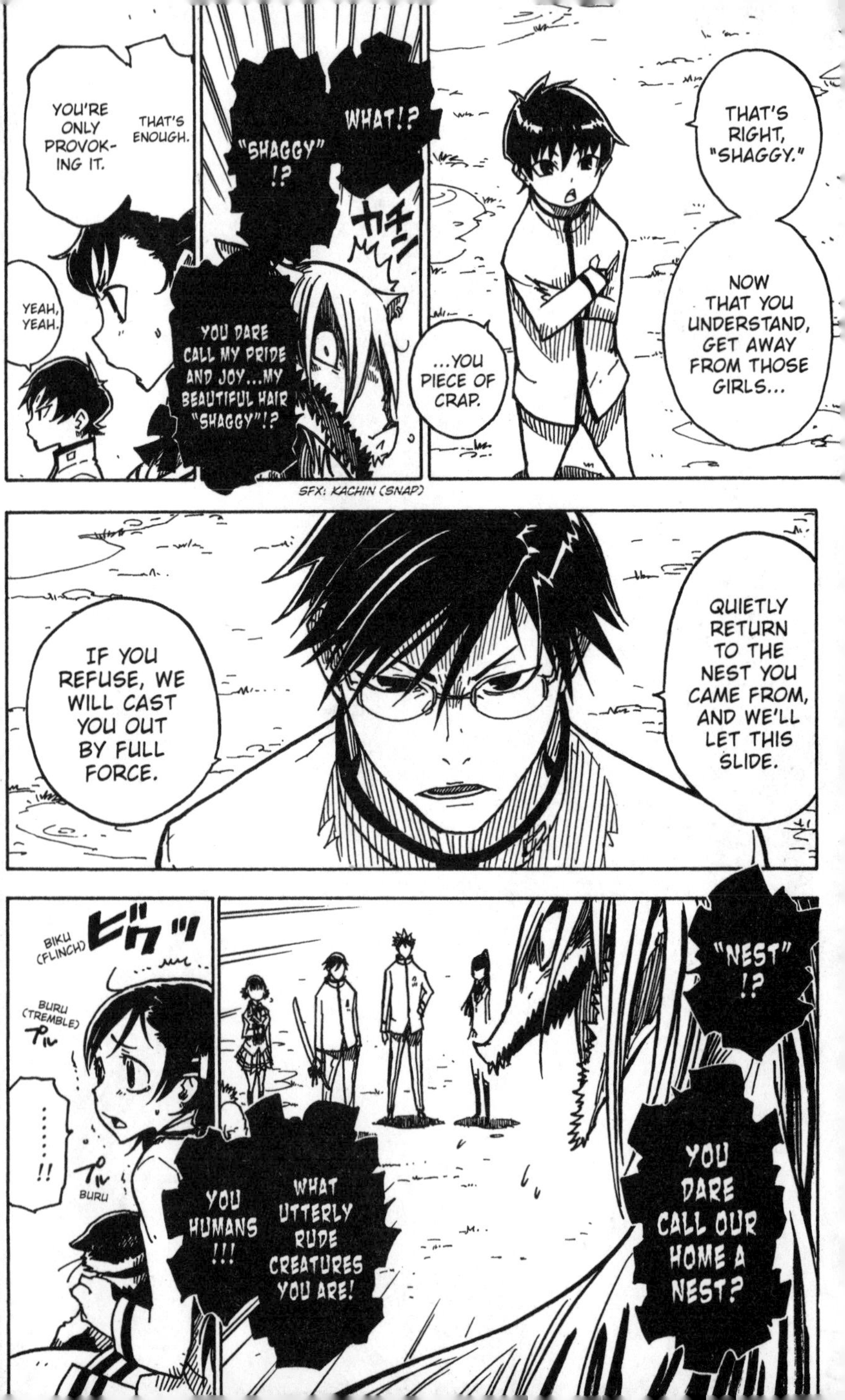
THAT'S RIGHT, "SHAGGY."
NOW THAT YOU UNDERSTAND, GET AWAY FROM THOSE GIRLS...
...YOU PIECE OF CRAP.
WHAT!?
"SHAGGY" !?
カチン
YOU DARE CALL MY PRIDE AND JOY...MY BEAUTIFUL HAIR "SHAGGY"!?
THAT'S ENOUGH.
YOU'RE ONLY PROVOK-ING IT.
YEAH, YEAH.
SFX: KACHIN (SNAP)
QUIETLY RETURN TO THE NEST YOU CAME FROM, AND WE'LL LET THIS SLIDE.
IF YOU REFUSE, WE WILL CAST YOU OUT BY FULL FORCE.
"NEST" !?
YOU DARE CALL OUR HOME A NEST?
WHAT UTTERLY RUDE CREATURES YOU ARE!
YOU HUMANS !!!
ビクッ
BIKU (FLINCH)
...
BURU (TREMBLE)
プル
......!!
プル
BURU

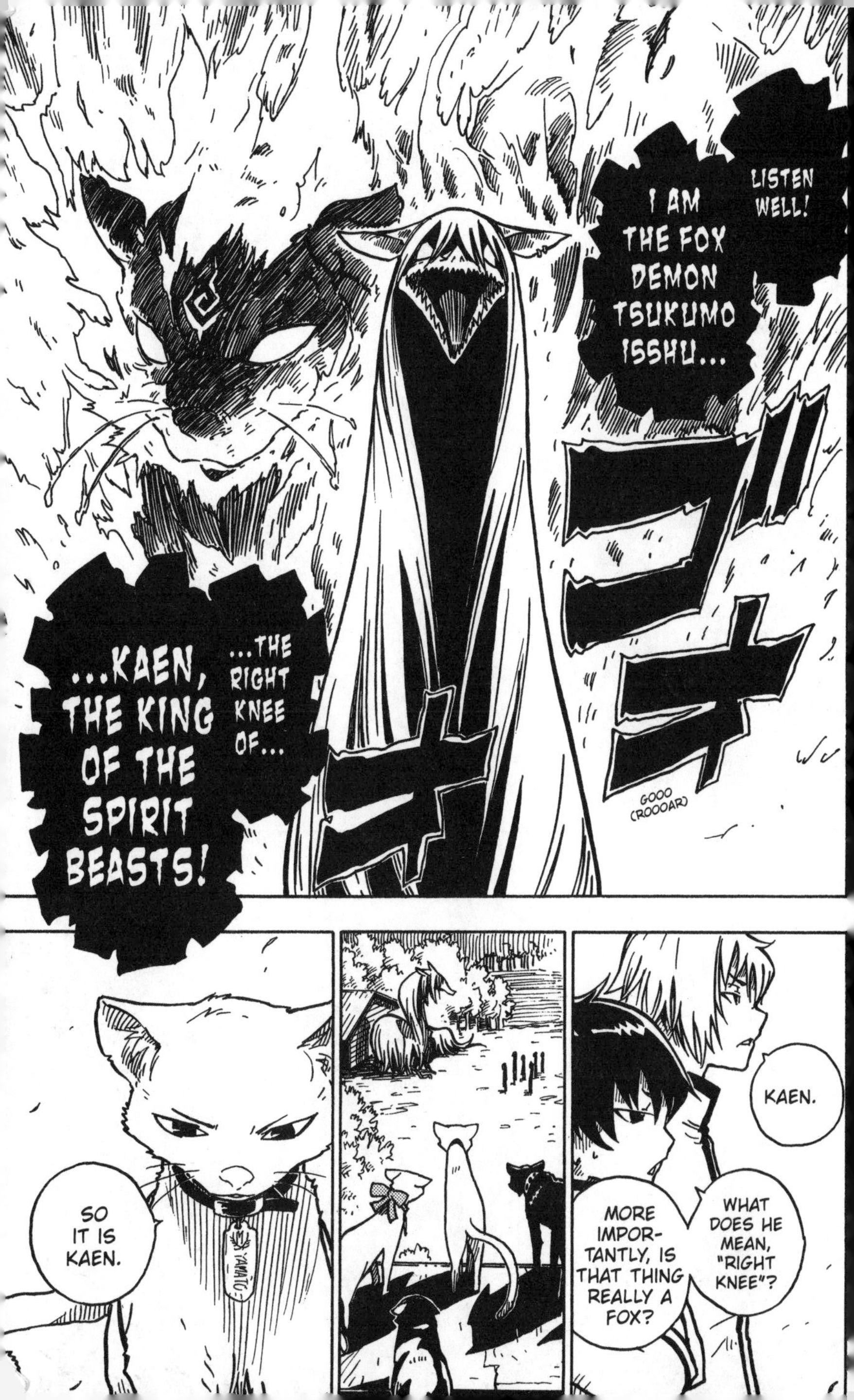
LISTEN WELL!
I AM THE FOX DEMON TSUKUMO ISSHU...
GOOO (ROOOAR)
...THE RIGHT KNEE OF...
...KAEN, THE KING OF THE SPIRIT BEASTS!
KAEN.
WHAT DOES HE MEAN, "RIGHT KNEE"?
MORE IMPORTANTLY, IS THAT THING REALLY A FOX?
SO IT IS KAEN.

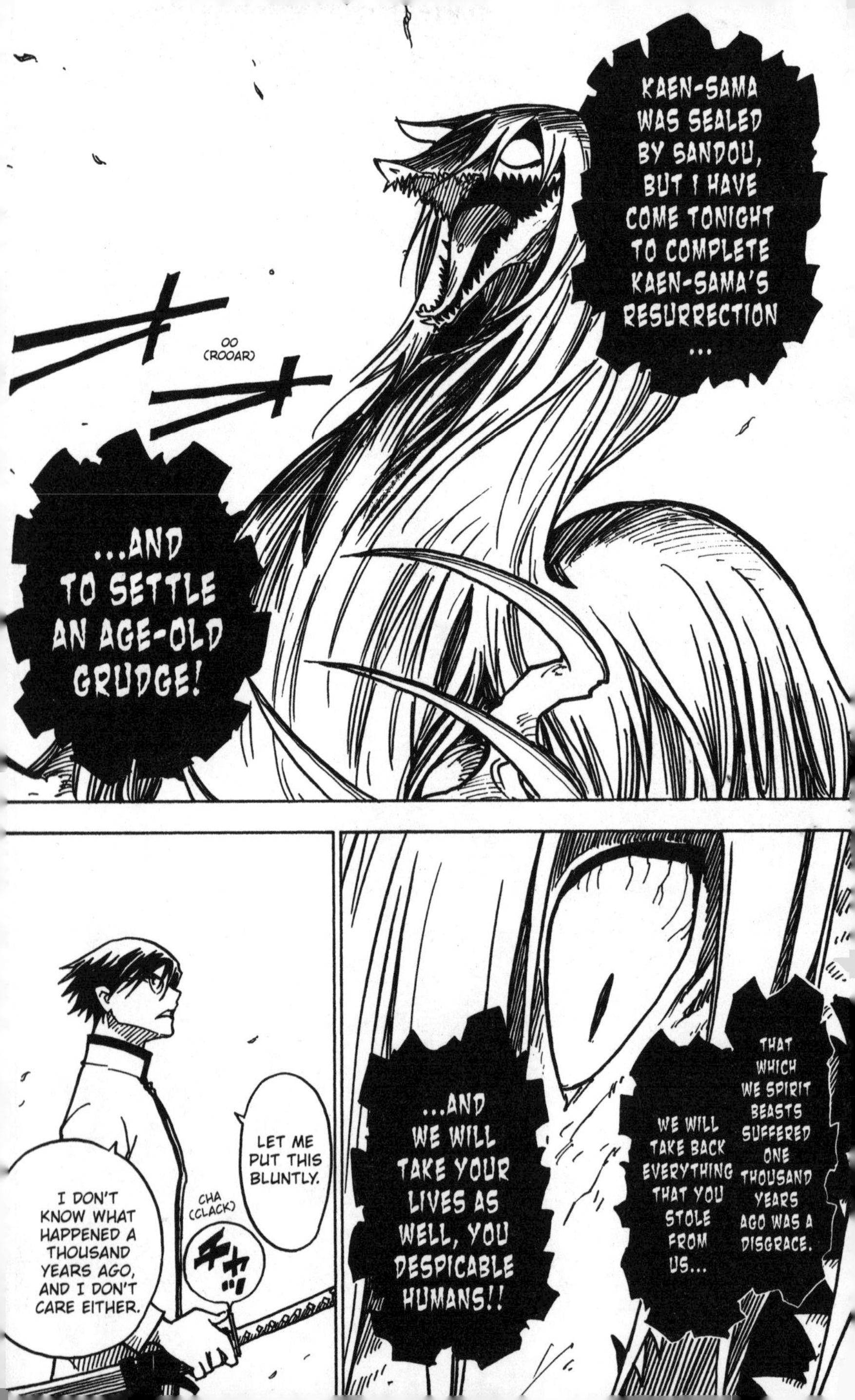
KAEN-SAMA WAS SEALED BY SANDOU, BUT I HAVE COME TONIGHT TO COMPLETE KAEN-SAMA'S RESURRECTION ...
OO (ROOAR)
...AND TO SETTLE AN AGE-OLD GRUDGE!
THAT WHICH WE SPIRIT BEASTS SUFFERED ONE THOUSAND YEARS AGO WAS A DISGRACE.
WE WILL TAKE BACK EVERYTHING THAT YOU STOLE FROM US...
...AND WE WILL TAKE YOUR LIVES AS WELL, YOU DESPICABLE HUMANS!!
LET ME PUT THIS BLUNTLY.
CHA (CLACK)
I DON'T KNOW WHAT HAPPENED A THOUSAND YEARS AGO, AND I DON'T CARE EITHER.

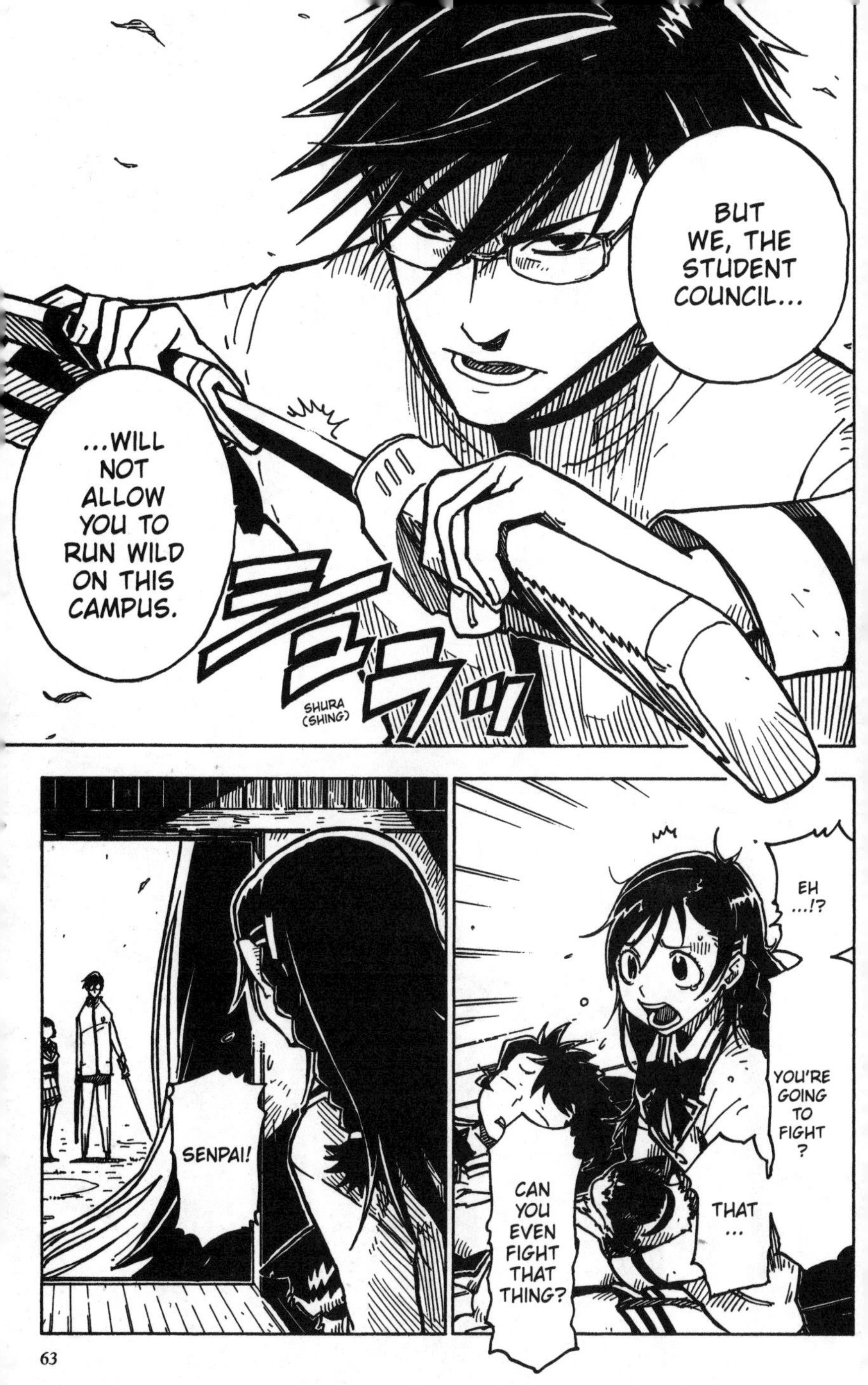
BUT WE, THE STUDENT COUNCIL...
...WILL NOT ALLOW YOU TO RUN WILD ON THIS CAMPUS.
SHURA (SHING)
EH ...!?
YOU'RE GOING TO FIGHT?
THAT ...
CAN YOU EVEN FIGHT THAT THING?
SENPAI!

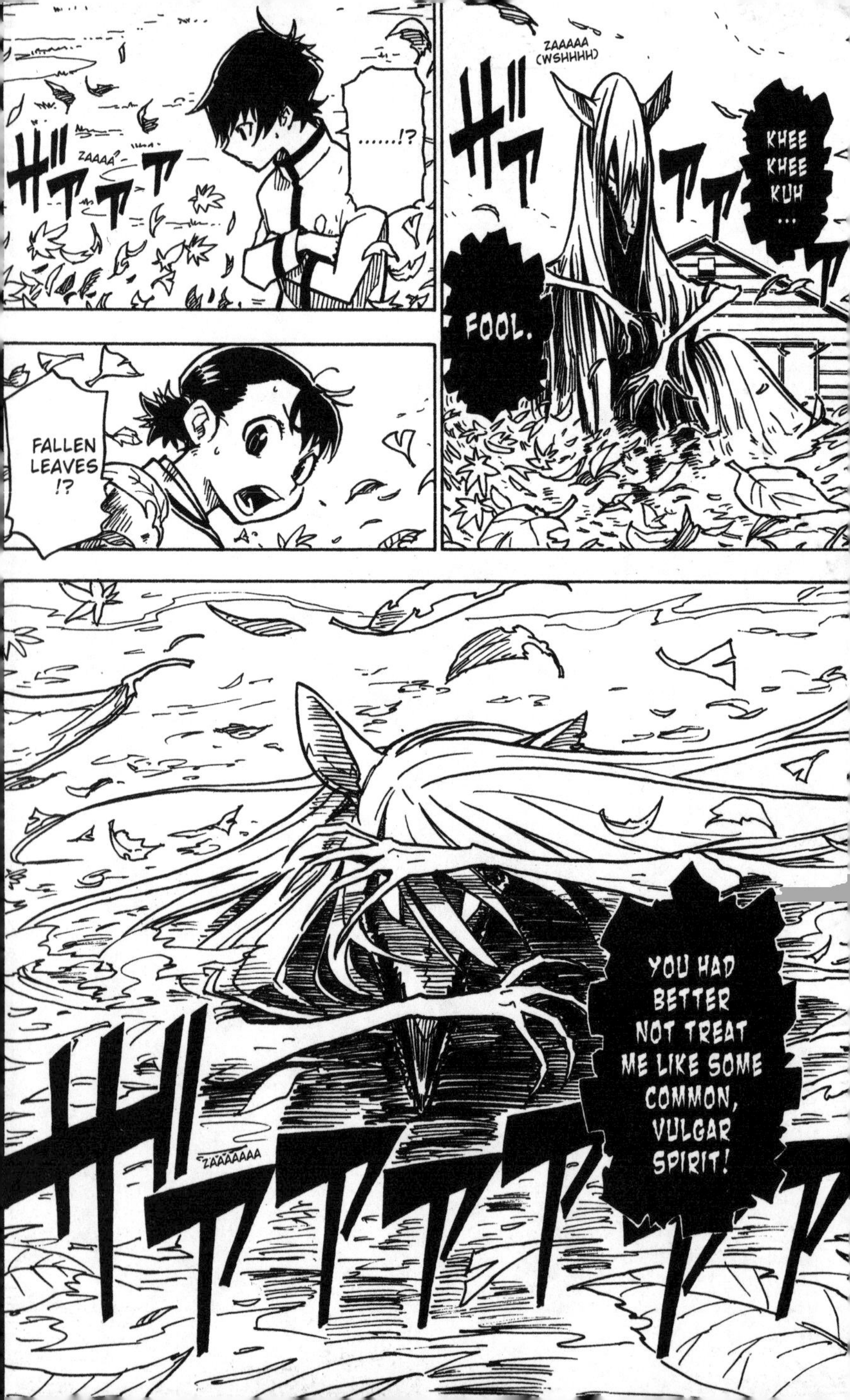
ZAAAAA (WSHHHH)
KHEE KHEE KUH ...
FOOL.
......!?
ZAAAA
FALLEN LEAVES !?
YOU HAD BETTER NOT TREAT ME LIKE SOME COMMON, VULGAR SPIRIT!
ZAAAAAAA

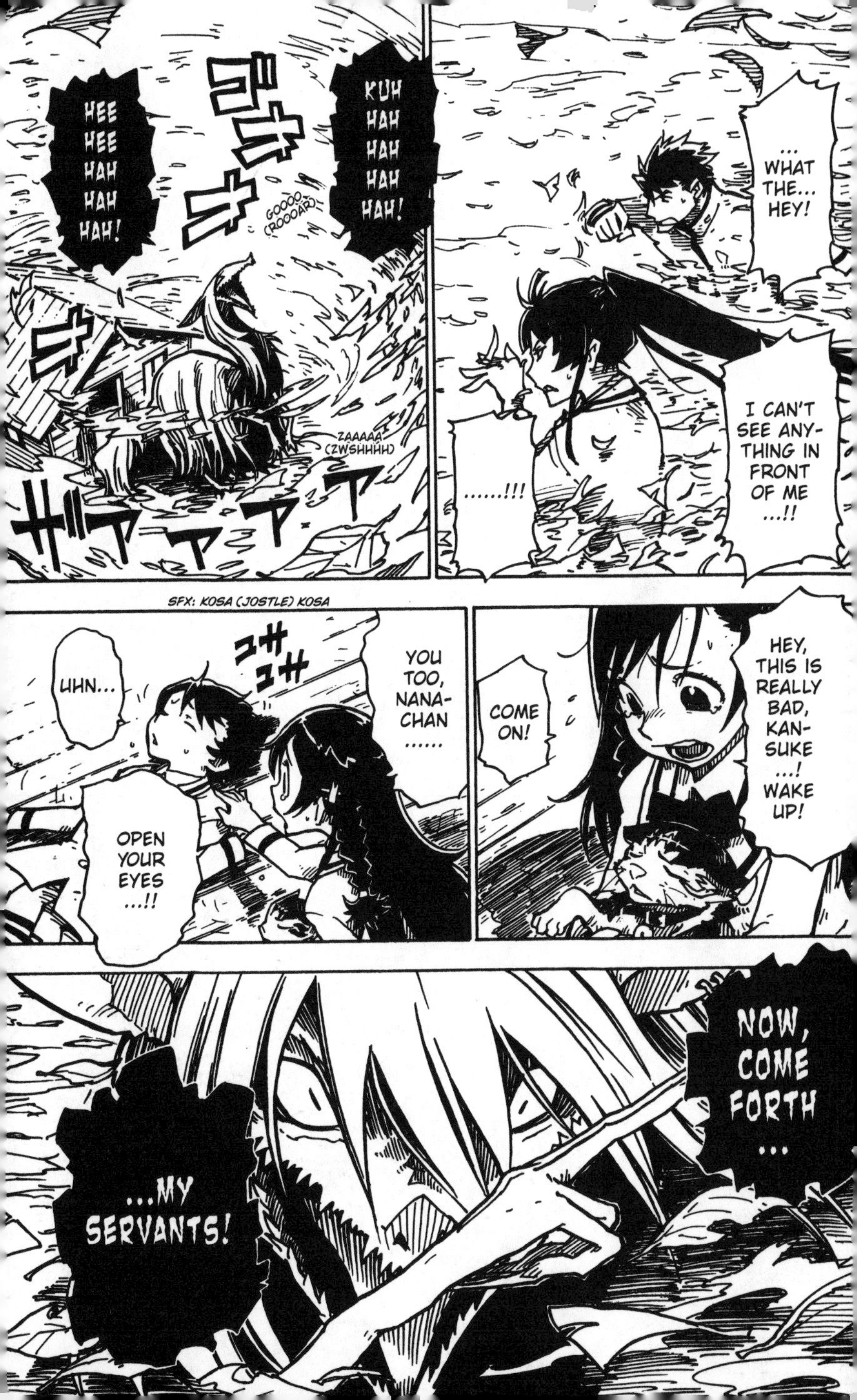
... WHAT THE... HEY!
I CAN'T SEE ANY-THING IN FRONT OF ME ...!!
......!!!
KUH HAH HAH HAH HAH!
GOOOO (ROOOAR)
HEE HEE HAH HAH HAH!
ZAAAAA (ZWSHHHH)
SFX: KOSA (JOSTLE) KOSA
HEY, THIS IS REALLY BAD, KAN-SUKE ...! WAKE UP!
COME ON!
YOU TOO, NANA-CHAN ......
UHN...
OPEN YOUR EYES ...!!
NOW, COME FORTH ...
...MY SERVANTS!

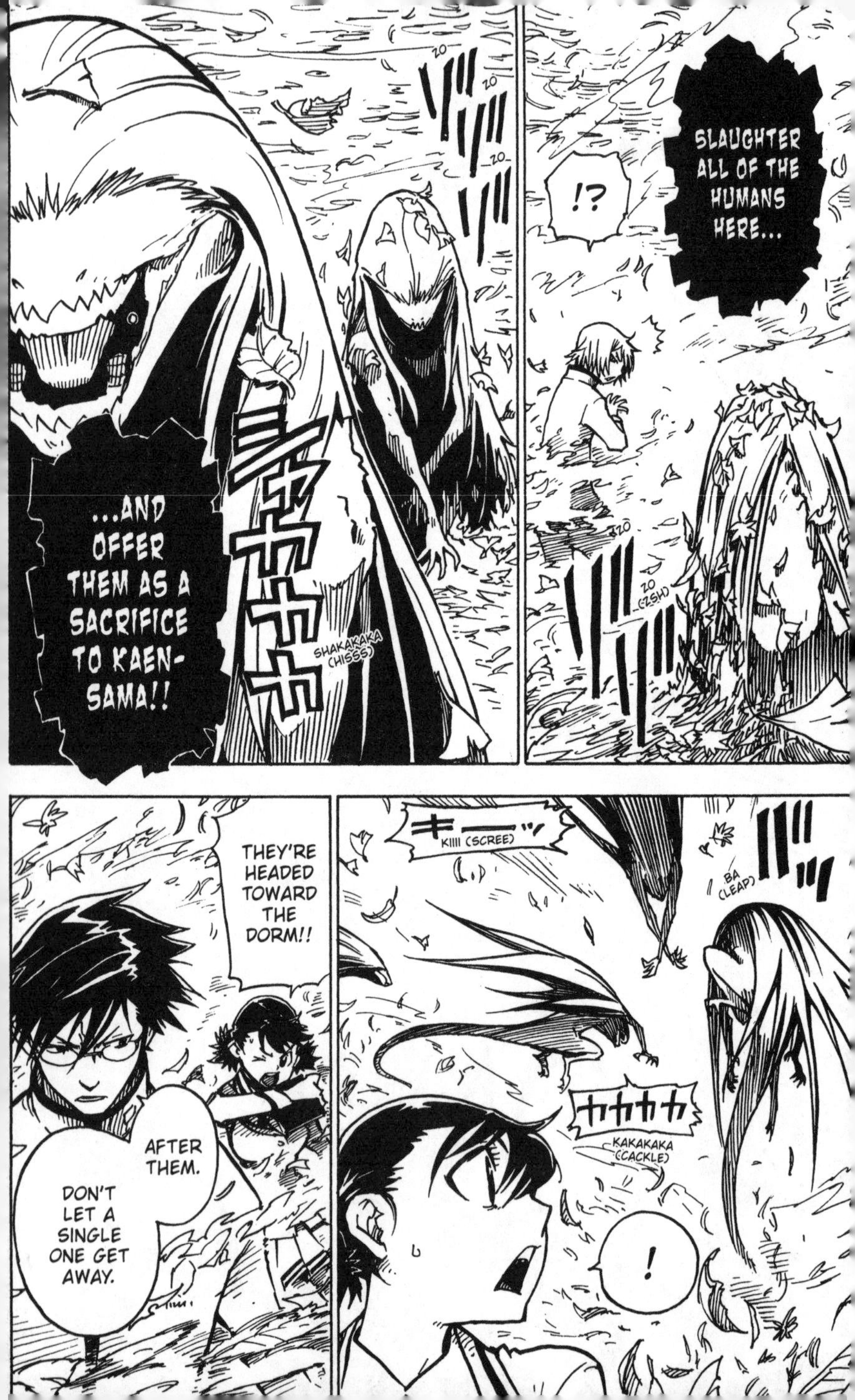
SLAUGHTER ALL OF THE HUMANS HERE...
!?
ZO (ZSH)
...AND OFFER THEM AS A SACRIFICE TO KAEN-SAMA!!
シャカカカ
SHAKAKAKA (HISSS)
ZO
キーッ
KIIII (SCREE)
BA (LEAP)
カカカカ
KAKAKAKA (CACKLE)
!
THEY'RE HEADED TOWARD THE DORM!!
AFTER THEM.
DON'T LET A SINGLE ONE GET AWAY.

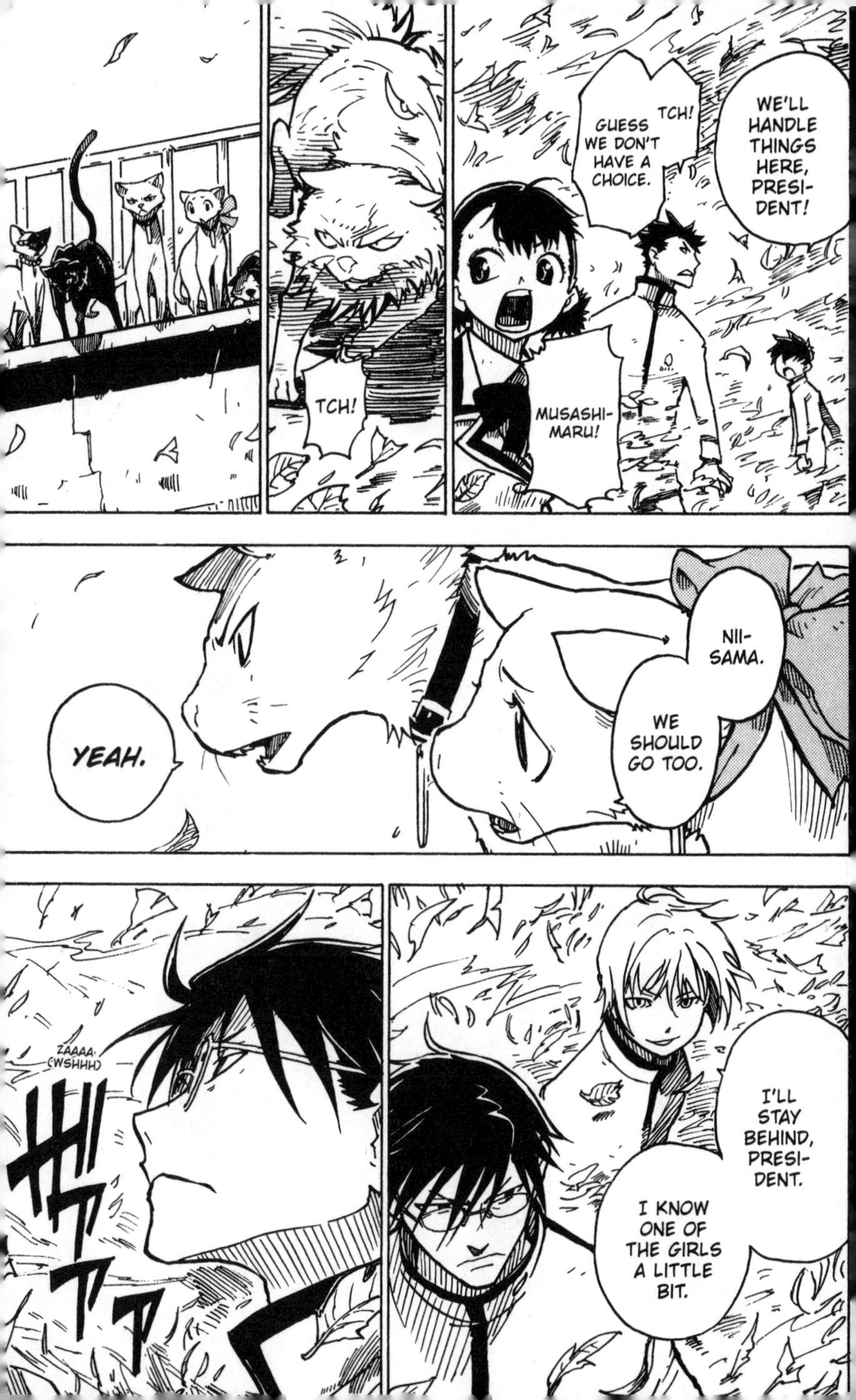
WE'LL HANDLE THINGS HERE, PRESIDENT!
TCH! GUESS WE DON'T HAVE A CHOICE.
MUSASHI-MARU!
TCH!
NII-SAMA.
WE SHOULD GO TOO.
YEAH.
I'LL STAY BEHIND, PRESIDENT.
I KNOW ONE OF THE GIRLS A LITTLE BIT.
ZAAAA (WSHHH)

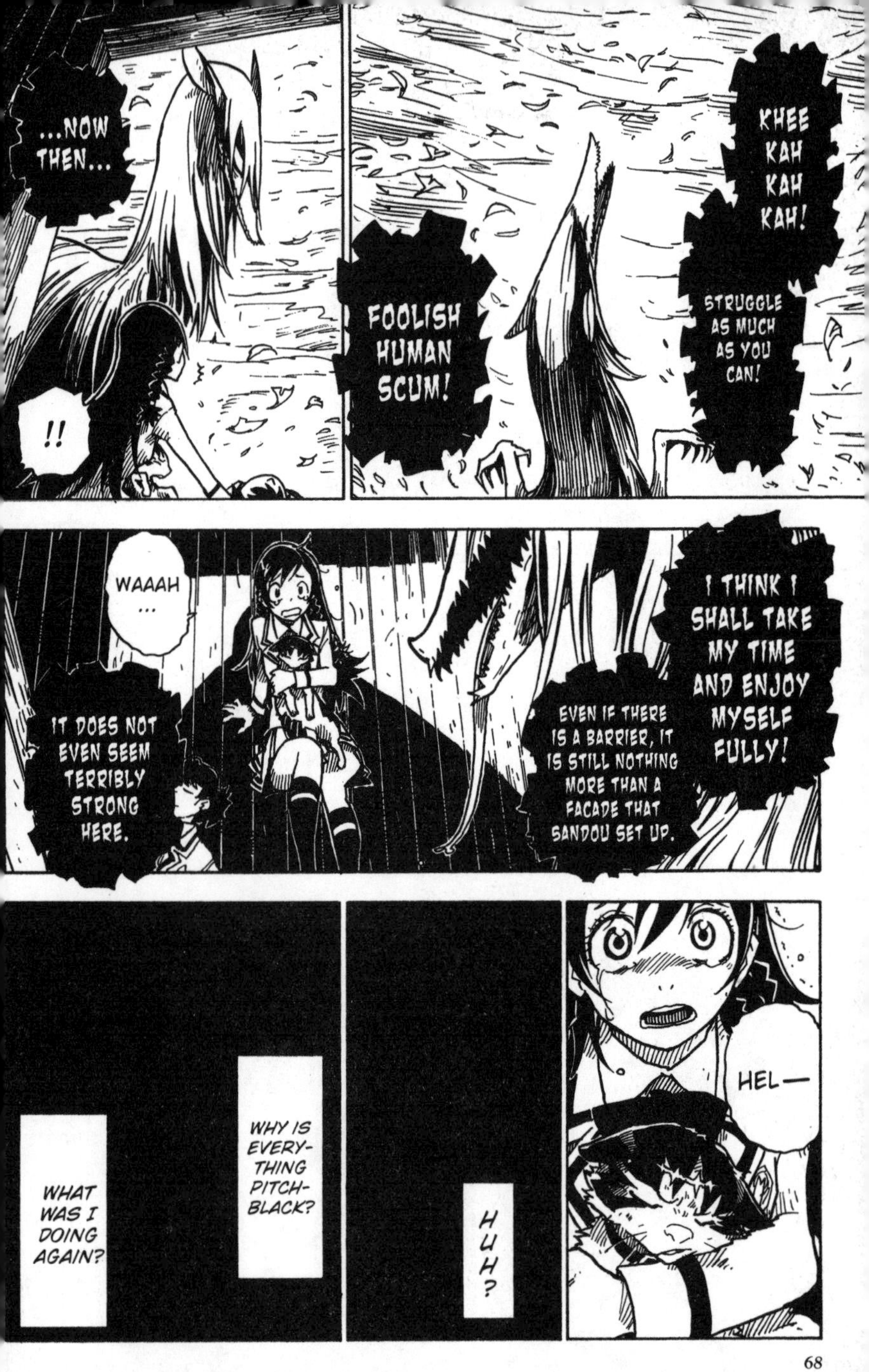
KHEE KAH KAH KAH!
STRUGGLE AS MUCH AS YOU CAN!
FOOLISH HUMAN SCUM!
...NOW THEN...
!!
I THINK I SHALL TAKE MY TIME AND ENJOY MYSELF FULLY!
EVEN IF THERE IS A BARRIER, IT IS STILL NOTHING MORE THAN A FACADE THAT SANDOU SET UP.
WAAAH ...
IT DOES NOT EVEN SEEM TERRIBLY STRONG HERE.
HEL—
HUH?
WHY IS EVERYTHING PITCH-BLACK?
WHAT WAS I DOING AGAIN?

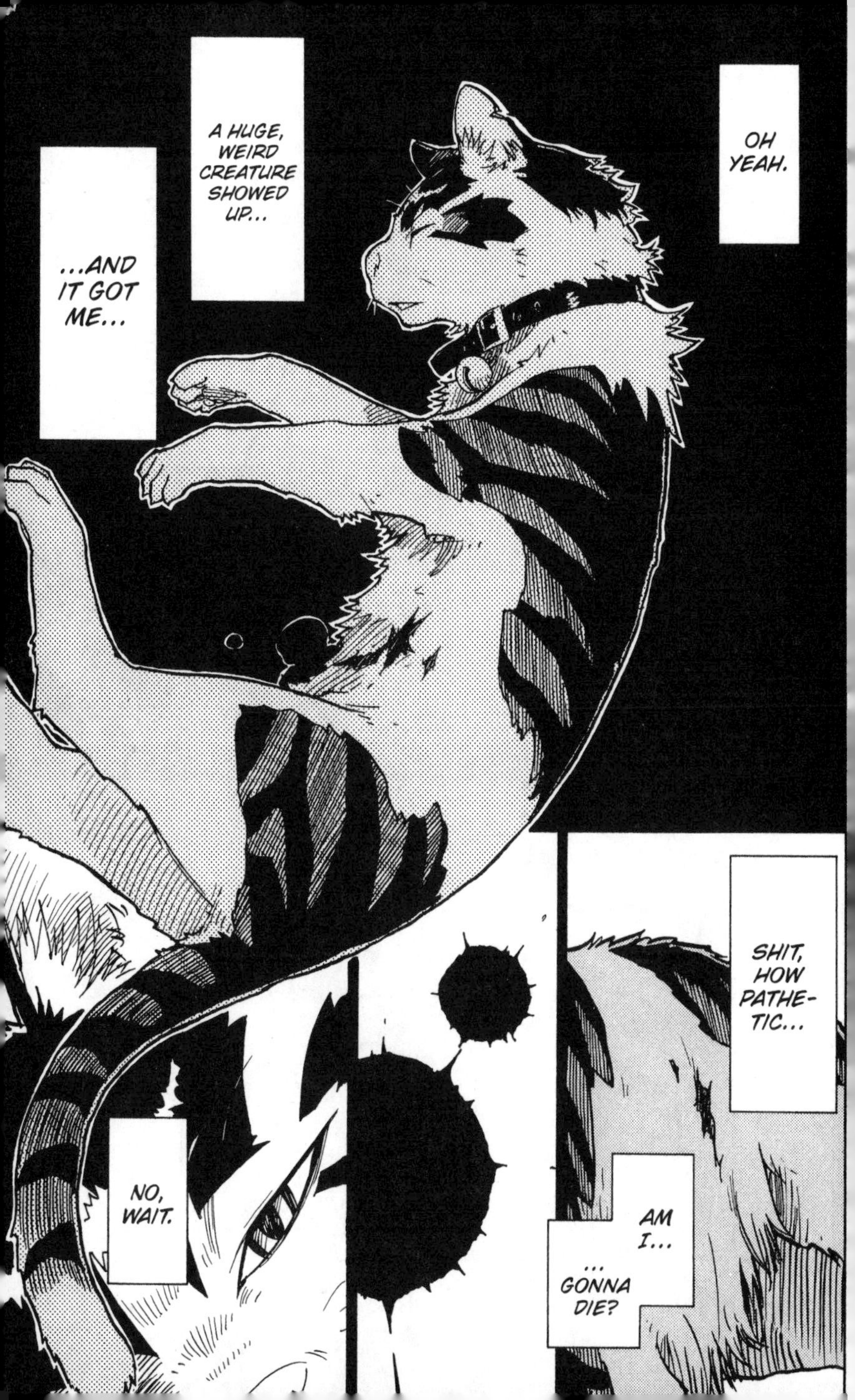
OH YEAH.
A HUGE, WEIRD CREATURE SHOWED UP...
...AND IT GOT ME...
SHIT, HOW PATHETIC...
AM I...
...GONNA DIE?
NO, WAIT.

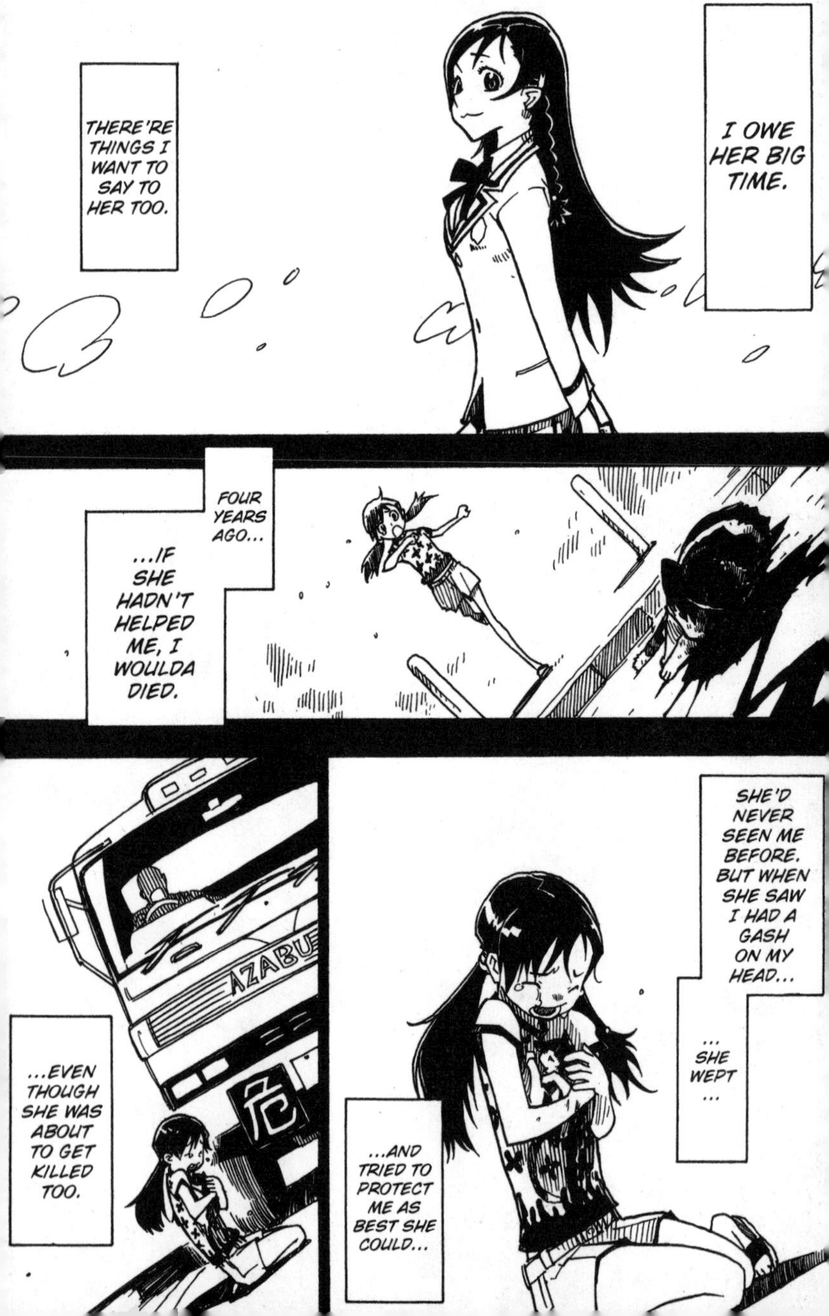
I OWE HER BIG TIME.
THERE'RE THINGS I WANT TO SAY TO HER TOO.
FOUR YEARS AGO...
...IF SHE HADN'T HELPED ME, I WOULDA DIED.
SHE'D NEVER SEEN ME BEFORE. BUT WHEN SHE SAW I HAD A GASH ON MY HEAD...
...SHE WEPT...
...AND TRIED TO PROTECT ME AS BEST SHE COULD...
AZABU
危
...EVEN THOUGH SHE WAS ABOUT TO GET KILLED TOO.

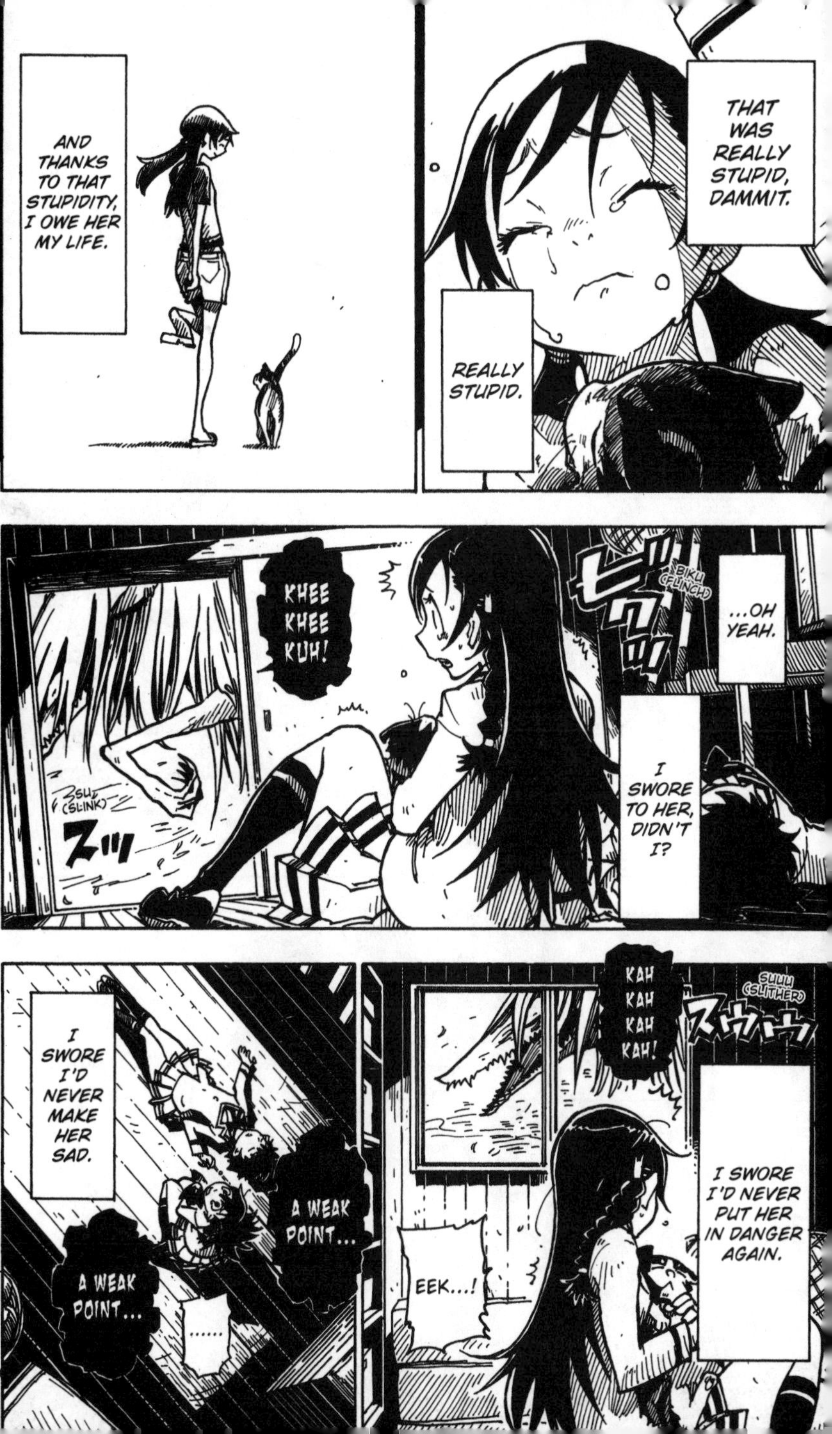
THAT WAS REALLY STUPID, DAMMIT.
REALLY STUPID.
AND THANKS TO THAT STUPIDITY, I OWE HER MY LIFE.
BIKU (FLINCH)
...OH YEAH.
I SWORE TO HER, DIDN'T I?
KHEE KHEE KUH!
ZSU (SLINK)
SUUU (SLITHER)
KAH KAH KAH KAH!
I SWORE I'D NEVER PUT HER IN DANGER AGAIN.
EEK...!
I SWORE I'D NEVER MAKE HER SAD.
A WEAK POINT...
A WEAK POINT...
......

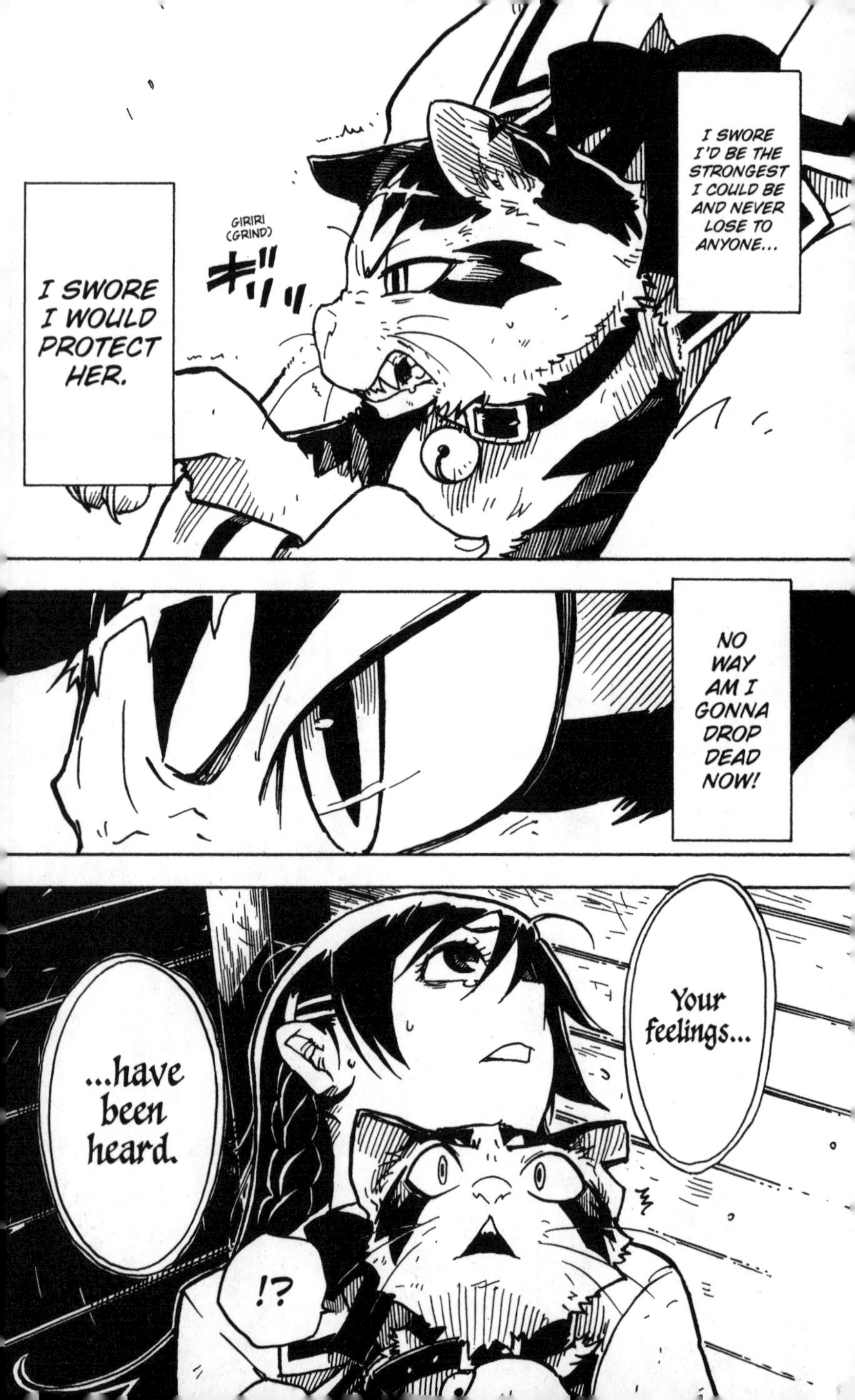
I SWORE I'D BE THE STRONGEST I COULD BE AND NEVER LOSE TO ANYONE...
GIRIRI (GRIND)
I SWORE I WOULD PROTECT HER.
NO WAY AM I GONNA DROP DEAD NOW!
Your feelings...
...have been heard.
!?

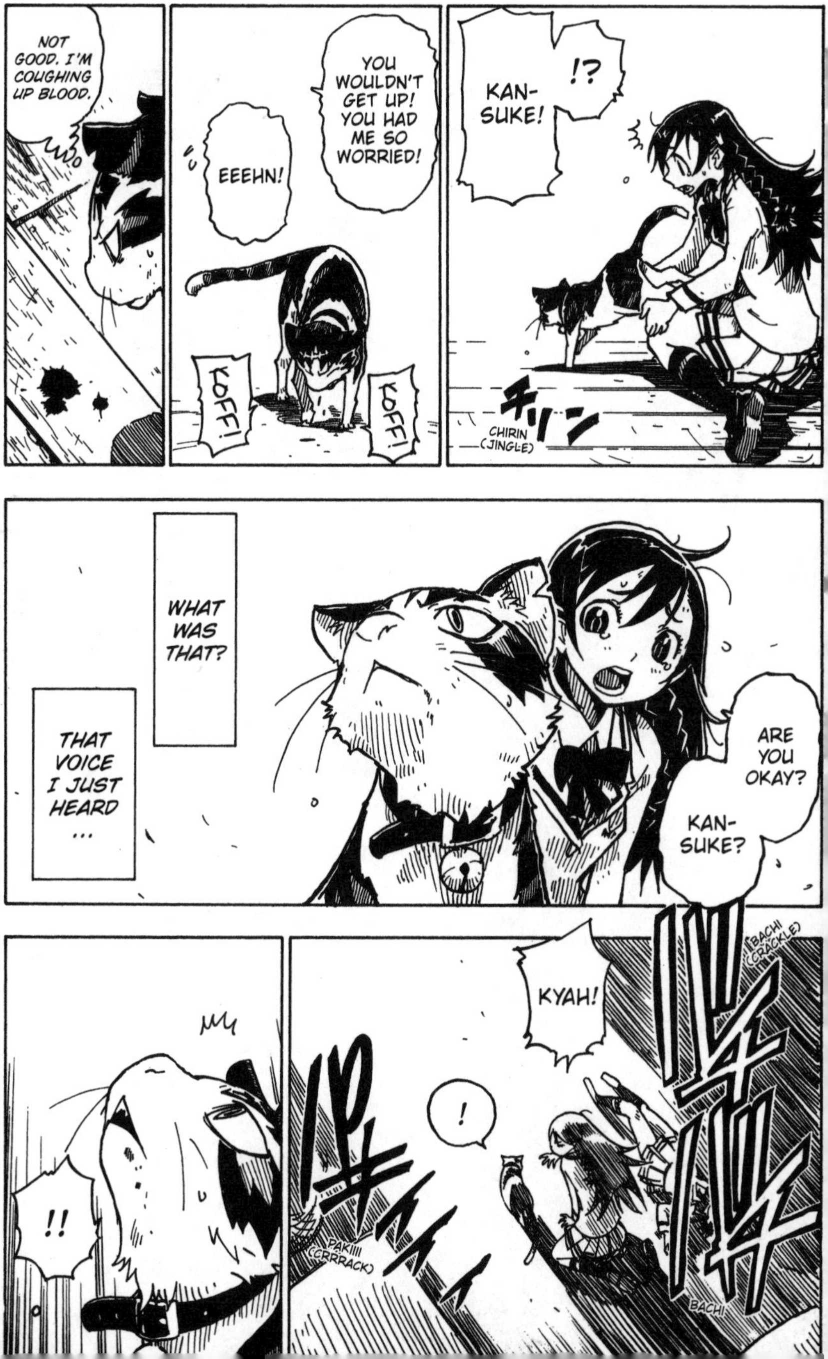
KAN-SUKE!
!?
チリン
CHIRIN (JINGLE)
YOU WOULDN'T GET UP! YOU HAD ME SO WORRIED!
EEEHN!
KOFF!
KOFF!
NOT GOOD. I'M COUGHING UP BLOOD.
ARE YOU OKAY?
KAN-SUKE?
WHAT WAS THAT?
THAT VOICE I JUST HEARD ...
BACHI (CRACKLE)
KYAH!
!
PAKIIII (CRRRACK)
BACHI
!!

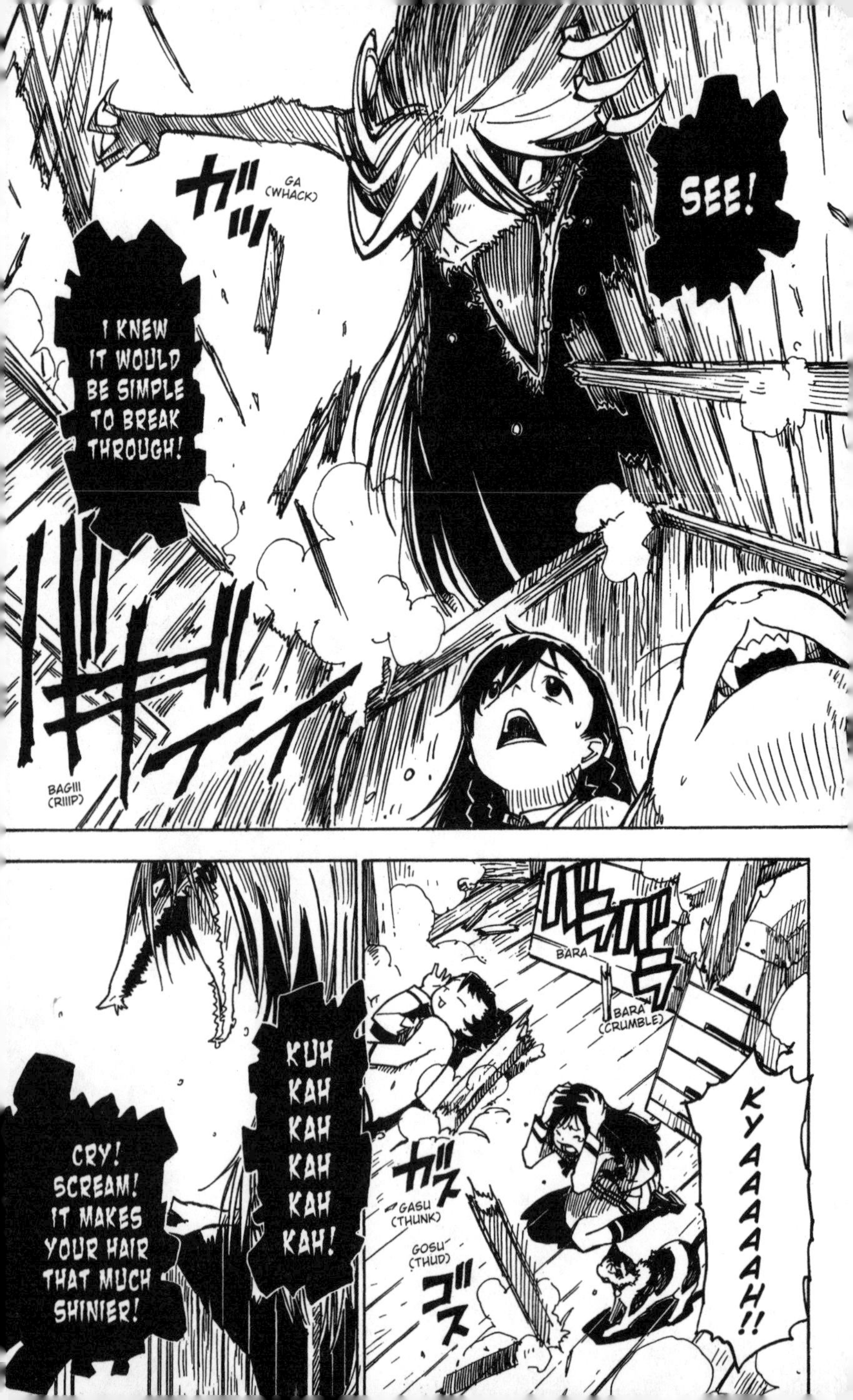
SEE!
GA (WHACK)
I KNEW IT WOULD BE SIMPLE TO BREAK THROUGH!
BAGIII (RIIIP)
BARA
BARA (CRUMBLE)
KYAAAAAAH!!
GASU (THUNK)
GOSU (THUD)
KUH KAH KAH KAH KAH KAH!
CRY! SCREAM! IT MAKES YOUR HAIR THAT MUCH SHINIER!

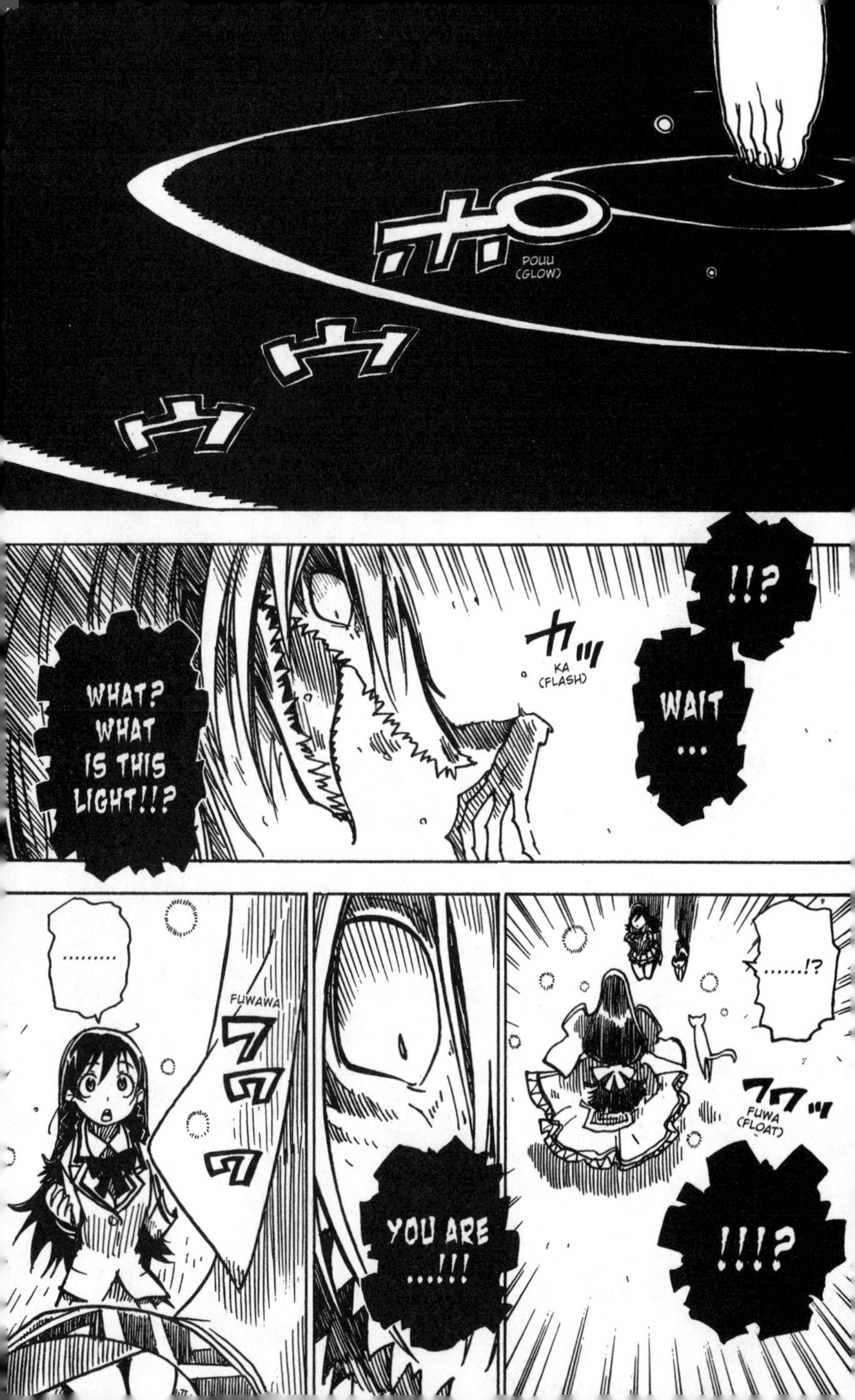
POUU
(GLOW)
!!?
WAIT ...
KA
(FLASH)
WHAT? WHAT IS THIS LIGHT!!?
......!?
FUWA
(FLOAT)
!!!?
YOU ARE ...!!!
FUWAWA
....

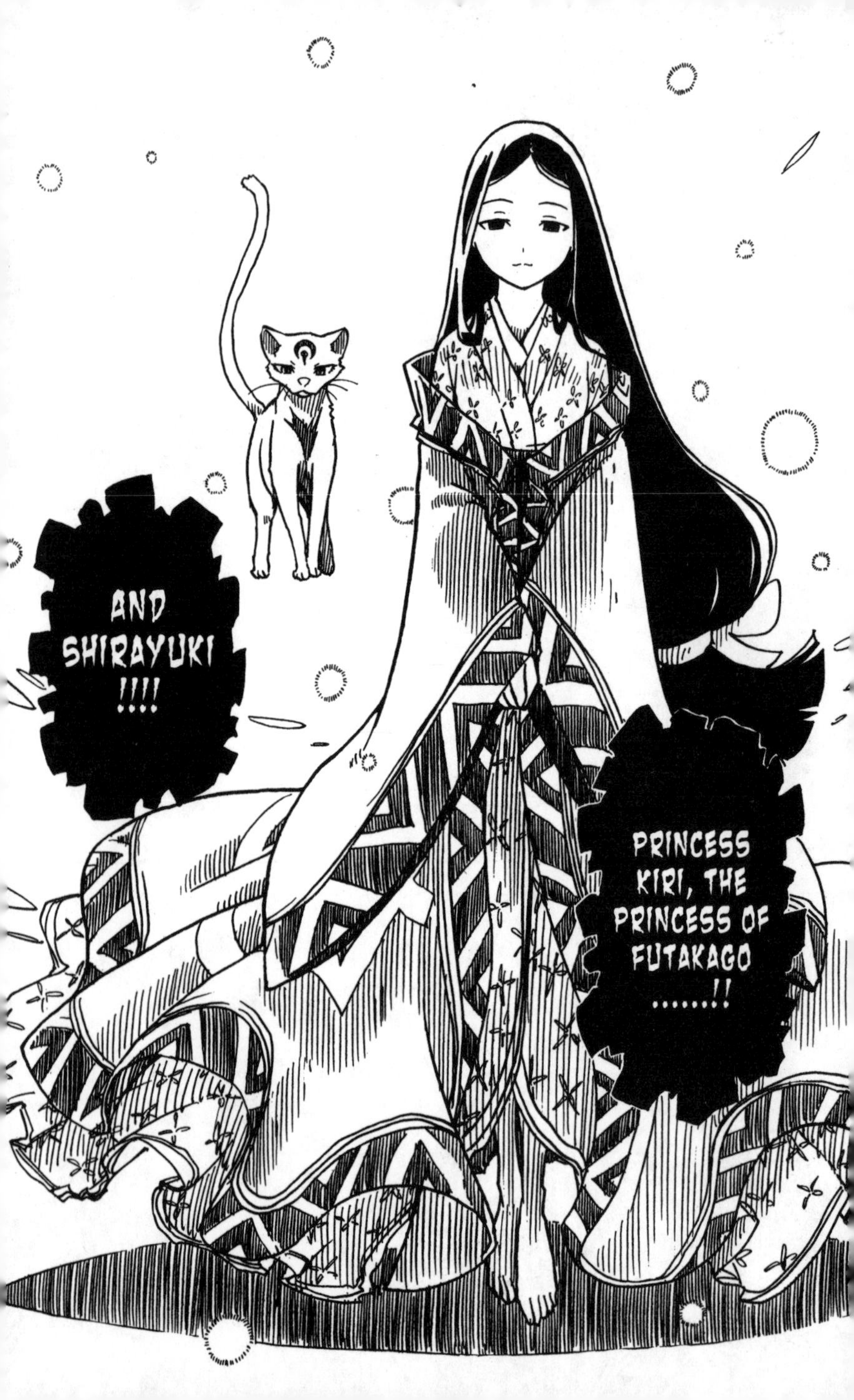
PRINCESS KIRI, THE PRINCESS OF FUTAKAGO ......!!
AND SHIRAYUKI !!!!

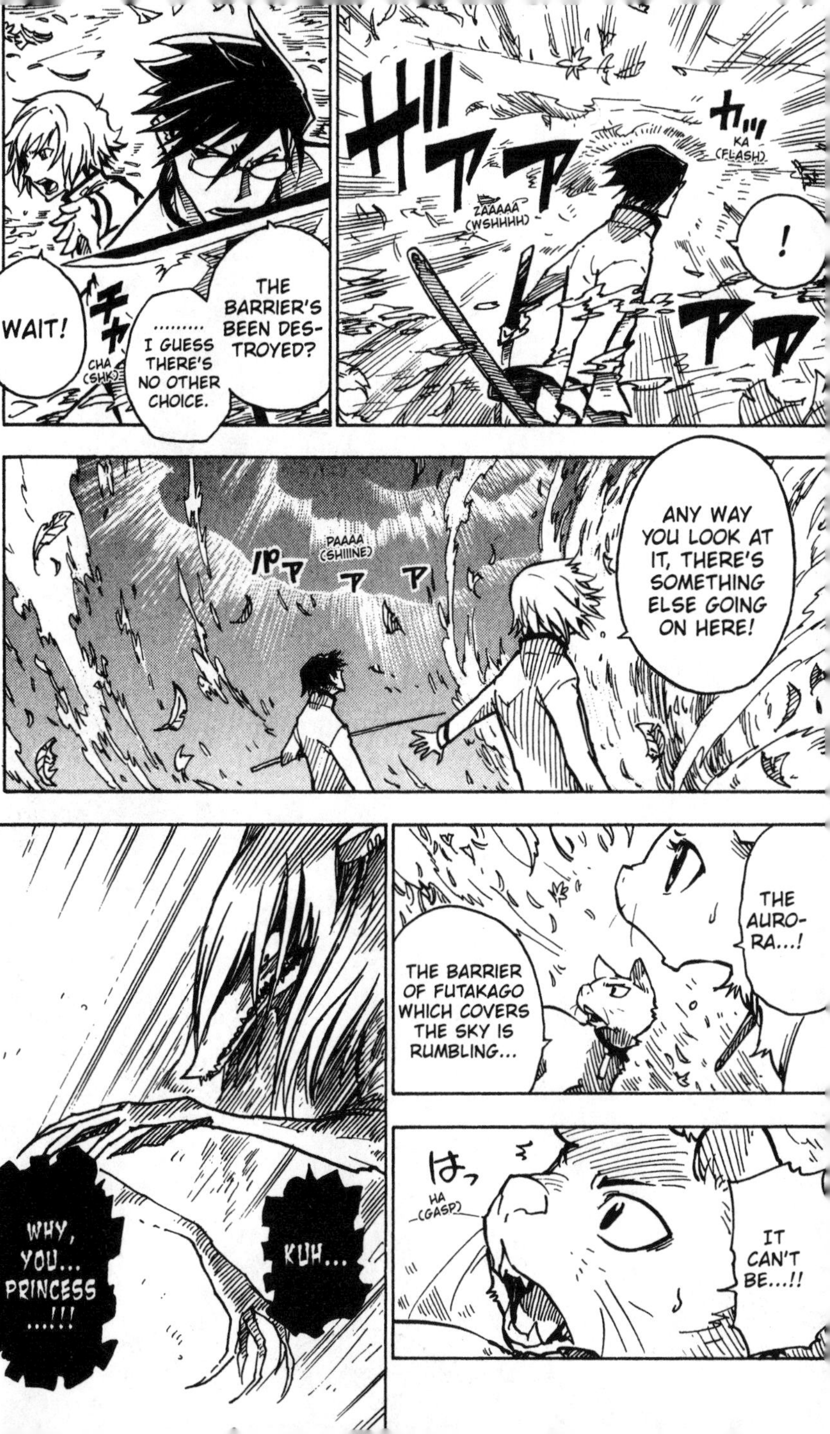
カッ
KA (FLASH)
!
ザァァァァ
ZAAAAA (WSHHHH)
THE BARRIER'S BEEN DES-TROYED?
.... I GUESS THERE'S NO OTHER CHOICE.
チャ
CHA (SHK)
WAIT!
ANY WAY YOU LOOK AT IT, THERE'S SOMETHING ELSE GOING ON HERE!
パァァァ
PAAAA (SHIIINE)
THE AURO-RA...!
THE BARRIER OF FUTAKAGO WHICH COVERS THE SKY IS RUMBLING...
IT CAN'T BE...!!
はっ
HA (GASP)
KUH...
WHY, YOU... PRINCESS ....!!!

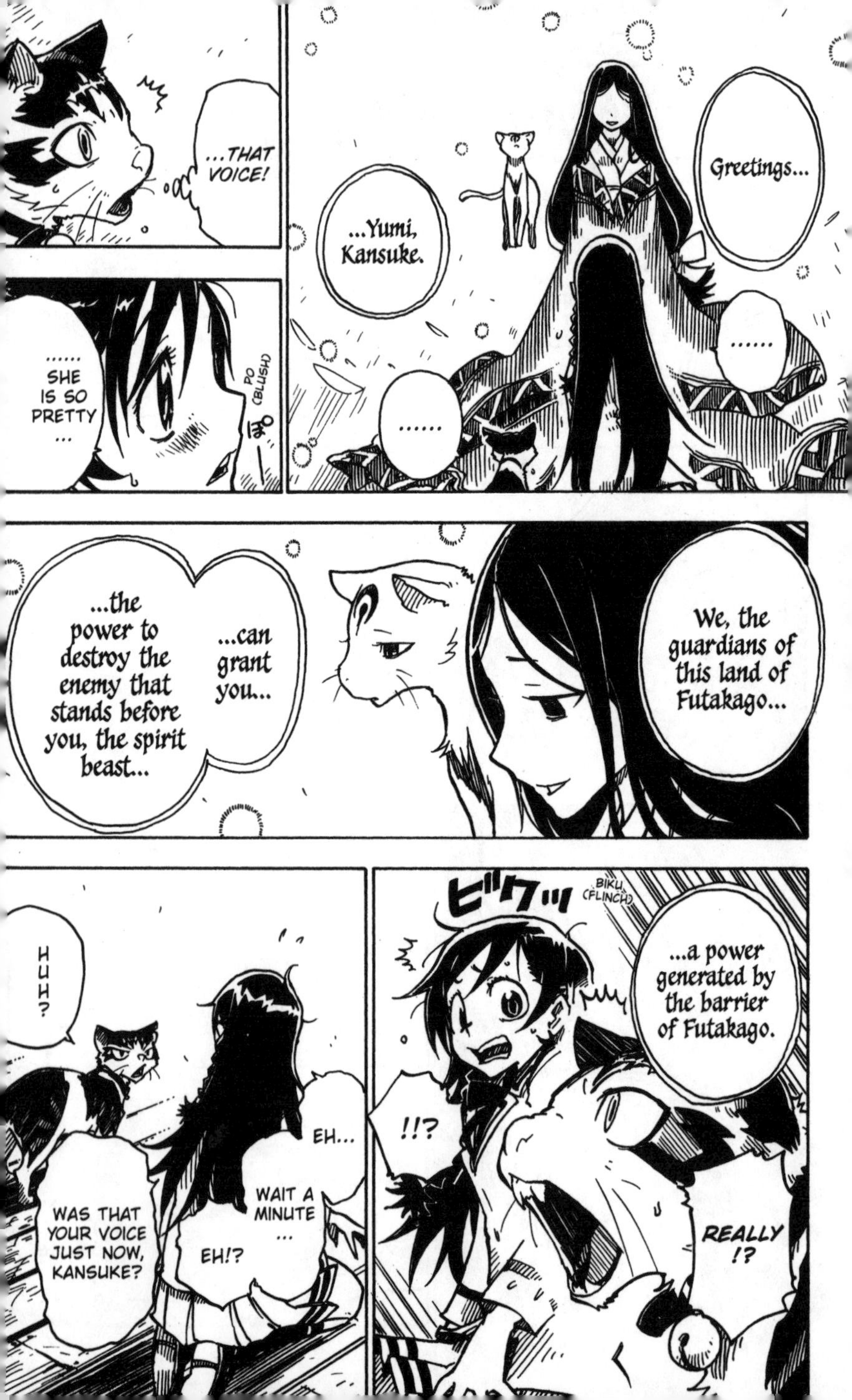
Greetings...
...Yumi, Kansuke.
......
......
...THAT VOICE!
...... SHE IS SO PRETTY ...
PO (BLUSH)
We, the guardians of this land of Futakago...
...can grant you...
...the power to destroy the enemy that stands before you, the spirit beast...
ビクッ
BIKU (FLINCH)
...a power generated by the barrier of Futakago.
!!?
REALLY !?
HUH?
EH...
WAIT A MINUTE ...
EH!?
WAS THAT YOUR VOICE JUST NOW, KANSUKE?

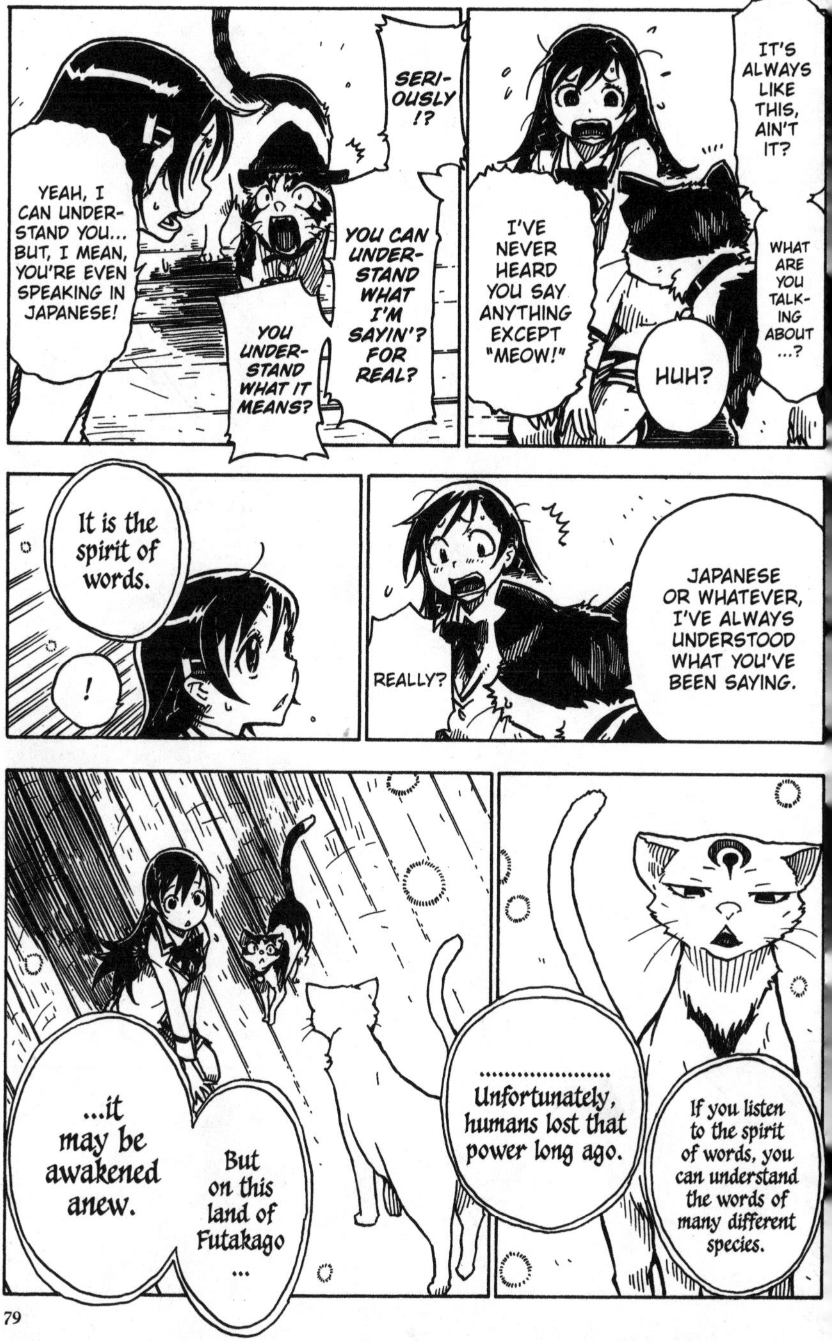
IT'S ALWAYS LIKE THIS, AIN'T IT?
WHAT ARE YOU TALKING ABOUT ...?
HUH?
I'VE NEVER HEARD YOU SAY ANYTHING EXCEPT "MEOW!"
SERIOUSLY !?
YOU CAN UNDERSTAND WHAT I'M SAYIN'? FOR REAL?
YOU UNDERSTAND WHAT IT MEANS?
YEAH, I CAN UNDERSTAND YOU... BUT, I MEAN, YOU'RE EVEN SPEAKING IN JAPANESE!
JAPANESE OR WHATEVER, I'VE ALWAYS UNDERSTOOD WHAT YOU'VE BEEN SAYING.
REALLY?
It is the spirit of words.
!
If you listen to the spirit of words, you can understand the words of many different species.
......................Unfortunately, humans lost that power long ago.
But on this land of Futakago ...
...it may be awakened anew.

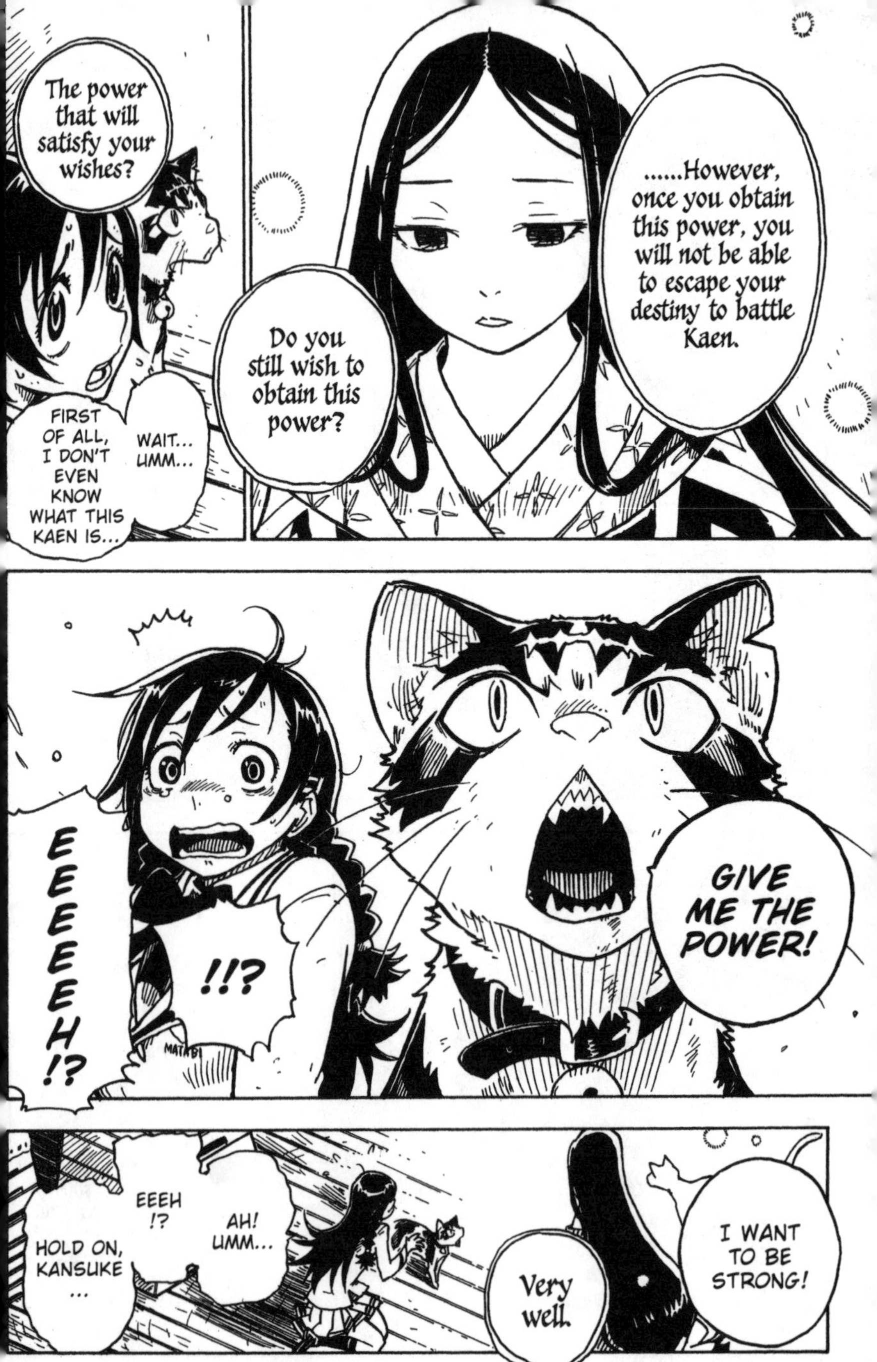
......However, once you obtain this power, you will not be able to escape your destiny to battle Kaen.
Do you still wish to obtain this power?
The power that will satisfy your wishes?
WAIT... UMM...
FIRST OF ALL, I DON'T EVEN KNOW WHAT THIS KAEN IS...
GIVE ME THE POWER!
!!?
EEEEEEH!?
MATABI
I WANT TO BE STRONG!
Very well.
AH! UMM...
EEEH !?
HOLD ON, KANSUKE ...

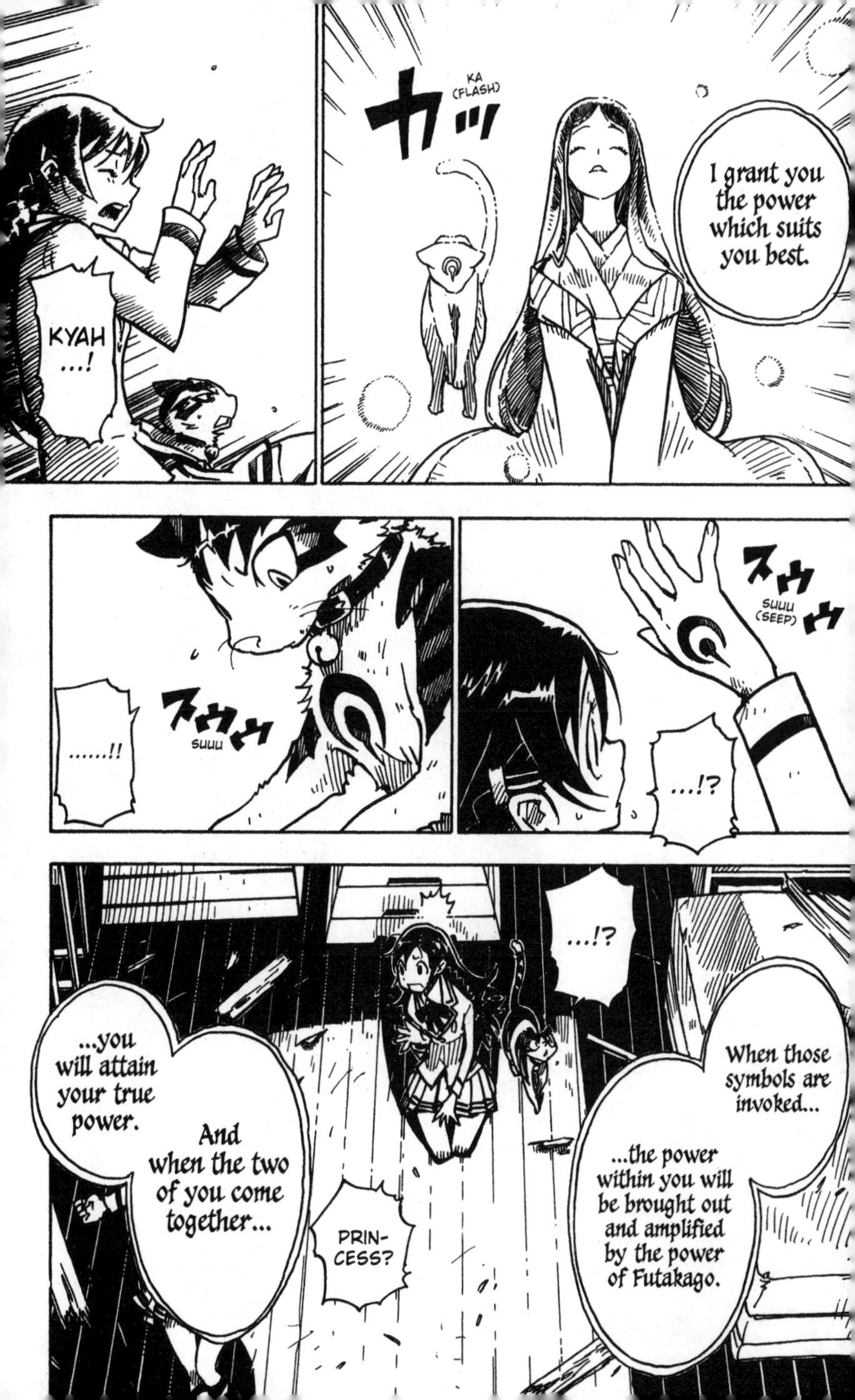
KA (FLASH)
I grant you the power which suits you best.
KYAH ...!
SUUU (SEEP)
...!?
......!!
SUUU
...!?
When those symbols are invoked...
...the power within you will be brought out and amplified by the power of Futakago.
PRIN-CESS?
And when the two of you come together...
...you will attain your true power.

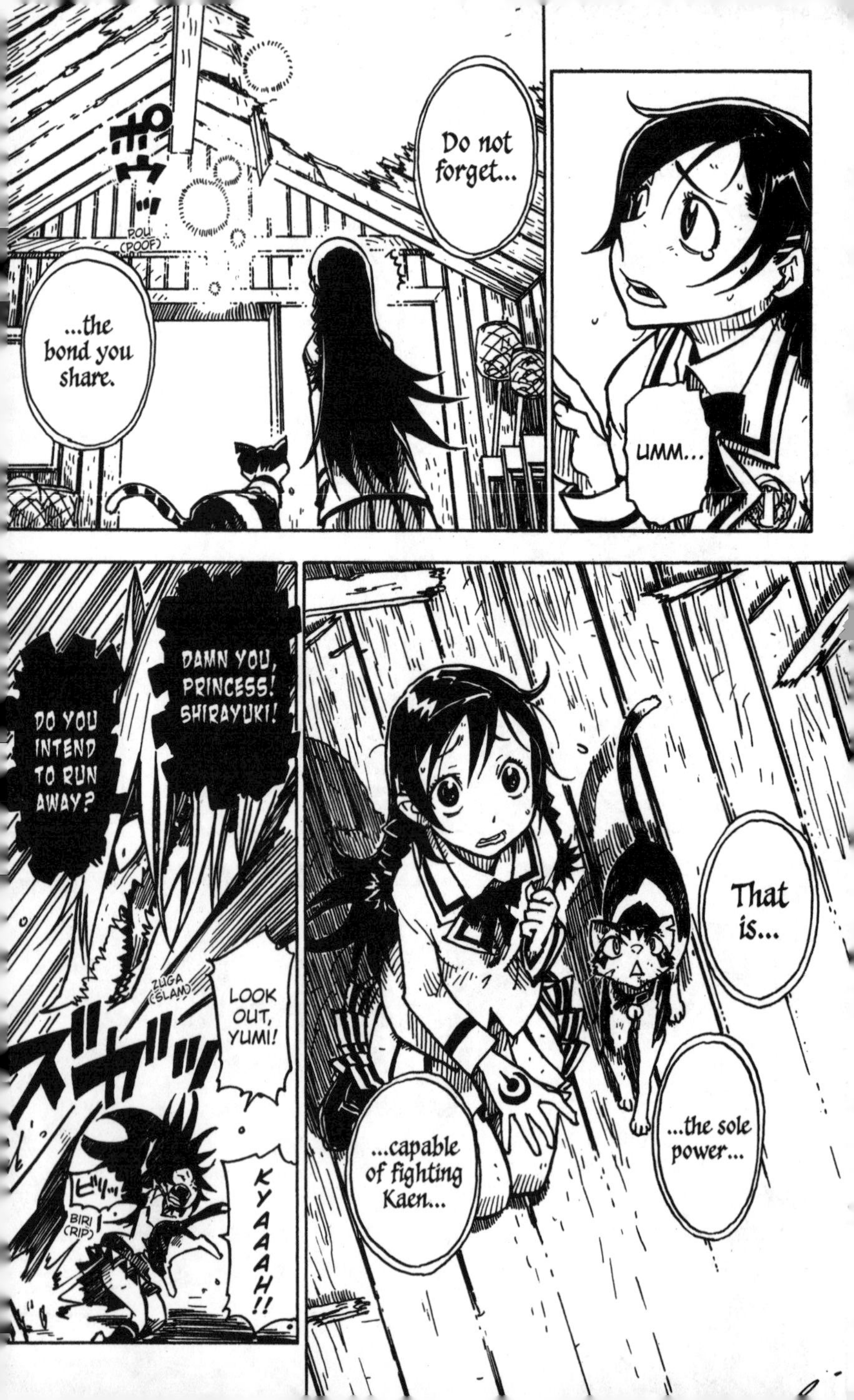
UMM...
Do not forget...
POU (POOF)
...the bond you share.
That is...
...the sole power...
...capable of fighting Kaen...
DAMN YOU, PRINCESS! SHIRAYUKI!
DO YOU INTEND TO RUN AWAY?
ZUGA (SLAM)
LOOK OUT, YUMI!
KYAAAAH!!
BIRI (RIP)

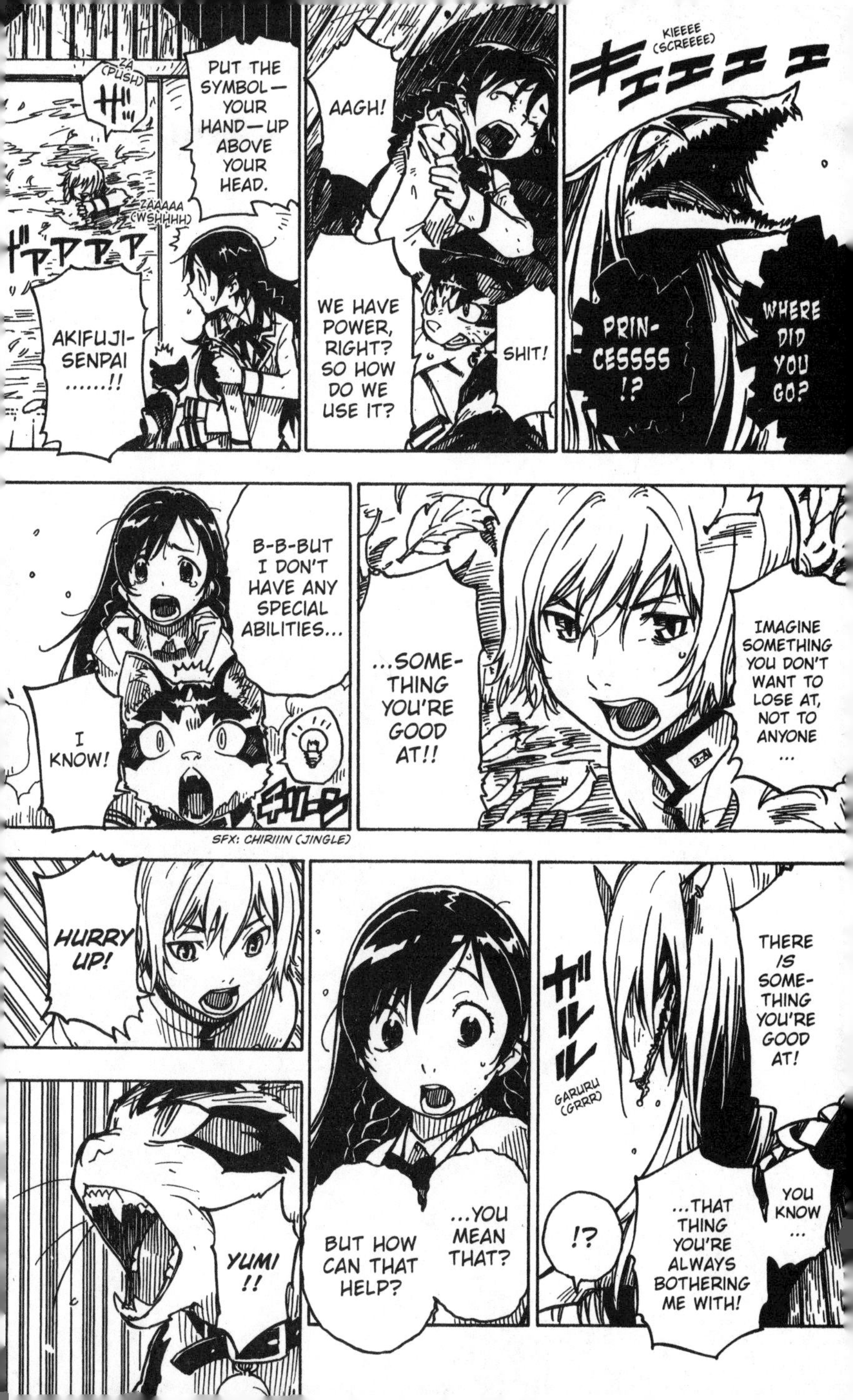
KIEEEE (SCREEEE)
PRIN-CESSSS!?
WHERE DID YOU GO?
AAGH!
SHIT!
WE HAVE POWER, RIGHT? SO HOW DO WE USE IT?
PUT THE SYMBOL—YOUR HAND—UP ABOVE YOUR HEAD.
ZA (PUSH)
ZAAAAA (WSHHHH)
AKIFUJI-SENPAI ......!!
IMAGINE SOMETHING YOU DON'T WANT TO LOSE AT, NOT TO ANYONE ...
...SOME-THING YOU'RE GOOD AT!!
B-B-BUT I DON'T HAVE ANY SPECIAL ABILITIES...
I KNOW!
SFX: CHIRIIIN (JINGLE)
THERE IS SOME-THING YOU'RE GOOD AT!
GARURU (GRRR)
YOU KNOW ...
...THAT THING YOU'RE ALWAYS BOTHERING ME WITH!
!?
...YOU MEAN THAT?
BUT HOW CAN THAT HELP?
HURRY UP!
YUMI !!

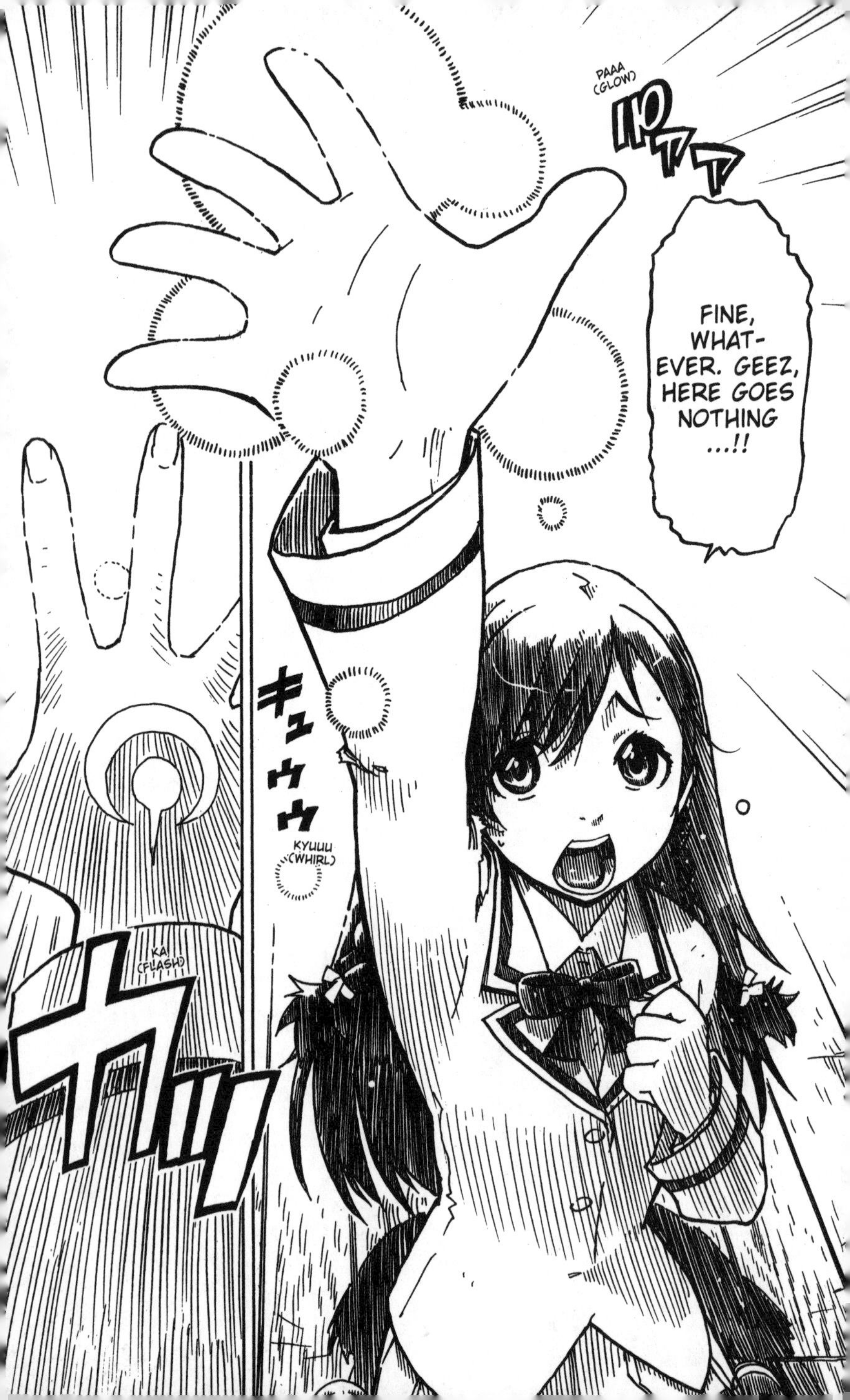
PAAA (GLOW)
FINE, WHAT-EVER. GEEZ, HERE GOES NOTHING ...!!
KYUUU (WHIRL)
KA (FLASH)

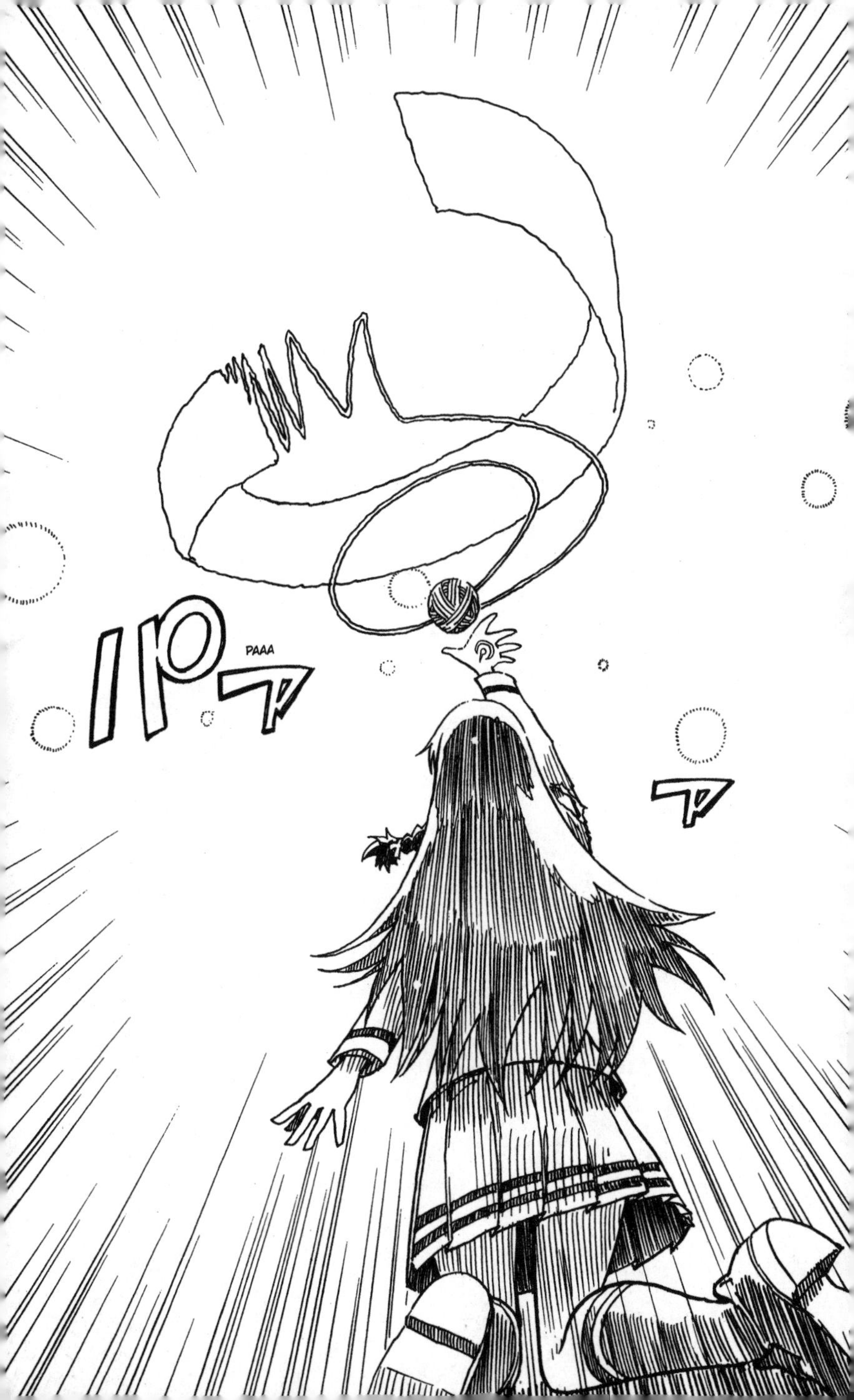
パァ
PAAA
ァ

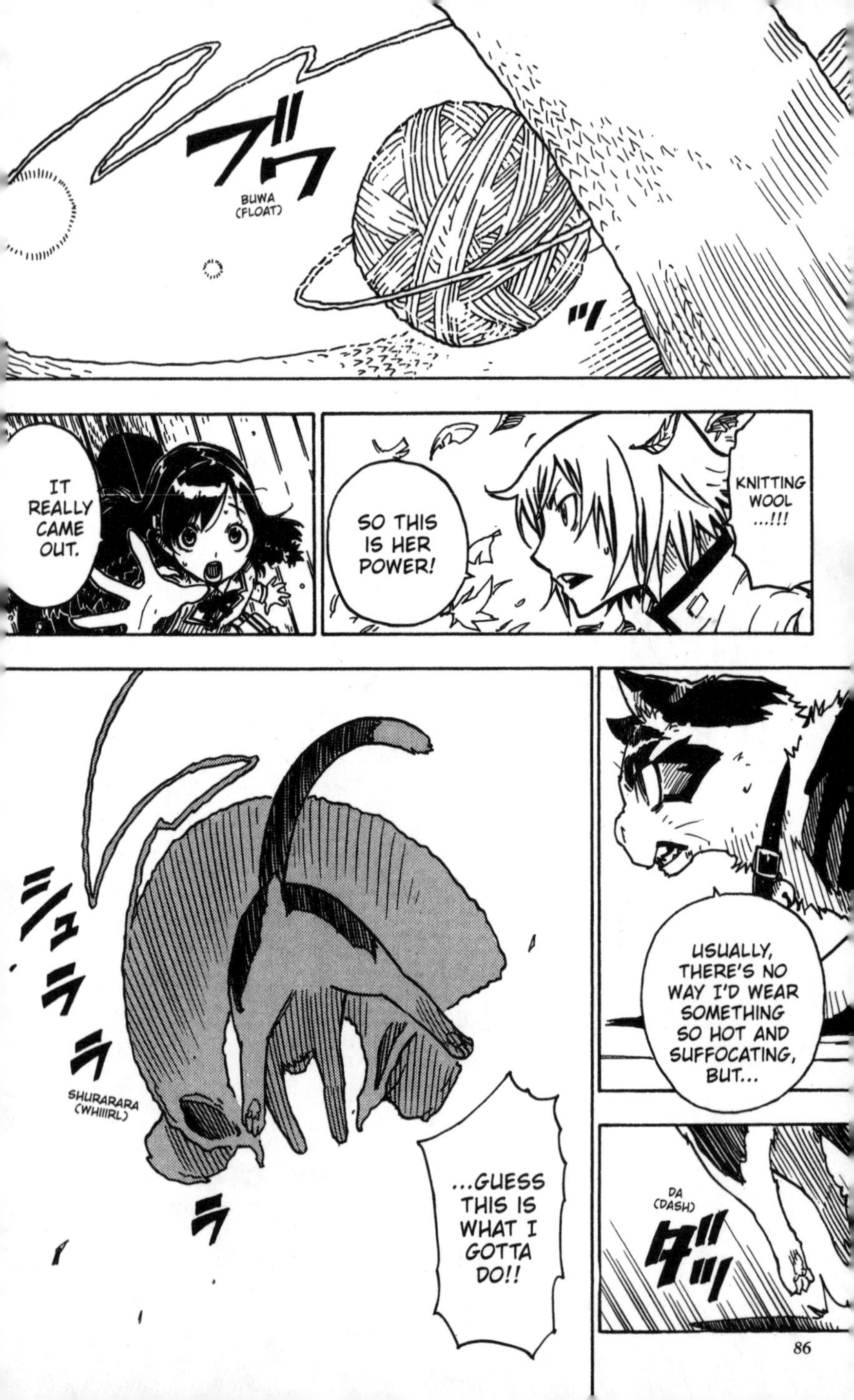
ブワ
ッ
BUWA (FLOAT)
KNITTING WOOL ...!!!
SO THIS IS HER POWER!
IT REALLY CAME OUT.
USUALLY, THERE'S NO WAY I'D WEAR SOMETHING SO HOT AND SUFFOCATING, BUT...
ダッ
DA (DASH)
シュラララ
SHURARARA (WHIIIRL)
...GUESS THIS IS WHAT I GOTTA DO!!

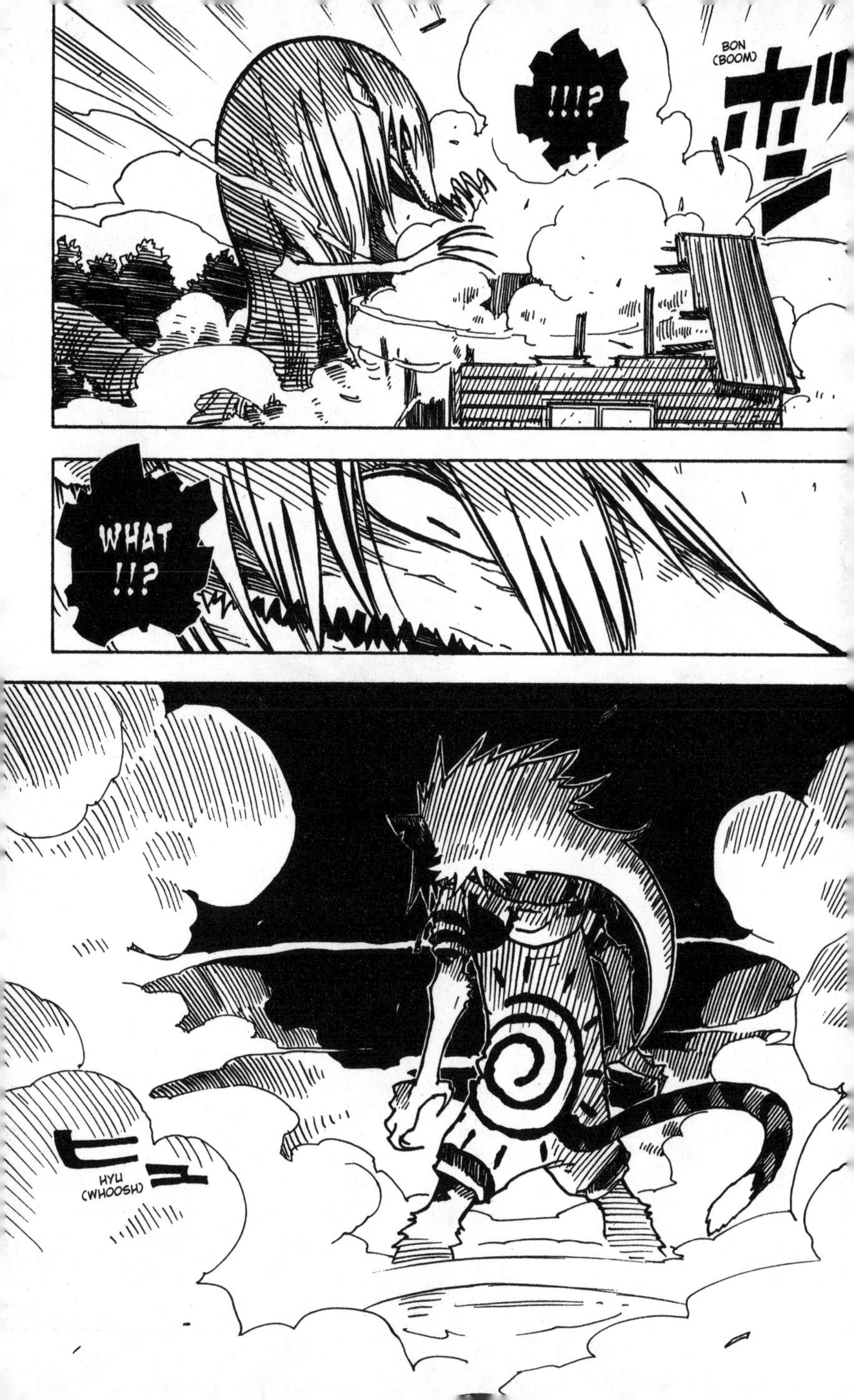

ボン
BON (BOOM)
!!!?
WHAT !!?
ヒュ
HYU (WHOOSH)

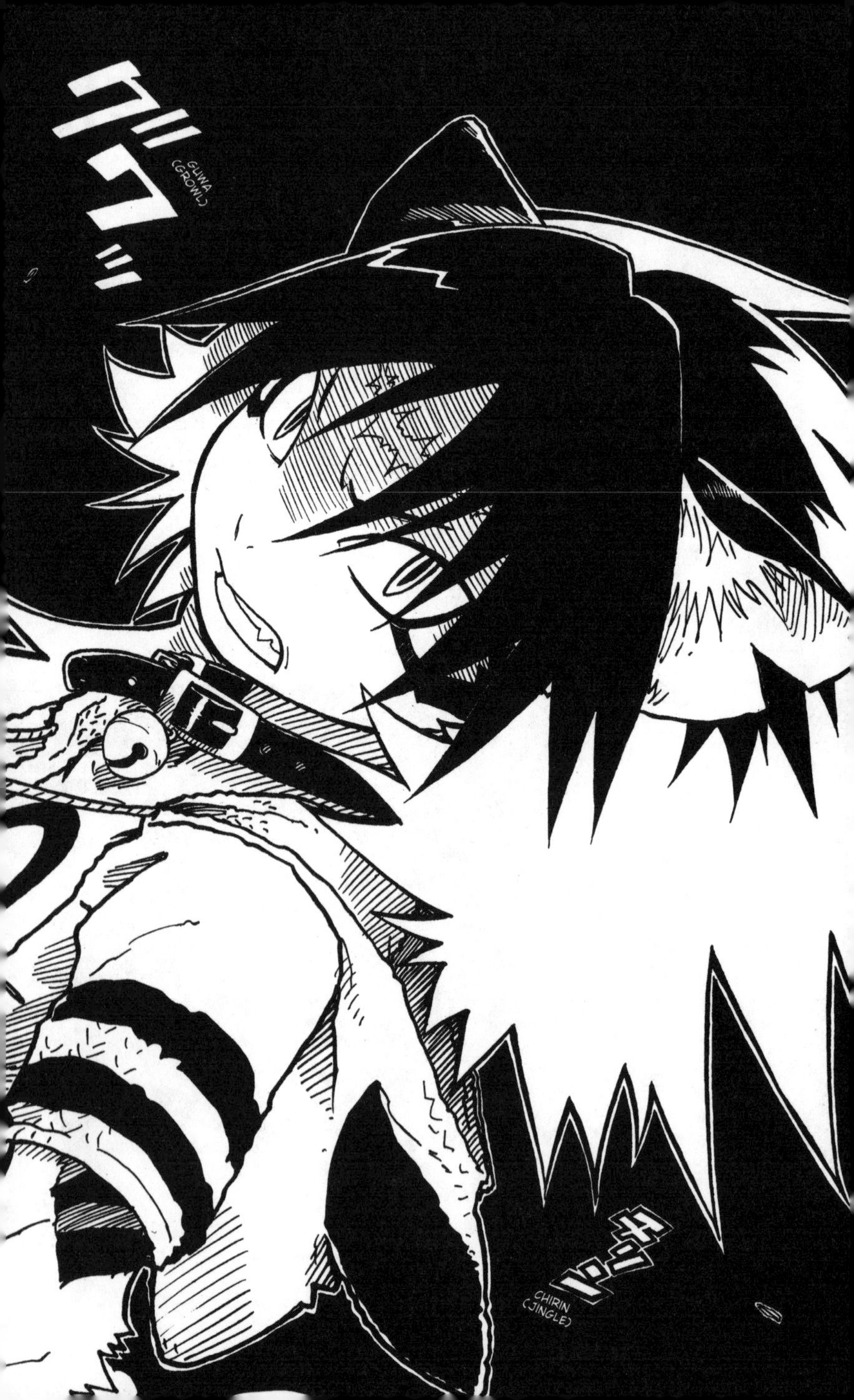
GUWA (GROWL)
CHIRIN (JINGLE)

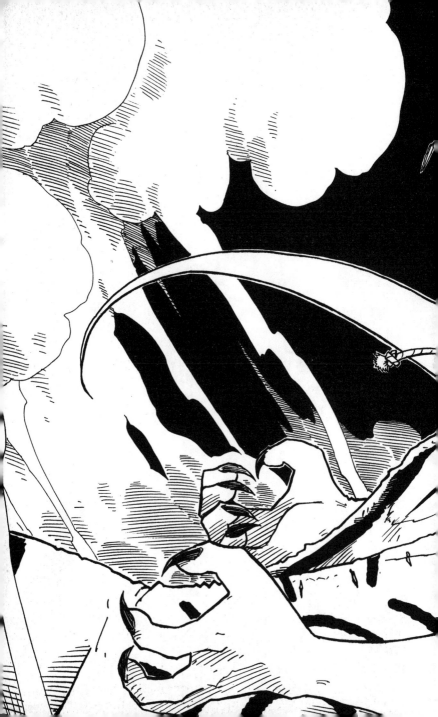

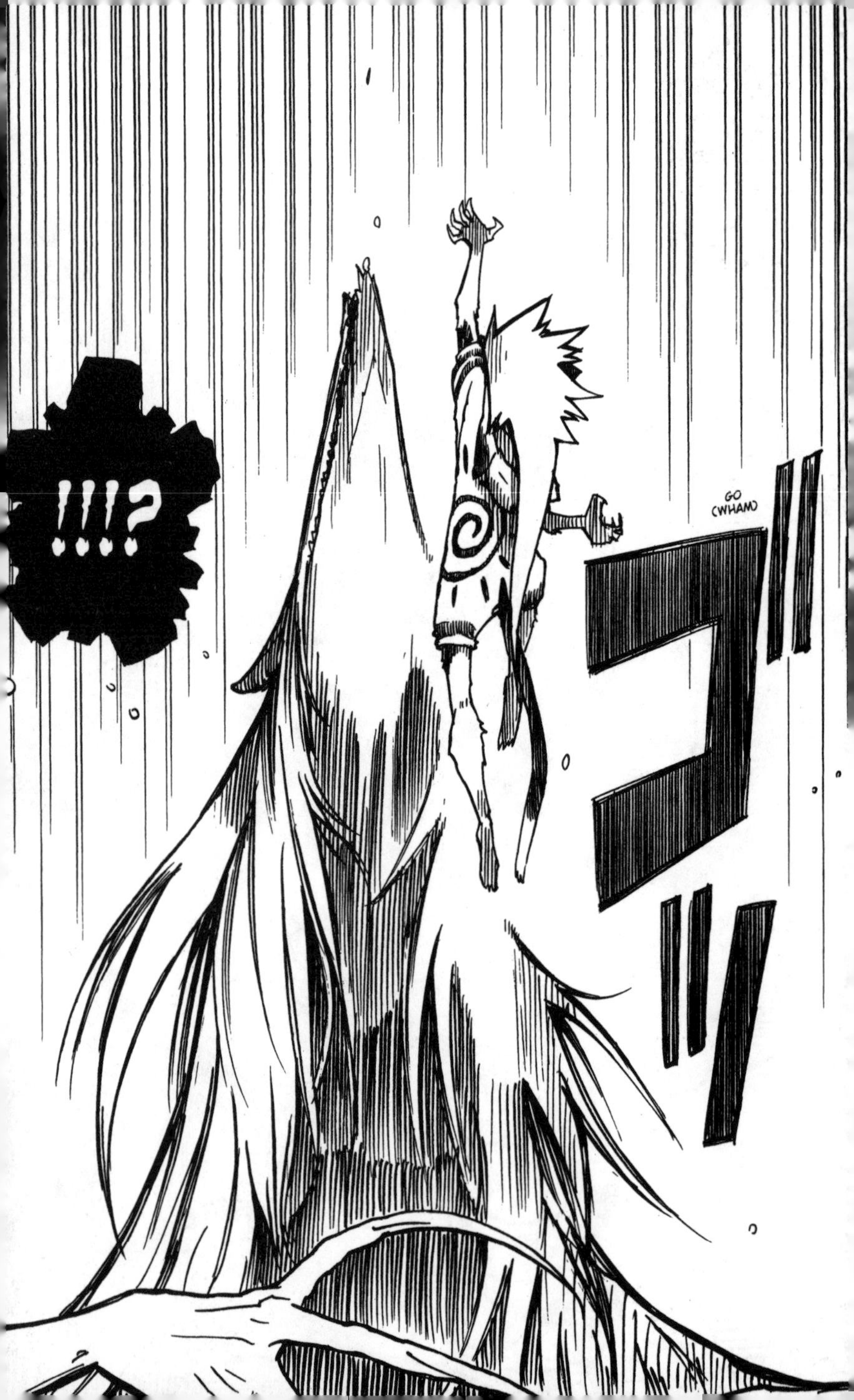
!!!?
GO
(WHAM)

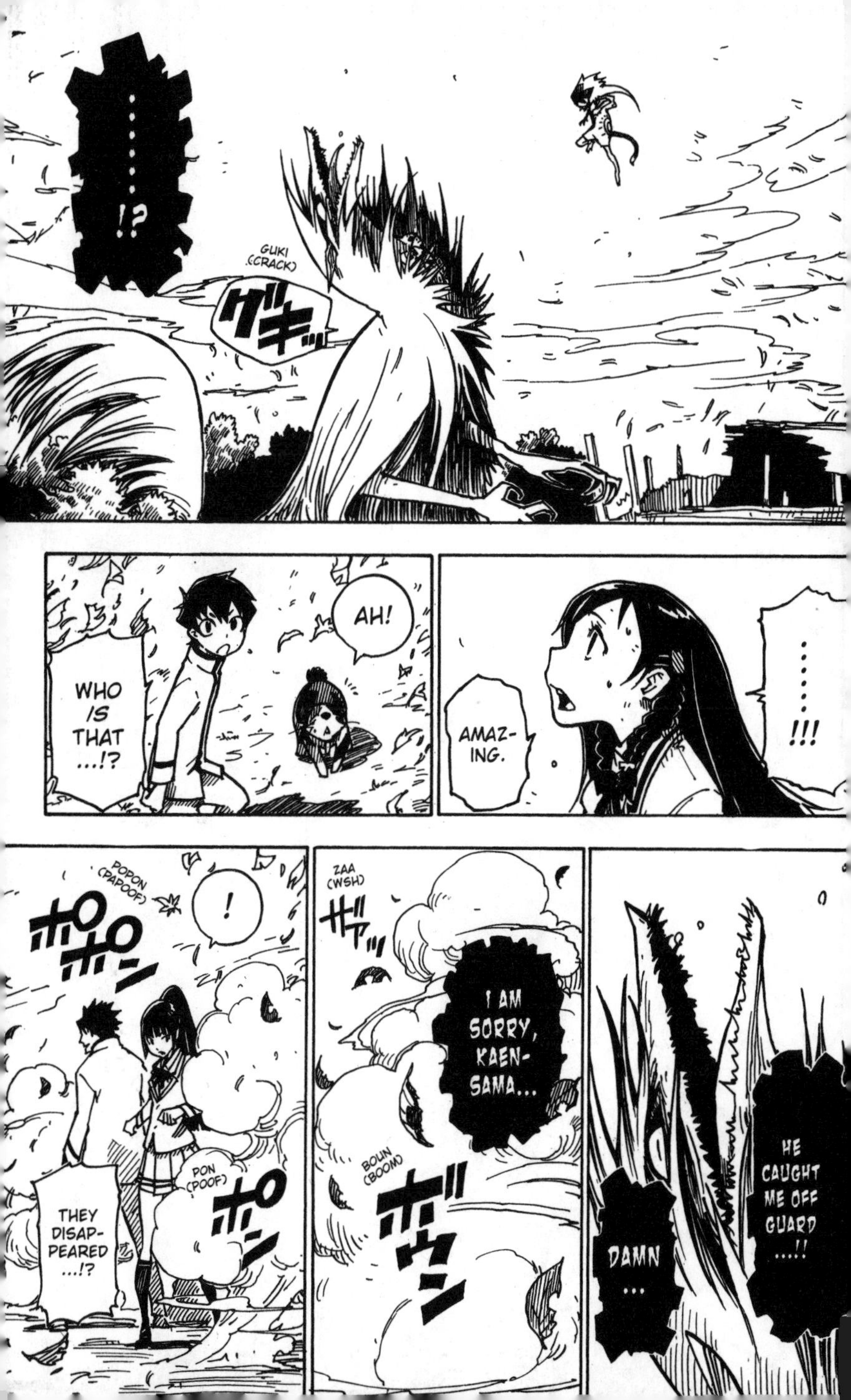

......!?
GUKI (CRACK)
グギッ
......!!!
AMAZ-ING.
AH!
WHO IS THAT ...!?
HE CAUGHT ME OFF GUARD ....!!
DAMN ...
ZAA (WSH)
ザァッ
I AM SORRY, KAEN-SAMA...
BOUN (BOOM)
ボウン
POPON (PAPOOF)
ポポン
!
PON (POOF)
ポン
THEY DISAP-PEARED ...!?

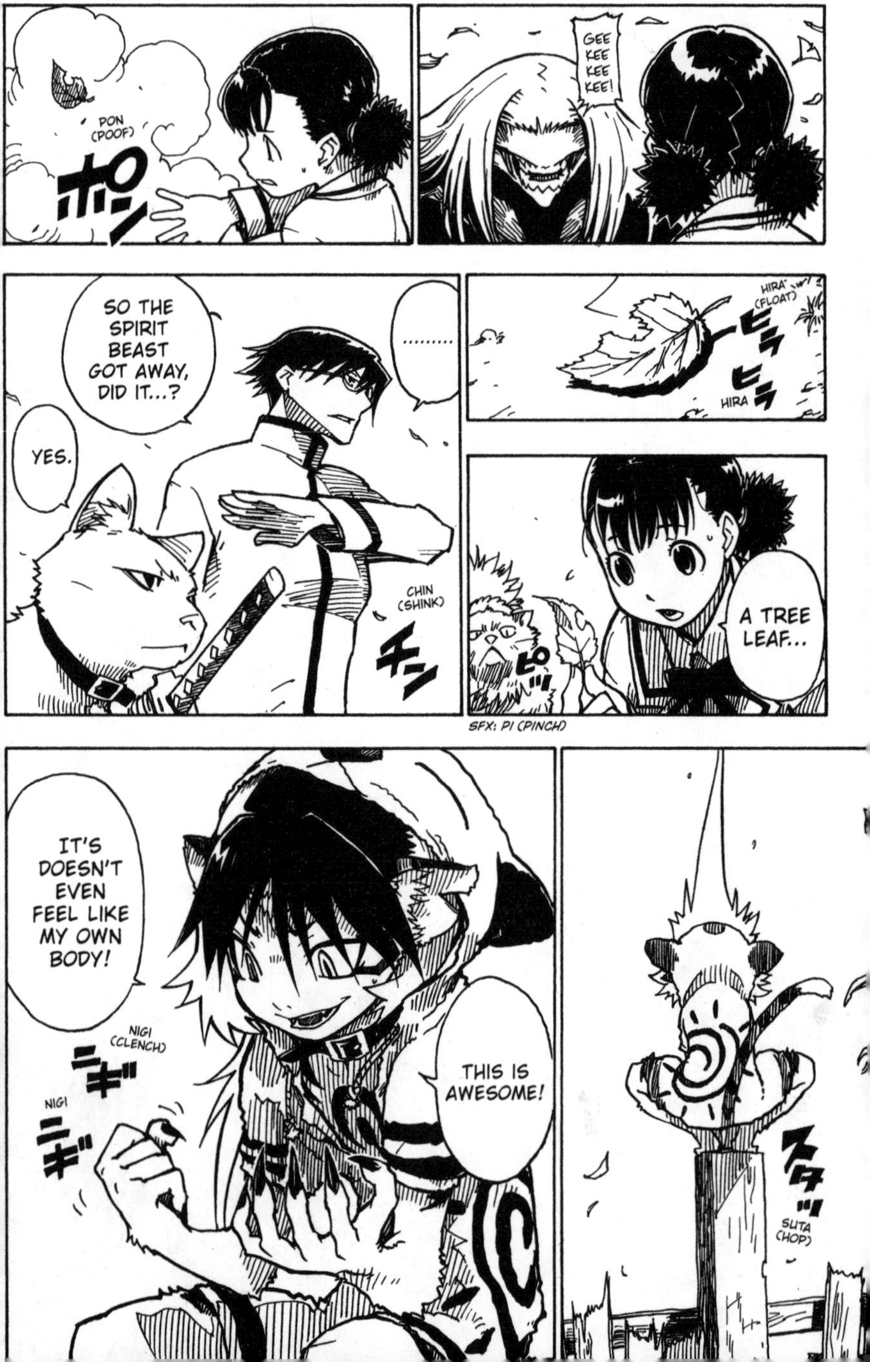
GEE KEE KEE KEE!
PON (POOF)
HIRA (FLOAT)
HIRA
A TREE LEAF...
SFX: PI (PINCH)
....
SO THE SPIRIT BEAST GOT AWAY, DID IT...?
YES.
CHIN (SHINK)
SUTA (HOP)
IT'S DOESN'T EVEN FEEL LIKE MY OWN BODY!
THIS IS AWESOME!
NIGI (CLENCH)
NIGI

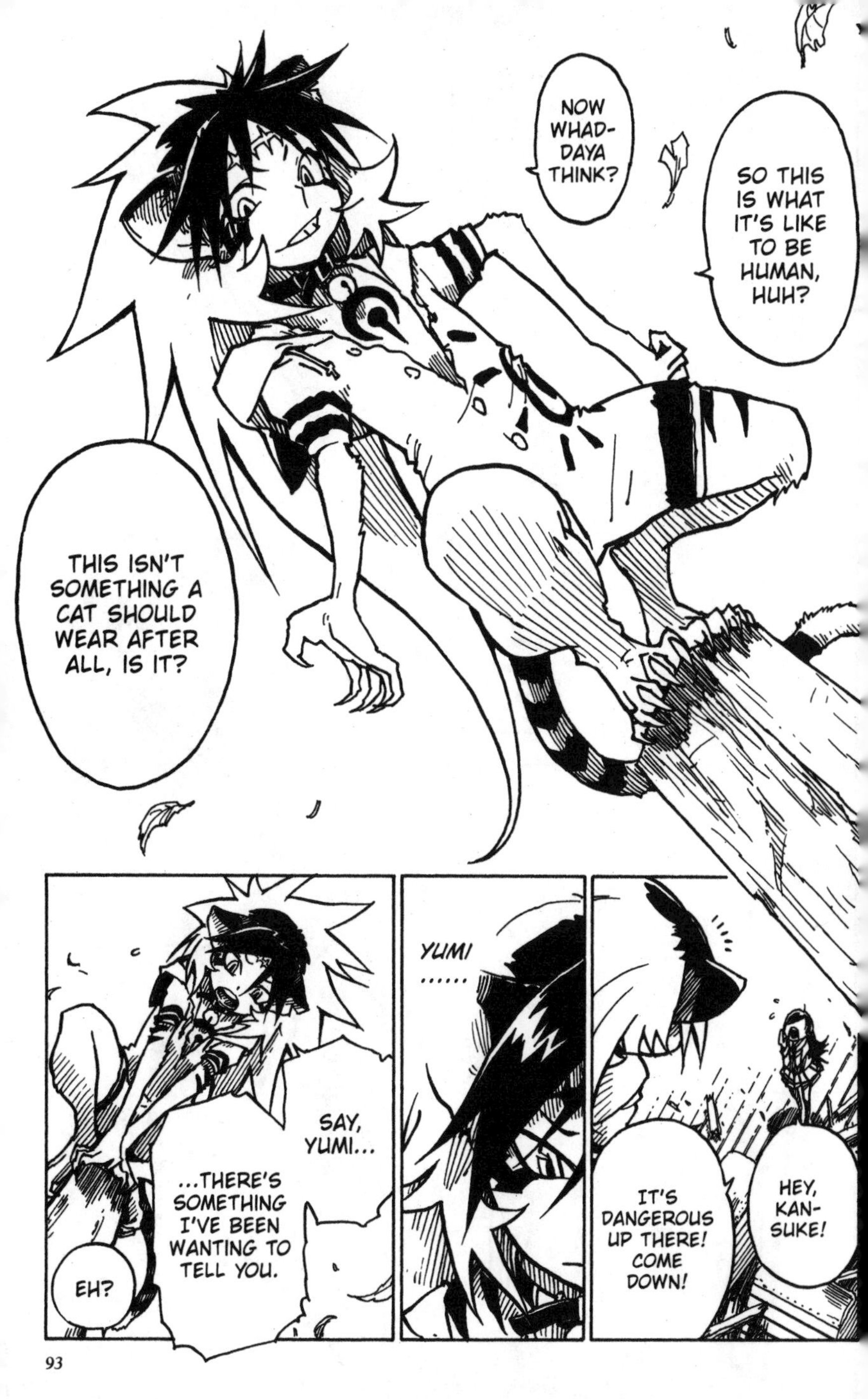
SO THIS IS WHAT IT'S LIKE TO BE HUMAN, HUH?
NOW WHAD-DAYA THINK?
THIS ISN'T SOMETHING A CAT SHOULD WEAR AFTER ALL, IS IT?
HEY, KAN-SUKE!
IT'S DANGEROUS UP THERE! COME DOWN!
YUMI ......
SAY, YUMI...
...THERE'S SOMETHING I'VE BEEN WANTING TO TELL YOU.
EH?

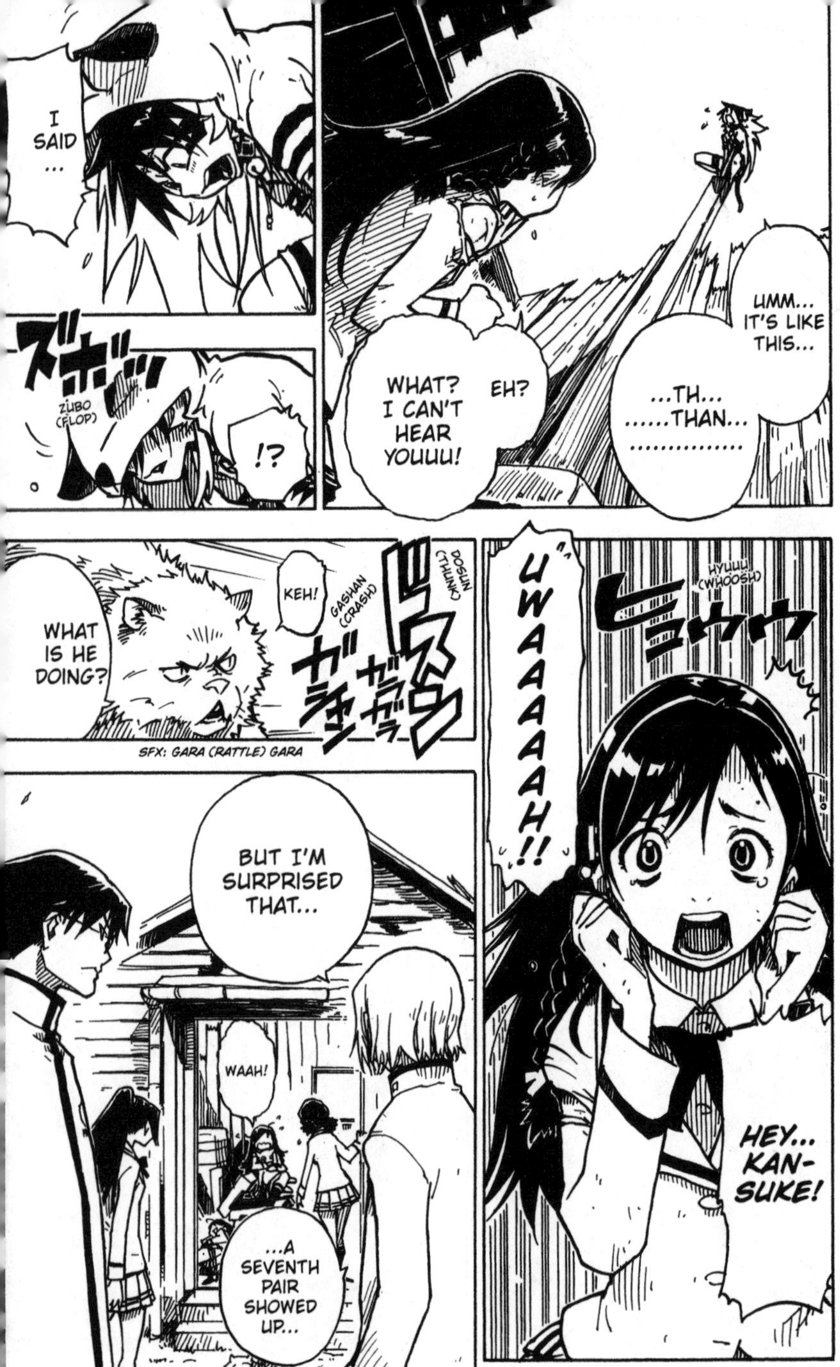
UMM... IT'S LIKE THIS...
...TH... ......THAN... ....
EH?
WHAT? I CAN'T HEAR YOUUU!
I SAID ...
ZUBO (FLOP)
!?
HYUUU (WHOOSH)
UWAAAAAAAH!!
HEY... KAN-SUKE!
DOSUN (THUNK)
KEH!
GASHAN (CRASH)
WHAT IS HE DOING?
SFX: GARA (RATTLE) GARA
BUT I'M SURPRISED THAT...
WAAH!
...A SEVENTH PAIR SHOWED UP...

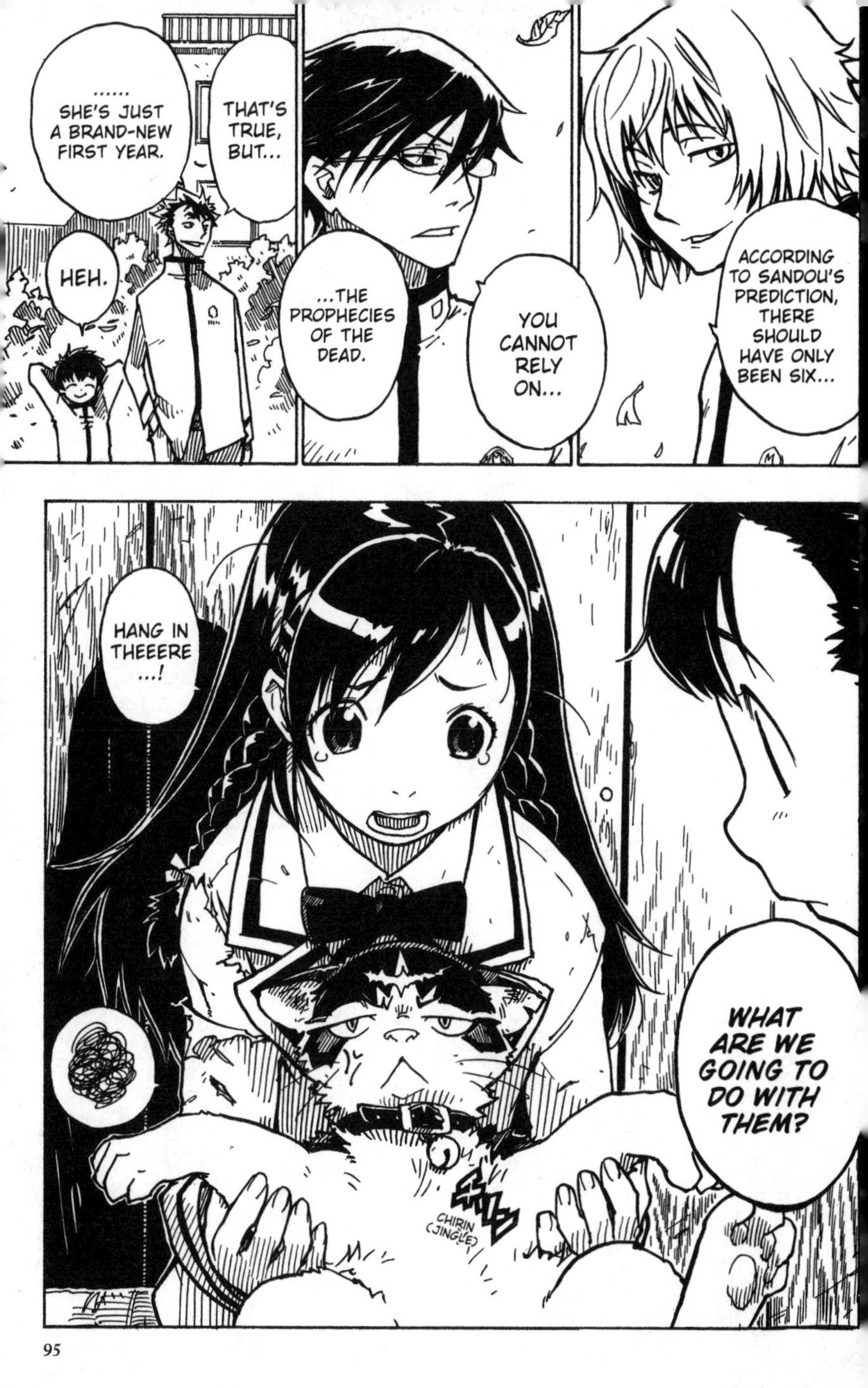
ACCORDING TO SANDOU'S PREDICTION, THERE SHOULD HAVE ONLY BEEN SIX...
YOU CANNOT RELY ON...
...THE PROPHECIES OF THE DEAD.
THAT'S TRUE, BUT...
...... SHE'S JUST A BRAND-NEW FIRST YEAR.
HEH.
WHAT ARE WE GOING TO DO WITH THEM?
HANG IN THEEERE ...!
CHIRIN (JINGLE)

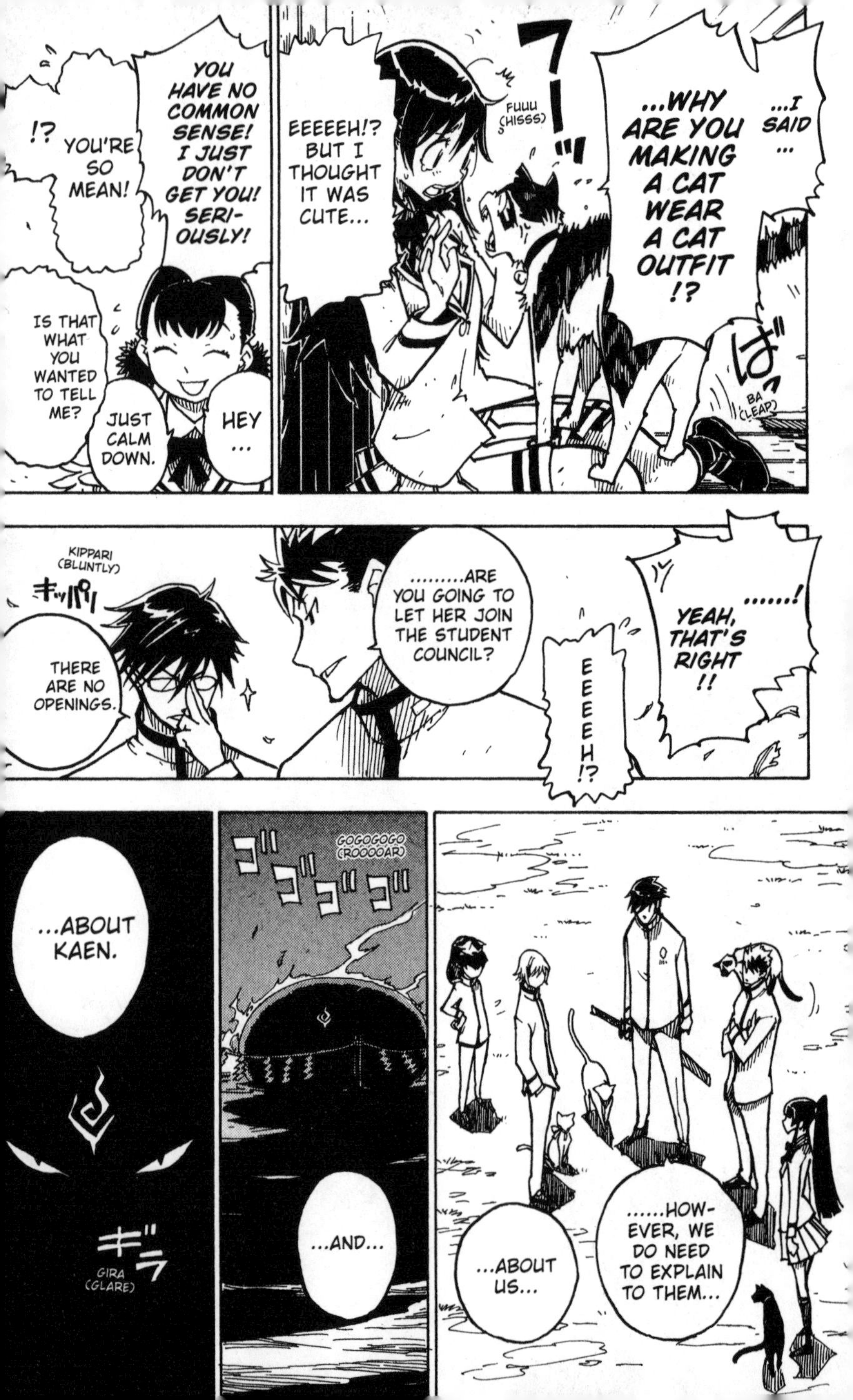
...I SAID ...
...WHY ARE YOU MAKING A CAT WEAR A CAT OUTFIT!?
FUUU (HISSS)
EEEEEH!? BUT I THOUGHT IT WAS CUTE...
BA (LEAP)
YOU HAVE NO COMMON SENSE! I JUST DON'T GET YOU! SERI-OUSLY!
!? YOU'RE SO MEAN!
HEY ...
JUST CALM DOWN.
IS THAT WHAT YOU WANTED TO TELL ME?
......!
YEAH, THAT'S RIGHT!!
EEEEEH!?
.........ARE YOU GOING TO LET HER JOIN THE STUDENT COUNCIL?
KIPPARI (BLUNTLY)
THERE ARE NO OPENINGS.
......HOW-EVER, WE DO NEED TO EXPLAIN TO THEM...
...ABOUT US...
GOGOGOGO (ROOOOAR)
...AND...
...ABOUT KAEN.
GIRA (GLARE)

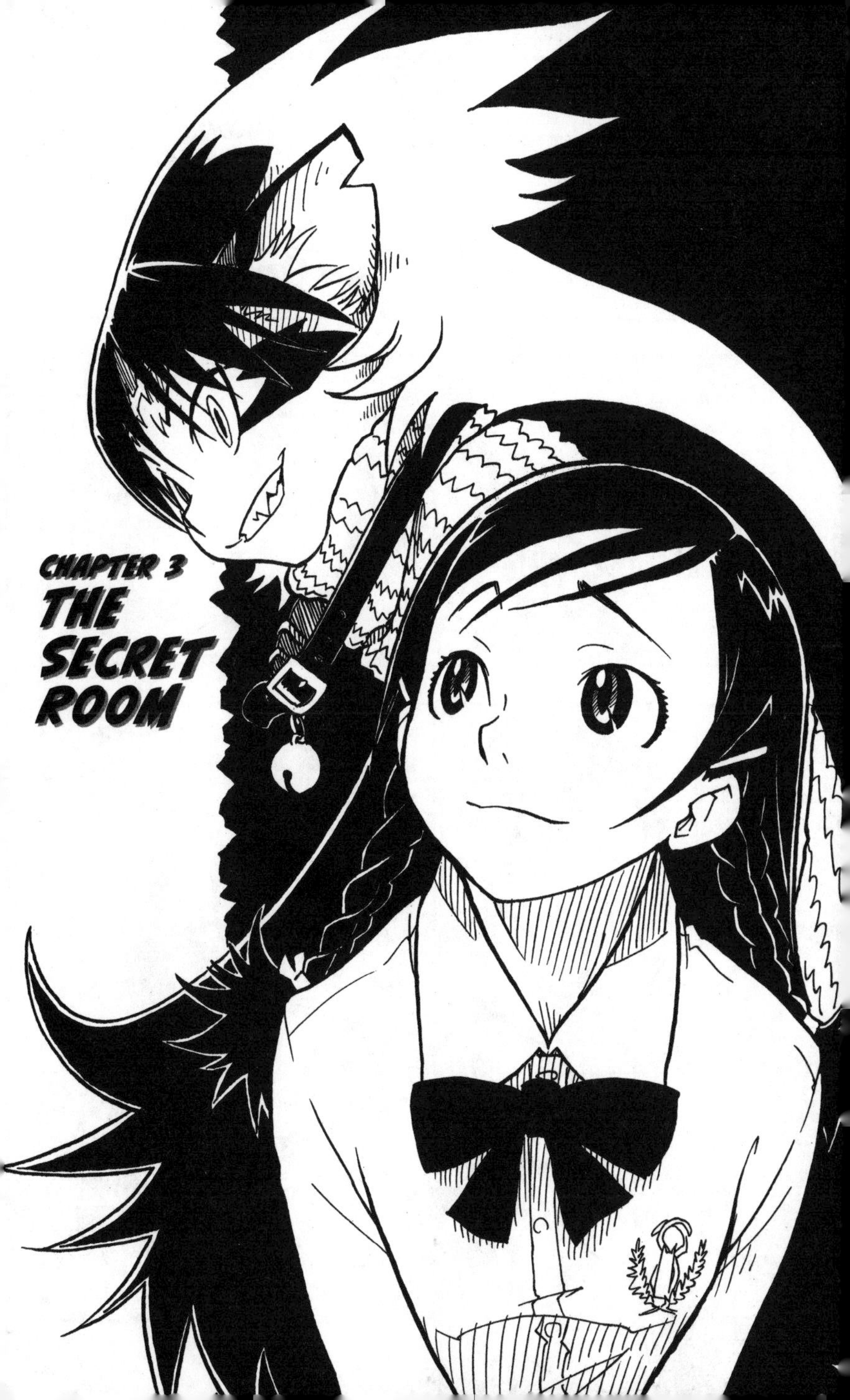
CHAPTER 3
THE SECRET ROOM

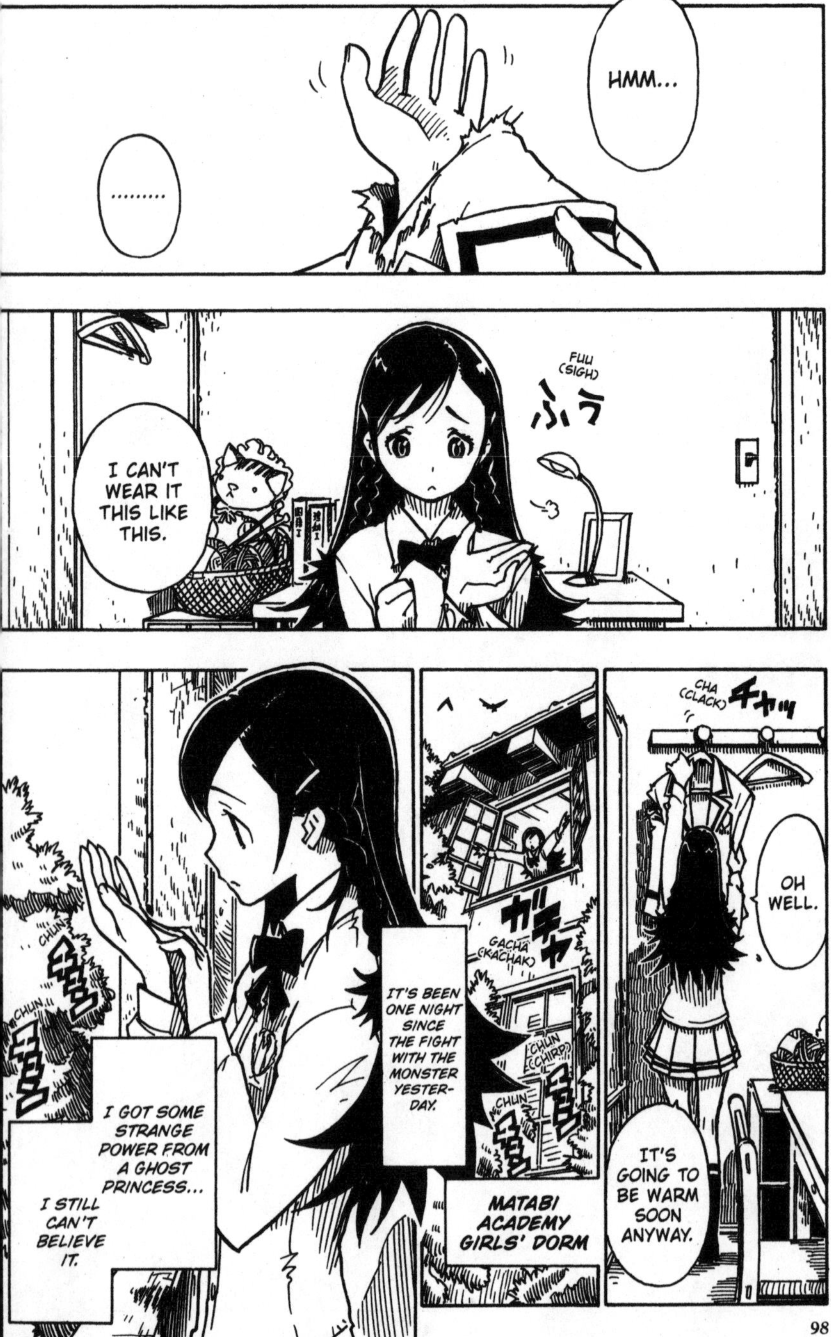
HMM...
....
FUU (SIGH)
ふう
I CAN'T WEAR IT THIS LIKE THIS.
CHA (CLACK)
チャッ
OH WELL.
IT'S GOING TO BE WARM SOON ANYWAY.
ガチャ
GACHA (KACHAK)
CHUN (CHIRP)
CHUN
MATABI ACADEMY GIRLS' DORM
IT'S BEEN ONE NIGHT SINCE THE FIGHT WITH THE MONSTER YESTER-DAY.
CHUN
CHUN
I GOT SOME STRANGE POWER FROM A GHOST PRINCESS...
I STILL CAN'T BELIEVE IT.

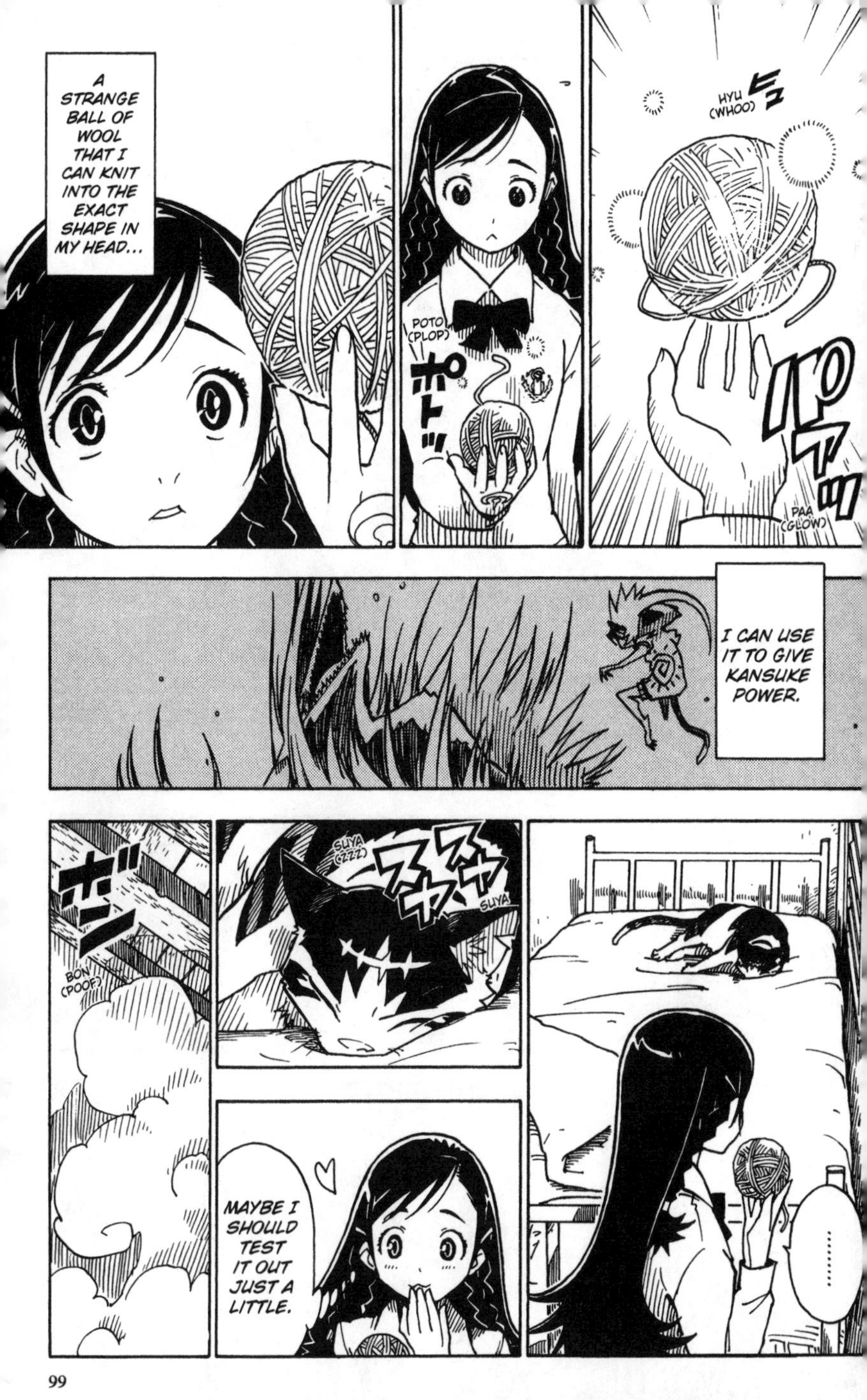
HYU (WHOO)
PAA (GLOW)
POTO (PLOP)
A STRANGE BALL OF WOOL THAT I CAN KNIT INTO THE EXACT SHAPE IN MY HEAD...
I CAN USE IT TO GIVE KANSUKE POWER.
......
SUYA (ZZZ)
SUYA
MAYBE I SHOULD TEST IT OUT JUST A LITTLE.
BON (POOF)

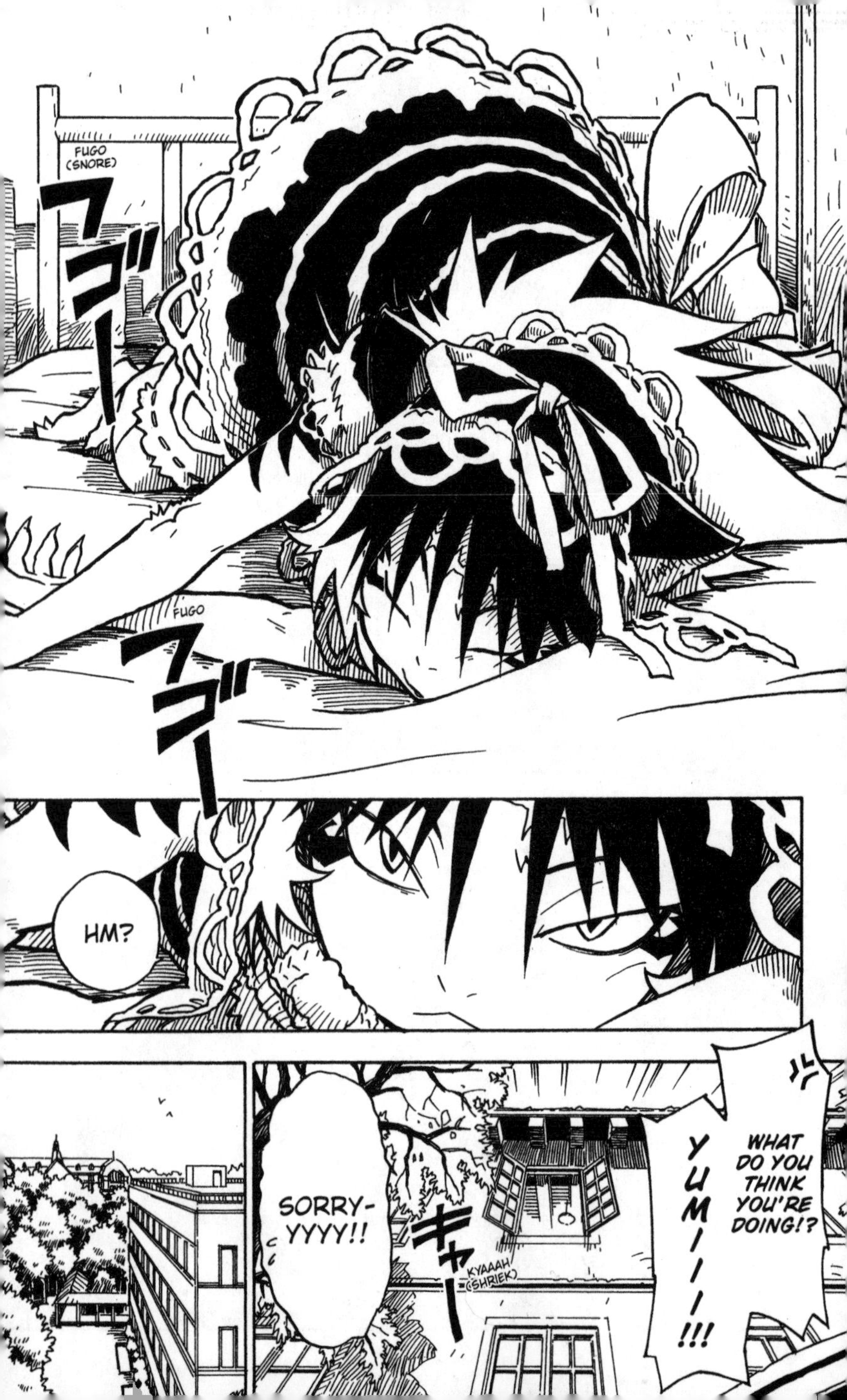

FUGO (SNORE)
フゴー
FUGO
フゴー
HM?
WHAT DO YOU THINK YOU'RE DOING!?
YUMI------!!!
キャー
KYAAAH (SHRIEK)
SORRY-YYYY!!

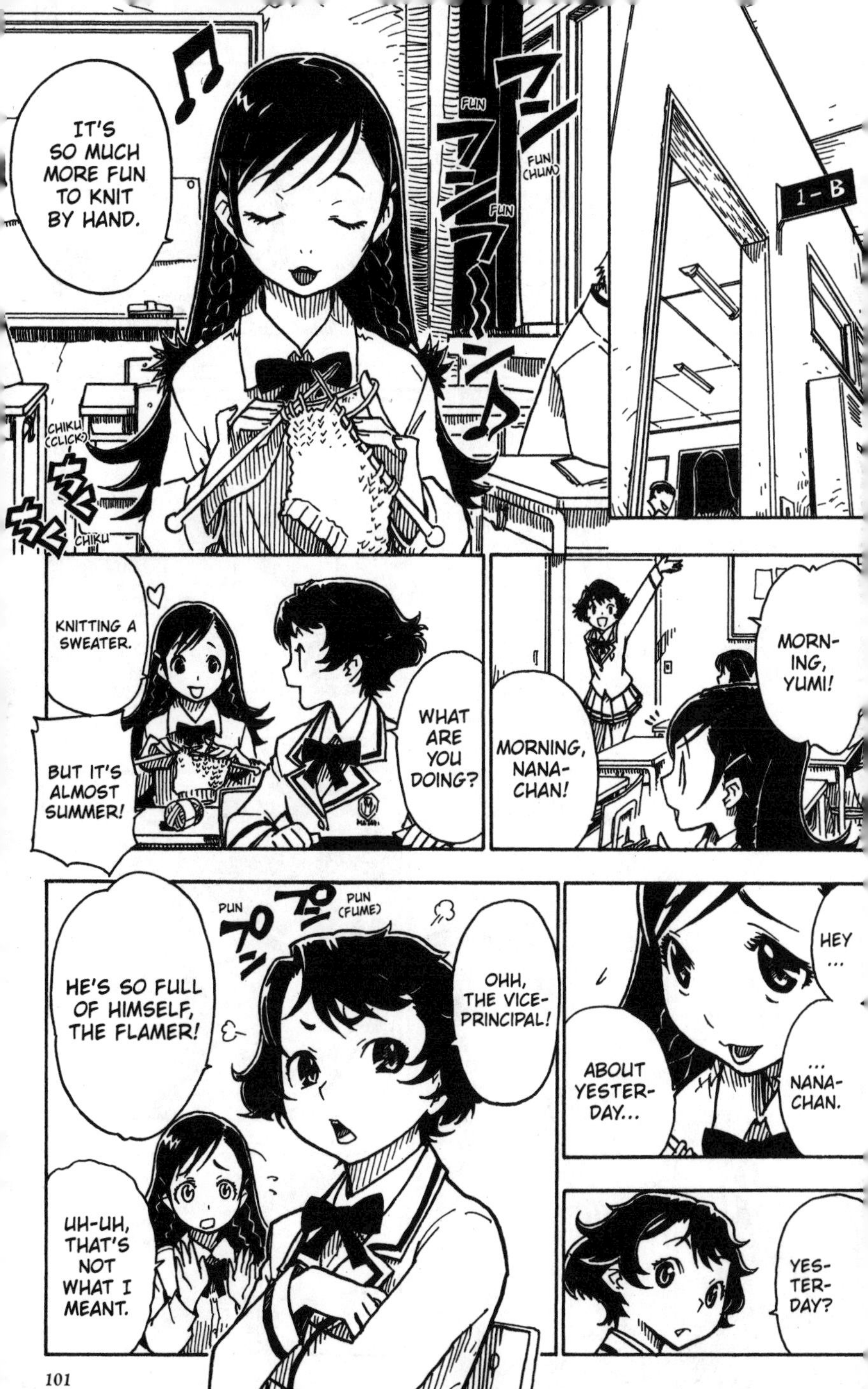

FUN
FUN (HUM)
FUN
IT'S SO MUCH MORE FUN TO KNIT BY HAND.
CHIKU (CLICK)
CHIKU
MORNING, YUMI!
MORNING, NANA-CHAN!
WHAT ARE YOU DOING?
KNITTING A SWEATER.
BUT IT'S ALMOST SUMMER!
HEY ...
... NANA-CHAN.
ABOUT YESTERDAY...
YESTERDAY?
PUN (FUME)
PUN
OHH, THE VICE-PRINCIPAL!
HE'S SO FULL OF HIMSELF, THE FLAMER!
UH-UH, THAT'S NOT WHAT I MEANT.

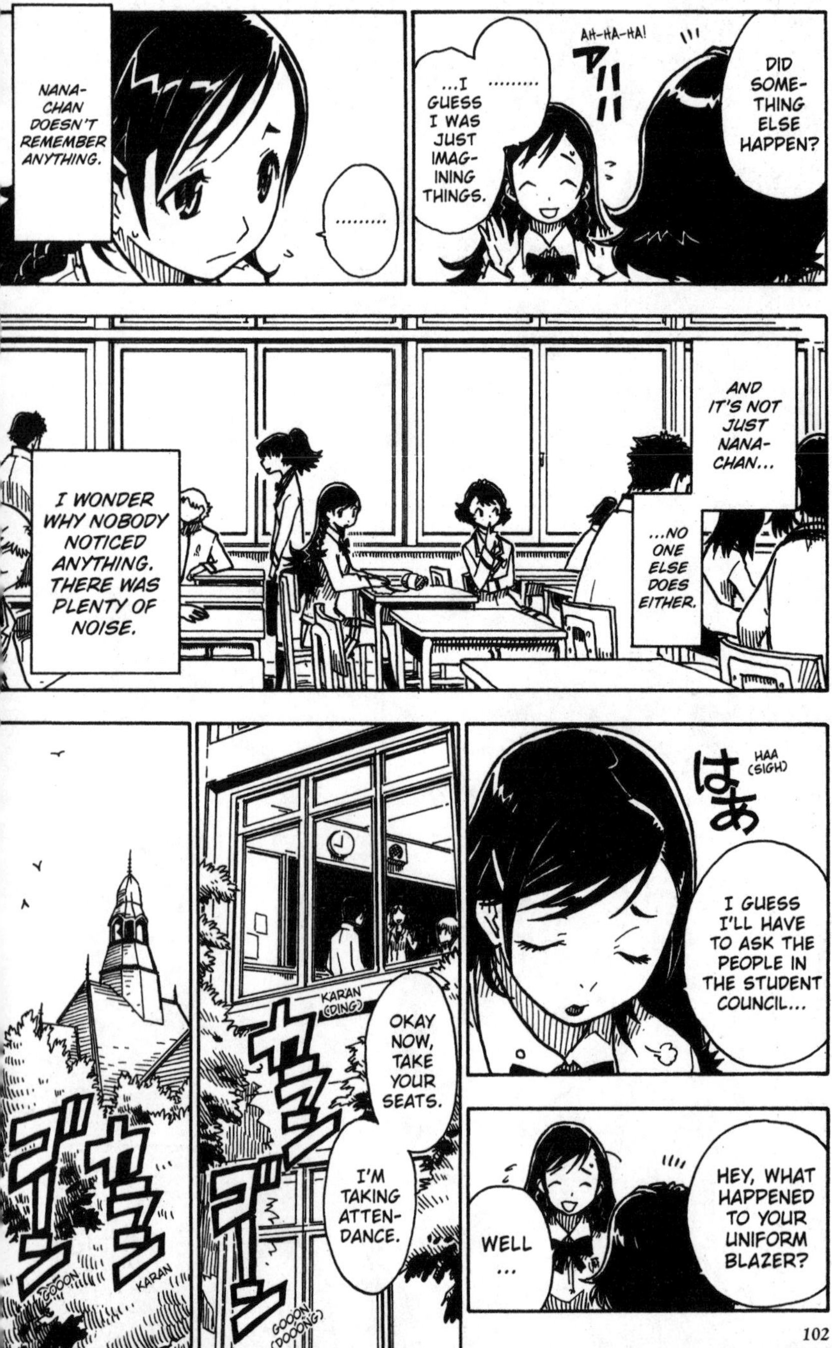
DID SOMETHING ELSE HAPPEN?
AH-HA-HA!
....
...I GUESS I WAS JUST IMAGINING THINGS.
NANA-CHAN DOESN'T REMEMBER ANYTHING.
....
AND IT'S NOT JUST NANA-CHAN...
...NO ONE ELSE DOES EITHER.
I WONDER WHY NOBODY NOTICED ANYTHING. THERE WAS PLENTY OF NOISE.
はあ
HAA (SIGH)
I GUESS I'LL HAVE TO ASK THE PEOPLE IN THE STUDENT COUNCIL...
HEY, WHAT HAPPENED TO YOUR UNIFORM BLAZER?
WELL...
KARAN (DING)
OKAY NOW, TAKE YOUR SEATS.
I'M TAKING ATTENDANCE.
GOOON (DOOONG)
KARAN
GOOON

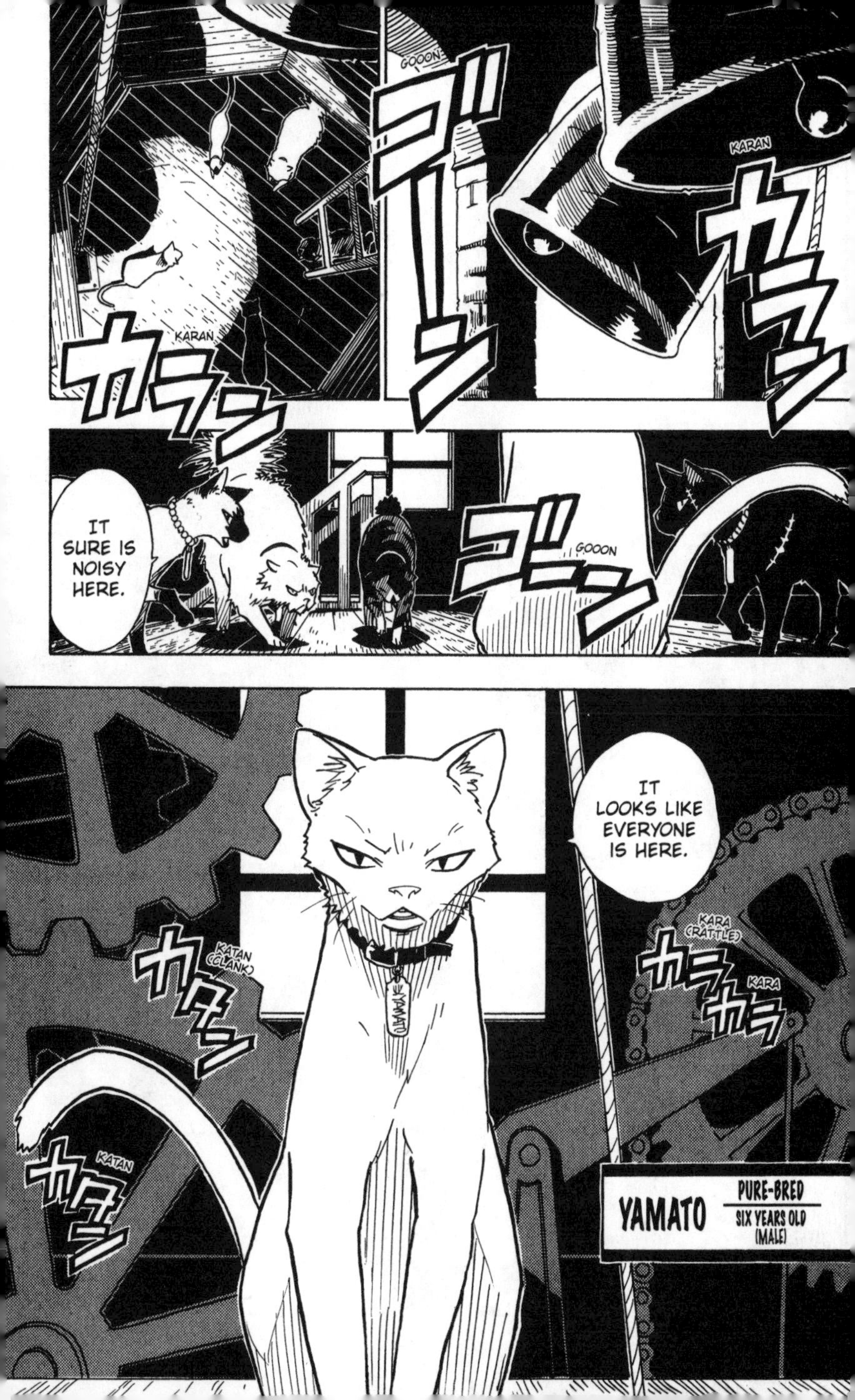
KARAN
カラン
GOOON
ゴーン
KARAN
カラン
GOOON
ゴーン
IT SURE IS NOISY HERE.
IT LOOKS LIKE EVERYONE IS HERE.
YAMATO
KARA (RATTLE)
カラ
KARA
カラ
KATAN (CLANK)
カタン
KATAN
カタン
YAMATO
PURE-BRED
SIX YEARS OLD (MALE)

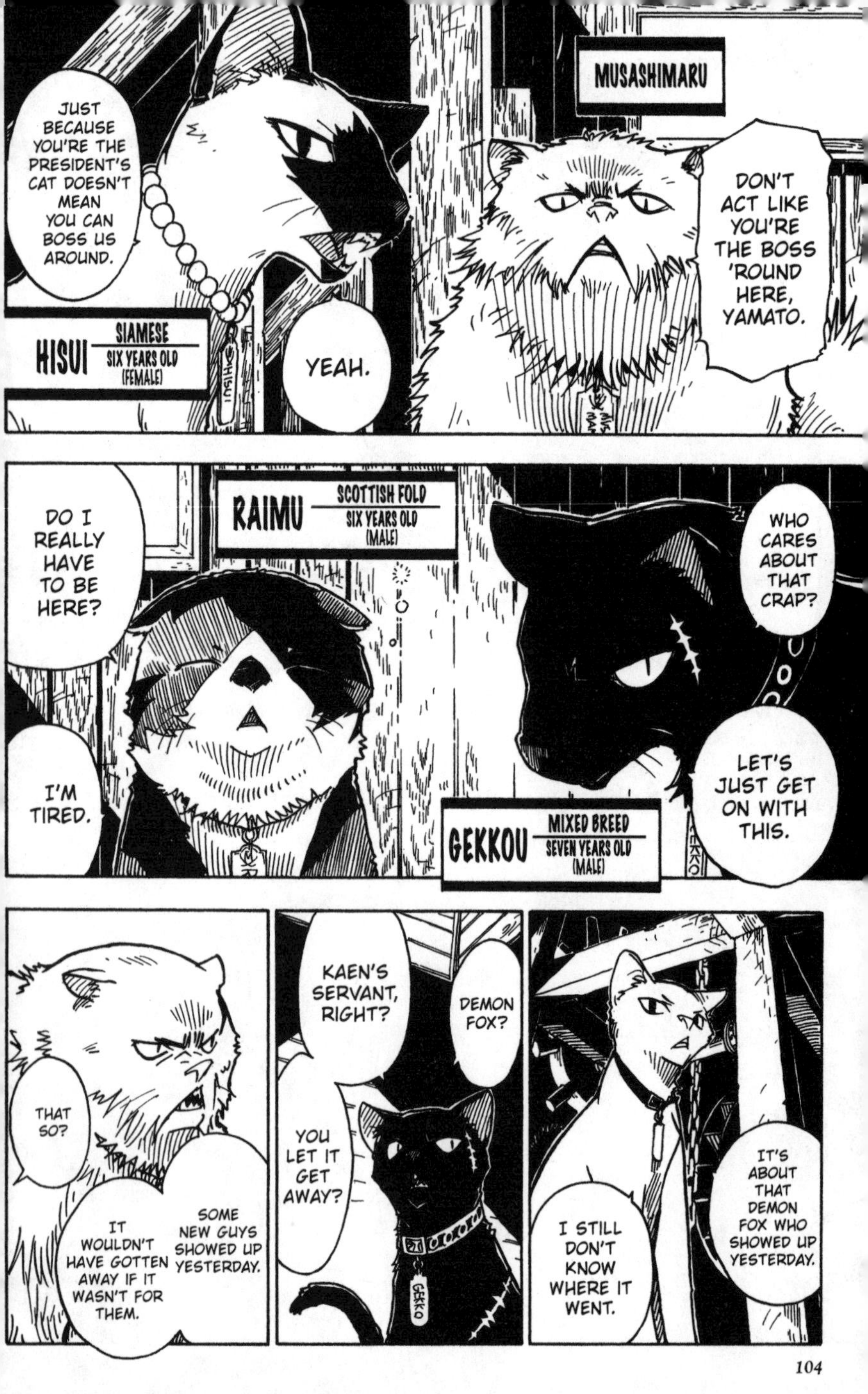
MUSASHIMARU
DON'T ACT LIKE YOU'RE THE BOSS 'ROUND HERE, YAMATO.
JUST BECAUSE YOU'RE THE PRESIDENT'S CAT DOESN'T MEAN YOU CAN BOSS US AROUND.
YEAH.
HISUI SIAMESE SIX YEARS OLD (FEMALE)
WHO CARES ABOUT THAT CRAP?
LET'S JUST GET ON WITH THIS.
GEKKOU MIXED BREED SEVEN YEARS OLD (MALE)
RAIMU SCOTTISH FOLD SIX YEARS OLD (MALE)
DO I REALLY HAVE TO BE HERE?
I'M TIRED.
IT'S ABOUT THAT DEMON FOX WHO SHOWED UP YESTERDAY.
I STILL DON'T KNOW WHERE IT WENT.
DEMON FOX?
KAEN'S SERVANT, RIGHT?
YOU LET IT GET AWAY?
THAT SO?
SOME NEW GUYS SHOWED UP YESTERDAY.
IT WOULDN'T HAVE GOTTEN AWAY IF IT WASN'T FOR THEM.

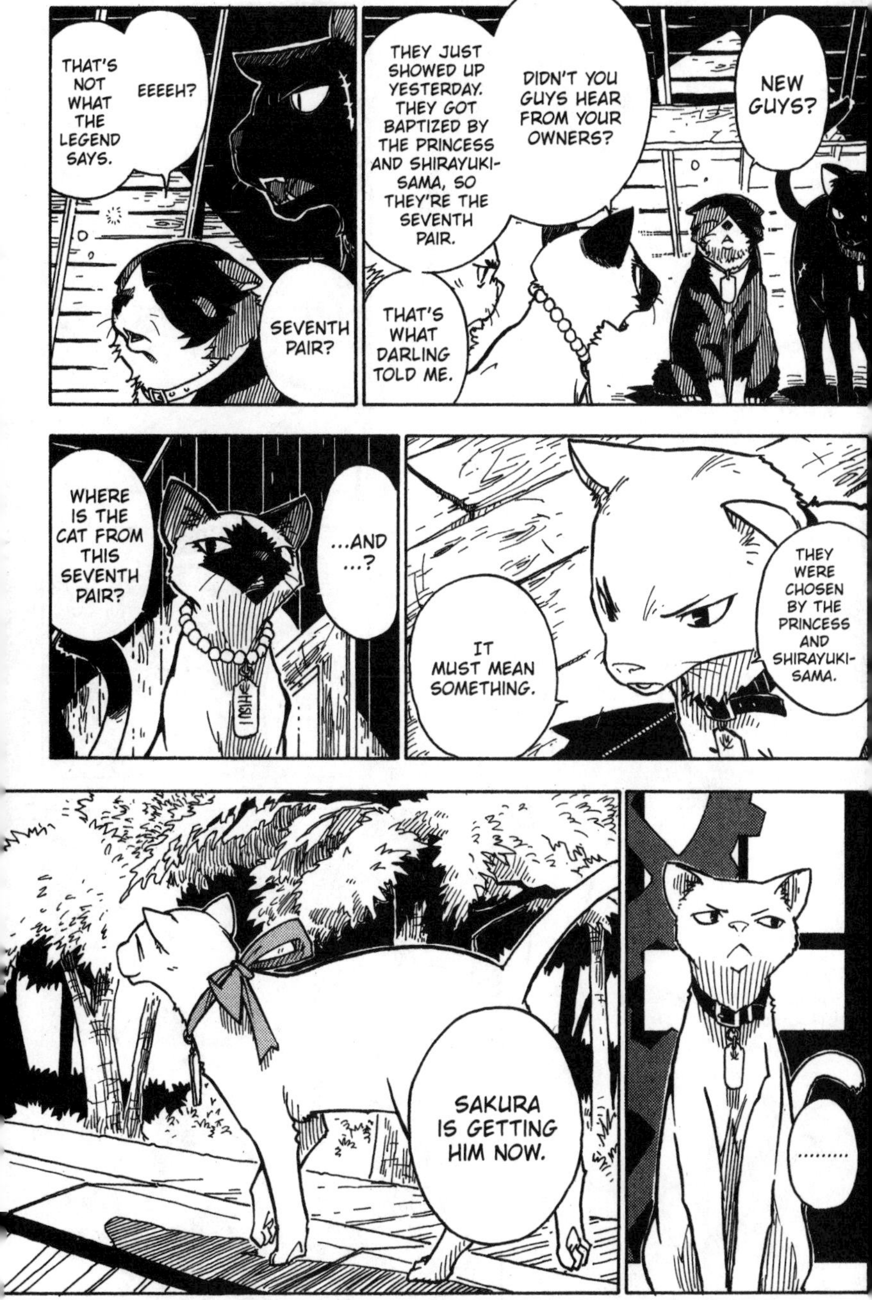
NEW GUYS?
DIDN'T YOU GUYS HEAR FROM YOUR OWNERS?
THEY JUST SHOWED UP YESTERDAY. THEY GOT BAPTIZED BY THE PRINCESS AND SHIRAYUKI-SAMA, SO THEY'RE THE SEVENTH PAIR.
THAT'S WHAT DARLING TOLD ME.
EEEEH?
THAT'S NOT WHAT THE LEGEND SAYS.
SEVENTH PAIR?
THEY WERE CHOSEN BY THE PRINCESS AND SHIRAYUKI-SAMA.
IT MUST MEAN SOMETHING.
...AND ...?
WHERE IS THE CAT FROM THIS SEVENTH PAIR?
....
SAKURA IS GETTING HIM NOW.

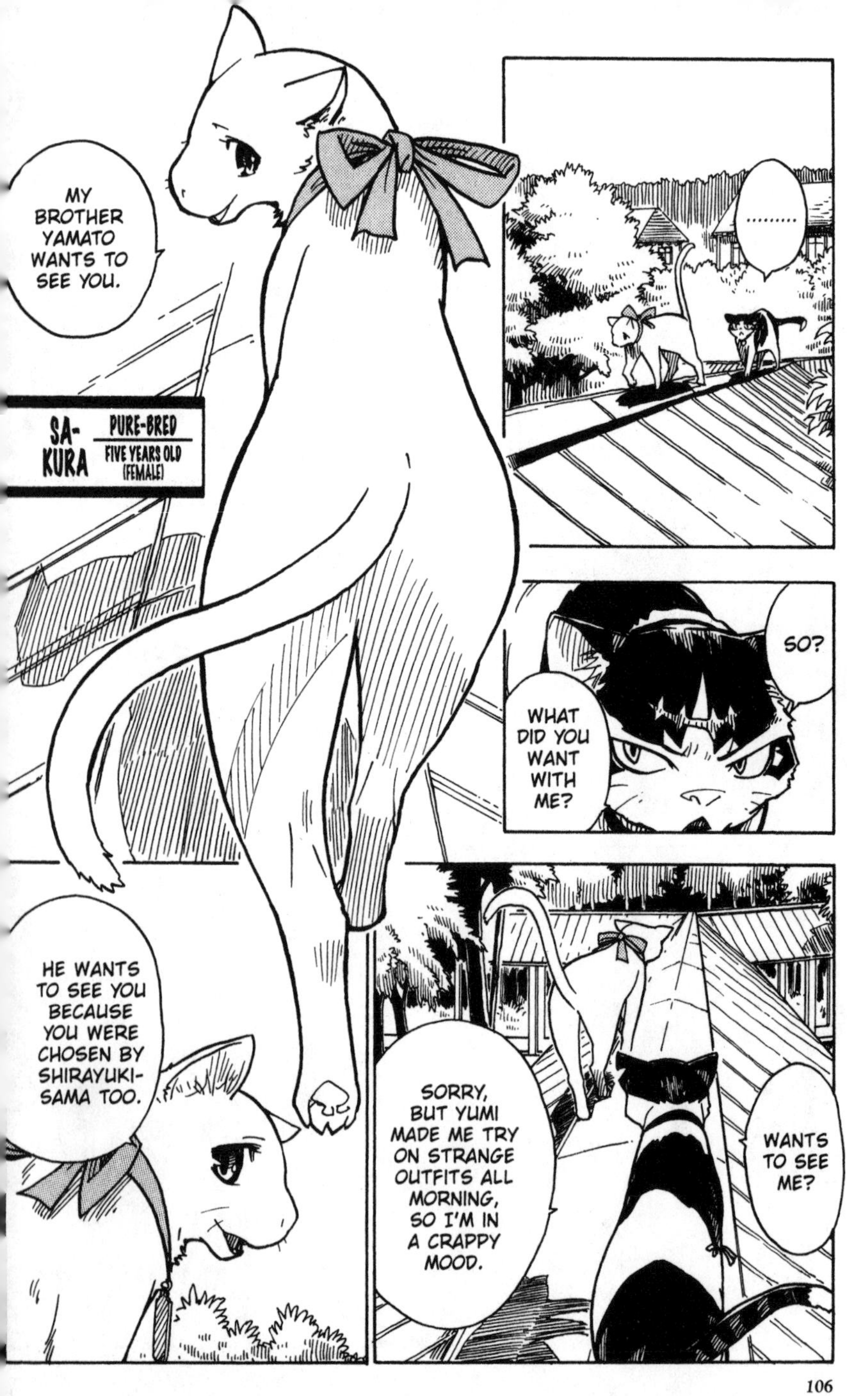
....
SO?
WHAT DID YOU WANT WITH ME?
MY BROTHER YAMATO WANTS TO SEE YOU.
SAKURA
PURE-BRED
FIVE YEARS OLD (FEMALE)
WANTS TO SEE ME?
SORRY, BUT YUMI MADE ME TRY ON STRANGE OUTFITS ALL MORNING, SO I'M IN A CRAPPY MOOD.
HE WANTS TO SEE YOU BECAUSE YOU WERE CHOSEN BY SHIRAYUKI-SAMA TOO.

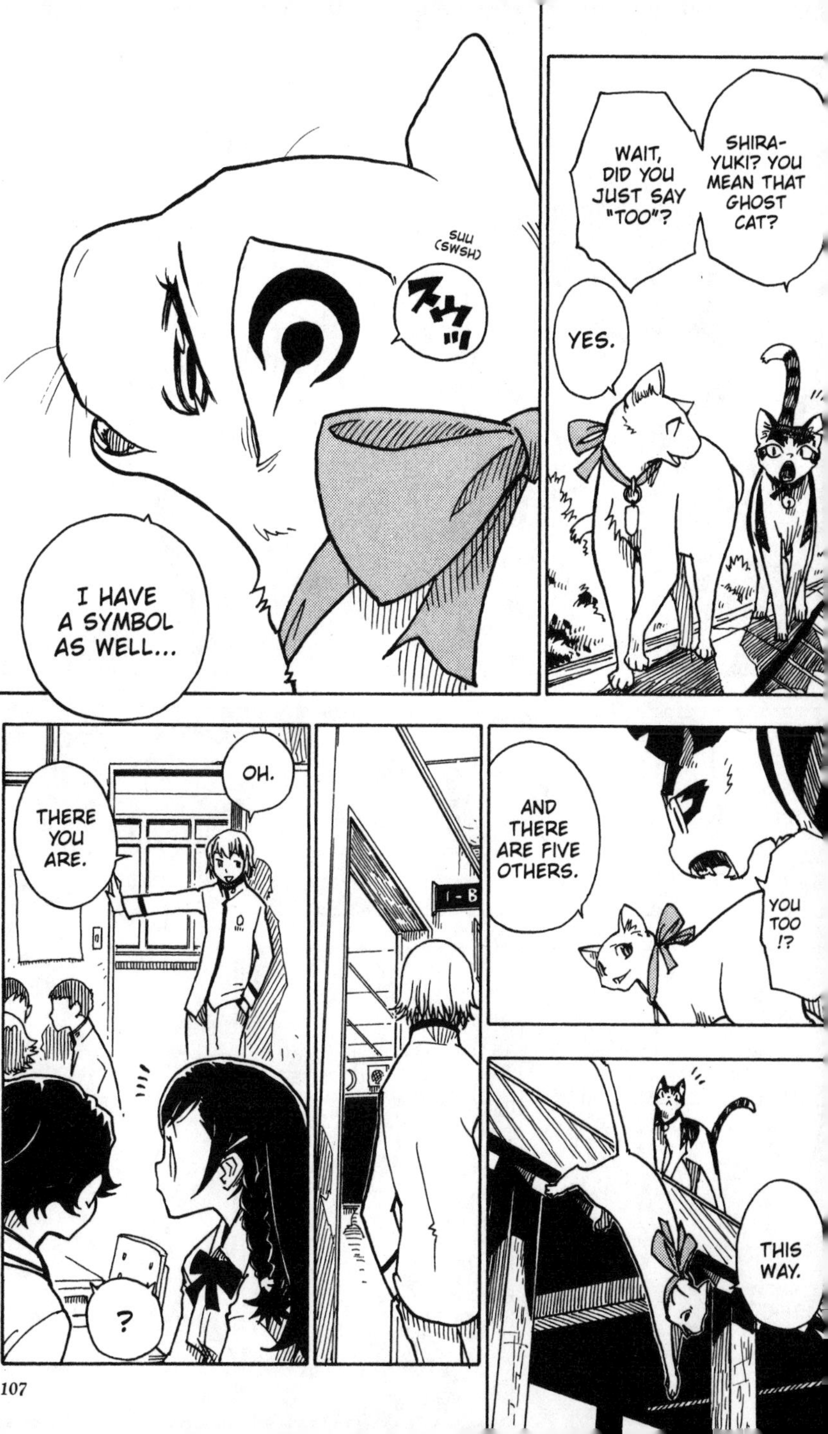
SHIRA-YUKI? YOU MEAN THAT GHOST CAT?
WAIT, DID YOU JUST SAY "TOO"?
YES.
SUU (SWSH)
I HAVE A SYMBOL AS WELL...
YOU TOO !?
AND THERE ARE FIVE OTHERS.
THIS WAY.
1-B
OH.
THERE YOU ARE.
?

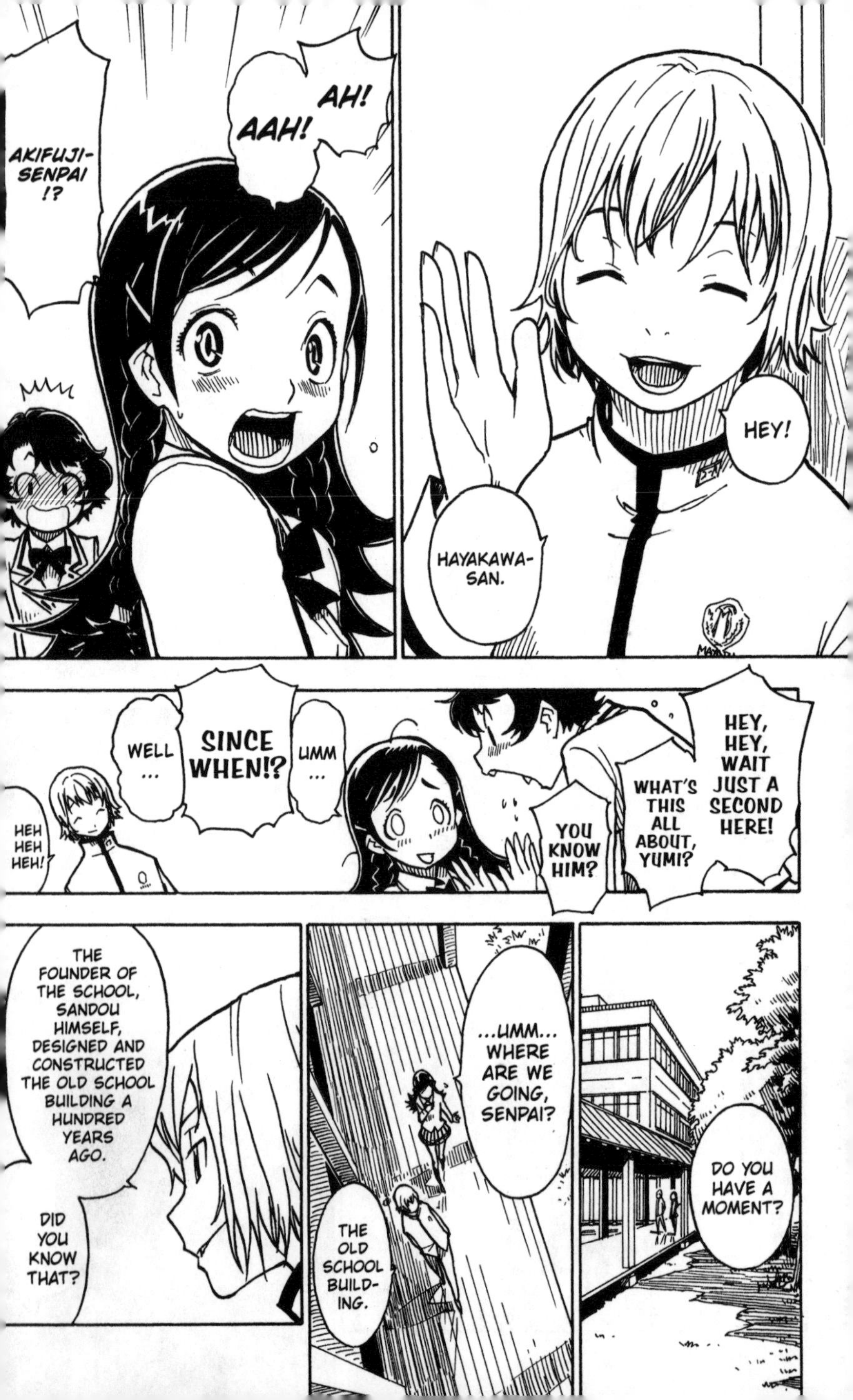
HEY!
HAYAKAWA-SAN.
AH! AAH!
AKIFUJI-SENPAI !?
HEY, HEY, WAIT JUST A SECOND HERE!
WHAT'S THIS ALL ABOUT, YUMI?
YOU KNOW HIM?
UMM ...
SINCE WHEN!?
WELL ...
HEH HEH HEH!
DO YOU HAVE A MOMENT?
...UMM... WHERE ARE WE GOING, SENPAI?
THE OLD SCHOOL BUILDING.
THE FOUNDER OF THE SCHOOL, SANDOU HIMSELF, DESIGNED AND CONSTRUCTED THE OLD SCHOOL BUILDING A HUNDRED YEARS AGO.
DID YOU KNOW THAT?

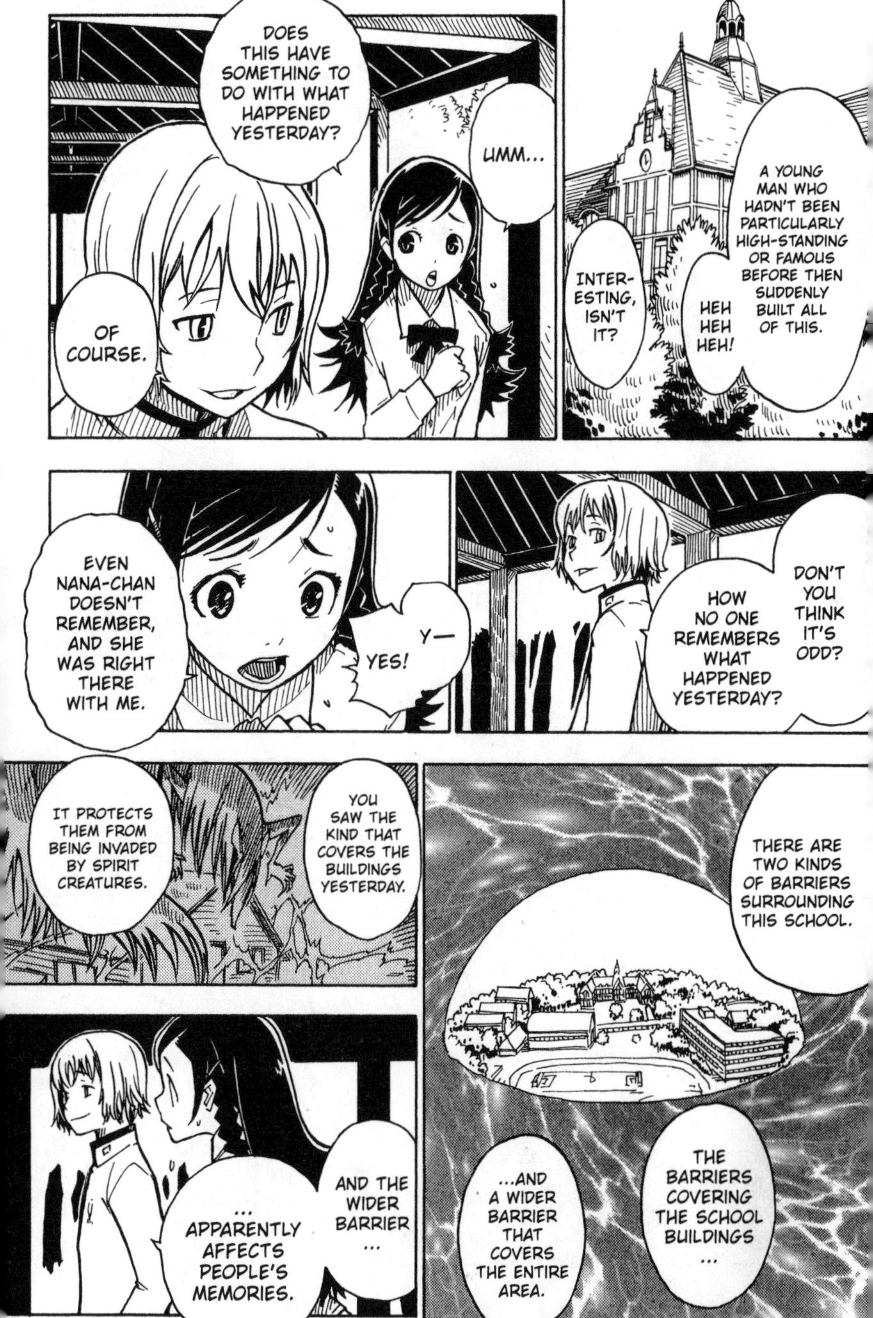
A YOUNG MAN WHO HADN'T BEEN PARTICULARLY HIGH-STANDING OR FAMOUS BEFORE THEN SUDDENLY BUILT ALL OF THIS.
HEH HEH HEH!
INTERESTING, ISN'T IT?
DOES THIS HAVE SOMETHING TO DO WITH WHAT HAPPENED YESTERDAY?
UMM...
OF COURSE.
DON'T YOU THINK IT'S ODD?
HOW NO ONE REMEMBERS WHAT HAPPENED YESTERDAY?
Y— YES!
EVEN NANA-CHAN DOESN'T REMEMBER, AND SHE WAS RIGHT THERE WITH ME.
THERE ARE TWO KINDS OF BARRIERS SURROUNDING THIS SCHOOL.
THE BARRIERS COVERING THE SCHOOL BUILDINGS ...
...AND A WIDER BARRIER THAT COVERS THE ENTIRE AREA.
YOU SAW THE KIND THAT COVERS THE BUILDINGS YESTERDAY.
IT PROTECTS THEM FROM BEING INVADED BY SPIRIT CREATURES.
AND THE WIDER BARRIER ...
... APPARENTLY AFFECTS PEOPLE'S MEMORIES.

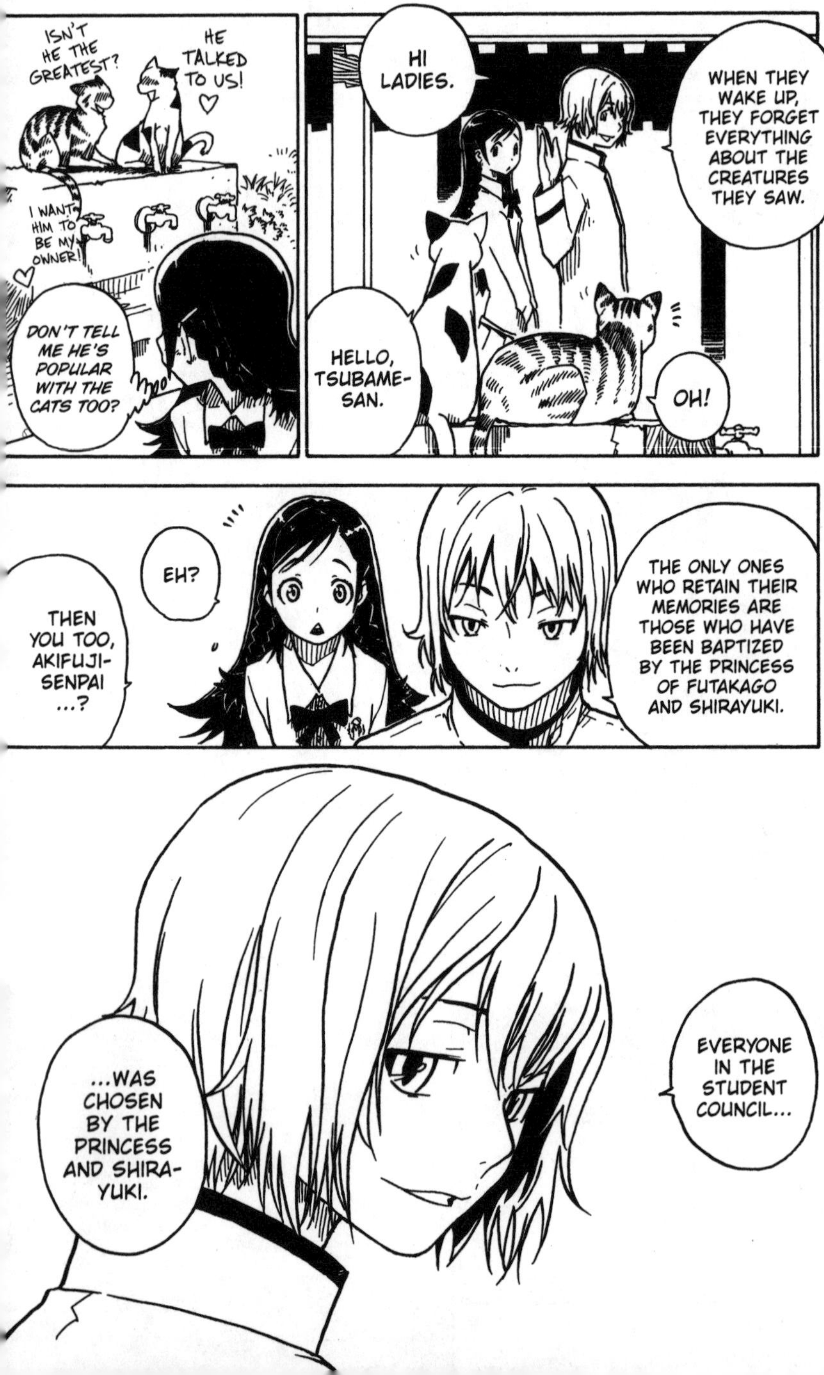
WHEN THEY WAKE UP, THEY FORGET EVERYTHING ABOUT THE CREATURES THEY SAW.
HI LADIES.
OH!
HELLO, TSUBAME-SAN.
HE TALKED TO US!
ISN'T HE THE GREATEST?
I WANT HIM TO BE MY OWNER!
DON'T TELL ME HE'S POPULAR WITH THE CATS TOO?
THE ONLY ONES WHO RETAIN THEIR MEMORIES ARE THOSE WHO HAVE BEEN BAPTIZED BY THE PRINCESS OF FUTAKAGO AND SHIRAYUKI.
EH?
THEN YOU TOO, AKIFUJI-SENPAI ...?
EVERYONE IN THE STUDENT COUNCIL...
...WAS CHOSEN BY THE PRINCESS AND SHIRAYUKI.

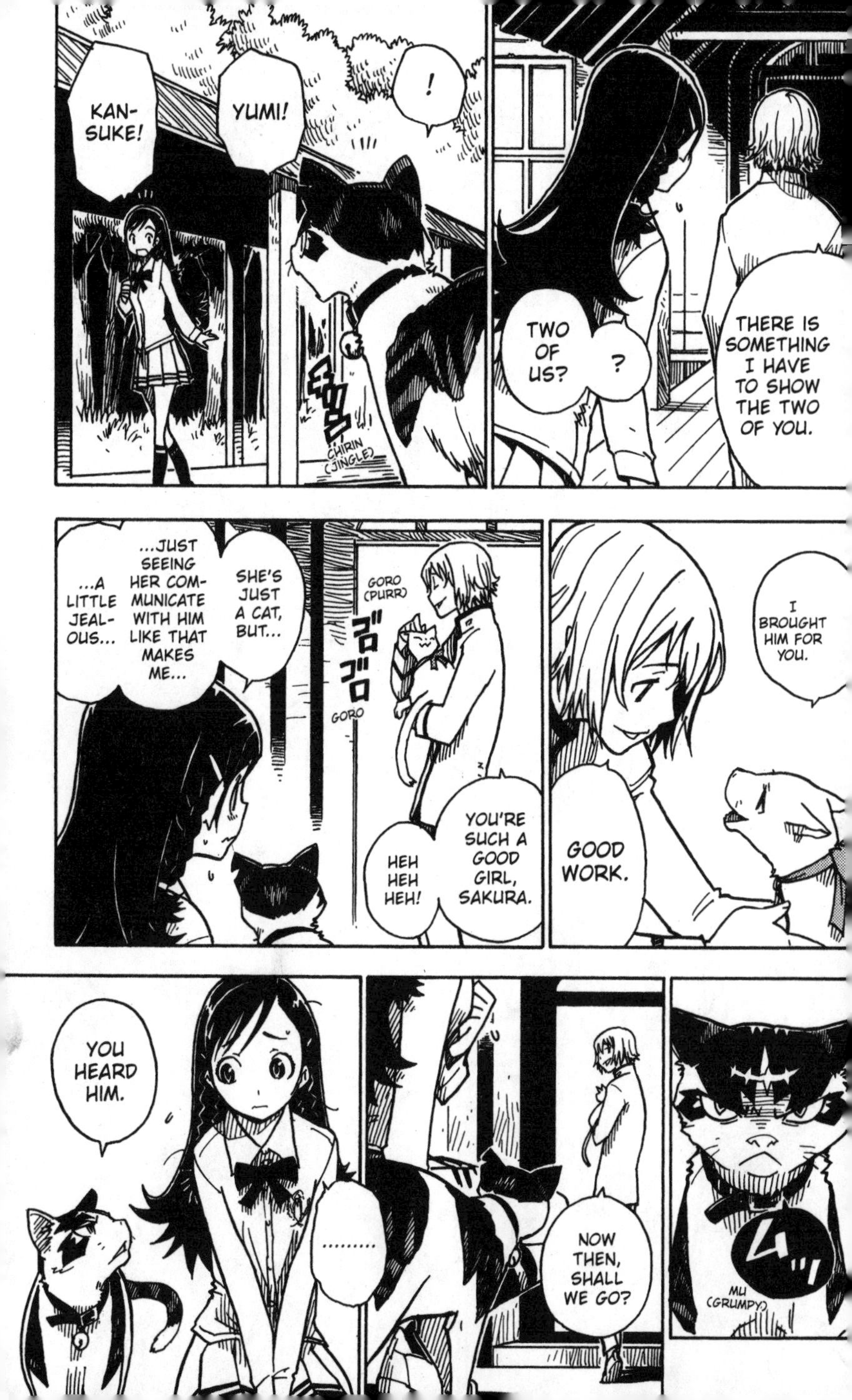
THERE IS SOMETHING I HAVE TO SHOW THE TWO OF YOU.
?
TWO OF US?
!
YUMI!
KAN-SUKE!
CHIRIN (JINGLE)
I BROUGHT HIM FOR YOU.
GOOD WORK.
GORO (PURR)
GORO
SHE'S JUST A CAT, BUT...
...JUST SEEING HER COMMUNICATE WITH HIM LIKE THAT MAKES ME...
...A LITTLE JEALOUS...
YOU'RE SUCH A GOOD GIRL, SAKURA.
HEH HEH HEH!
MU (GRUMPY)
NOW THEN, SHALL WE GO?
YOU HEARD HIM.
....

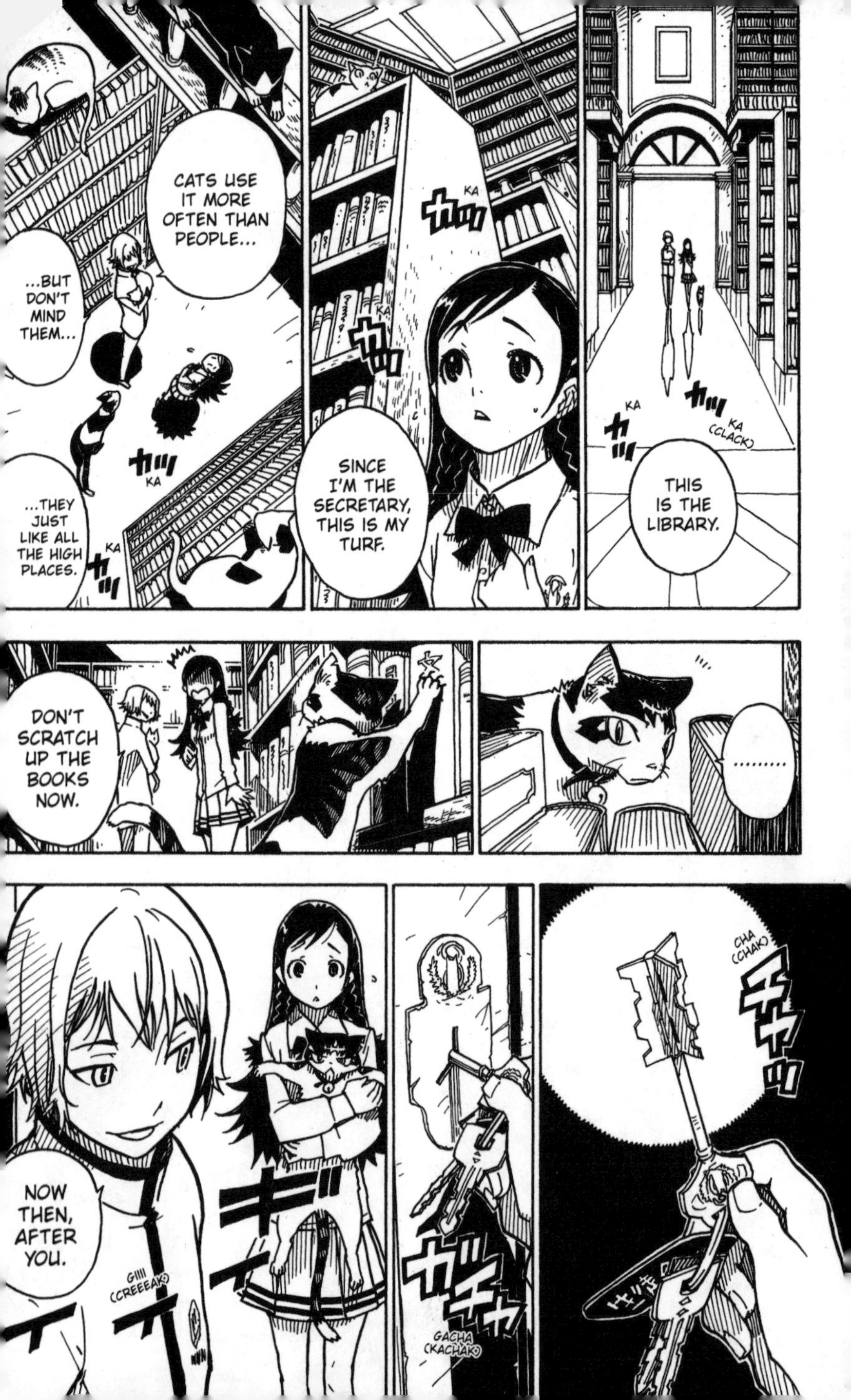
KA
KA (CLACK)
THIS IS THE LIBRARY.
KA
KA
SINCE I'M THE SECRETARY, THIS IS MY TURF.
CATS USE IT MORE OFTEN THAN PEOPLE...
...BUT DON'T MIND THEM...
KA
...THEY JUST LIKE ALL THE HIGH PLACES.
KA
....
DON'T SCRATCH UP THE BOOKS NOW.
CHA (CHAK)
GACHA (KACHAK)
NOW THEN, AFTER YOU.
GIIII (CREEEAK)

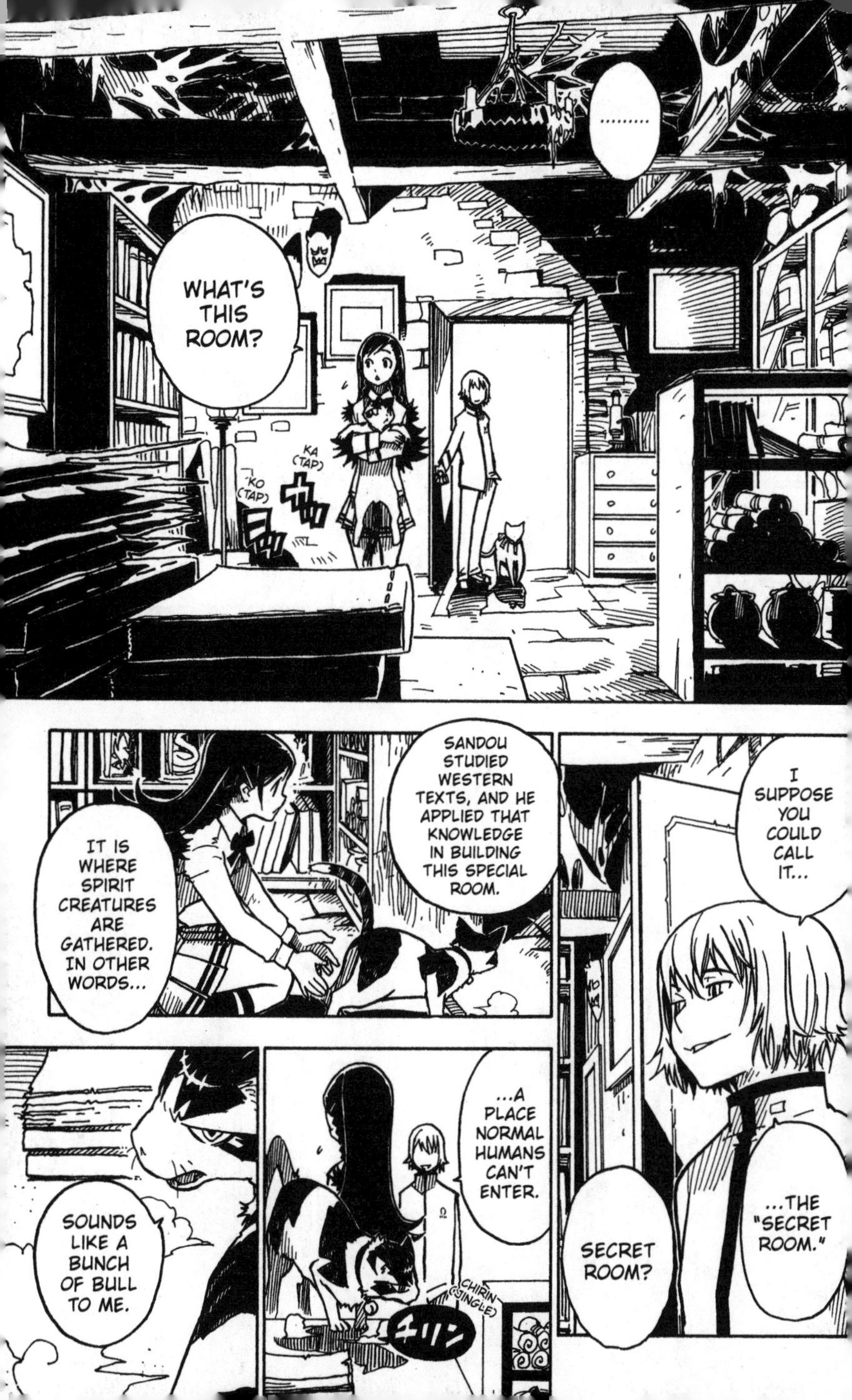
....
WHAT'S THIS ROOM?
KA (TAP)
KO (TAP)
I SUPPOSE YOU COULD CALL IT...
...THE "SECRET ROOM."
SECRET ROOM?
SANDOU STUDIED WESTERN TEXTS, AND HE APPLIED THAT KNOWLEDGE IN BUILDING THIS SPECIAL ROOM.
IT IS WHERE SPIRIT CREATURES ARE GATHERED. IN OTHER WORDS...
...A PLACE NORMAL HUMANS CAN'T ENTER.
CHIRIN (JINGLE)
SOUNDS LIKE A BUNCH OF BULL TO ME.

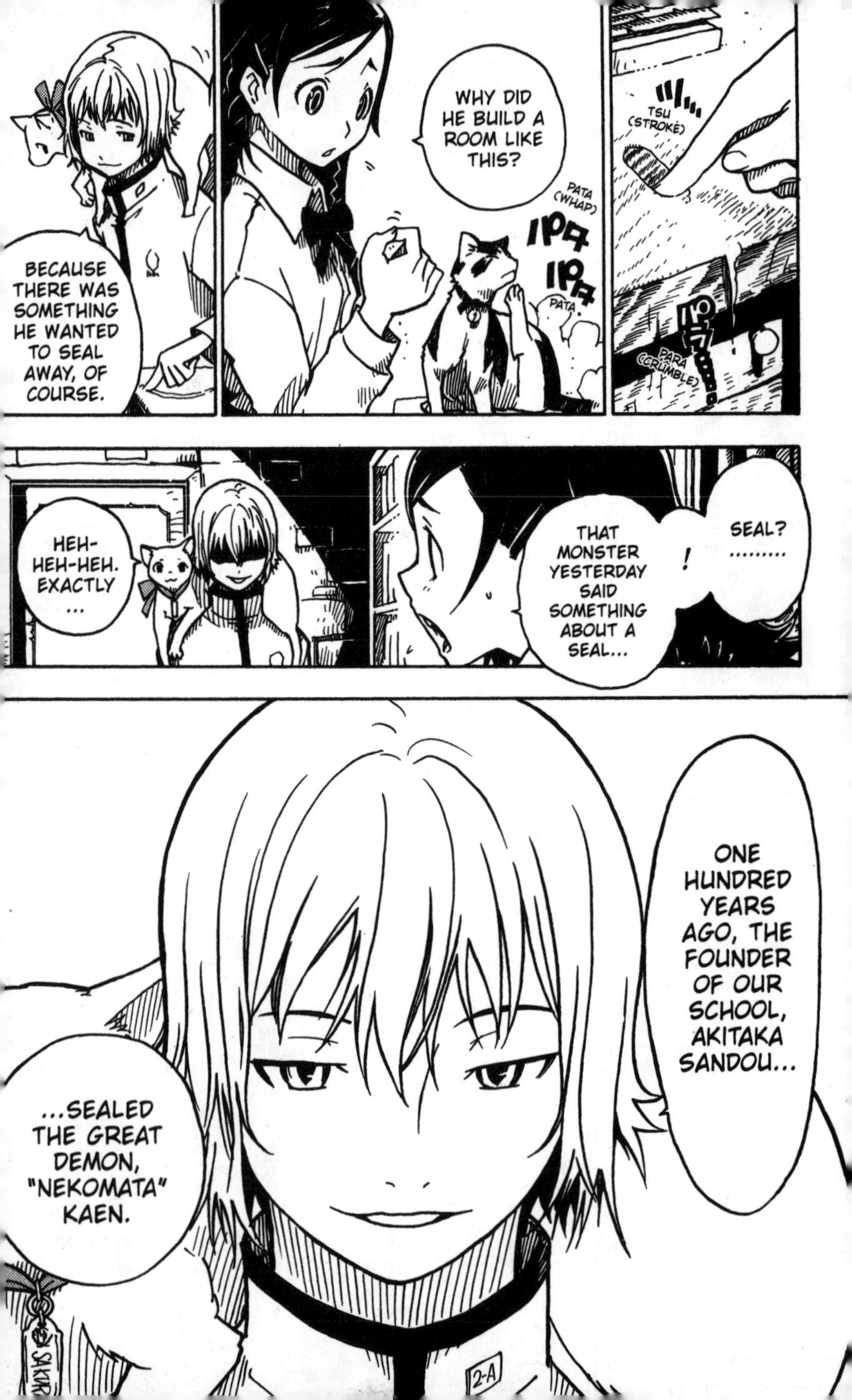
TSU (STROKE)
PARA (CRUMBLE)
WHY DID HE BUILD A ROOM LIKE THIS?
PATA (WHAP)
PATA
BECAUSE THERE WAS SOMETHING HE WANTED TO SEAL AWAY, OF COURSE.
SEAL? ....
!
THAT MONSTER YESTERDAY SAID SOMETHING ABOUT A SEAL...
HEH-HEH-HEH. EXACTLY ...
ONE HUNDRED YEARS AGO, THE FOUNDER OF OUR SCHOOL, AKITAKA SANDOU...
...SEALED THE GREAT DEMON, "NEKOMATA" KAEN.
2-A

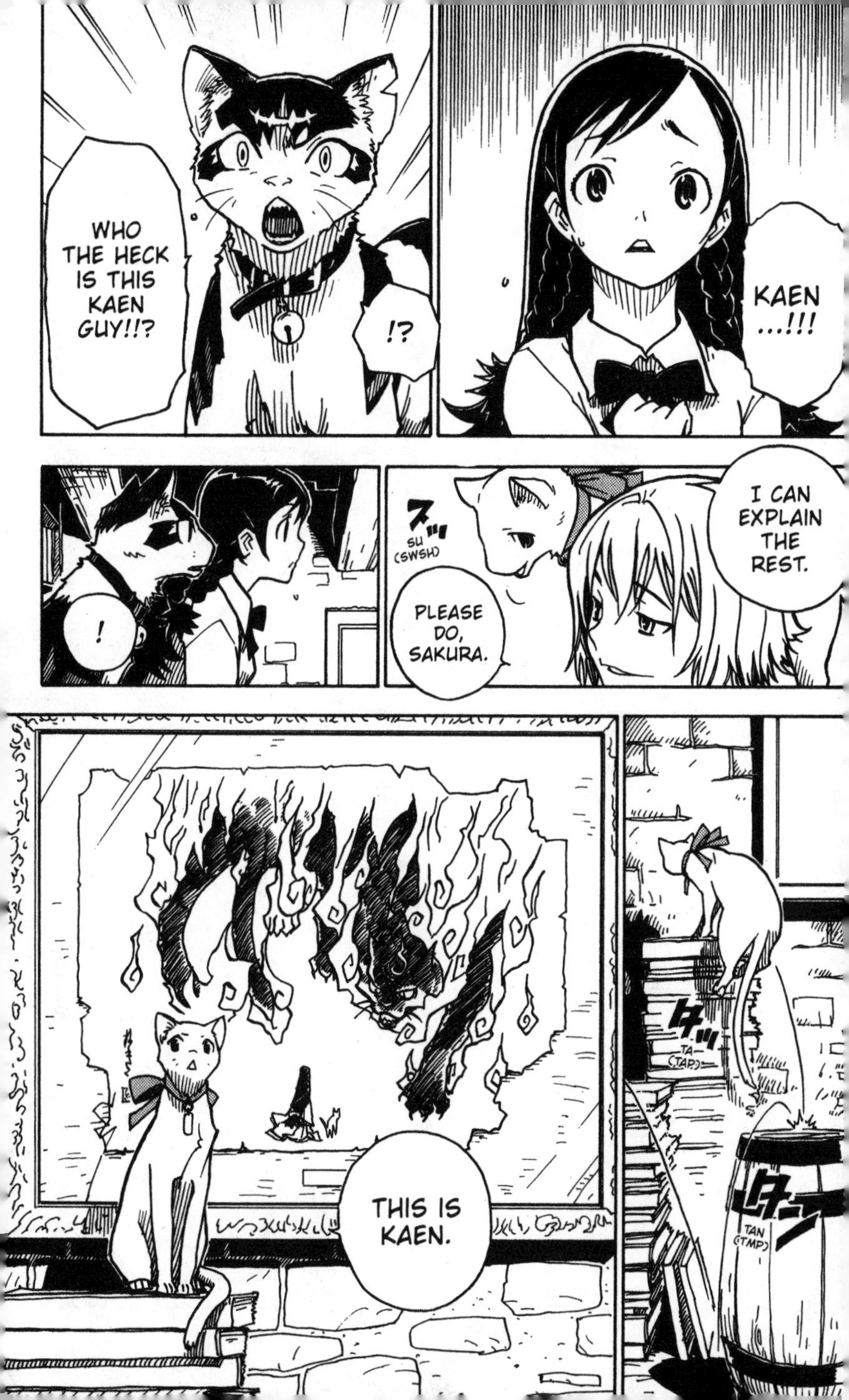
KAEN ...!!!
!?
WHO THE HECK IS THIS KAEN GUY!!?
I CAN EXPLAIN THE REST.
SU (SWSH)
PLEASE DO, SAKURA.
!
TA (TAP)
TAN (TMP)
THIS IS KAEN.

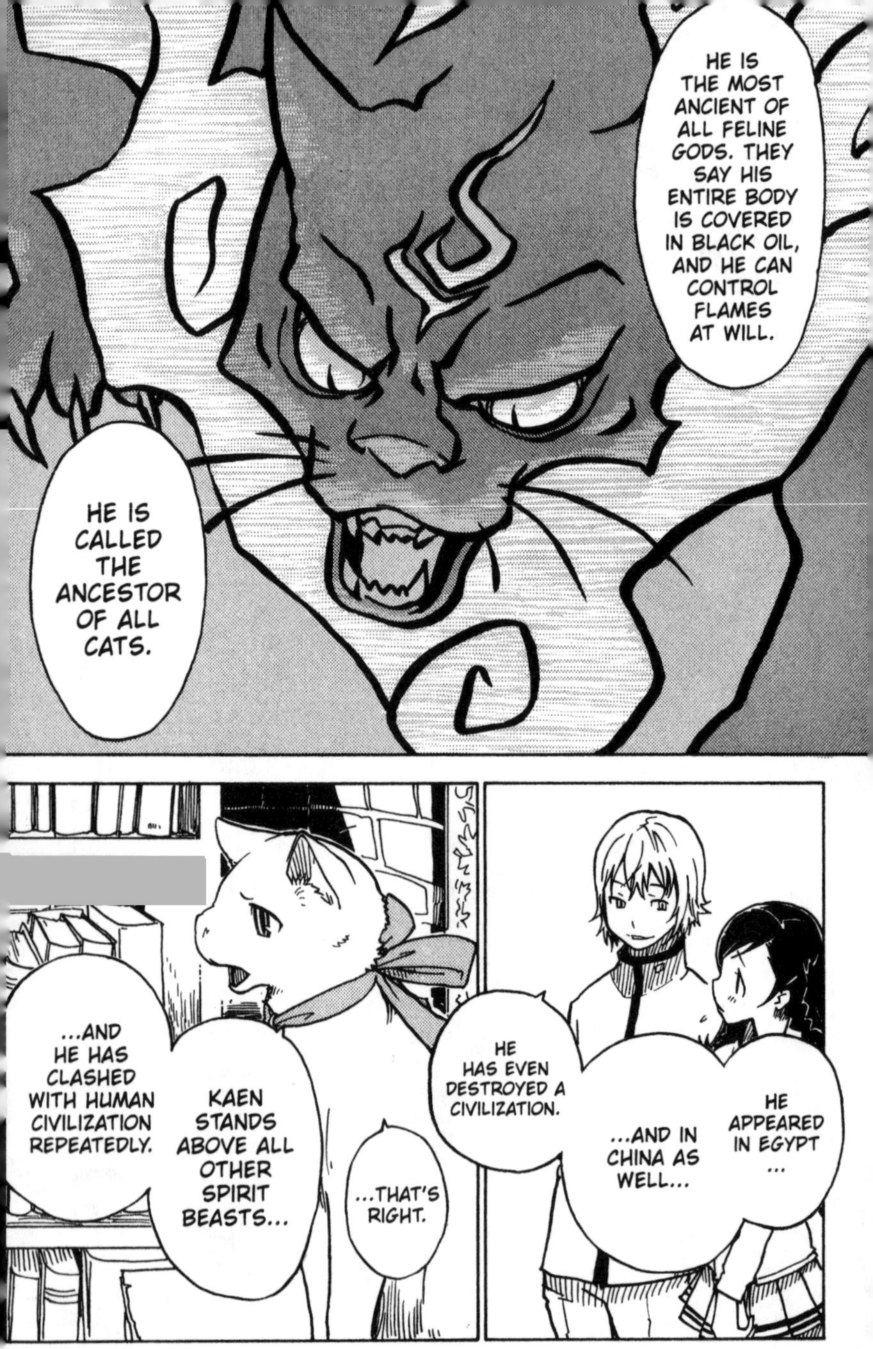
HE IS THE MOST ANCIENT OF ALL FELINE GODS. THEY SAY HIS ENTIRE BODY IS COVERED IN BLACK OIL, AND HE CAN CONTROL FLAMES AT WILL.
HE IS CALLED THE ANCESTOR OF ALL CATS.
HE APPEARED IN EGYPT ...
...AND IN CHINA AS WELL...
HE HAS EVEN DESTROYED A CIVILIZATION.
...THAT'S RIGHT.
KAEN STANDS ABOVE ALL OTHER SPIRIT BEASTS...
...AND HE HAS CLASHED WITH HUMAN CIVILIZATION REPEATEDLY.

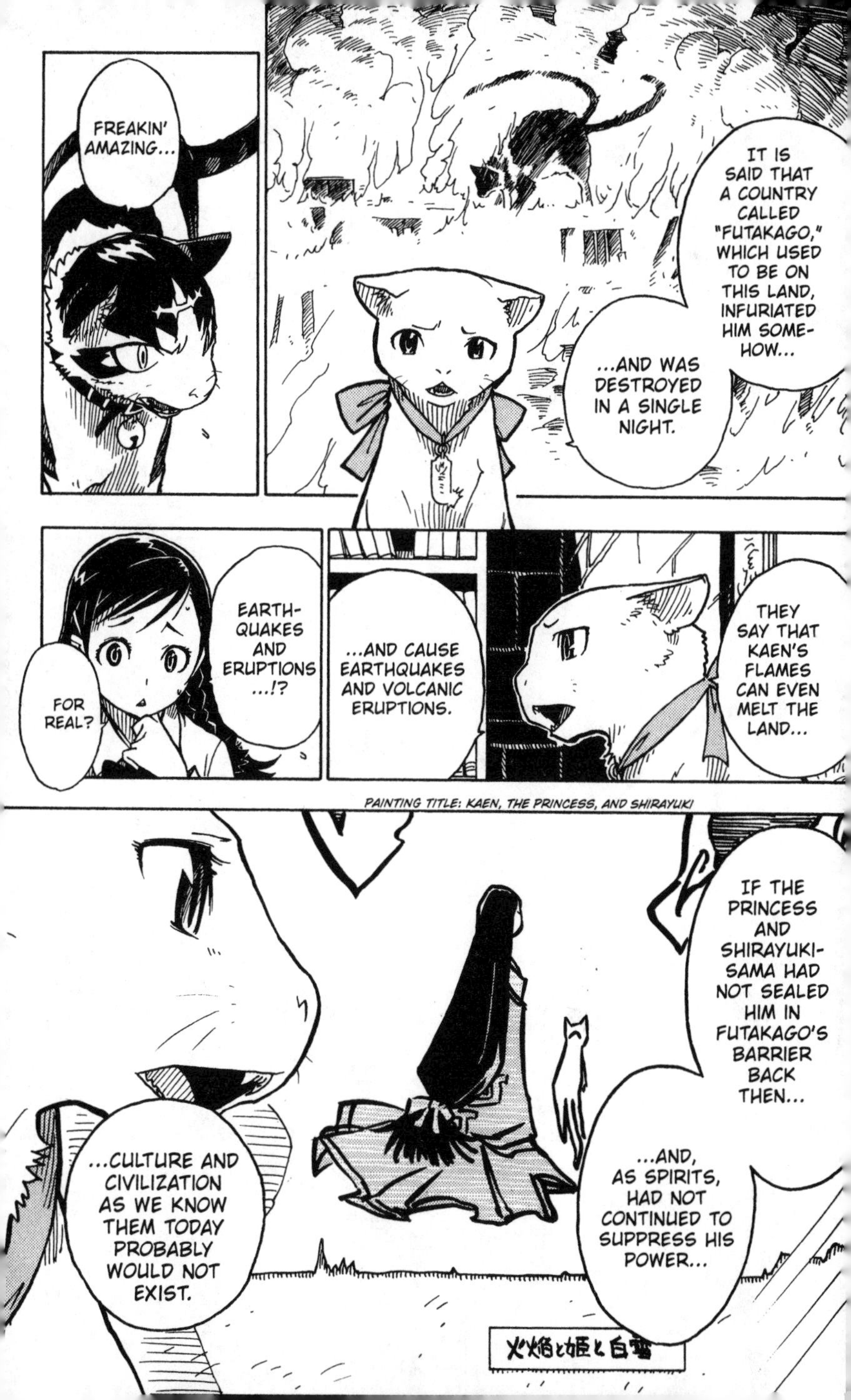
IT IS SAID THAT A COUNTRY CALLED "FUTAKAGO," WHICH USED TO BE ON THIS LAND, INFURIATED HIM SOME-HOW...
...AND WAS DESTROYED IN A SINGLE NIGHT.
FREAKIN' AMAZING...
THEY SAY THAT KAEN'S FLAMES CAN EVEN MELT THE LAND...
...AND CAUSE EARTHQUAKES AND VOLCANIC ERUPTIONS.
EARTH-QUAKES AND ERUPTIONS ...!?
FOR REAL?
PAINTING TITLE: KAEN, THE PRINCESS, AND SHIRAYUKI
IF THE PRINCESS AND SHIRAYUKI-SAMA HAD NOT SEALED HIM IN FUTAKAGO'S BARRIER BACK THEN...
...AND, AS SPIRITS, HAD NOT CONTINUED TO SUPPRESS HIS POWER...
...CULTURE AND CIVILIZATION AS WE KNOW THEM TODAY PROBABLY WOULD NOT EXIST.
火焔と姫と白雪

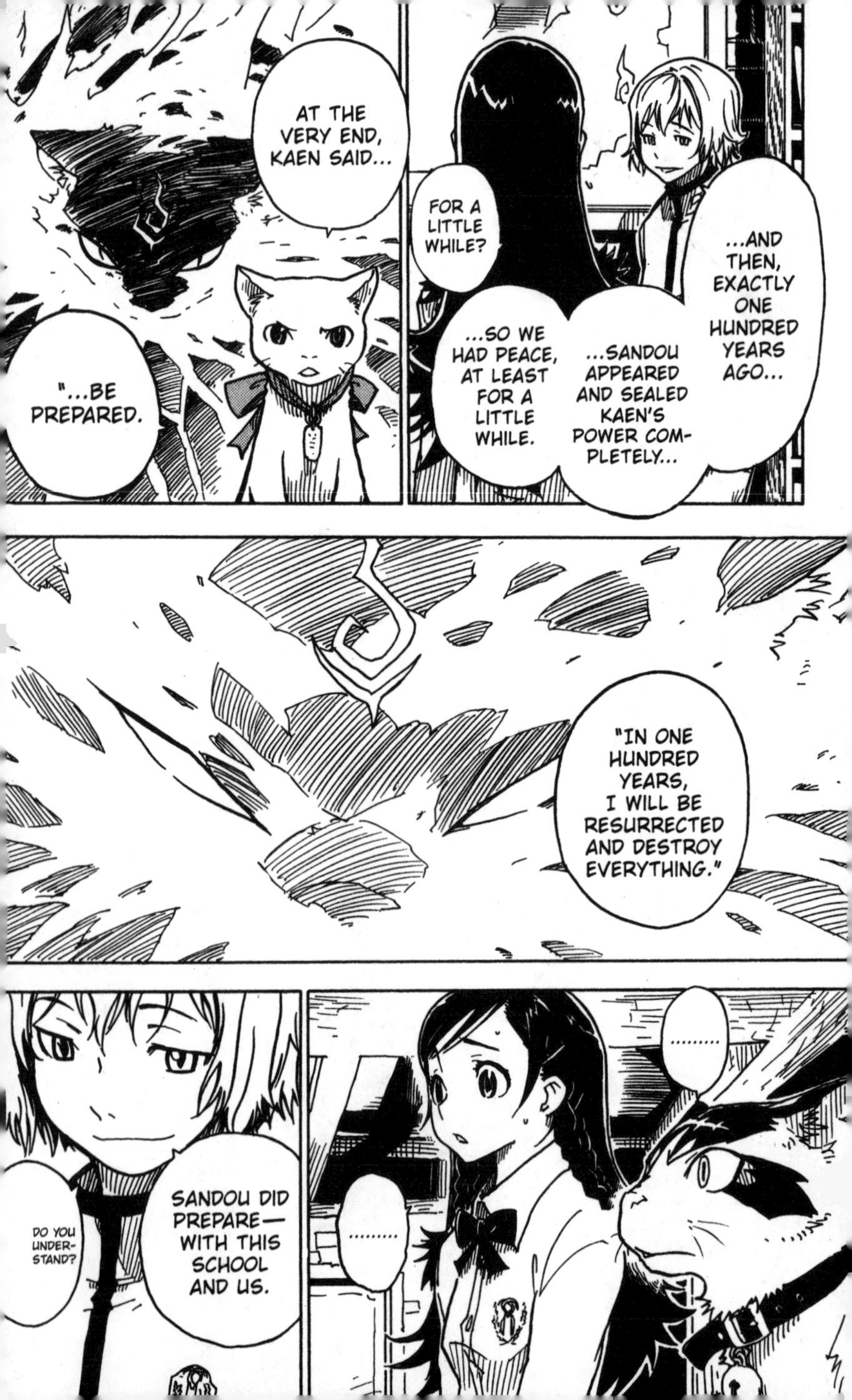
...AND THEN, EXACTLY ONE HUNDRED YEARS AGO...
...SANDOU APPEARED AND SEALED KAEN'S POWER COM-PLETELY...
...SO WE HAD PEACE, AT LEAST FOR A LITTLE WHILE.
FOR A LITTLE WHILE?
AT THE VERY END, KAEN SAID...
"...BE PREPARED.
"IN ONE HUNDRED YEARS, I WILL BE RESURRECTED AND DESTROY EVERYTHING."
....
....
SANDOU DID PREPARE— WITH THIS SCHOOL AND US.
DO YOU UNDER-STAND?

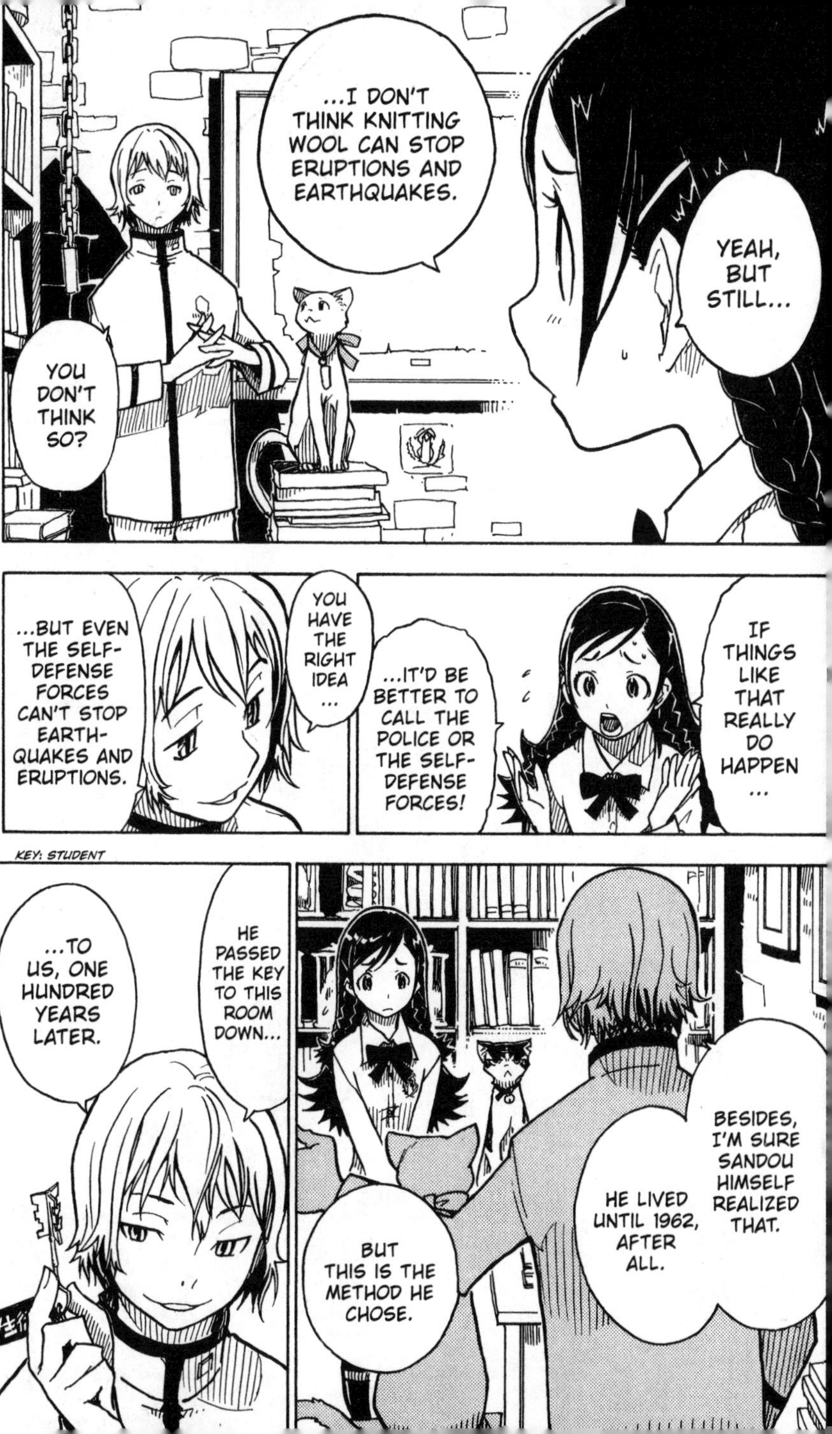
...I DON'T THINK KNITTING WOOL CAN STOP ERUPTIONS AND EARTHQUAKES.
YOU DON'T THINK SO?
YEAH, BUT STILL...
IF THINGS LIKE THAT REALLY DO HAPPEN...
...IT'D BE BETTER TO CALL THE POLICE OR THE SELF-DEFENSE FORCES!
YOU HAVE THE RIGHT IDEA...
...BUT EVEN THE SELF-DEFENSE FORCES CAN'T STOP EARTHQUAKES AND ERUPTIONS.
BESIDES, I'M SURE SANDOU HIMSELF REALIZED THAT.
HE LIVED UNTIL 1962, AFTER ALL.
BUT THIS IS THE METHOD HE CHOSE.
HE PASSED THE KEY TO THIS ROOM DOWN...
...TO US, ONE HUNDRED YEARS LATER.
KEY: STUDENT

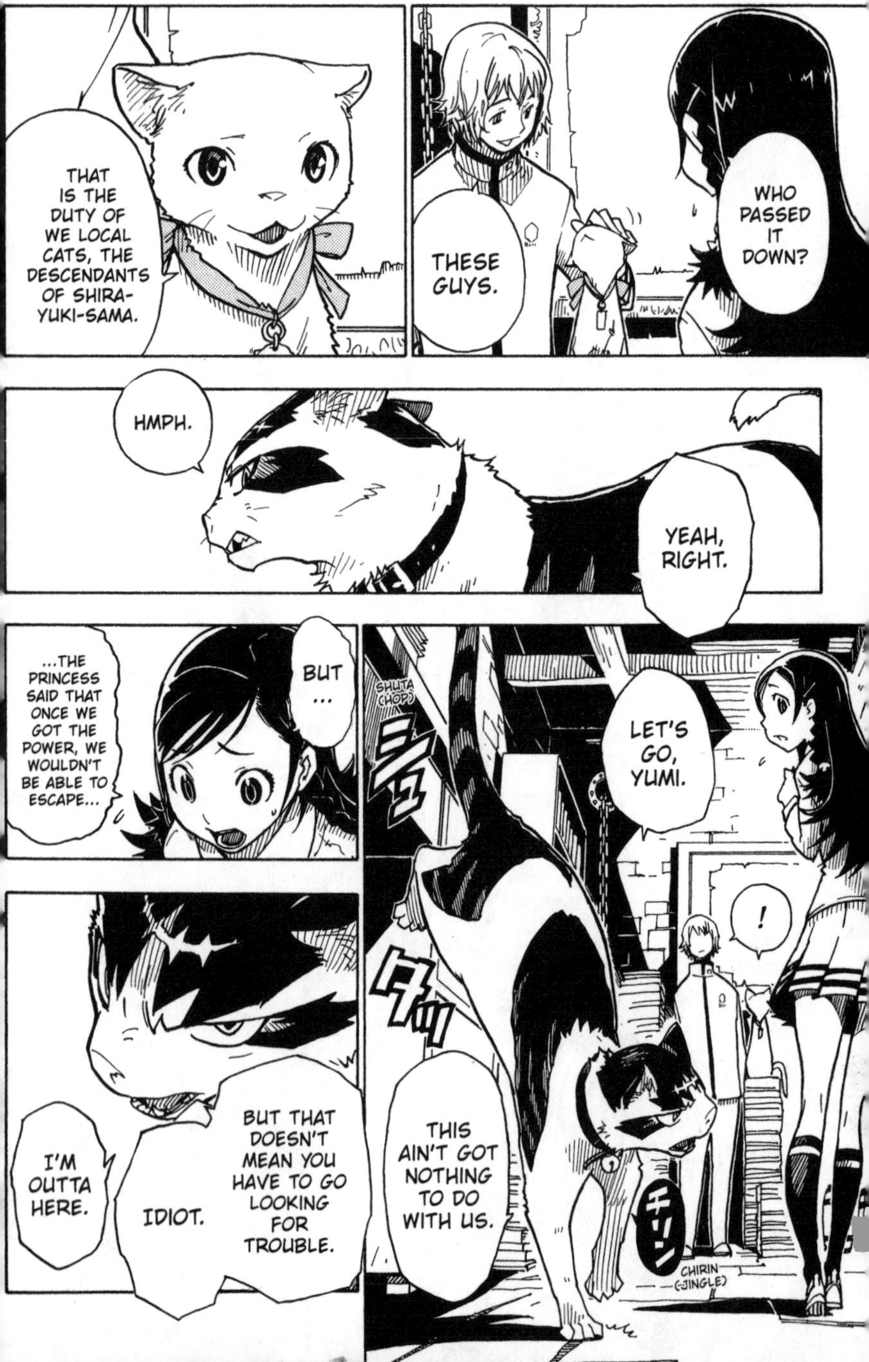
WHO PASSED IT DOWN?
THESE GUYS.
THAT IS THE DUTY OF WE LOCAL CATS, THE DESCENDANTS OF SHIRA-YUKI-SAMA.
HMPH.
YEAH, RIGHT.
LET'S GO, YUMI.
SHUTA (HOP)
!
THIS AIN'T GOT NOTHING TO DO WITH US.
CHIRIN (JINGLE)
BUT ...
...THE PRINCESS SAID THAT ONCE WE GOT THE POWER, WE WOULDN'T BE ABLE TO ESCAPE...
BUT THAT DOESN'T MEAN YOU HAVE TO GO LOOKING FOR TROUBLE.
IDIOT.
I'M OUTTA HERE.

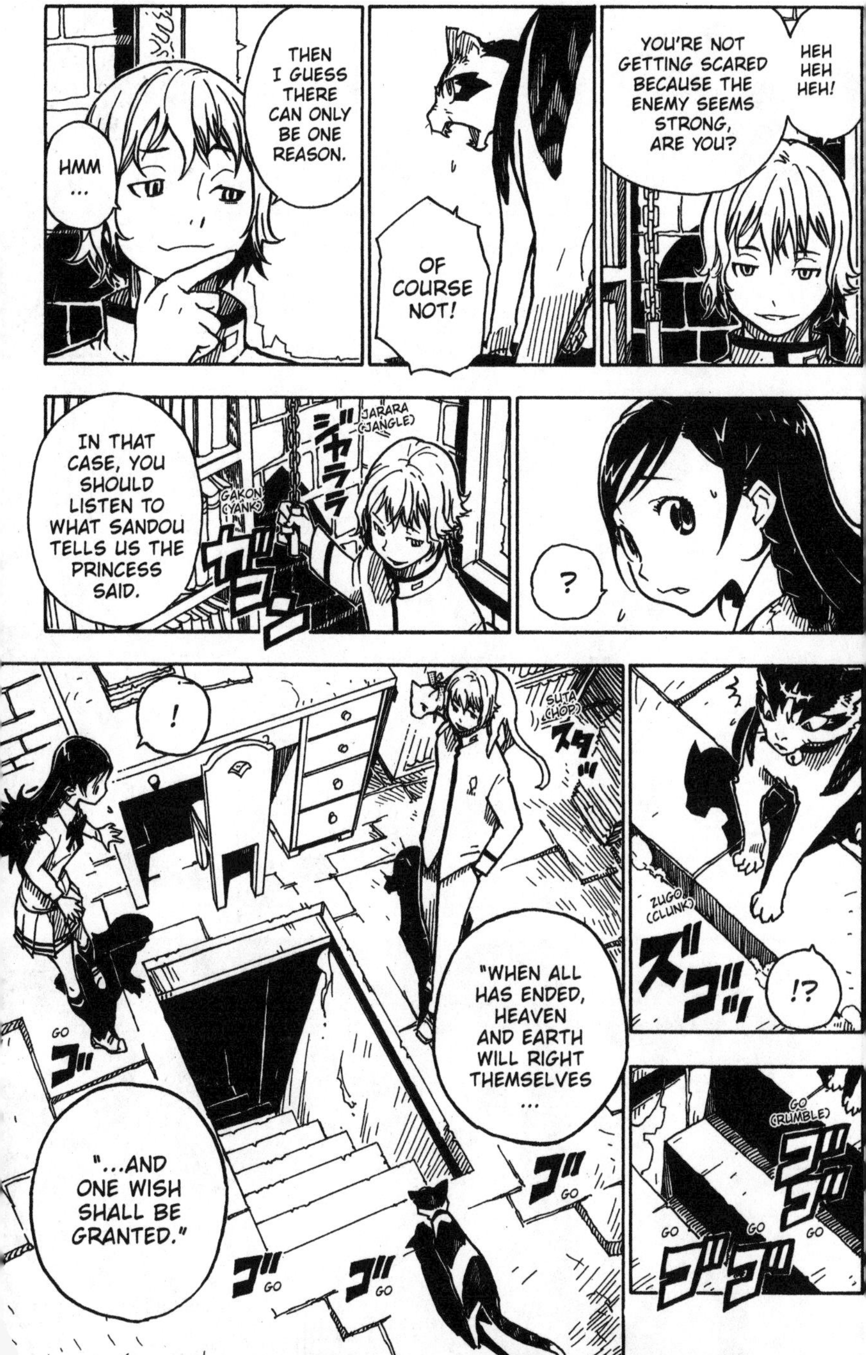
HEH HEH HEH!
YOU'RE NOT GETTING SCARED BECAUSE THE ENEMY SEEMS STRONG, ARE YOU?
OF COURSE NOT!
THEN I GUESS THERE CAN ONLY BE ONE REASON.
HMM ...
?
JARARA (JANGLE)
GAKON (YANK)
IN THAT CASE, YOU SHOULD LISTEN TO WHAT SANDOU TELLS US THE PRINCESS SAID.
ZUGO (CLUNK)
!?
GO (RUMBLE)
GO
GO
GO
SUTA (HOP)
!
"WHEN ALL HAS ENDED, HEAVEN AND EARTH WILL RIGHT THEMSELVES ...
GO
GO
"...AND ONE WISH SHALL BE GRANTED."
GO
GO

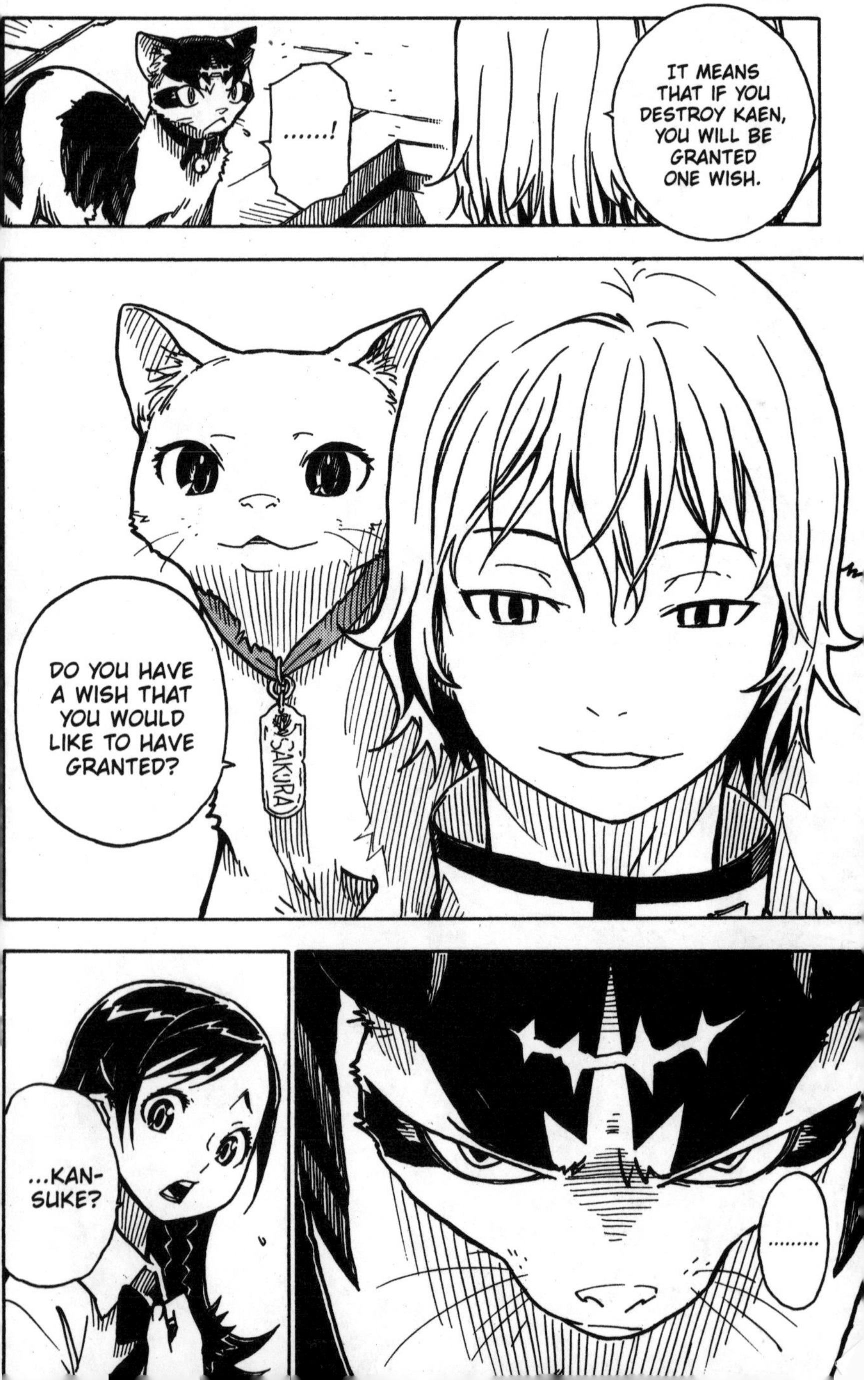
IT MEANS THAT IF YOU DESTROY KAEN, YOU WILL BE GRANTED ONE WISH.
......!
SAKURA
DO YOU HAVE A WISH THAT YOU WOULD LIKE TO HAVE GRANTED?
....
...KAN-SUKE?

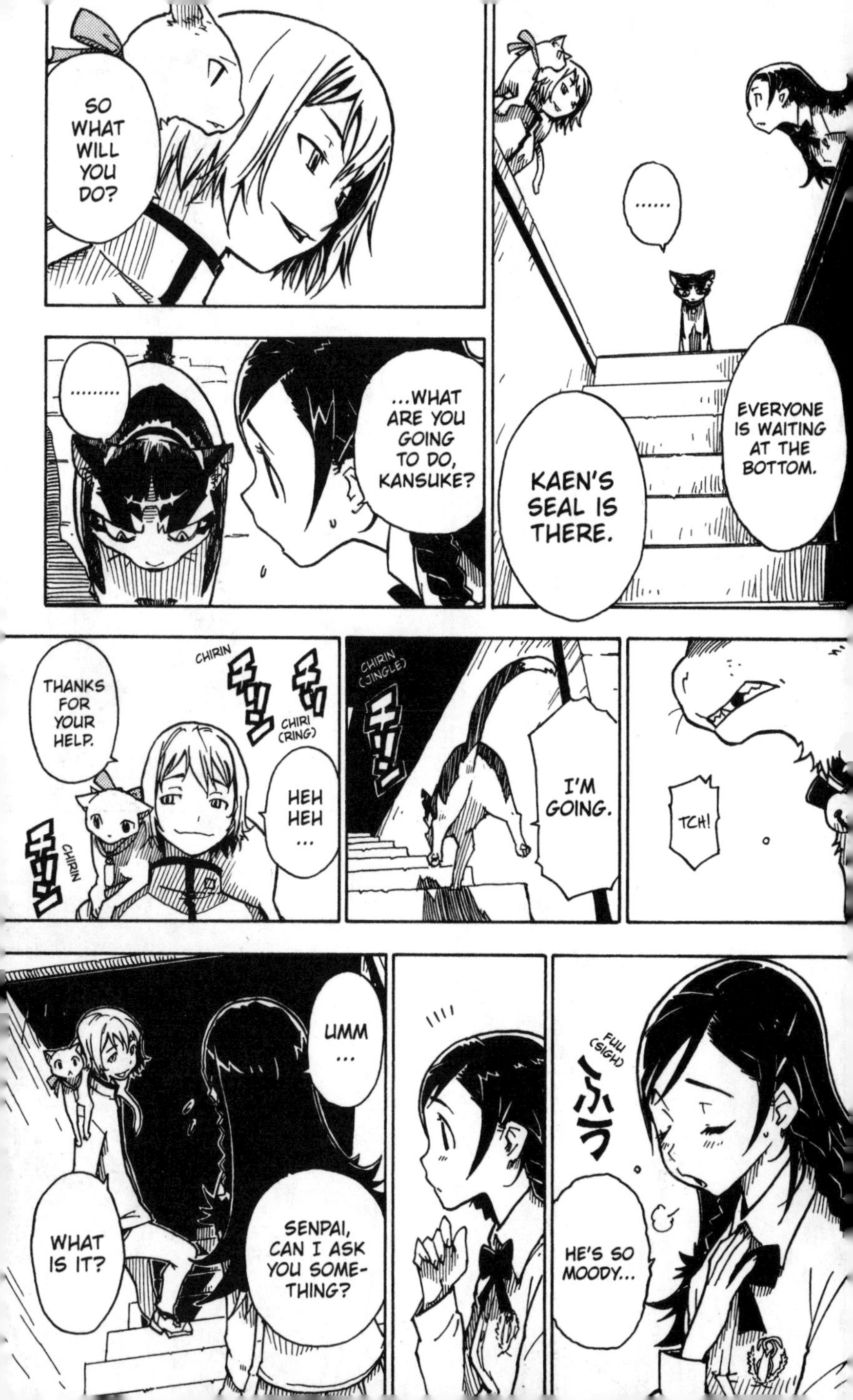
......
EVERYONE IS WAITING AT THE BOTTOM.
KAEN'S SEAL IS THERE.
SO WHAT WILL YOU DO?
...WHAT ARE YOU GOING TO DO, KANSUKE?
....
TCH!
CHIRIN (JINGLE)
I'M GOING.
CHIRIN
CHIRI (RING)
THANKS FOR YOUR HELP.
HEH HEH ...
CHIRIN
FUU (SIGH)
HE'S SO MOODY...
UMM ...
SENPAI, CAN I ASK YOU SOME-THING?
WHAT IS IT?

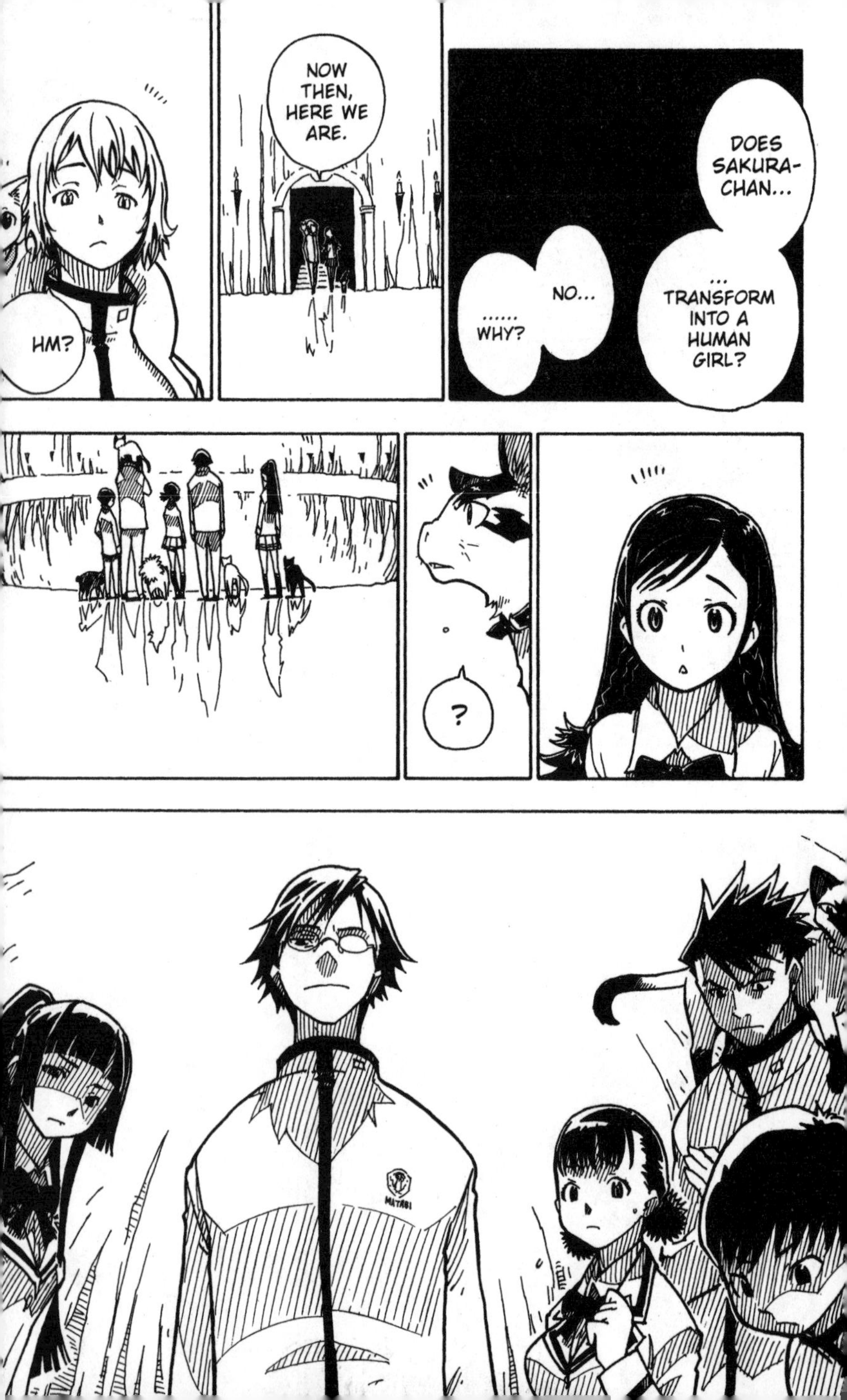
DOES SAKURA-CHAN...
... TRANSFORM INTO A HUMAN GIRL?
NO...
...... WHY?
NOW THEN, HERE WE ARE.
HM?
?

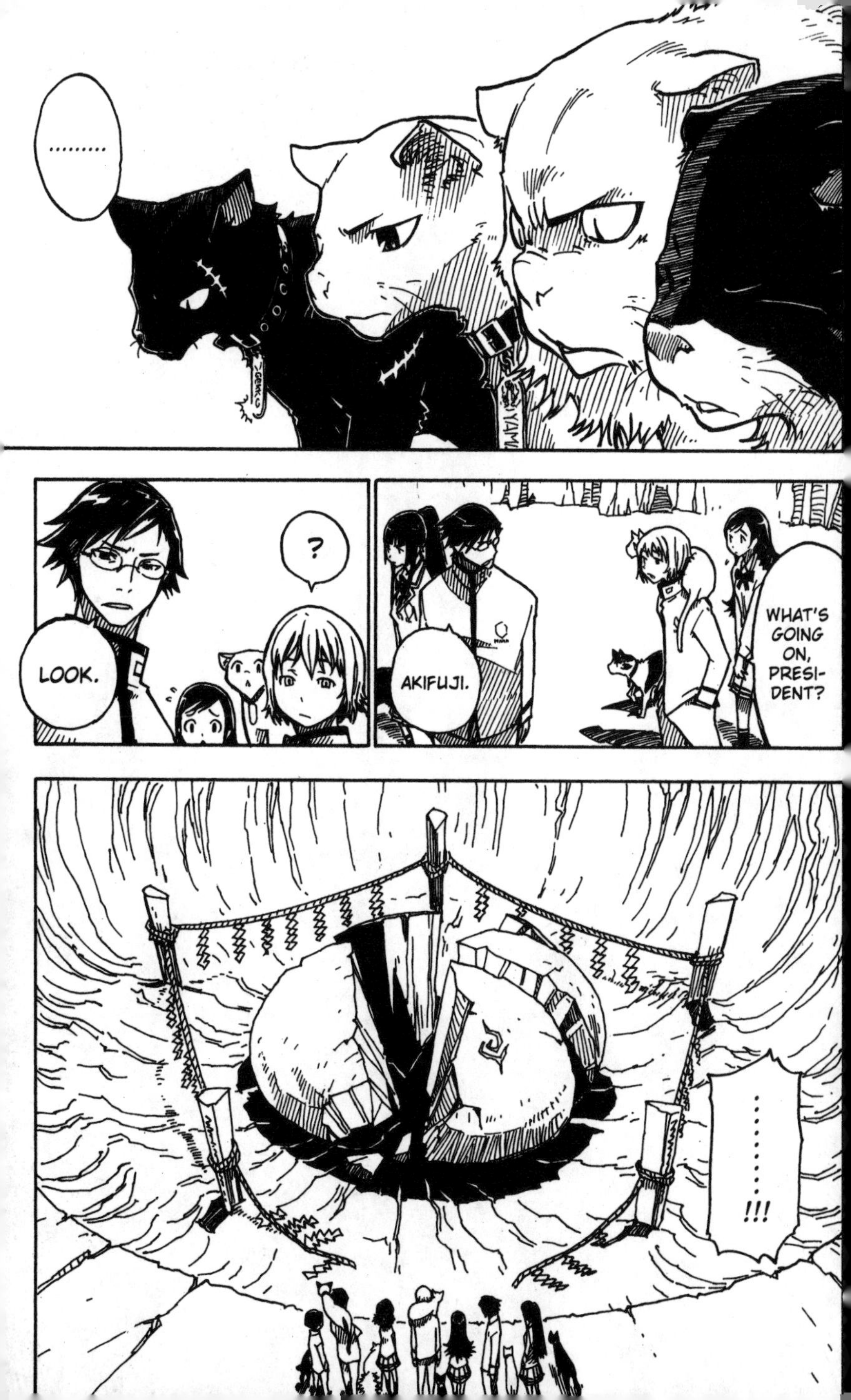
....
WHAT'S GOING ON, PRESIDENT?
AKIFUJI.
?
LOOK.
........!!!

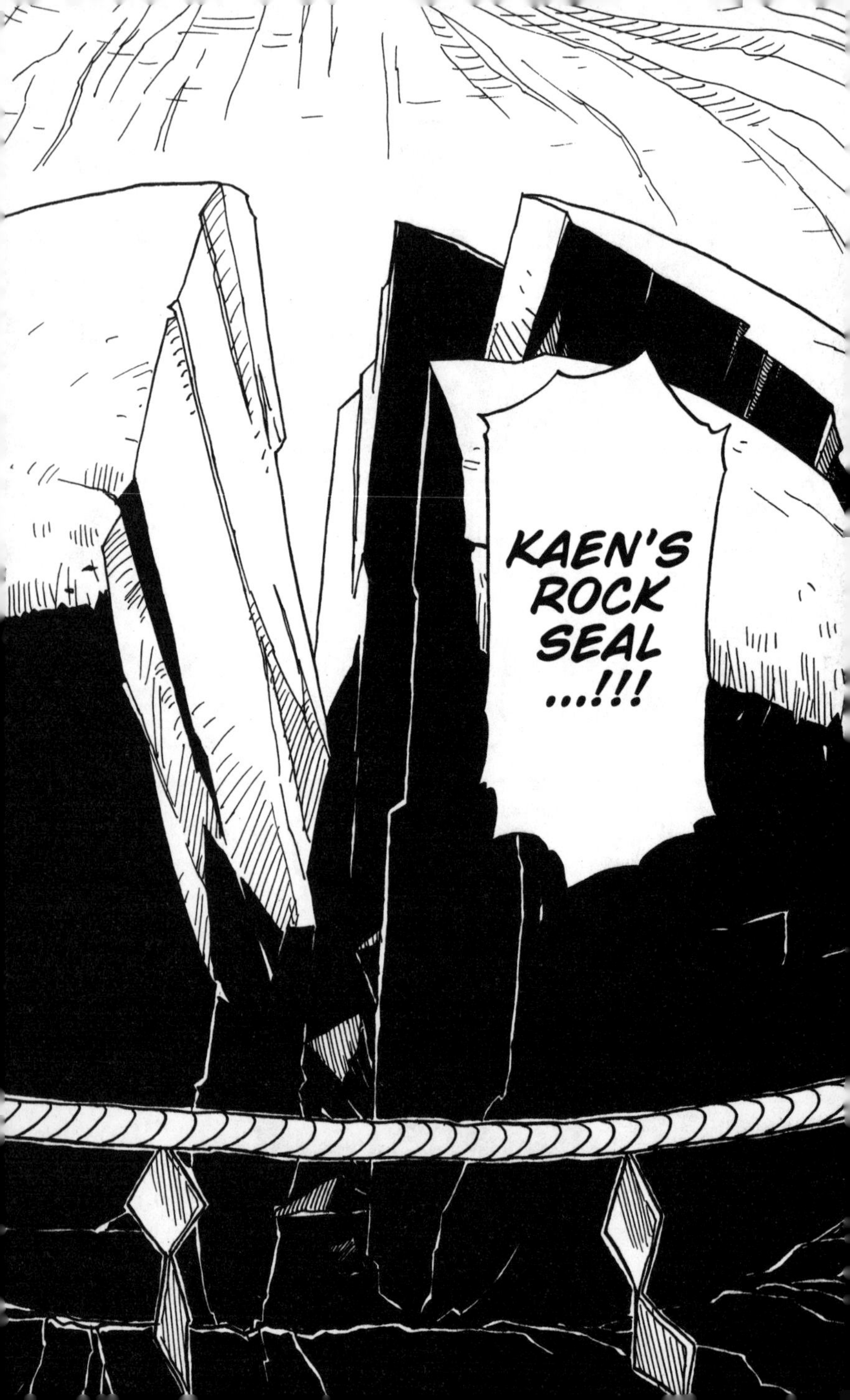
KAEN'S ROCK SEAL ...!!!

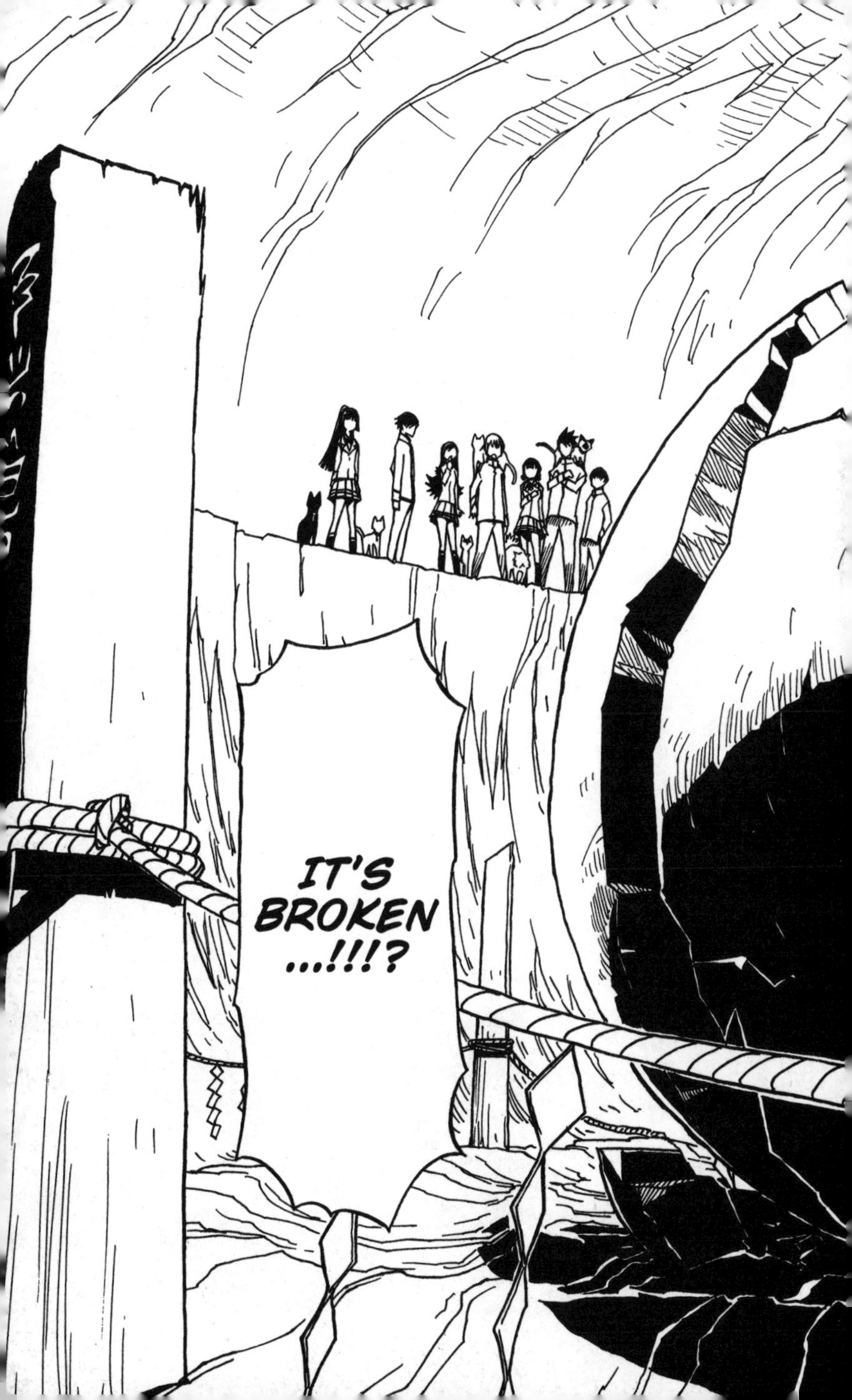
IT'S BROKEN ...!!!?

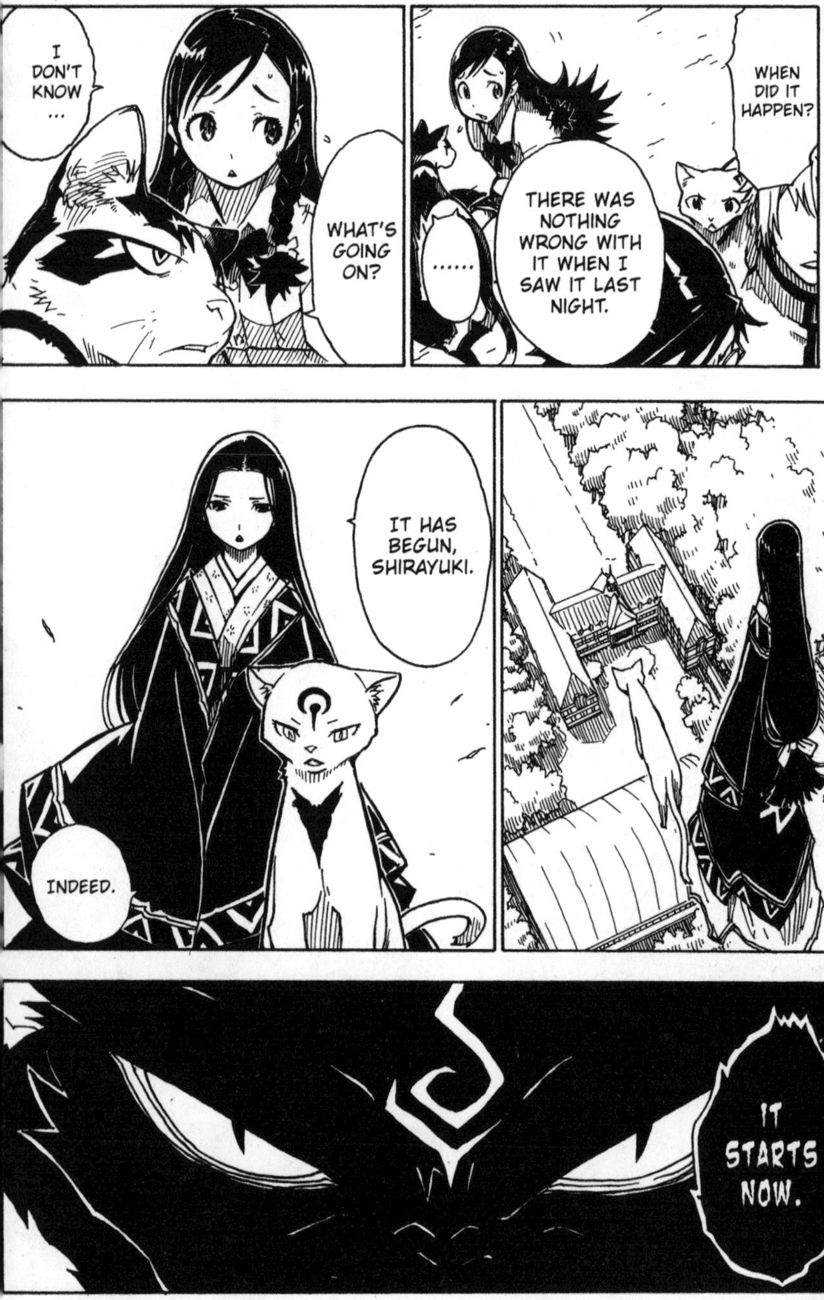
WHEN DID IT HAPPEN?
THERE WAS NOTHING WRONG WITH IT WHEN I SAW IT LAST NIGHT.
......
WHAT'S GOING ON?
I DON'T KNOW ...
IT HAS BEGUN, SHIRAYUKI.
INDEED.
IT STARTS NOW.

CHAPTER 4 · THE REQUEST

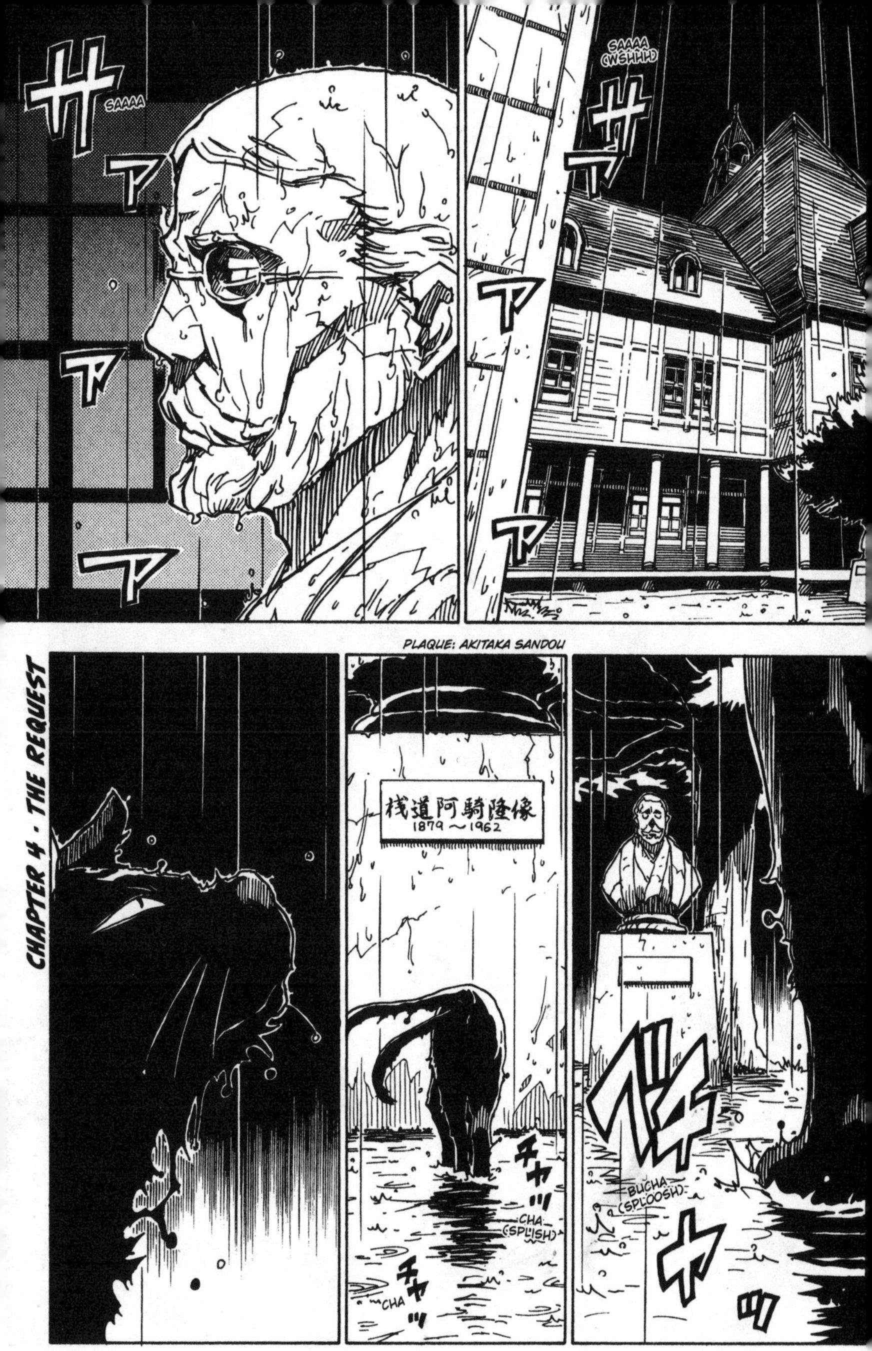

SAAAA (WSHHHD)
SAAAA
PLAQUE: AKITAKA SANDOU
BUCHA (SPLOOSH)
桟道阿騎隆像
1879～1962
CHA (SPLISH)
CHA

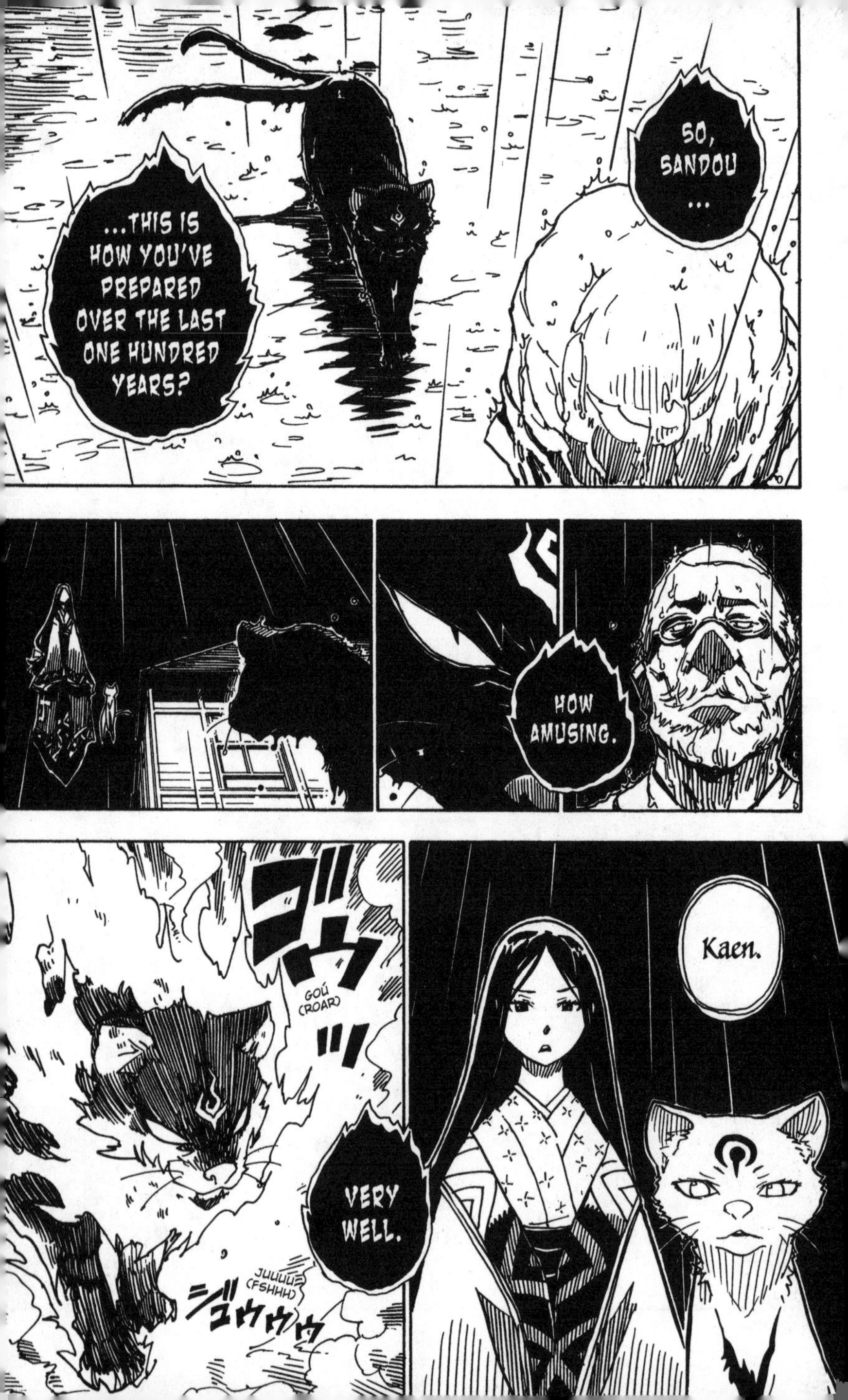
SO, SANDOU ...
...THIS IS HOW YOU'VE PREPARED OVER THE LAST ONE HUNDRED YEARS?
HOW AMUSING.
Kaen.
GOU (ROAR)
VERY WELL.
JUUUU (FSHHH)

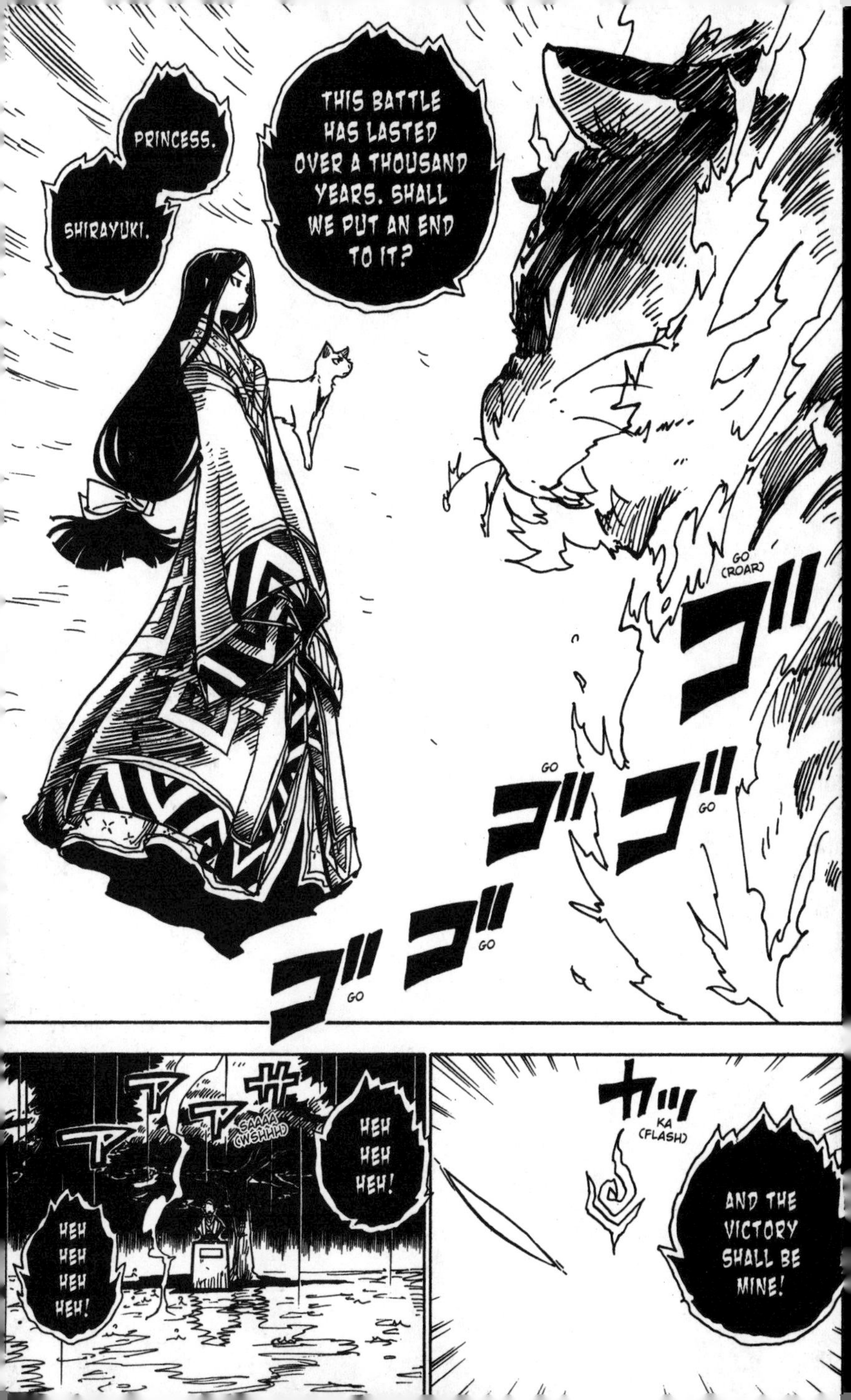
THIS BATTLE HAS LASTED OVER A THOUSAND YEARS. SHALL WE PUT AN END TO IT?
PRINCESS.
SHIRAYUKI.
ゴ
GO (ROAR)
ゴ
GO
ゴ
GO
ゴ
GO
ゴ
GO
カッ
KA (FLASH)
AND THE VICTORY SHALL BE MINE!
ザァァァ
SAAAA (WSHHH)
HEH HEH HEH!
HEH HEH HEH HEH!

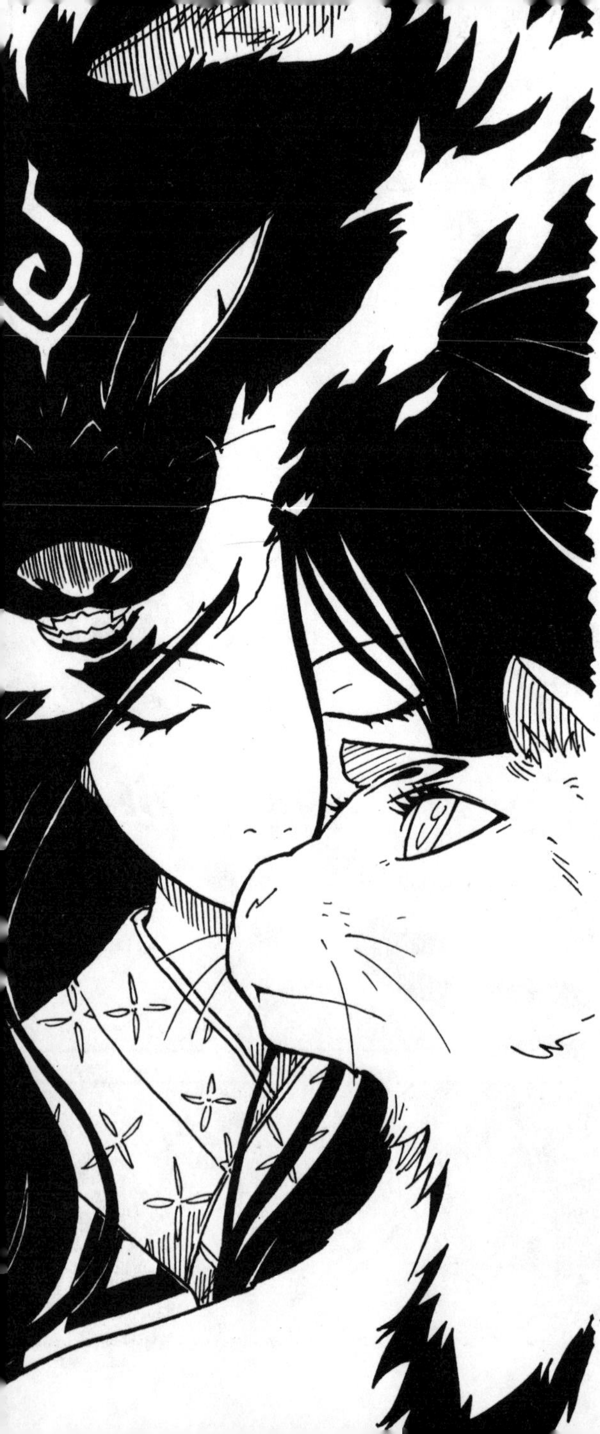

CHAPTER 4
THE REQUEST

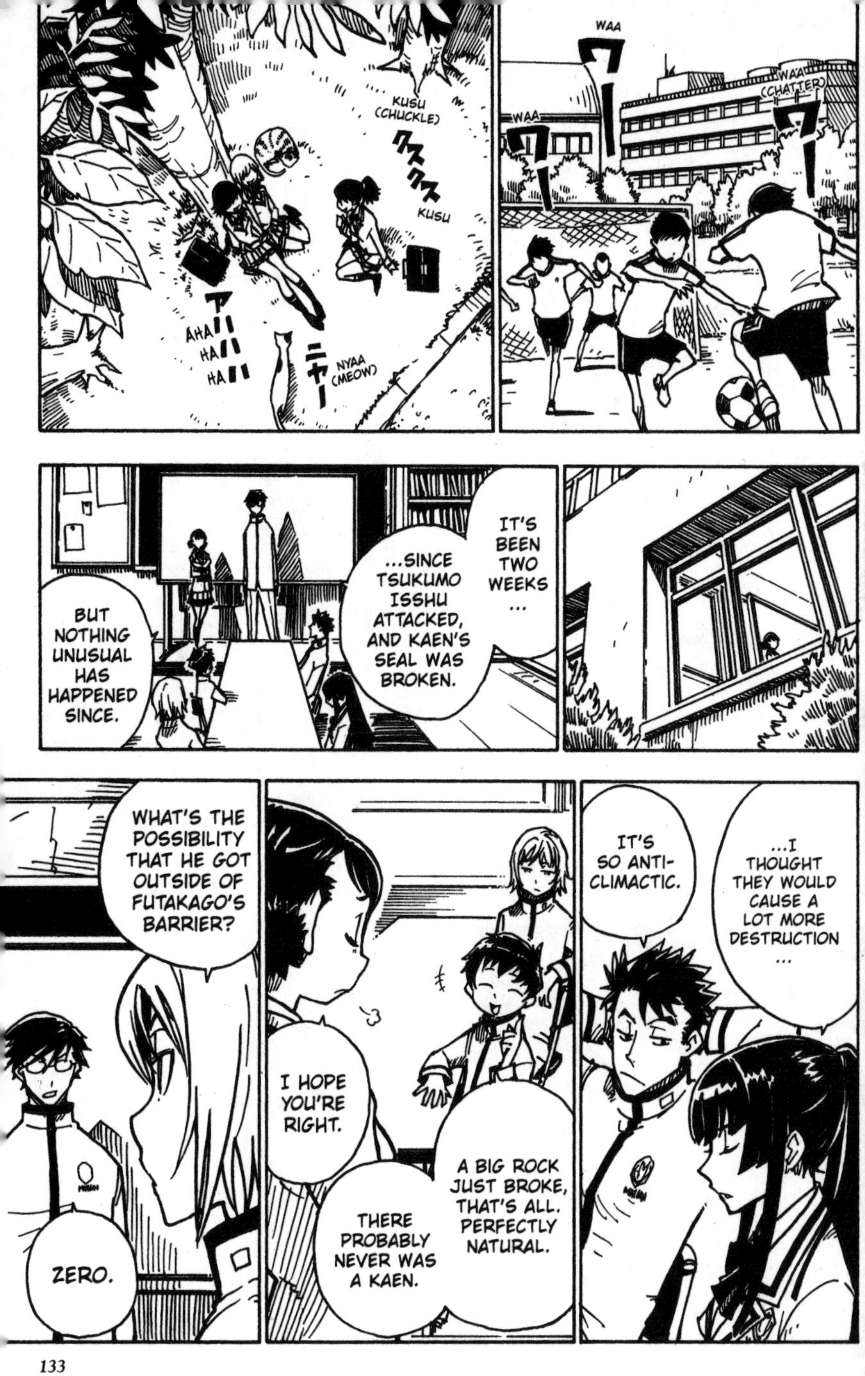
WAA
ワー
WAA (CHATTER)
ワー
WAA
ワー
KUSU (CHUCKLE)
クスクス
KUSU
AHA HA HA
アハハ
NYAA (MEOW)
ニャー
IT'S BEEN TWO WEEKS...
...SINCE TSUKUMO ISSHU ATTACKED, AND KAEN'S SEAL WAS BROKEN.
BUT NOTHING UNUSUAL HAS HAPPENED SINCE.
...I THOUGHT THEY WOULD CAUSE A LOT MORE DESTRUCTION...
IT'S SO ANTI-CLIMACTIC.
A BIG ROCK JUST BROKE, THAT'S ALL. PERFECTLY NATURAL.
THERE PROBABLY NEVER WAS A KAEN.
I HOPE YOU'RE RIGHT.
WHAT'S THE POSSIBILITY THAT HE GOT OUTSIDE OF FUTAKAGO'S BARRIER?
ZERO.

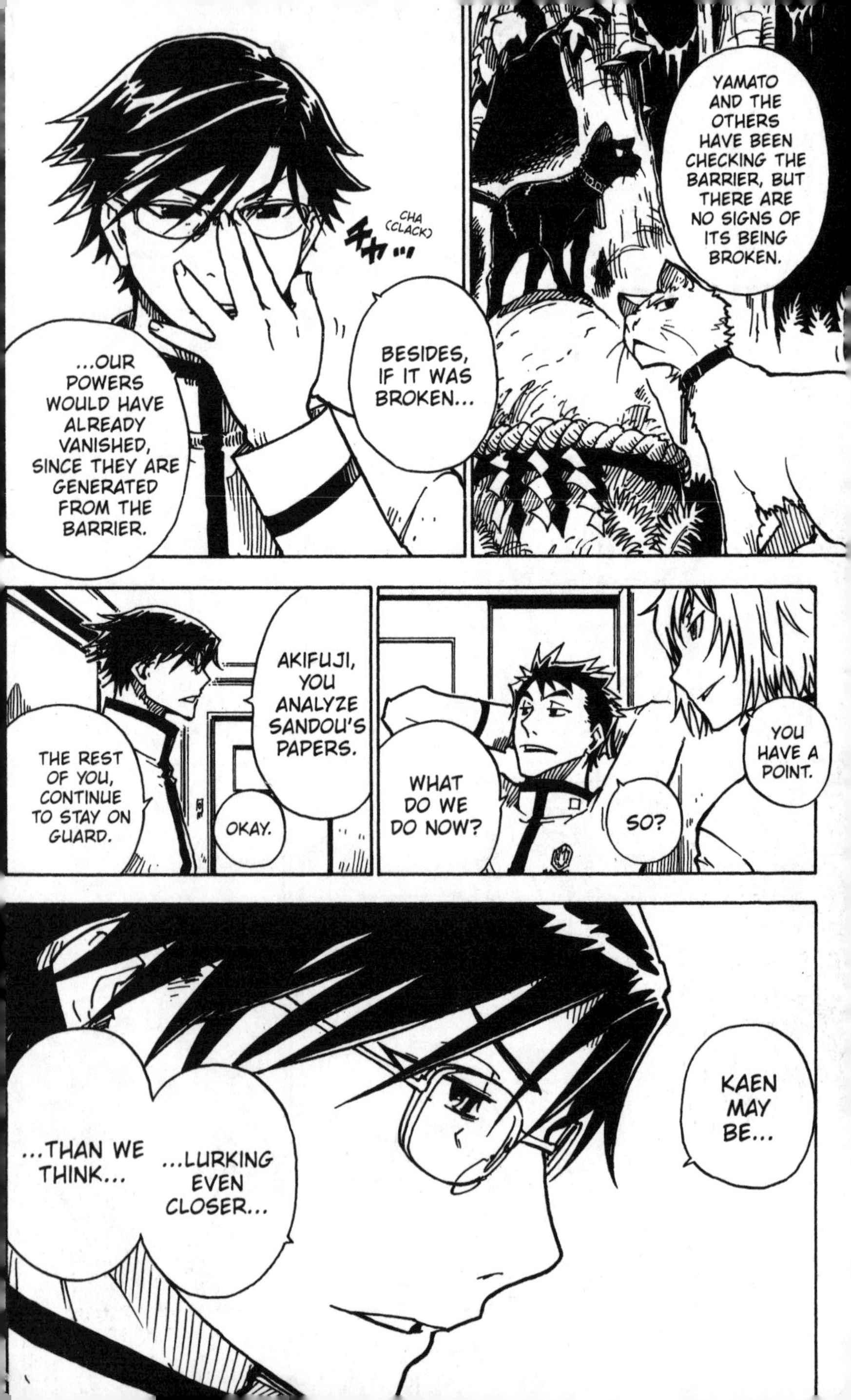
YAMATO AND THE OTHERS HAVE BEEN CHECKING THE BARRIER, BUT THERE ARE NO SIGNS OF ITS BEING BROKEN.
CHA (CLACK)
BESIDES, IF IT WAS BROKEN...
...OUR POWERS WOULD HAVE ALREADY VANISHED, SINCE THEY ARE GENERATED FROM THE BARRIER.
YOU HAVE A POINT.
SO?
WHAT DO WE DO NOW?
AKIFUJI, YOU ANALYZE SANDOU'S PAPERS.
OKAY.
THE REST OF YOU, CONTINUE TO STAY ON GUARD.
KAEN MAY BE...
...LURKING EVEN CLOSER...
...THAN WE THINK...

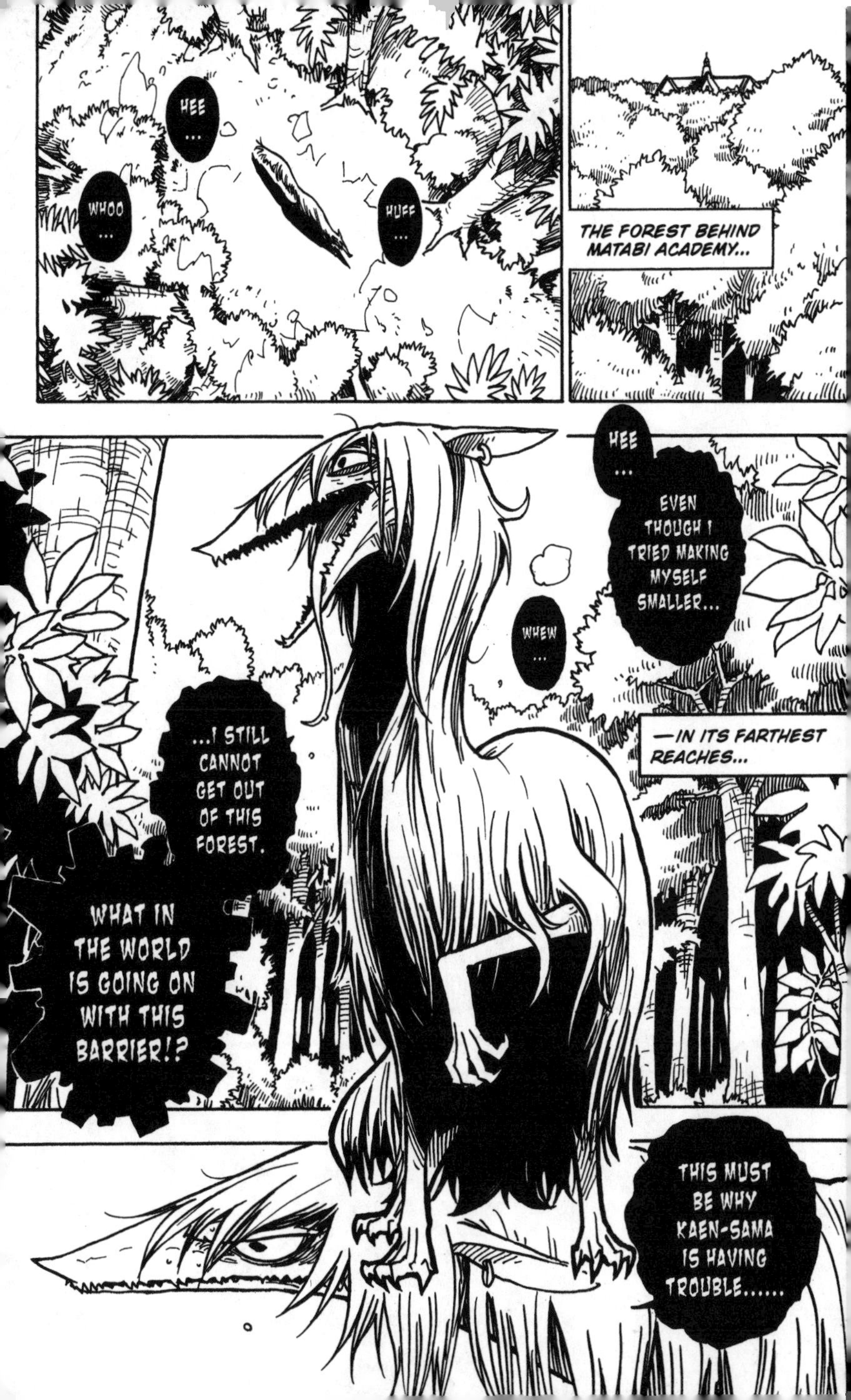
THE FOREST BEHIND MATABI ACADEMY...
HUFF...
HEE...
WHOO...
HEE... EVEN THOUGH I TRIED MAKING MYSELF SMALLER...
WHEW...
—IN ITS FARTHEST REACHES...
...I STILL CANNOT GET OUT OF THIS FOREST.
WHAT IN THE WORLD IS GOING ON WITH THIS BARRIER!?
THIS MUST BE WHY KAEN-SAMA IS HAVING TROUBLE......

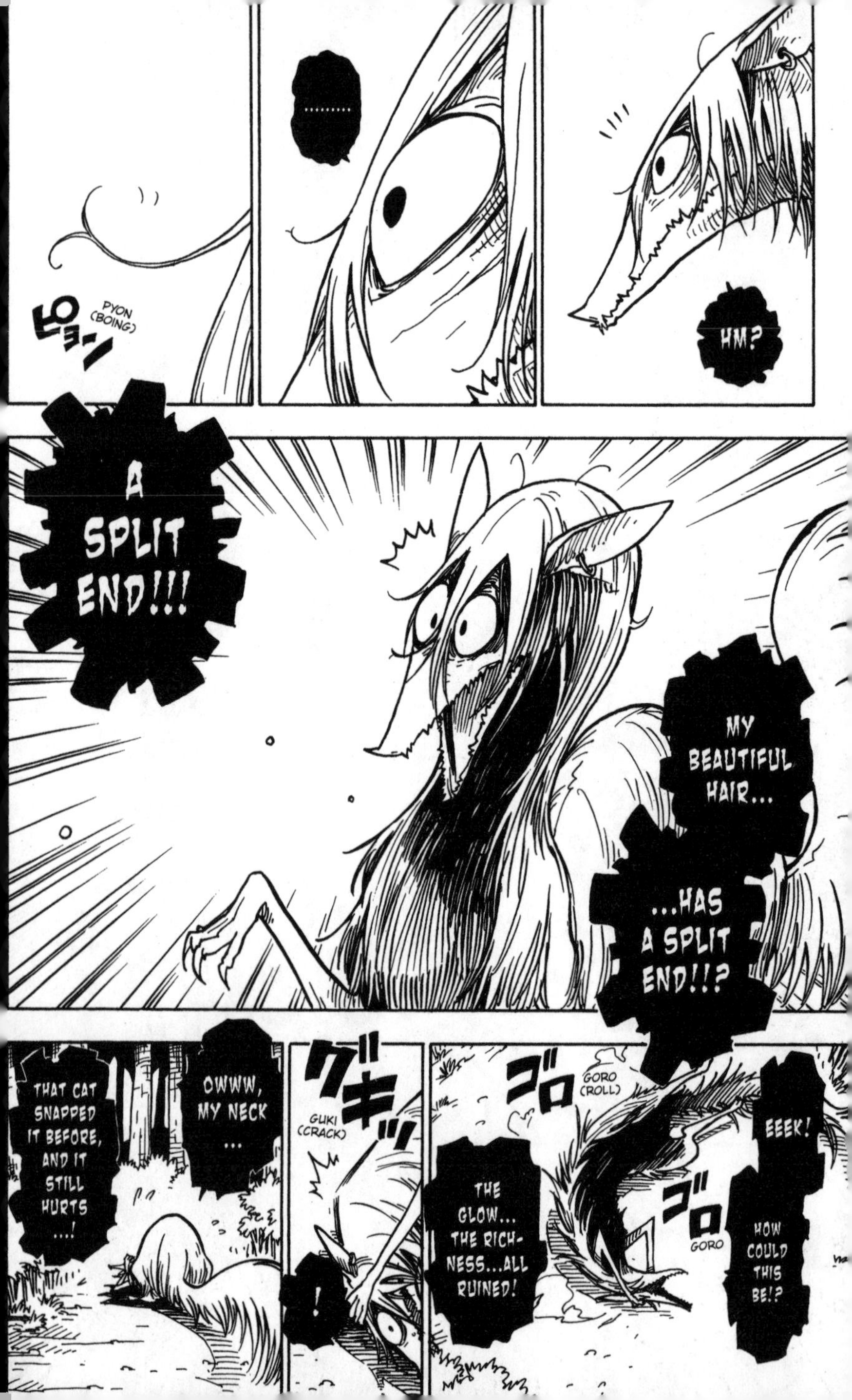
HM?
....
ピョン
PYON (BOING)
A SPLIT END!!!
MY BEAUTIFUL HAIR...
...HAS A SPLIT END!!?
EEEK!
ゴロ
GORO (ROLL)
ゴロ
GORO
HOW COULD THIS BE!?
THE GLOW... THE RICHNESS...ALL RUINED!
グキッ
GUKI (CRACK)
!
OWWW, MY NECK...
THAT CAT SNAPPED IT BEFORE, AND IT STILL HURTS...!

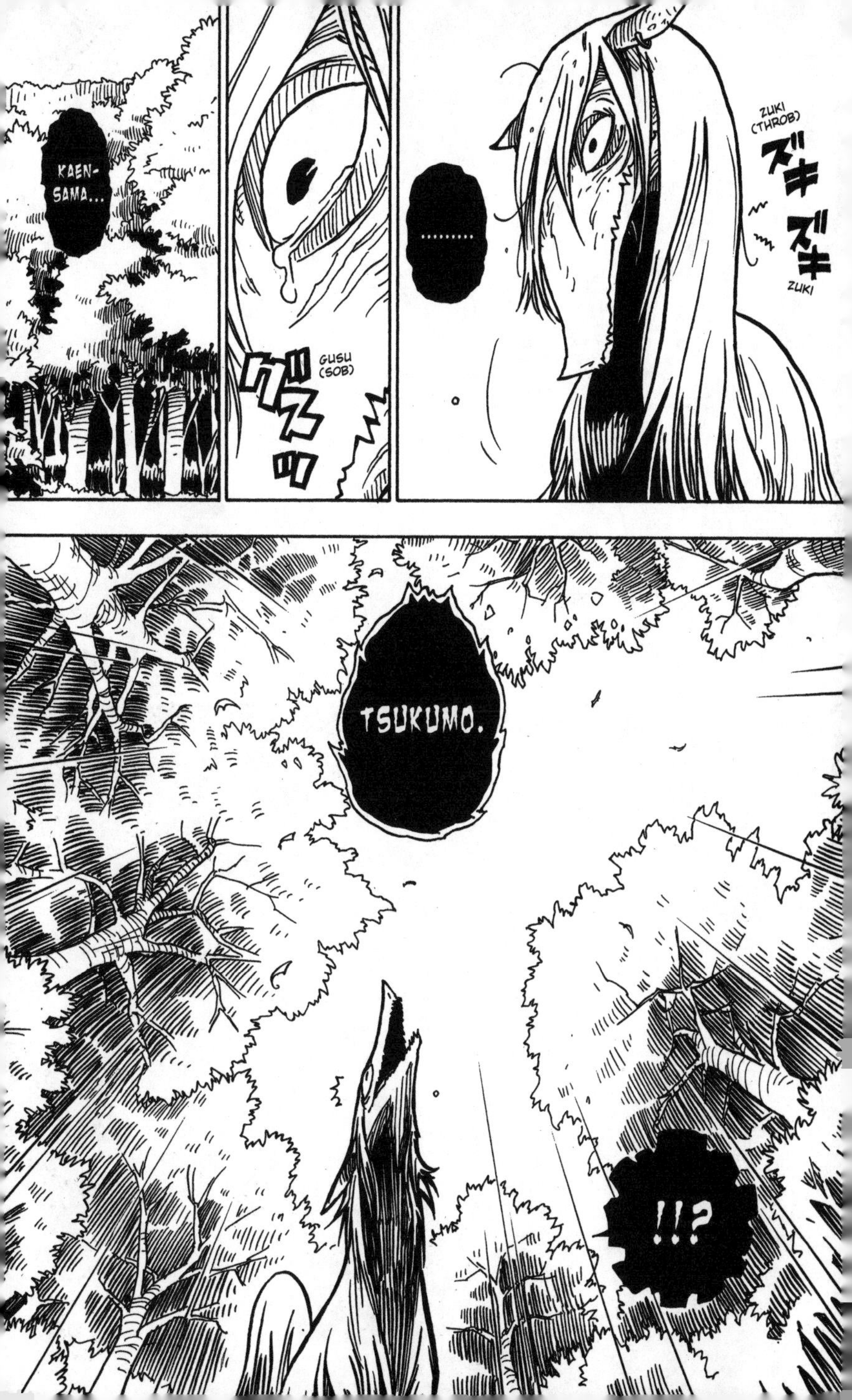
ZUKI (THROB)
ズキ
ズキ
ZUKI
....
GUSU (SOB)
KAEN-SAMA...
TSUKUMO.
!!?

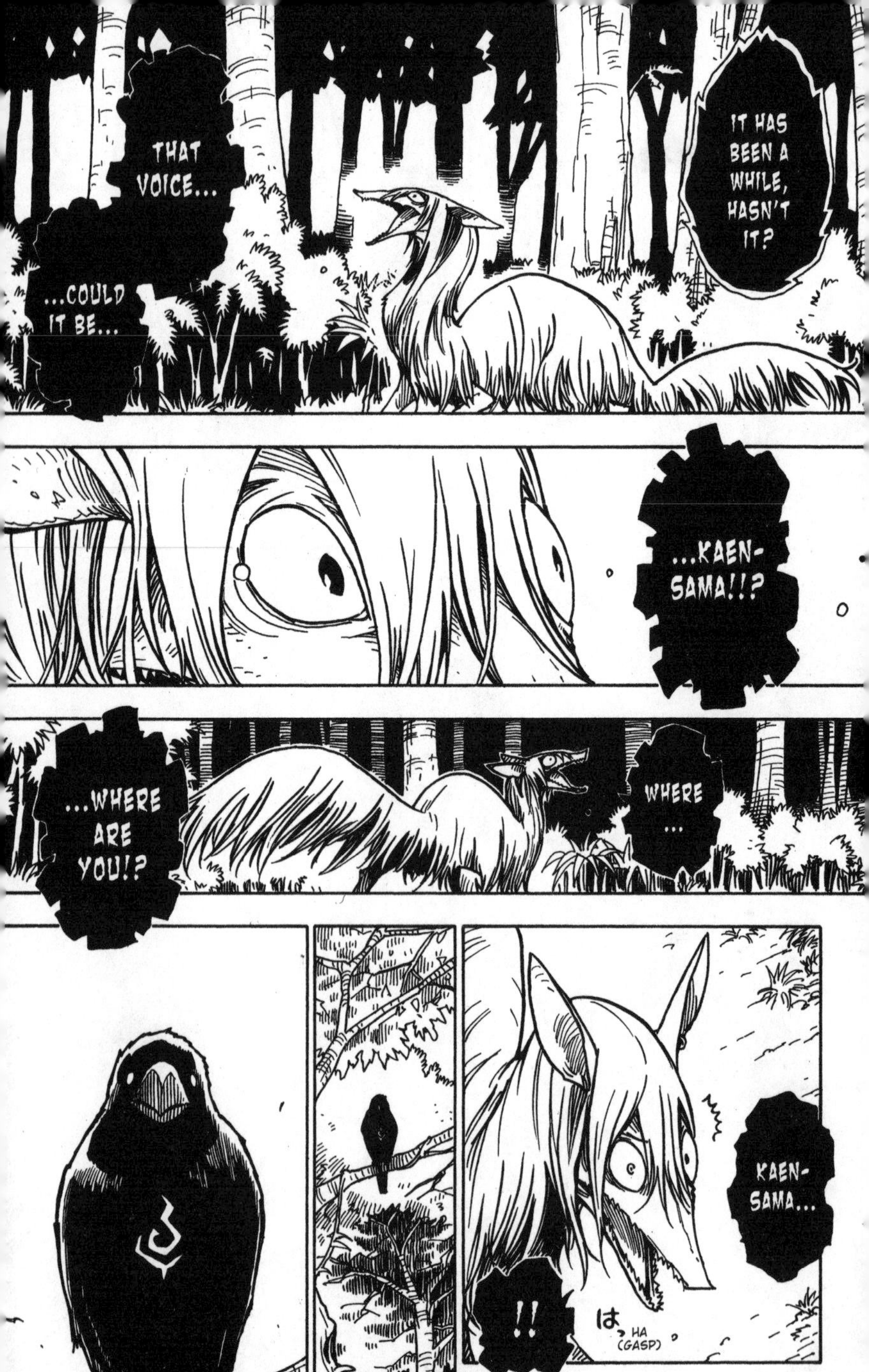
IT HAS BEEN A WHILE, HASN'T IT?
THAT VOICE...
...COULD IT BE...
...KAEN-SAMA!!?
WHERE...
...WHERE ARE YOU!?
KAEN-SAMA...
!!
は、 HA (GASP)

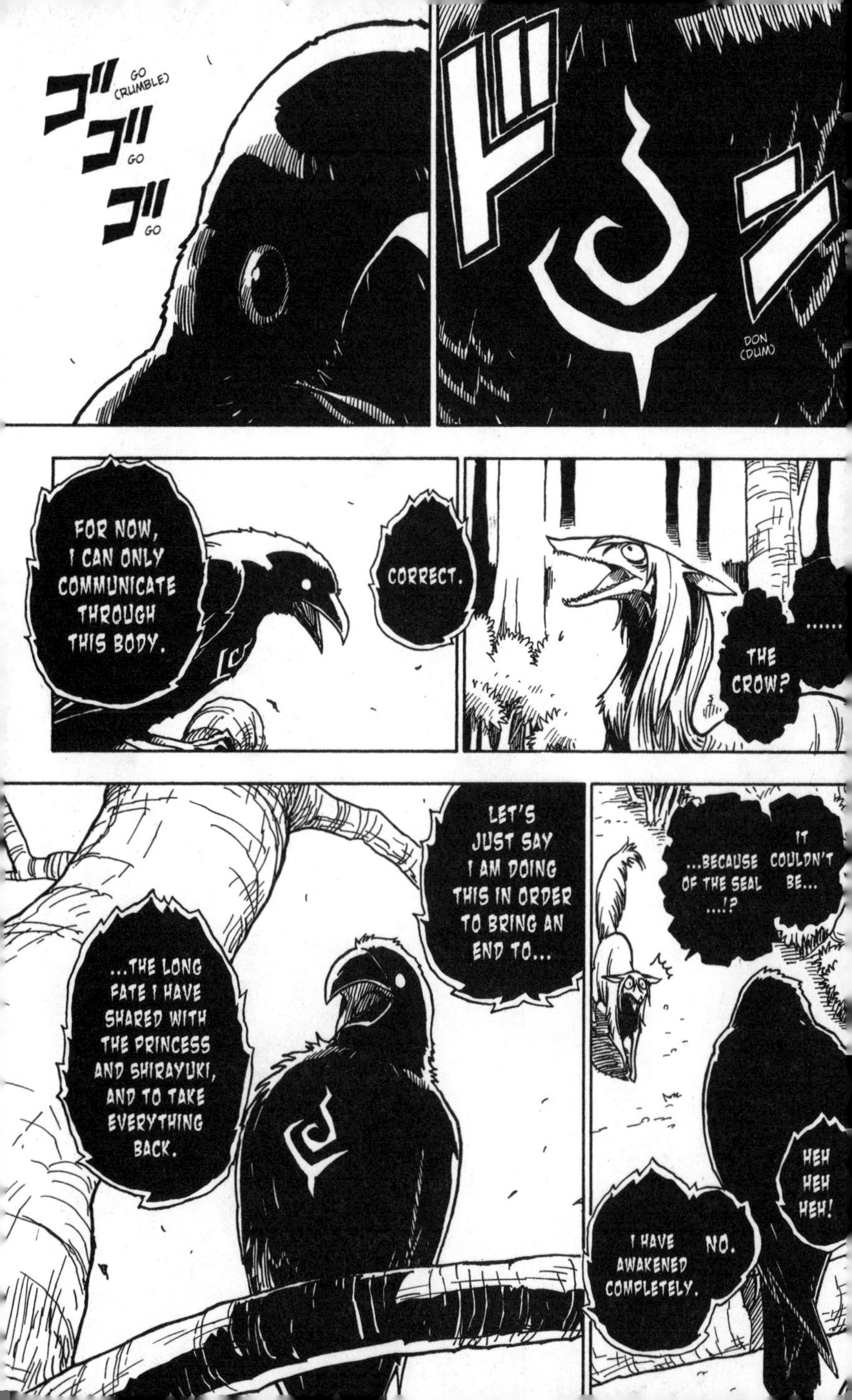

ドン
DON
(DUM)
ゴ
GO
(RUMBLE)
ゴ
GO
ゴ
GO
......
THE CROW?
CORRECT.
FOR NOW, I CAN ONLY COMMUNICATE THROUGH THIS BODY.
IT COULDN'T BE...
...BECAUSE OF THE SEAL ...!?
HEH HEH HEH!
NO.
I HAVE AWAKENED COMPLETELY.
LET'S JUST SAY I AM DOING THIS IN ORDER TO BRING AN END TO...
...THE LONG FATE I HAVE SHARED WITH THE PRINCESS AND SHIRAYUKI, AND TO TAKE EVERYTHING BACK.

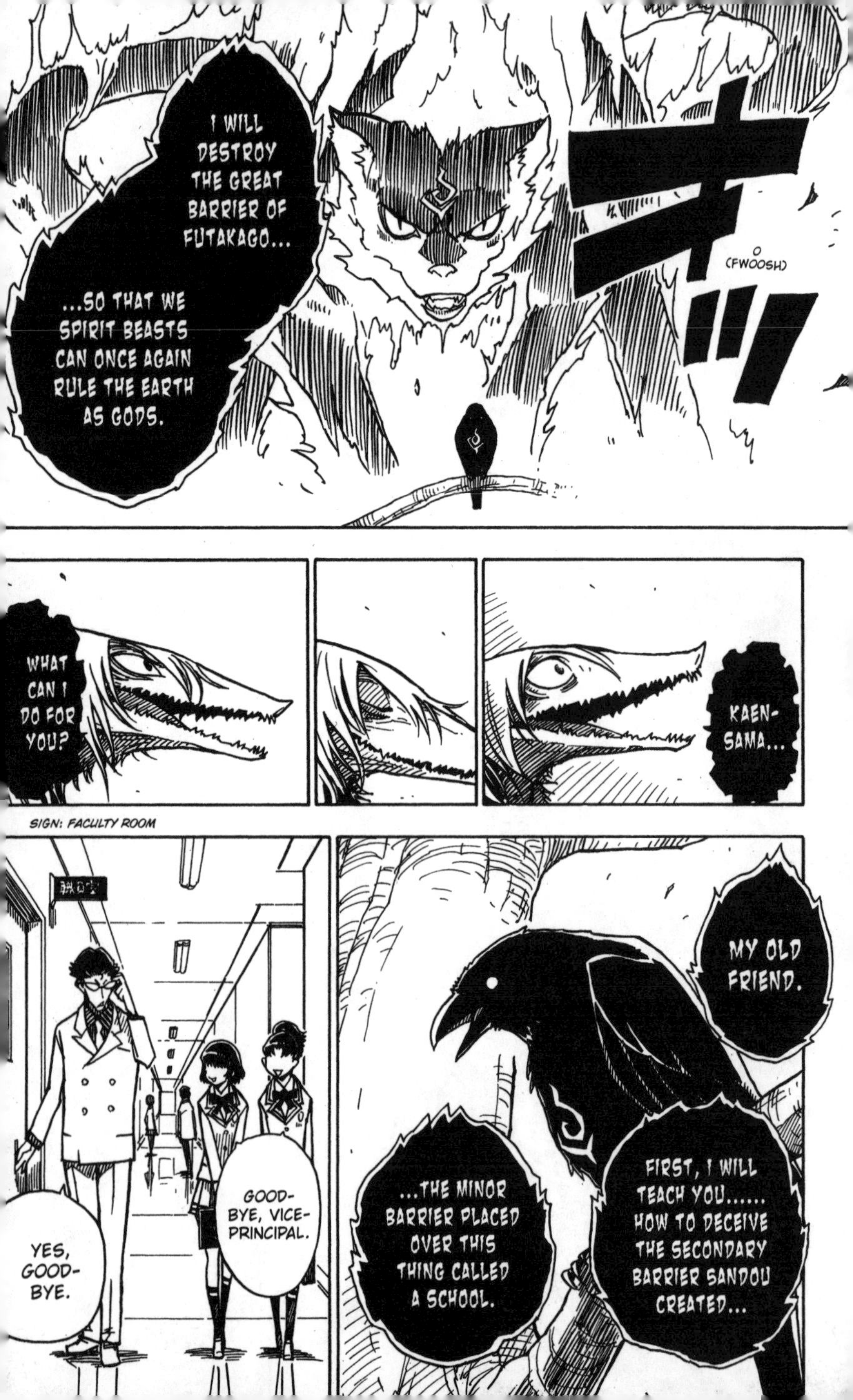
O (FWOOSH)
I WILL DESTROY THE GREAT BARRIER OF FUTAKAGO...
...SO THAT WE SPIRIT BEASTS CAN ONCE AGAIN RULE THE EARTH AS GODS.
KAEN-SAMA...
WHAT CAN I DO FOR YOU?
MY OLD FRIEND.
FIRST, I WILL TEACH YOU...... HOW TO DECEIVE THE SECONDARY BARRIER SANDOU CREATED...
...THE MINOR BARRIER PLACED OVER THIS THING CALLED A SCHOOL.
SIGN: FACULTY ROOM
GOOD-BYE, VICE-PRINCIPAL.
YES, GOOD-BYE.

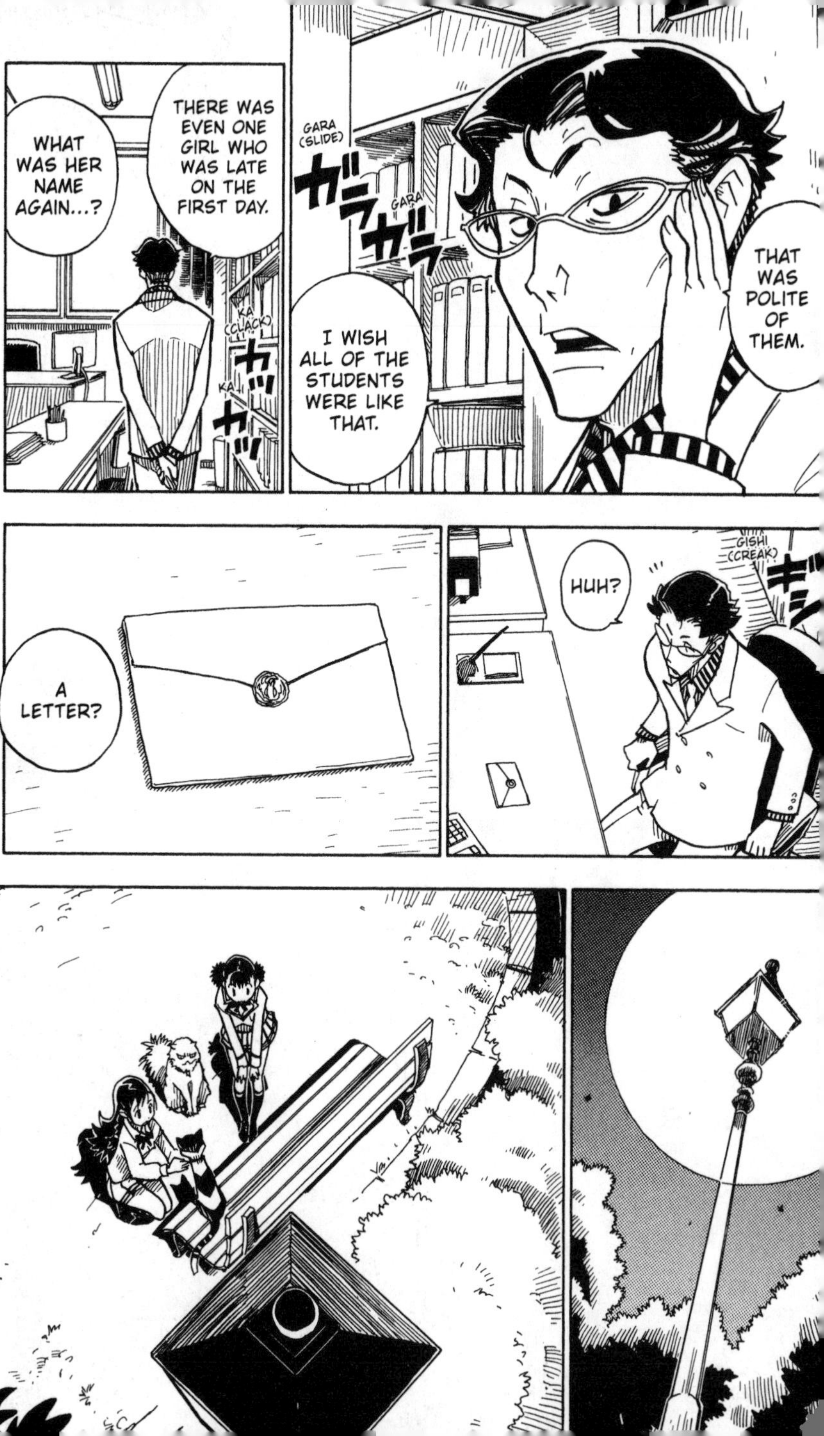
GARA (SLIDE)
GARA
THAT WAS POLITE OF THEM.
I WISH ALL OF THE STUDENTS WERE LIKE THAT.
KA (CLACK)
KA
THERE WAS EVEN ONE GIRL WHO WAS LATE ON THE FIRST DAY.
WHAT WAS HER NAME AGAIN...?
GISHI (CREAK)
HUH?
A LETTER?

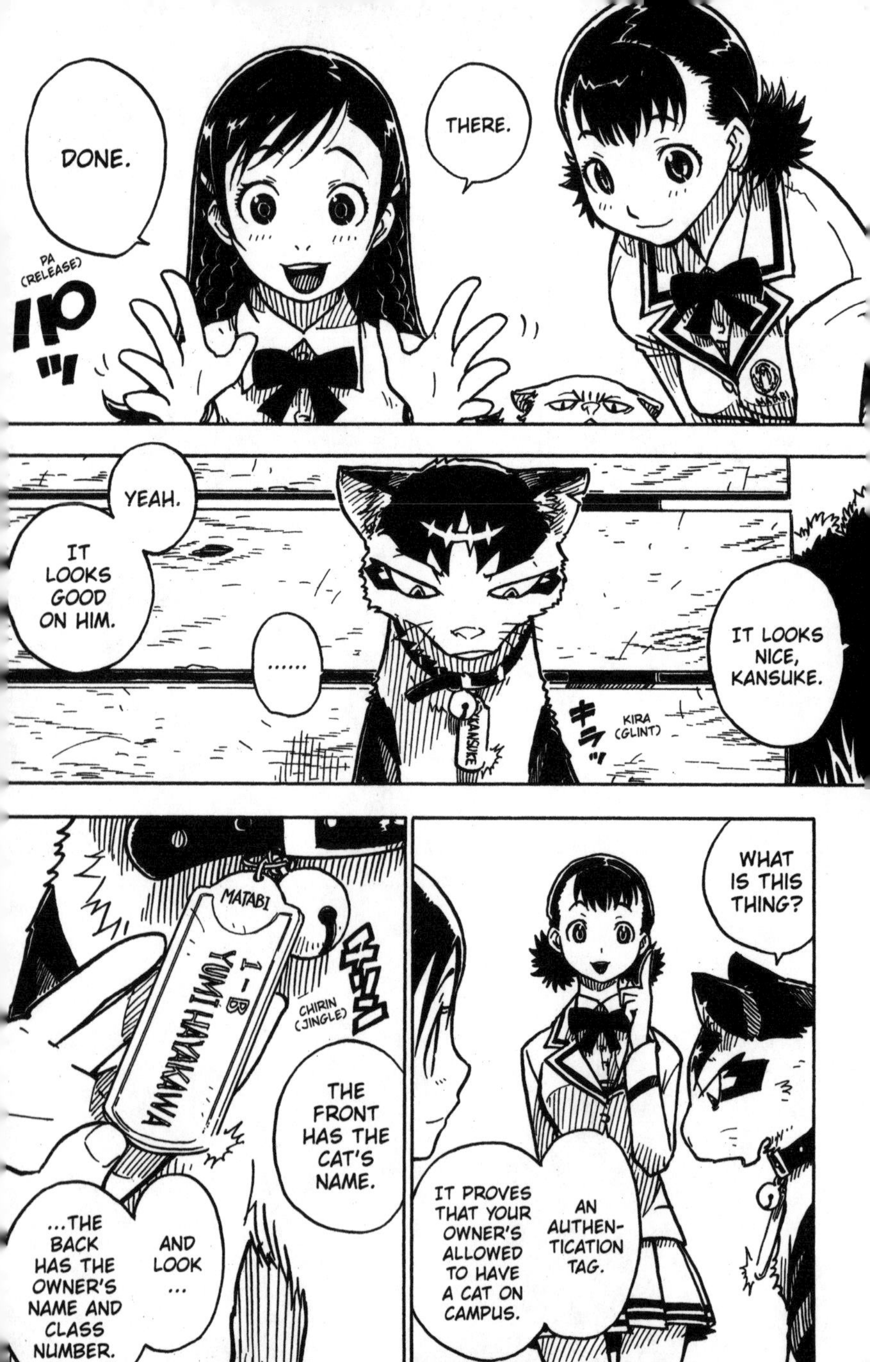
THERE.
DONE.
PA (RELEASE)
IT LOOKS NICE, KANSUKE.
KIRA (GLINT)
KANSUKE
......
YEAH.
IT LOOKS GOOD ON HIM.
WHAT IS THIS THING?
AN AUTHEN-TICATION TAG.
IT PROVES THAT YOUR OWNER'S ALLOWED TO HAVE A CAT ON CAMPUS.
MATABI
1-B YUMI HAYAKAWA
CHIRIN (JINGLE)
THE FRONT HAS THE CAT'S NAME.
AND LOOK...
...THE BACK HAS THE OWNER'S NAME AND CLASS NUMBER.

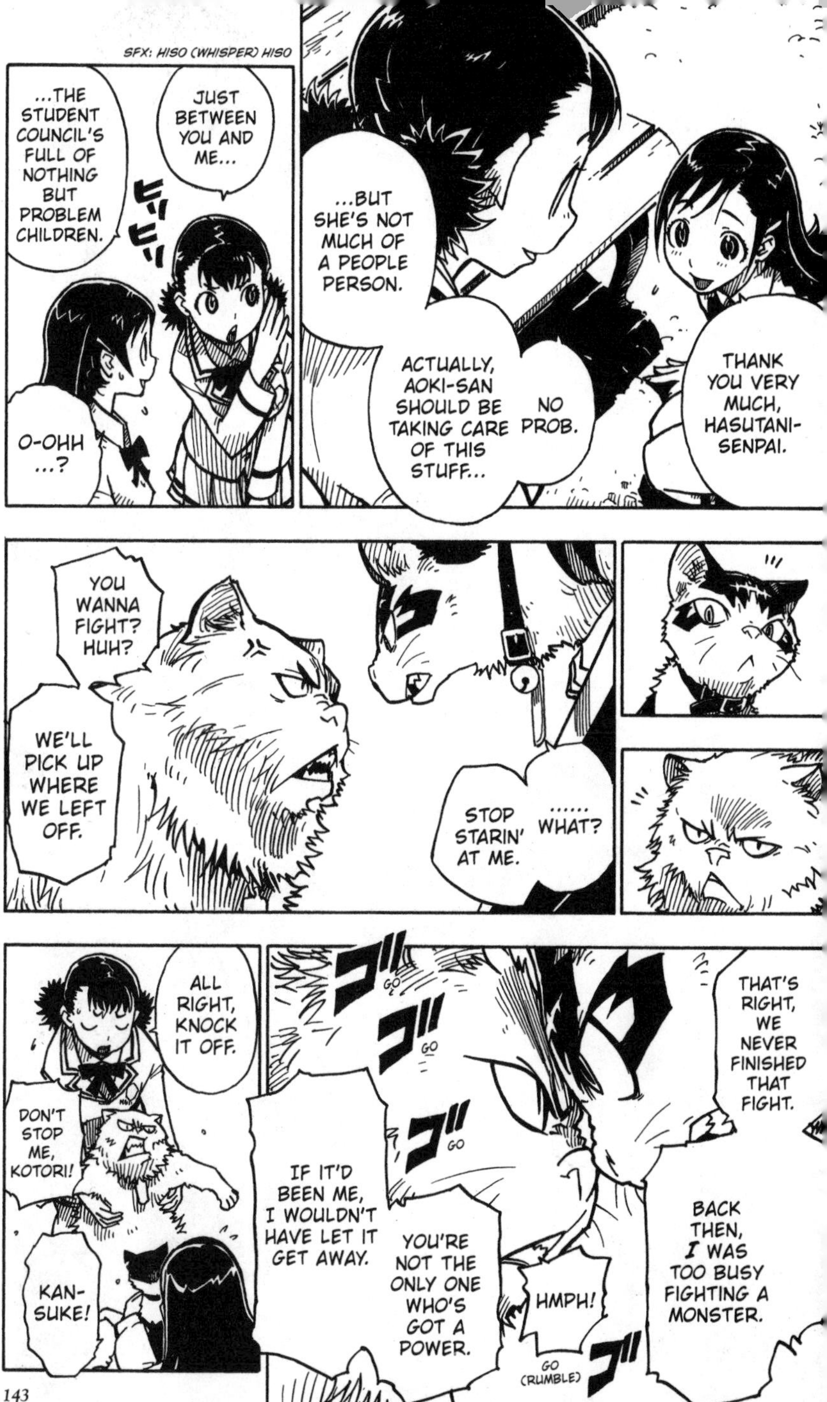
THANK YOU VERY MUCH, HASUTANI-SENPAI.
NO PROB.
ACTUALLY, AOKI-SAN SHOULD BE TAKING CARE OF THIS STUFF...
...BUT SHE'S NOT MUCH OF A PEOPLE PERSON.
SFX: HISO (WHISPER) HISO
JUST BETWEEN YOU AND ME...
...THE STUDENT COUNCIL'S FULL OF NOTHING BUT PROBLEM CHILDREN.
O-OHH ...?
...... WHAT?
STOP STARIN' AT ME.
YOU WANNA FIGHT? HUH?
WE'LL PICK UP WHERE WE LEFT OFF.
THAT'S RIGHT, WE NEVER FINISHED THAT FIGHT.
BACK THEN, *I* WAS TOO BUSY FIGHTING A MONSTER.
GO
GO
GO
HMPH!
YOU'RE NOT THE ONLY ONE WHO'S GOT A POWER.
IF IT'D BEEN ME, I WOULDN'T HAVE LET IT GET AWAY.
GO (RUMBLE)
ALL RIGHT, KNOCK IT OFF.
DON'T STOP ME, KOTORI!
KAN-SUKE!

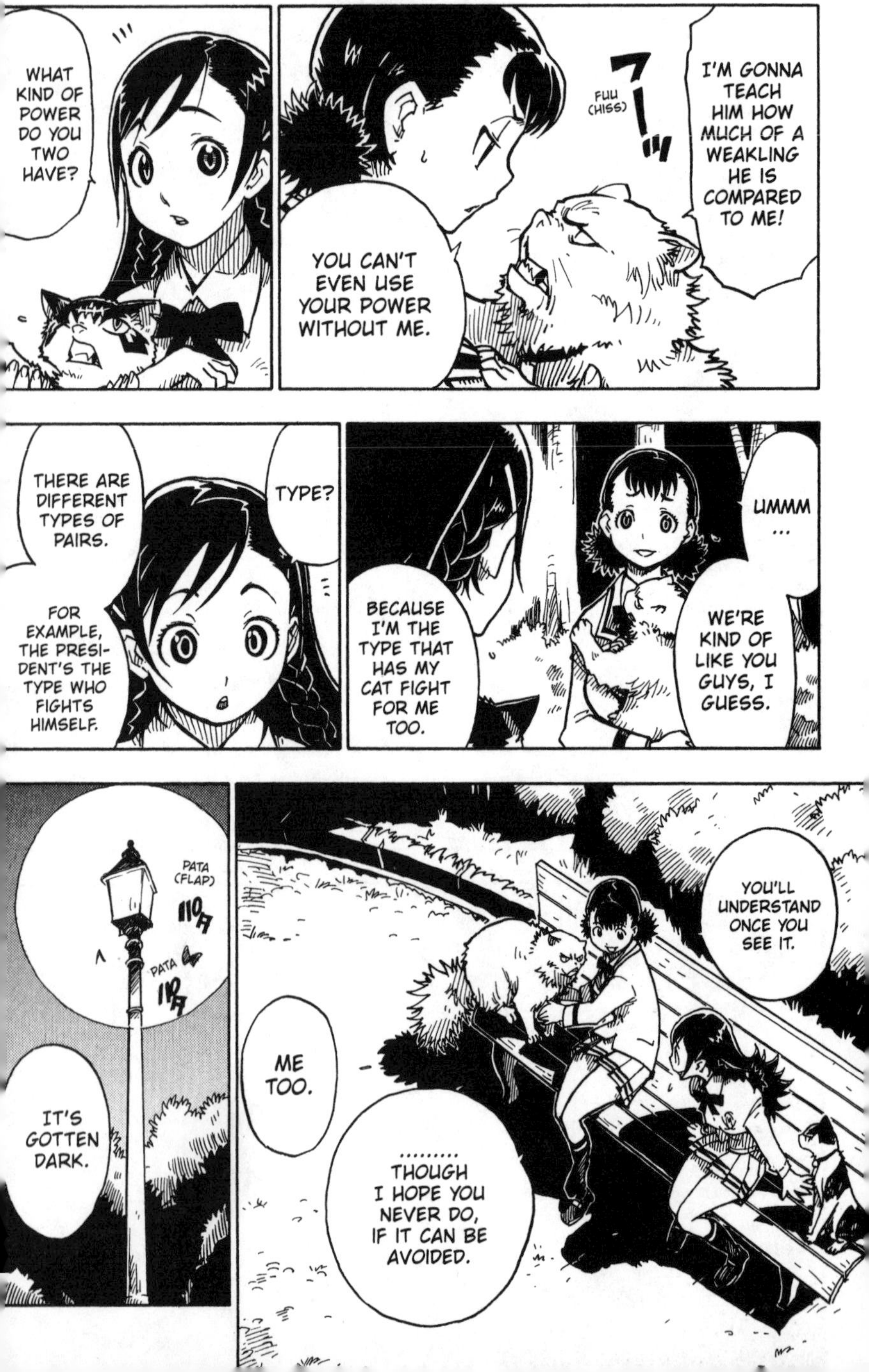
I'M GONNA TEACH HIM HOW MUCH OF A WEAKLING HE IS COMPARED TO ME!
FUU (HISS)
YOU CAN'T EVEN USE YOUR POWER WITHOUT ME.
WHAT KIND OF POWER DO YOU TWO HAVE?
UMMM ...
WE'RE KIND OF LIKE YOU GUYS, I GUESS.
BECAUSE I'M THE TYPE THAT HAS MY CAT FIGHT FOR ME TOO.
TYPE?
THERE ARE DIFFERENT TYPES OF PAIRS.
FOR EXAMPLE, THE PRESIDENT'S THE TYPE WHO FIGHTS HIMSELF.
YOU'LL UNDERSTAND ONCE YOU SEE IT.
ME TOO.
.... THOUGH I HOPE YOU NEVER DO, IF IT CAN BE AVOIDED.
PATA (FLAP)
PATA
IT'S GOTTEN DARK.

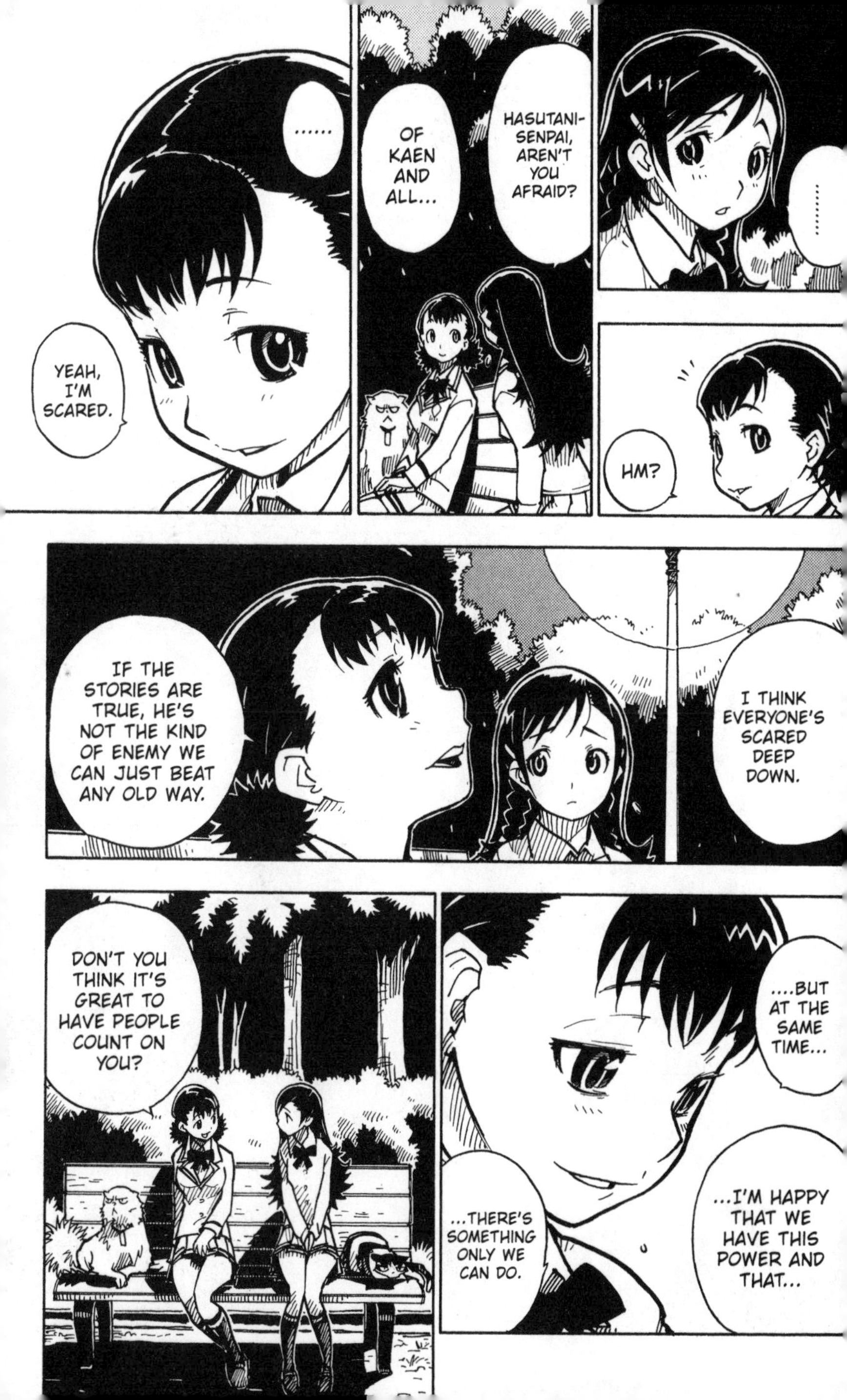
……
HM?
HASUTANI-SENPAI, AREN'T YOU AFRAID?
OF KAEN AND ALL…
……
YEAH, I'M SCARED.
I THINK EVERYONE'S SCARED DEEP DOWN.
IF THE STORIES ARE TRUE, HE'S NOT THE KIND OF ENEMY WE CAN JUST BEAT ANY OLD WAY.
....BUT AT THE SAME TIME…
…I'M HAPPY THAT WE HAVE THIS POWER AND THAT…
…THERE'S SOMETHING ONLY WE CAN DO.
DON'T YOU THINK IT'S GREAT TO HAVE PEOPLE COUNT ON YOU?

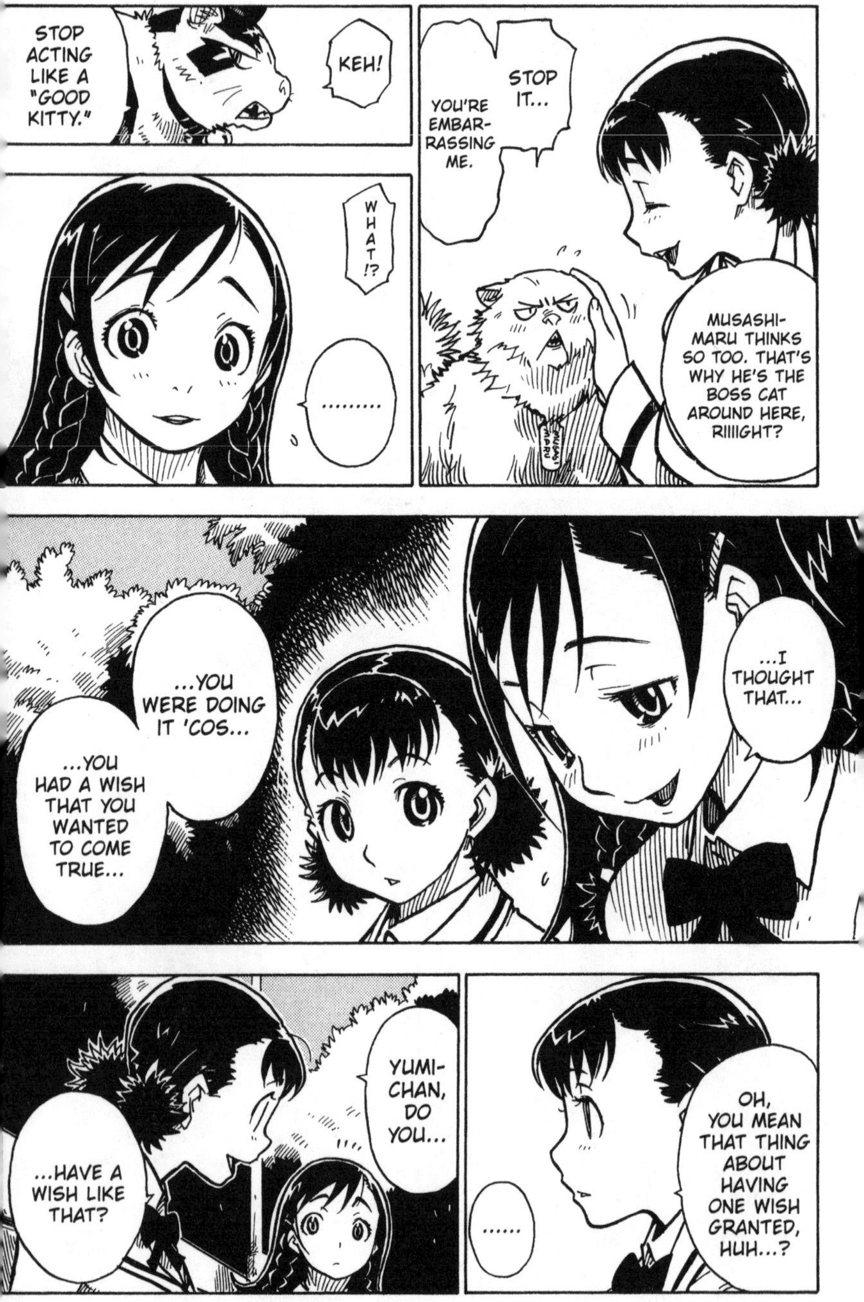
STOP IT... YOU'RE EMBARRASSING ME.
MUSASHIMARU THINKS SO TOO. THAT'S WHY HE'S THE BOSS CAT AROUND HERE, RIIIIGHT?
MUSASHIMARU
KEH!
STOP ACTING LIKE A "GOOD KITTY."
WHAT!?
....
...I THOUGHT THAT...
...YOU WERE DOING IT 'COS...
...YOU HAD A WISH THAT YOU WANTED TO COME TRUE...
OH, YOU MEAN THAT THING ABOUT HAVING ONE WISH GRANTED, HUH...?
......
YUMI-CHAN, DO YOU...
...HAVE A WISH LIKE THAT?

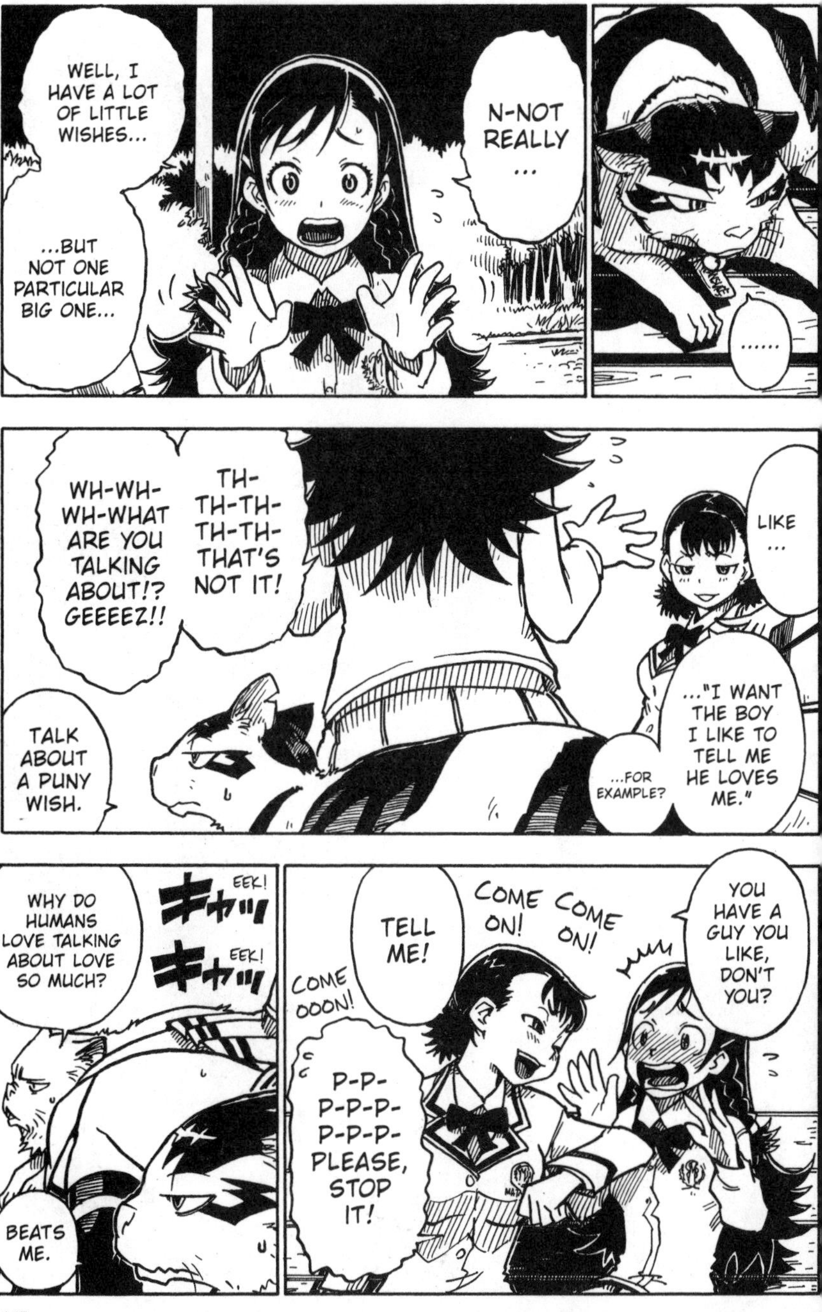
......
N-NOT REALLY ...
WELL, I HAVE A LOT OF LITTLE WISHES...
...BUT NOT ONE PARTICULAR BIG ONE...
LIKE ...
..."I WANT THE BOY I LIKE TO TELL ME HE LOVES ME."
...FOR EXAMPLE?
TH-TH-TH-TH-TH-THAT'S NOT IT!
WH-WH-WH-WHAT ARE YOU TALKING ABOUT!? GEEEEZ!!
TALK ABOUT A PUNY WISH.
YOU HAVE A GUY YOU LIKE, DON'T YOU?
COME ON!
COME ON!
TELL ME!
COME OOON!
P-P-P-P-P-P-P-P-P-P-PLEASE, STOP IT!
キャッ EEK!
キャッ EEK!
WHY DO HUMANS LOVE TALKING ABOUT LOVE SO MUCH?
BEATS ME.

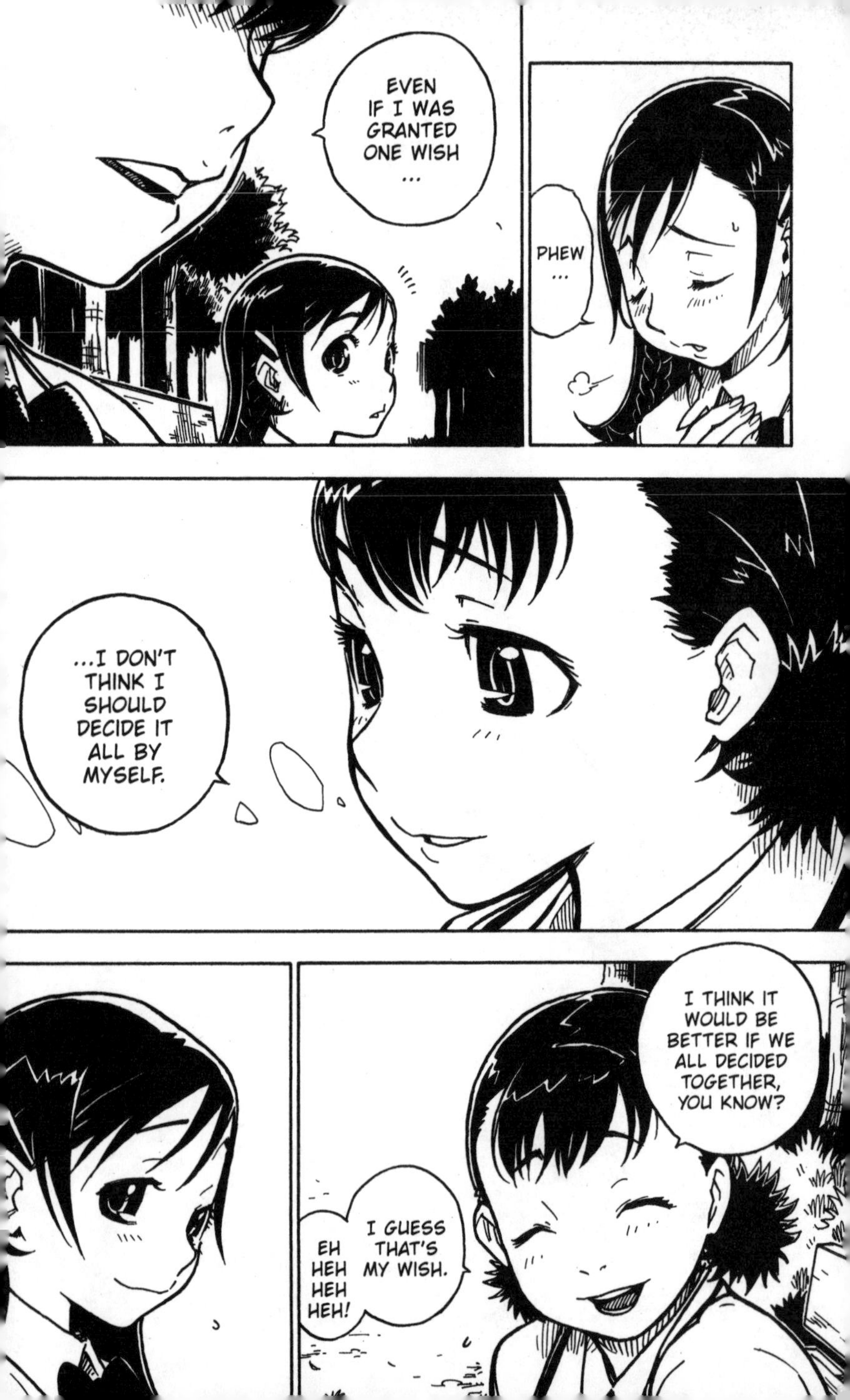
PHEW ...
EVEN IF I WAS GRANTED ONE WISH ...
...I DON'T THINK I SHOULD DECIDE IT ALL BY MYSELF.
I THINK IT WOULD BE BETTER IF WE ALL DECIDED TOGETHER, YOU KNOW?
I GUESS THAT'S MY WISH.
EH HEH HEH HEH!

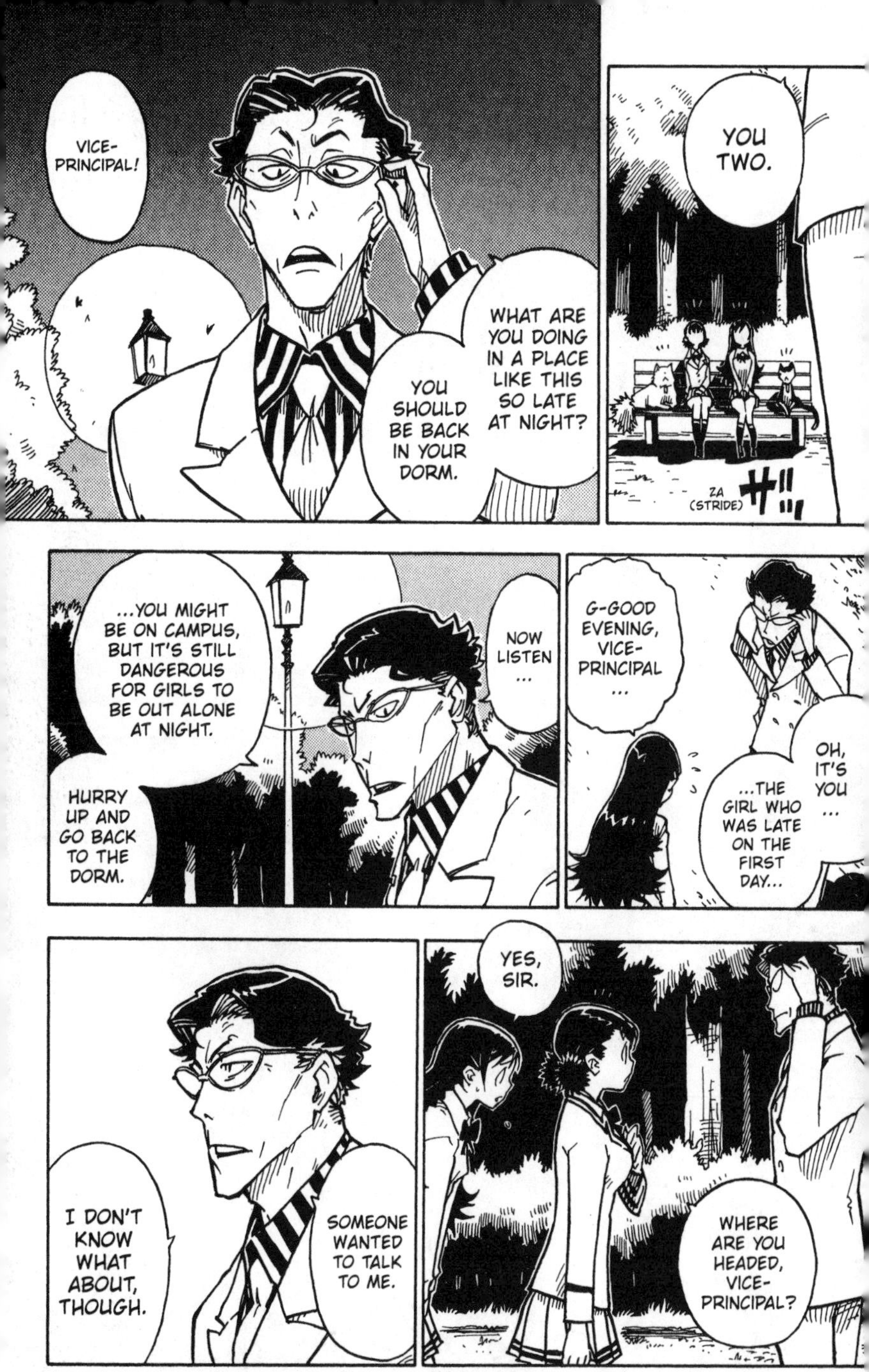
YOU TWO.
ZA (STRIDE)
VICE-PRINCIPAL!
WHAT ARE YOU DOING IN A PLACE LIKE THIS SO LATE AT NIGHT?
YOU SHOULD BE BACK IN YOUR DORM.
G-GOOD EVENING, VICE-PRINCIPAL...
OH, IT'S YOU...
...THE GIRL WHO WAS LATE ON THE FIRST DAY...
NOW LISTEN...
...YOU MIGHT BE ON CAMPUS, BUT IT'S STILL DANGEROUS FOR GIRLS TO BE OUT ALONE AT NIGHT.
HURRY UP AND GO BACK TO THE DORM.
YES, SIR.
WHERE ARE YOU HEADED, VICE-PRINCIPAL?
SOMEONE WANTED TO TALK TO ME.
I DON'T KNOW WHAT ABOUT, THOUGH.

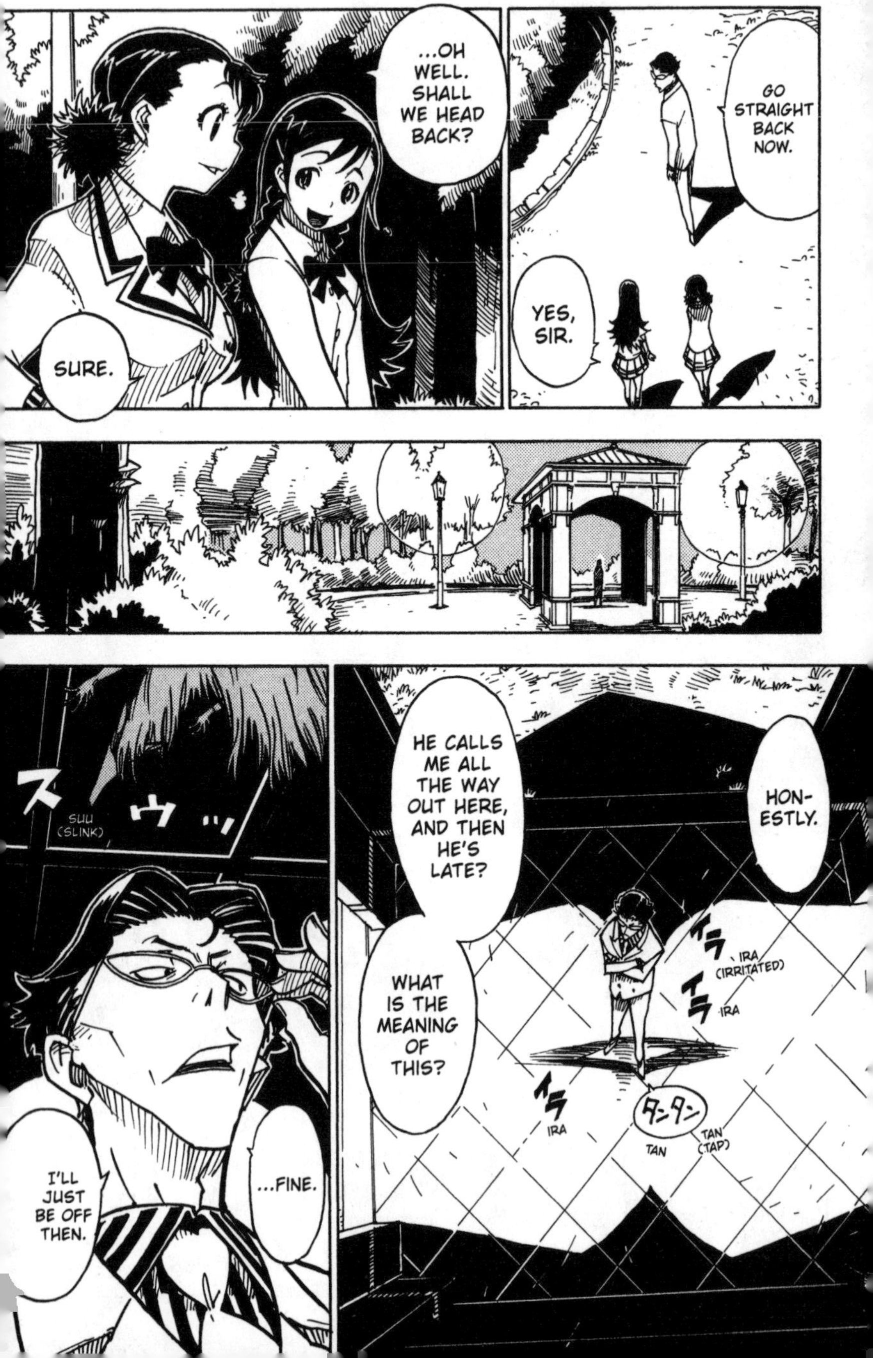
GO STRAIGHT BACK NOW.
YES, SIR.
...OH WELL. SHALL WE HEAD BACK?
SURE.
HON- ESTLY.
HE CALLS ME ALL THE WAY OUT HERE, AND THEN HE'S LATE?
WHAT IS THE MEANING OF THIS?
イラ IRA (IRRITATED)
イラ IRA
イラ IRA
タンタン TAN TAN (TAP)
スゥッ SUU (SLINK)
...FINE.
I'LL JUST BE OFF THEN.

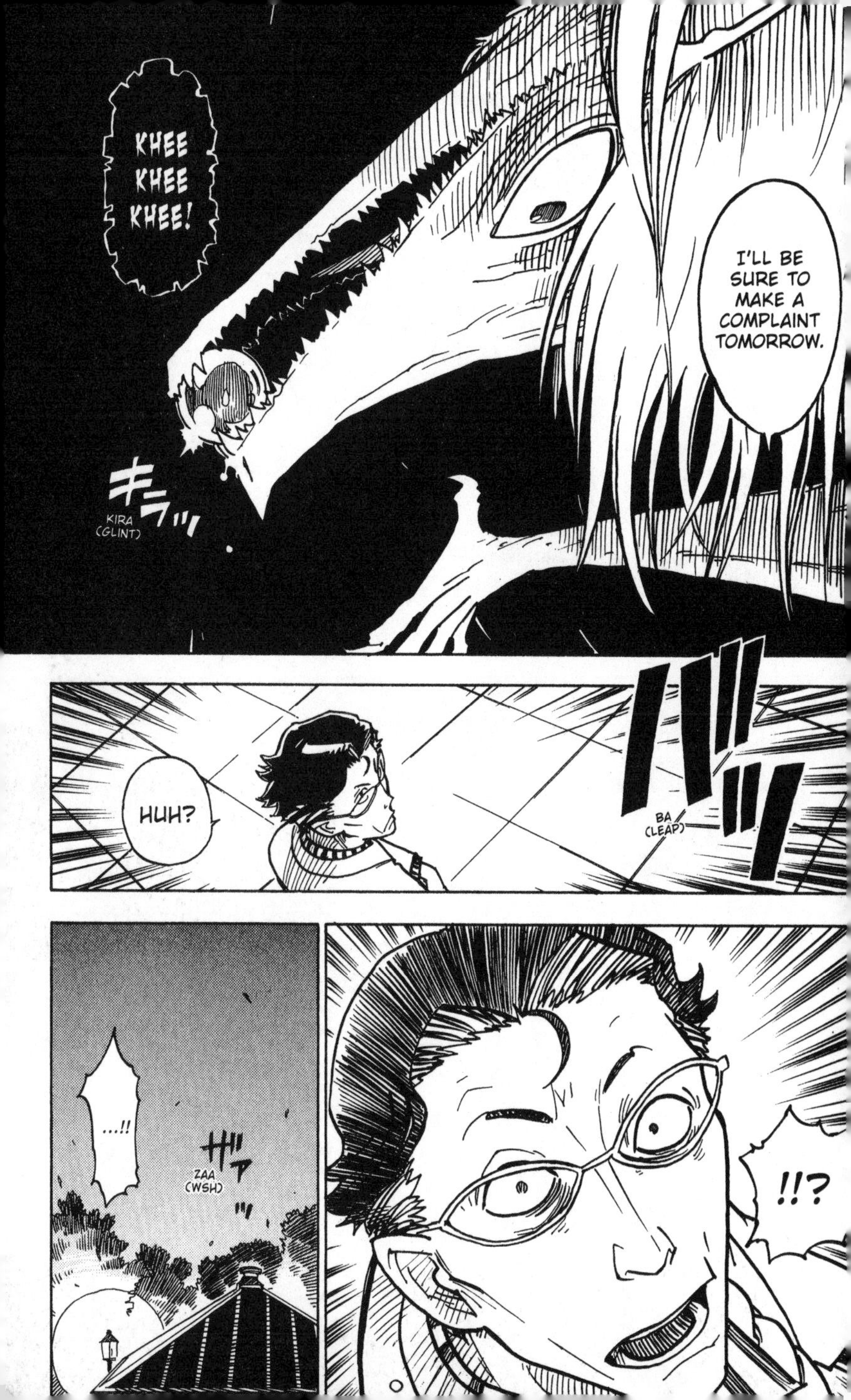
I'LL BE SURE TO MAKE A COMPLAINT TOMORROW.
KHEE KHEE KHEE!
キラッ
KIRA (GLINT)
バッ
BA (LEAP)
HUH?
!!?
...!!
ザァ
ZAA (WSH)

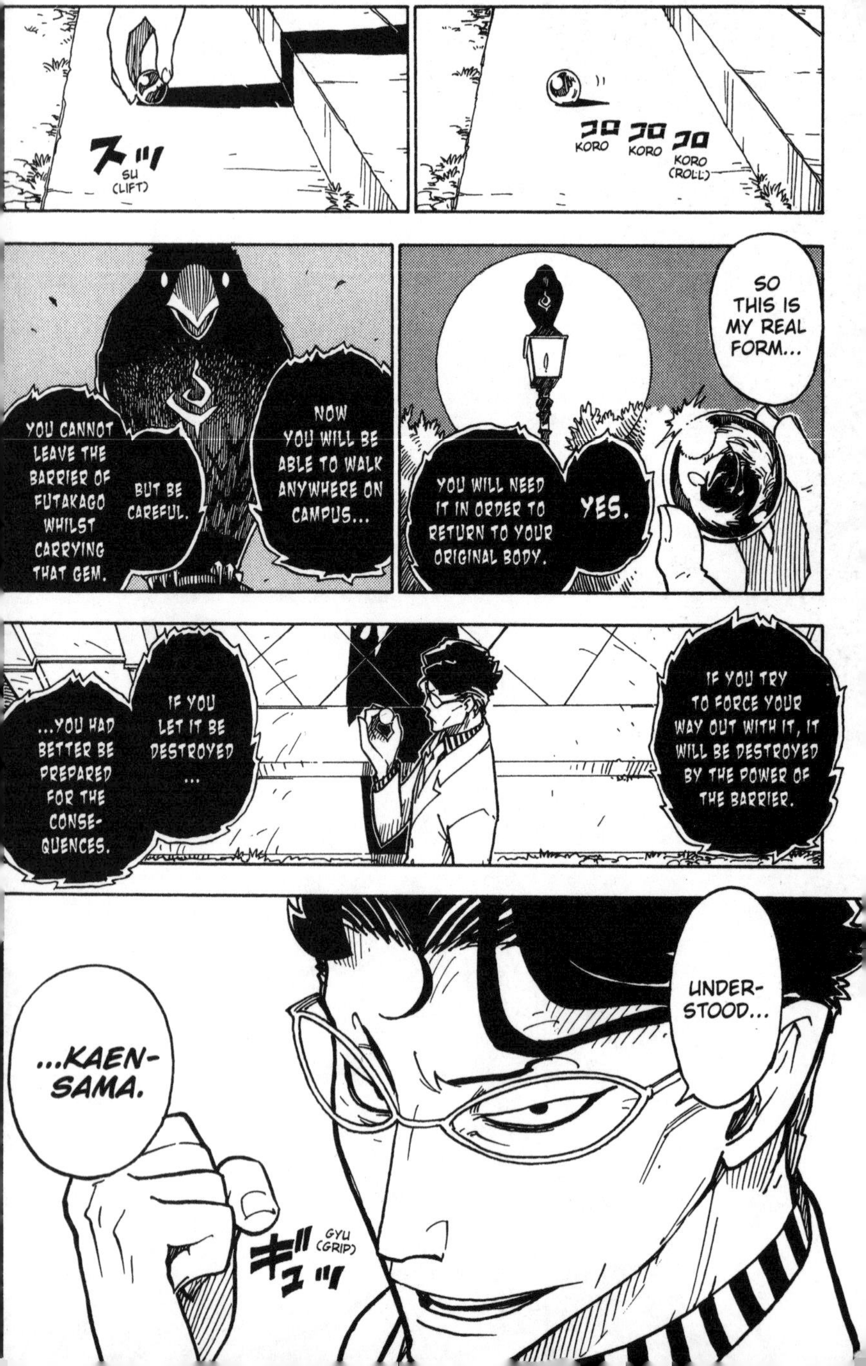
コロ KORO コロ KORO コロ KORO (ROLL)
スッ SU (LIFT)
SO THIS IS MY REAL FORM...
YES.
YOU WILL NEED IT IN ORDER TO RETURN TO YOUR ORIGINAL BODY.
NOW YOU WILL BE ABLE TO WALK ANYWHERE ON CAMPUS...
BUT BE CAREFUL.
YOU CANNOT LEAVE THE BARRIER OF FUTAKAGO WHILST CARRYING THAT GEM.
IF YOU TRY TO FORCE YOUR WAY OUT WITH IT, IT WILL BE DESTROYED BY THE POWER OF THE BARRIER.
IF YOU LET IT BE DESTROYED...
...YOU HAD BETTER BE PREPARED FOR THE CONSEQUENCES.
UNDER-STOOD...
...KAEN-SAMA.
ギュッ GYU (GRIP)

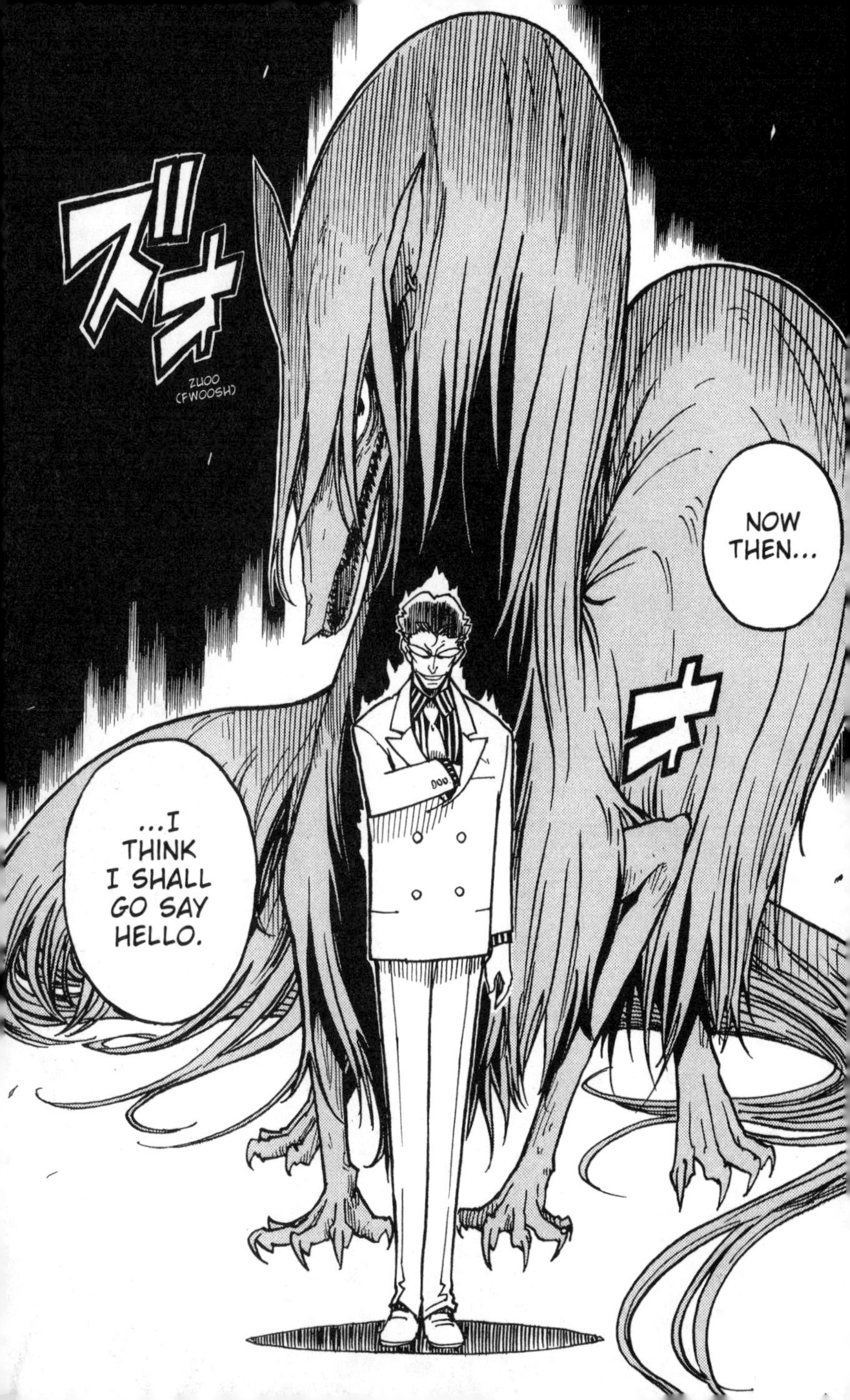
ズオ
ZUOO (FWOOSH)
NOW THEN...
...I THINK I SHALL GO SAY HELLO.

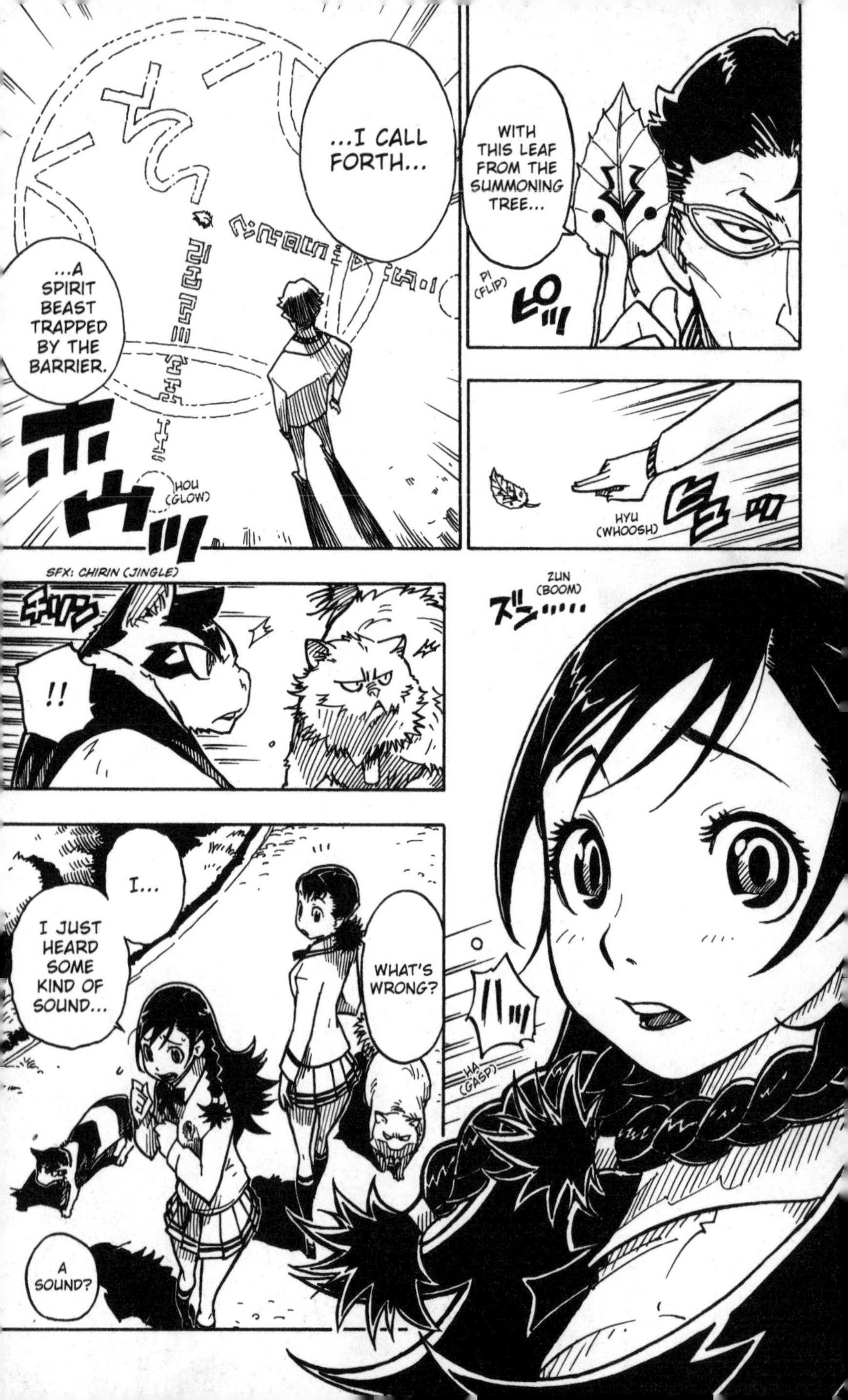
WITH THIS LEAF FROM THE SUMMONING TREE...
PI (FLIP)
HYU (WHOOSH)
...I CALL FORTH...
...A SPIRIT BEAST TRAPPED BY THE BARRIER.
HOU (GLOW)
ZUN (BOOM)
HA (GASP)
SFX: CHIRIN (JINGLE)
!!
WHAT'S WRONG?
I...
I JUST HEARD SOME KIND OF SOUND...
A SOUND?

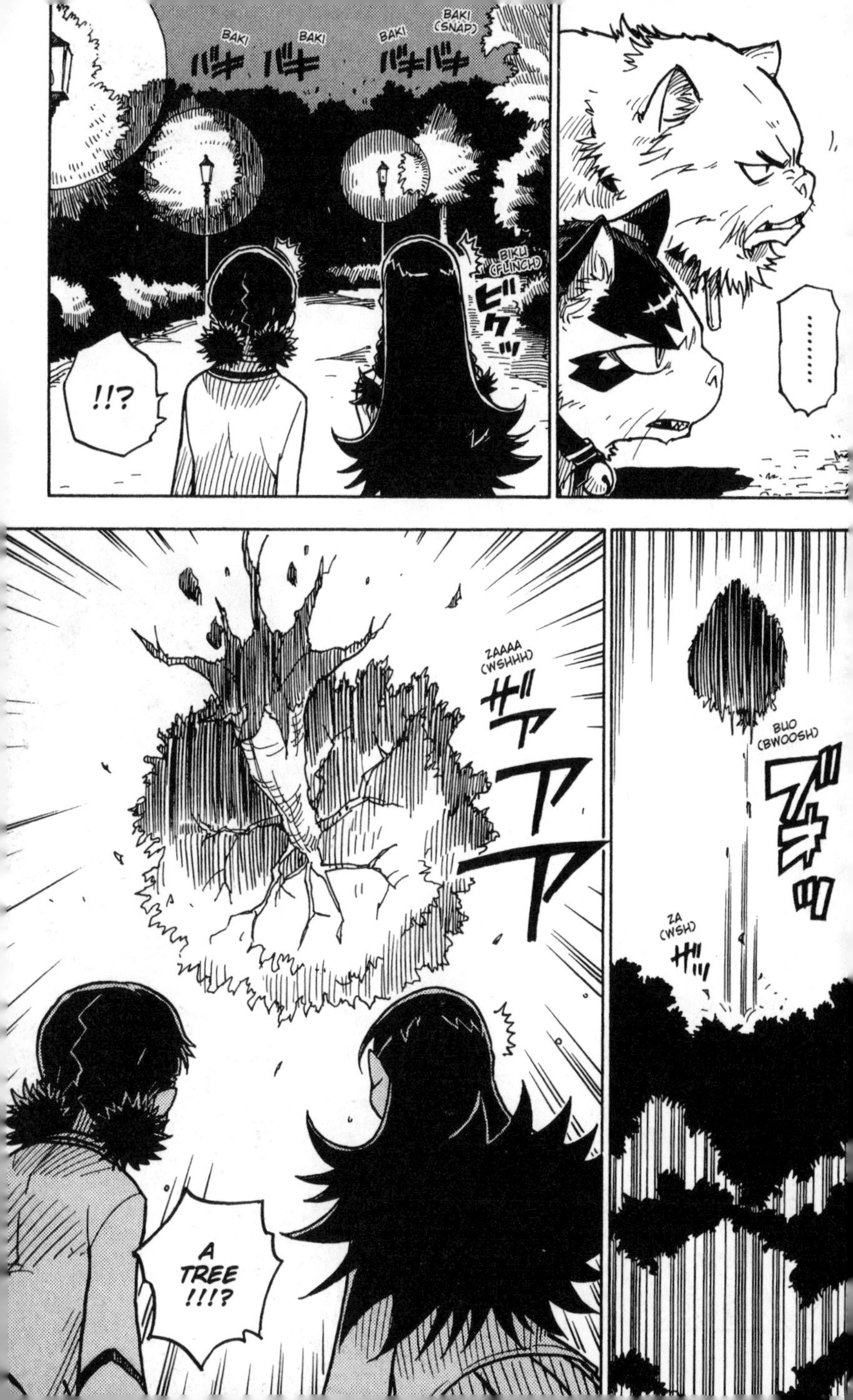
......
BAKI (SNAP)
BAKI
バキバキ
BAKI
バキ
BAKI
バキ
BIKU (FLINCH)
ビクッ
!!?
BUO (BWOOSH)
ブオッ
ZA (WSH)
ザッ
ZAAAA (WSHHH)
ザァアア
A TREE!!!?

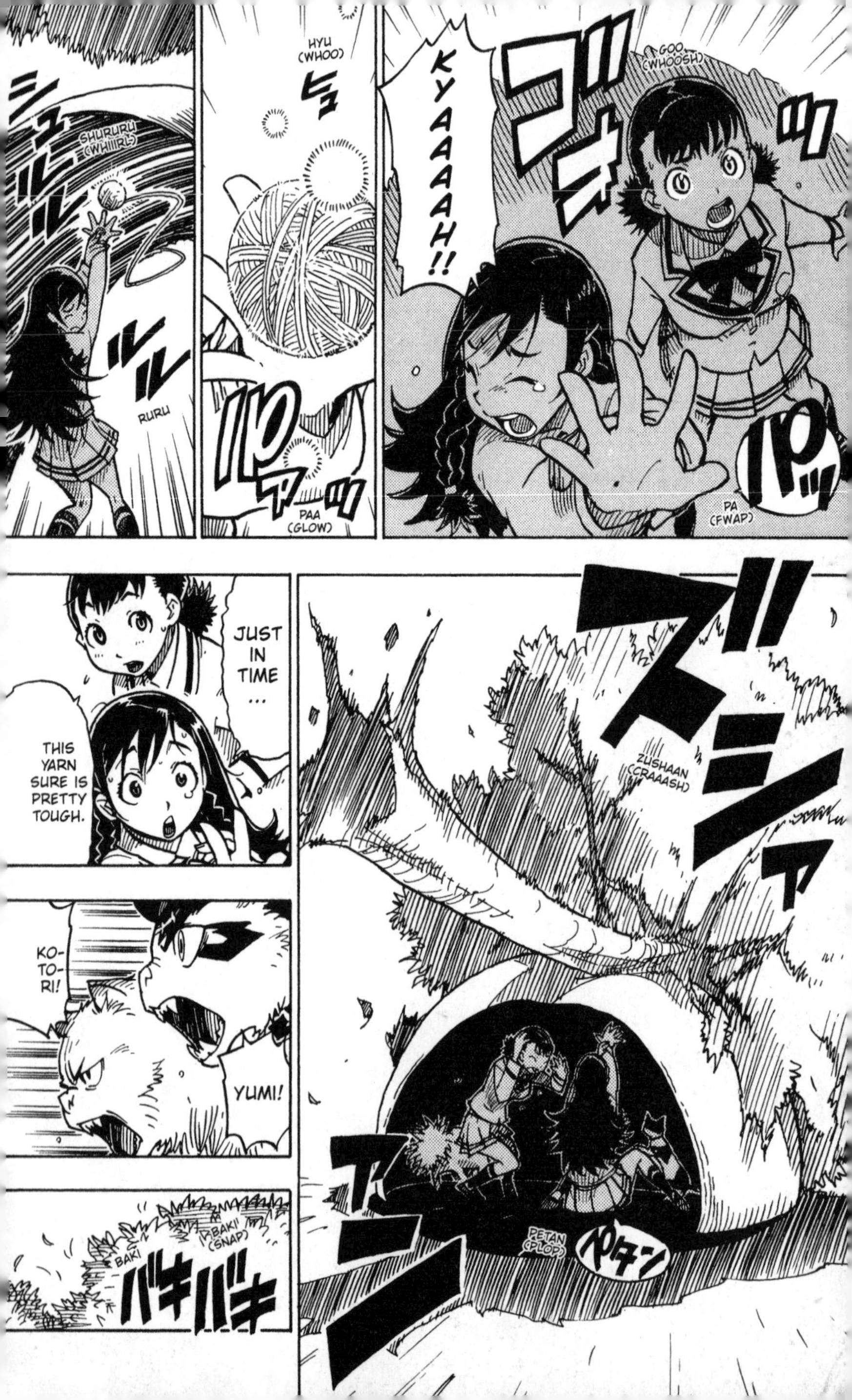
GOO (WHOOSH)
KYAAAAAH!!
PA (FWAP)
HYU (WHOO)
PAA (GLOW)
SHURURU (WHIRL)
RURU
ZUSHAAN (CRAAASH)
PETAN (PLOP)
JUST IN TIME...
THIS YARN SURE IS PRETTY TOUGH.
KO-TO-RI!
YUMI!
BAKI (SNAP)
BAKI

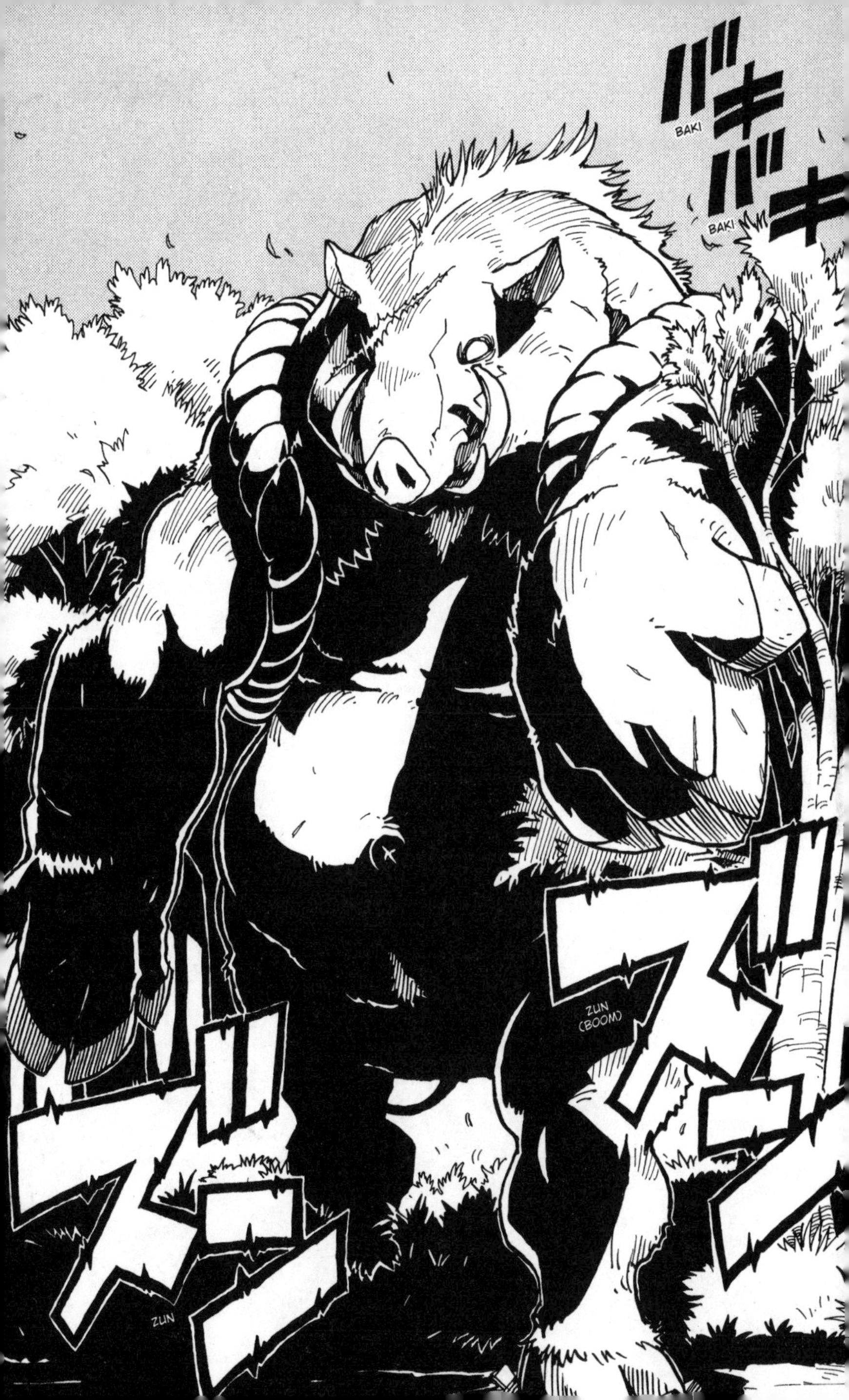
バキバキ
BAKI
BAKI
ズン
ZUN
(BOOM)
ズン
ZUN

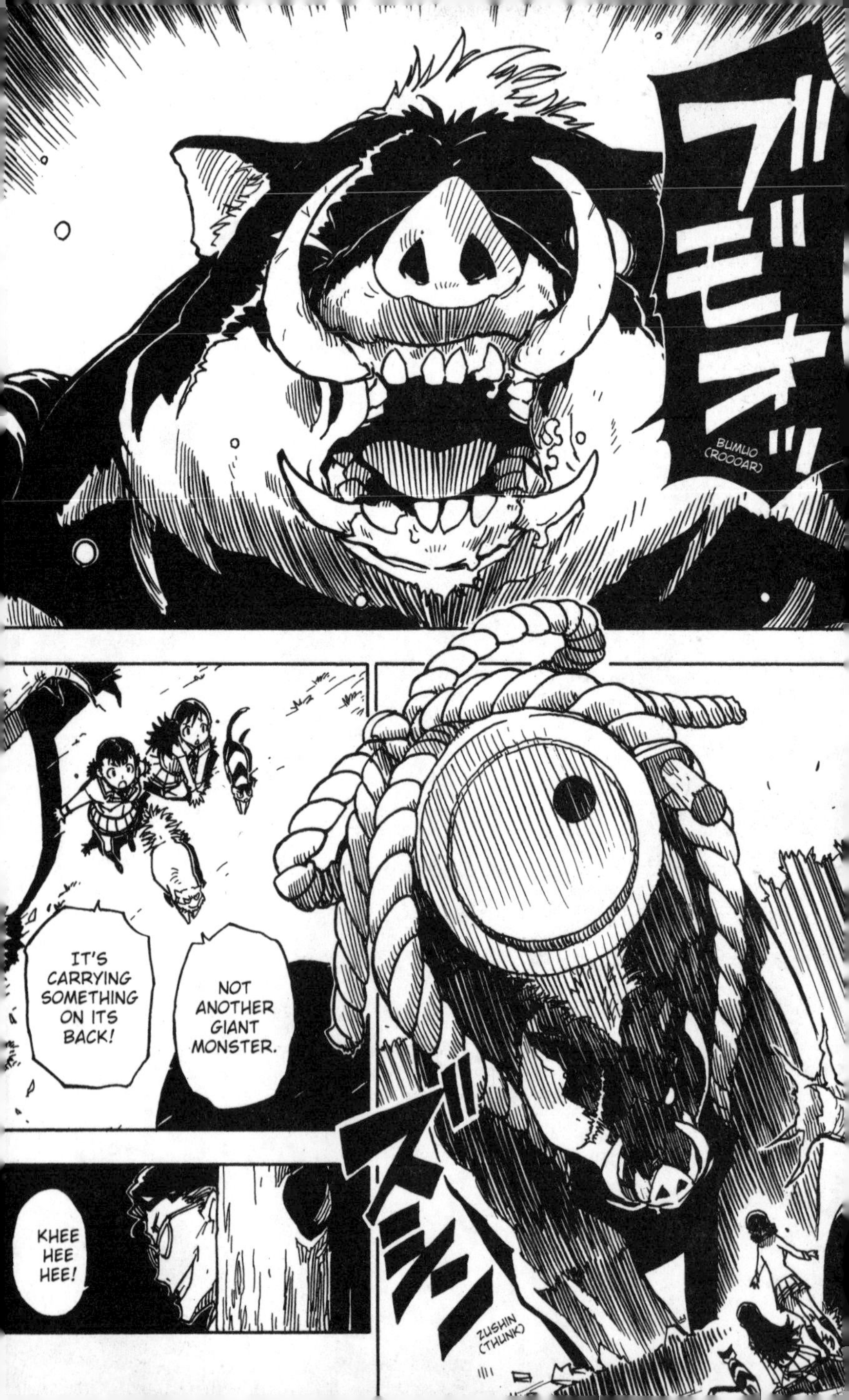
ブモオッ
BUMUO (ROOOAR)
ズシン
ZUSHIN (THUNK)
NOT ANOTHER GIANT MONSTER.
IT'S CARRYING SOMETHING ON ITS BACK!
KHEE HEE HEE!

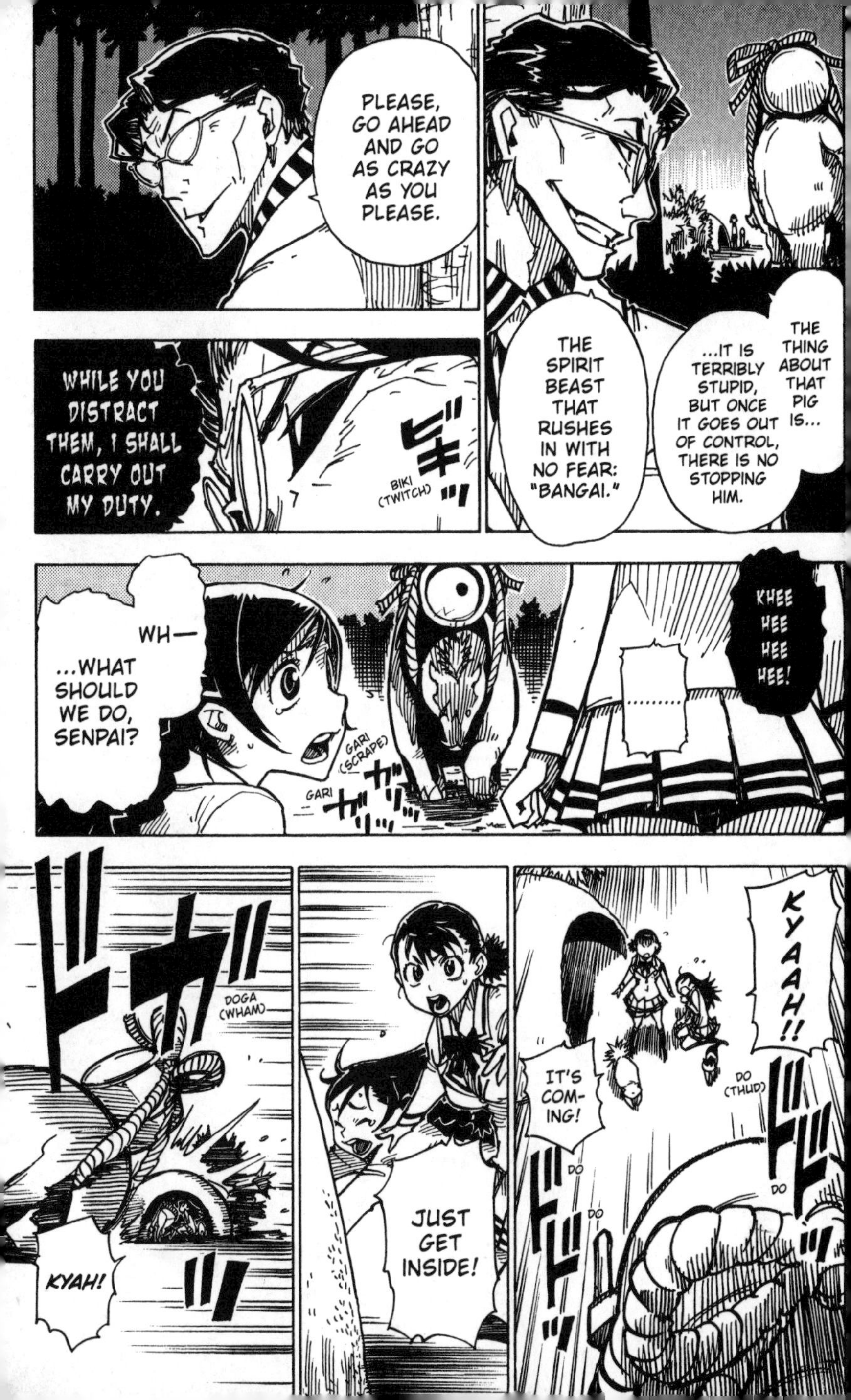
THE THING ABOUT THAT PIG IS...
...IT IS TERRIBLY STUPID, BUT ONCE IT GOES OUT OF CONTROL, THERE IS NO STOPPING HIM.
THE SPIRIT BEAST THAT RUSHES IN WITH NO FEAR: "BANGAI."
PLEASE, GO AHEAD AND GO AS CRAZY AS YOU PLEASE.
BIKI (TWITCH)
WHILE YOU DISTRACT THEM, I SHALL CARRY OUT MY DUTY.
KHEE HEE HEE HEE!
....
GARI (SCRAPE)
GARI
WH—
...WHAT SHOULD WE DO, SENPAI?
KYAAH!!
DO (THUD)
IT'S COMING!
DO
DO
DO
JUST GET INSIDE!
DOGA (WHAM)
KYAH!

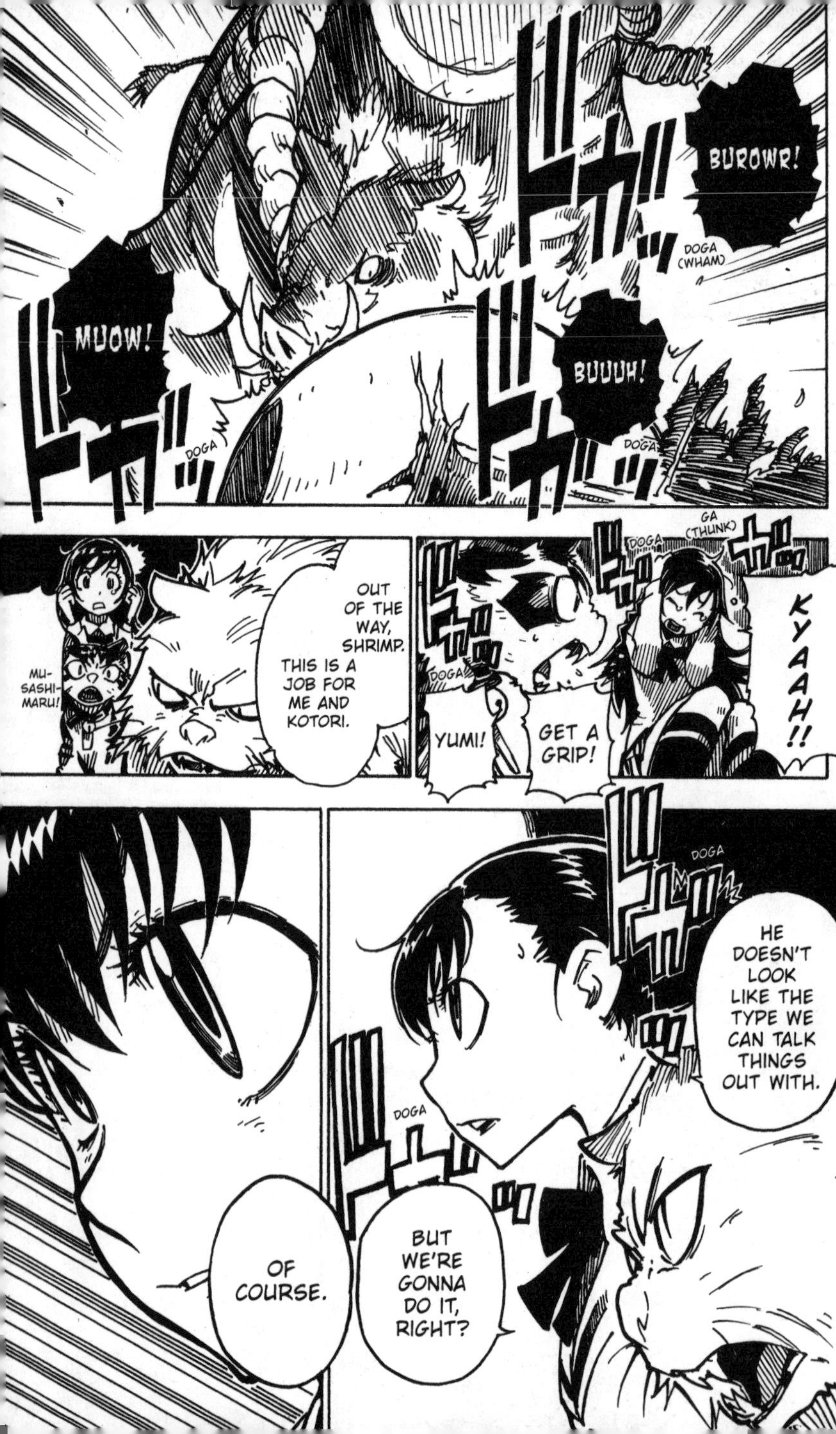
BUROWR!
DOGA (WHAM)
BUUUH!
DOGA
MUOW!
DOGA
GA (THUNK)
DOGA
KYAAAH!!
GET A GRIP!
YUMI!
DOGA
OUT OF THE WAY, SHRIMP.
THIS IS A JOB FOR ME AND KOTORI.
MU-SASHI-MARU!
DOGA
HE DOESN'T LOOK LIKE THE TYPE WE CAN TALK THINGS OUT WITH.
DOGA
BUT WE'RE GONNA DO IT, RIGHT?
OF COURSE.

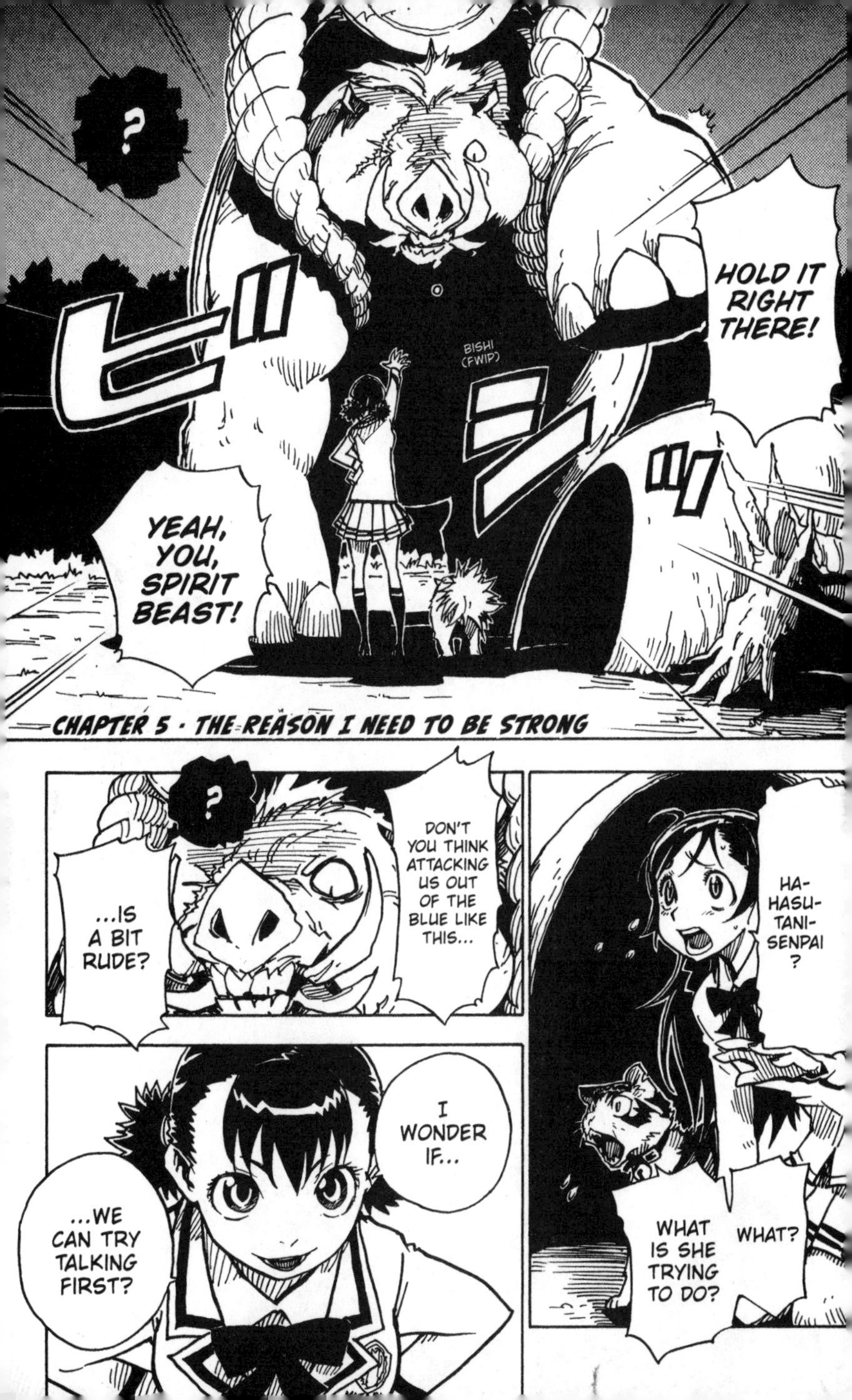

HOLD IT RIGHT THERE!
?
BISHI (FWIP)
YEAH, YOU, SPIRIT BEAST!
CHAPTER 5 · THE REASON I NEED TO BE STRONG
HA-HASUTANI-SENPAI?
WHAT?
WHAT IS SHE TRYING TO DO?
?
DON'T YOU THINK ATTACKING US OUT OF THE BLUE LIKE THIS...
...IS A BIT RUDE?
I WONDER IF...
...WE CAN TRY TALKING FIRST?

CHAPTER 5
THE REASON I NEED TO BE STRONG

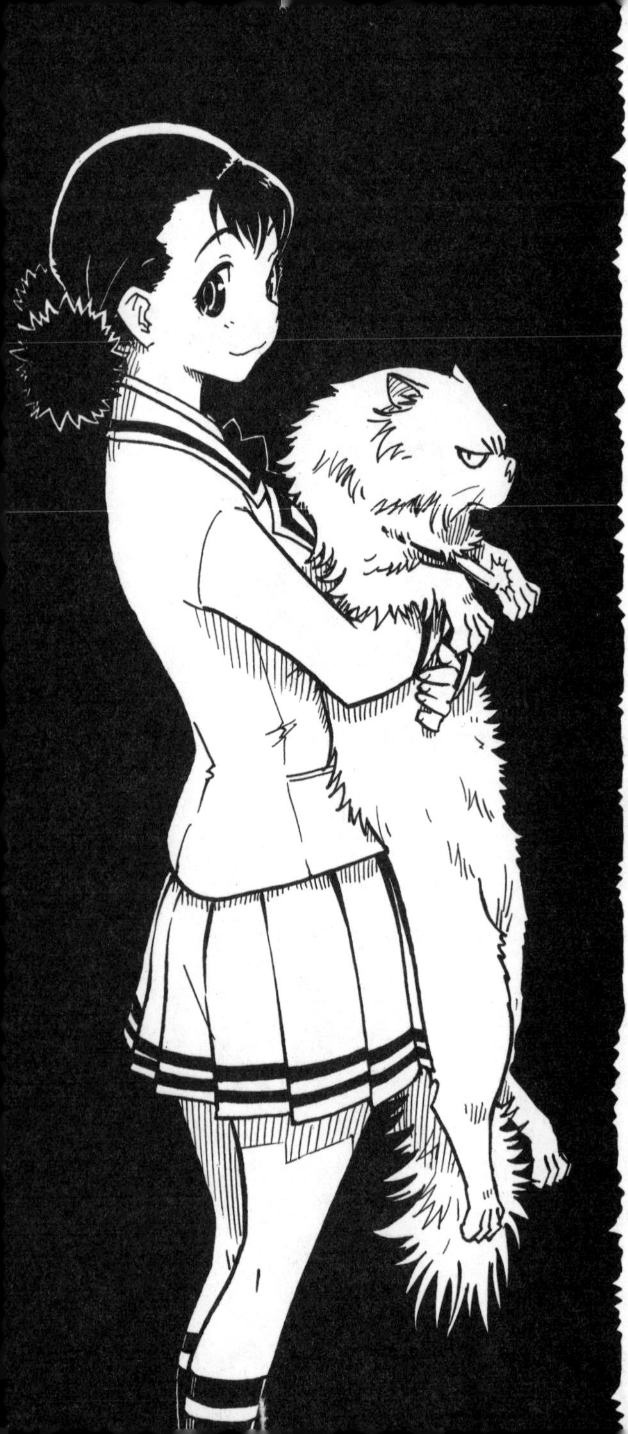

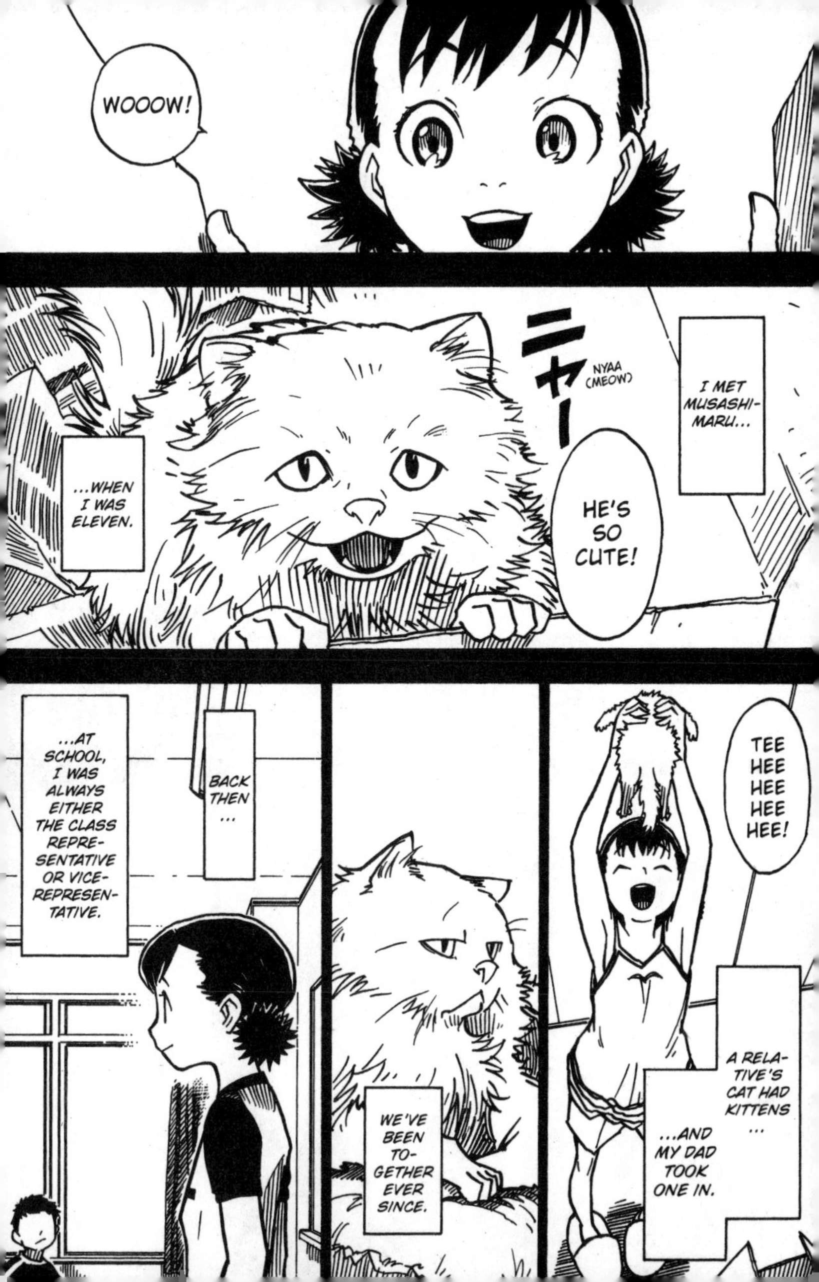
WOOOW!
I MET MUSASHI-MARU...
ニャー
NYAA (MEOW)
HE'S SO CUTE!
...WHEN I WAS ELEVEN.
TEE HEE HEE HEE HEE!
A RELATIVE'S CAT HAD KITTENS...
...AND MY DAD TOOK ONE IN.
WE'VE BEEN TOGETHER EVER SINCE.
BACK THEN...
...AT SCHOOL, I WAS ALWAYS EITHER THE CLASS REPRESENTATIVE OR VICE-REPRESENTATIVE.

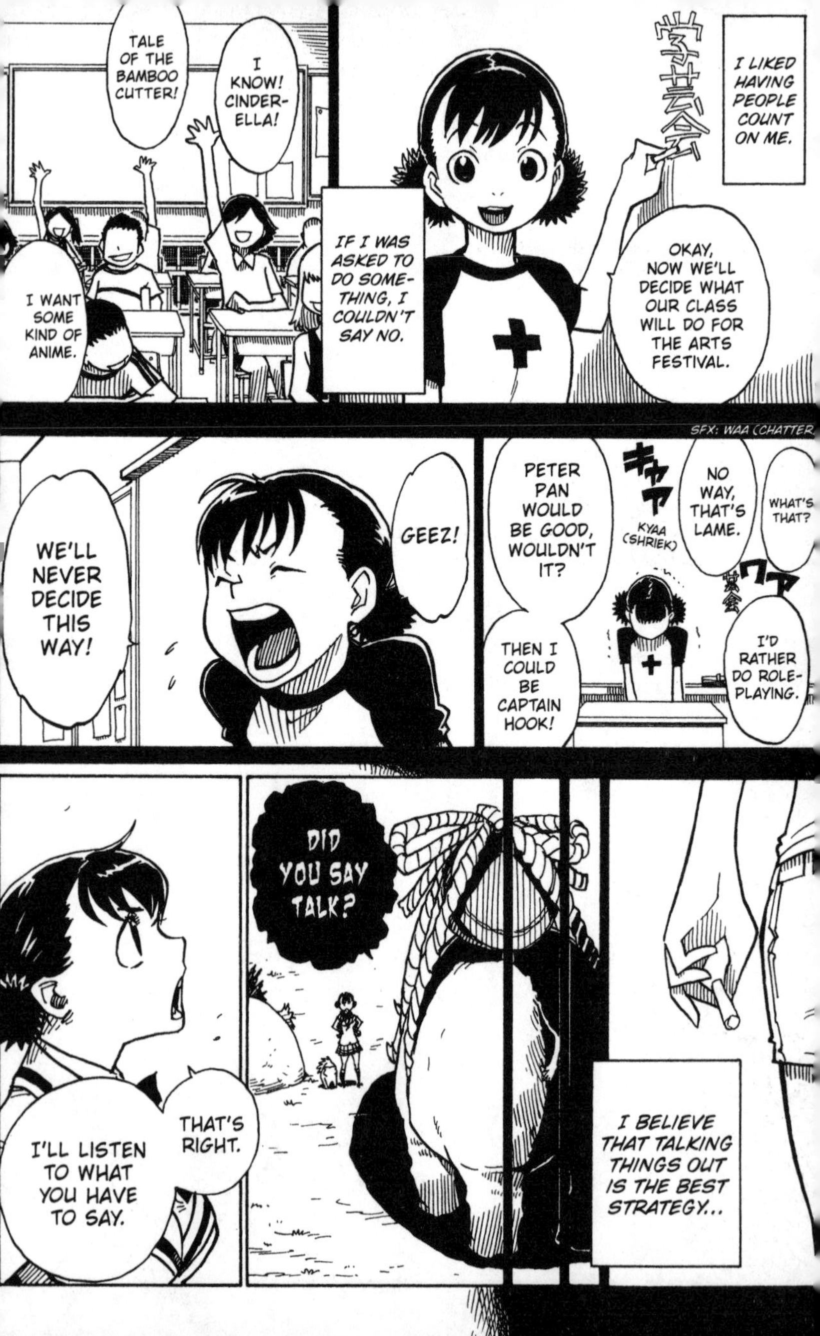
I LIKED HAVING PEOPLE COUNT ON ME.
OKAY, NOW WE'LL DECIDE WHAT OUR CLASS WILL DO FOR THE ARTS FESTIVAL.
IF I WAS ASKED TO DO SOME-THING, I COULDN'T SAY NO.
I KNOW! CINDER-ELLA!
TALE OF THE BAMBOO CUTTER!
I WANT SOME KIND OF ANIME.
SFX: WAA (CHATTER)
WHAT'S THAT?
NO WAY, THAT'S LAME.
KYAA (SHRIEK)
PETER PAN WOULD BE GOOD, WOULDN'T IT?
I'D RATHER DO ROLE-PLAYING.
THEN I COULD BE CAPTAIN HOOK!
GEEZ!
WE'LL NEVER DECIDE THIS WAY!
I BELIEVE THAT TALKING THINGS OUT IS THE BEST STRATEGY...
DID YOU SAY TALK?
THAT'S RIGHT.
I'LL LISTEN TO WHAT YOU HAVE TO SAY.

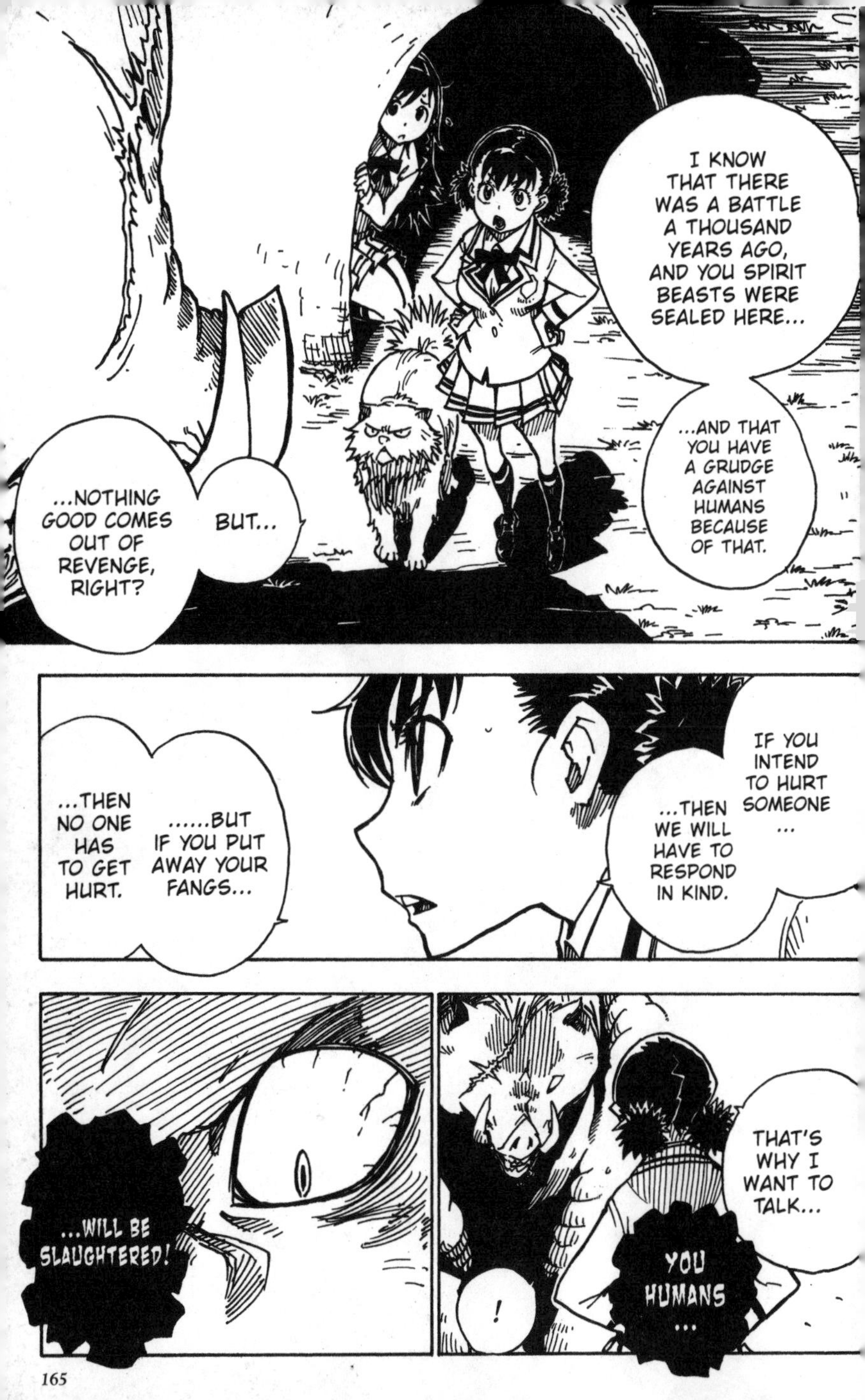
I KNOW THAT THERE WAS A BATTLE A THOUSAND YEARS AGO, AND YOU SPIRIT BEASTS WERE SEALED HERE...
...AND THAT YOU HAVE A GRUDGE AGAINST HUMANS BECAUSE OF THAT.
BUT...
...NOTHING GOOD COMES OUT OF REVENGE, RIGHT?
IF YOU INTEND TO HURT SOMEONE...
...THEN WE WILL HAVE TO RESPOND IN KIND.
......BUT IF YOU PUT AWAY YOUR FANGS...
...THEN NO ONE HAS TO GET HURT.
THAT'S WHY I WANT TO TALK...
YOU HUMANS...
!
...WILL BE SLAUGHTERED!

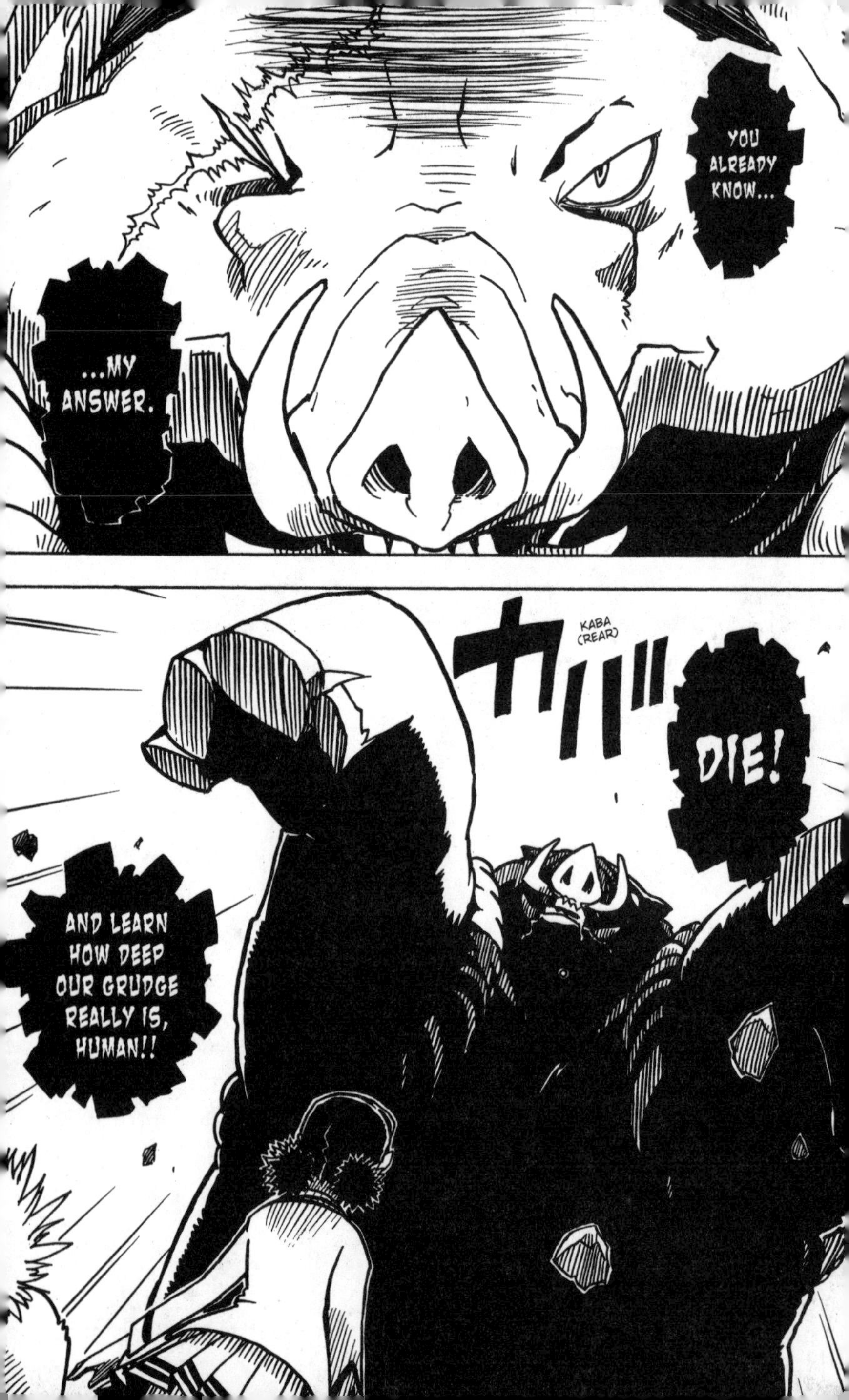
YOU ALREADY KNOW...
...MY ANSWER.
カバ
KABA (REAR)
DIE!
AND LEARN HOW DEEP OUR GRUDGE REALLY IS, HUMAN!!

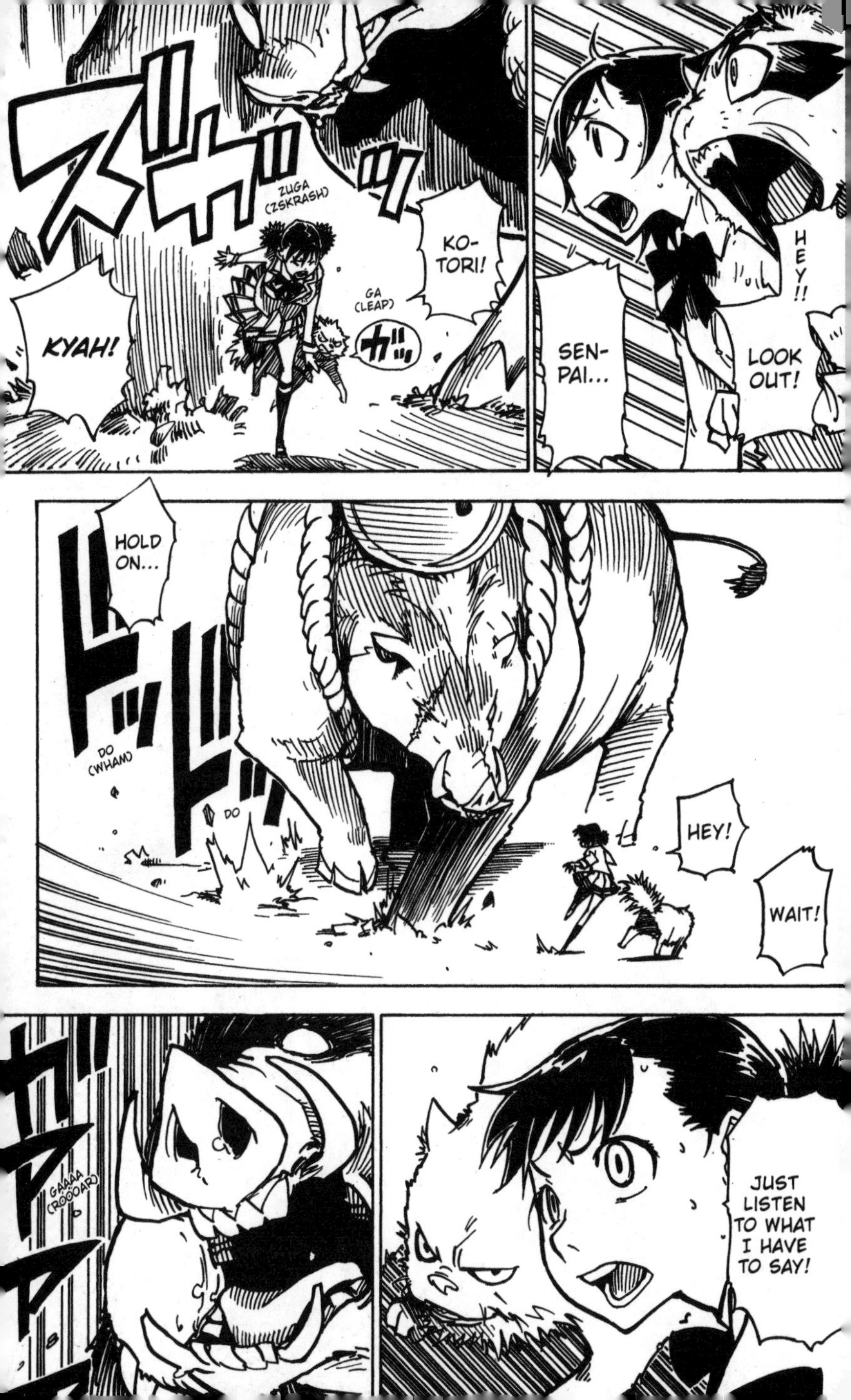
HEY!!
LOOK OUT!
SEN-PAI...
ZUGA (ZSKRASH)
KO-TORI!
GA (LEAP)
KYAH!
HEY!
WAIT!
HOLD ON...
DO (WHAM)
DO
JUST LISTEN TO WHAT I HAVE TO SAY!
GAAAA (ROOOAR)

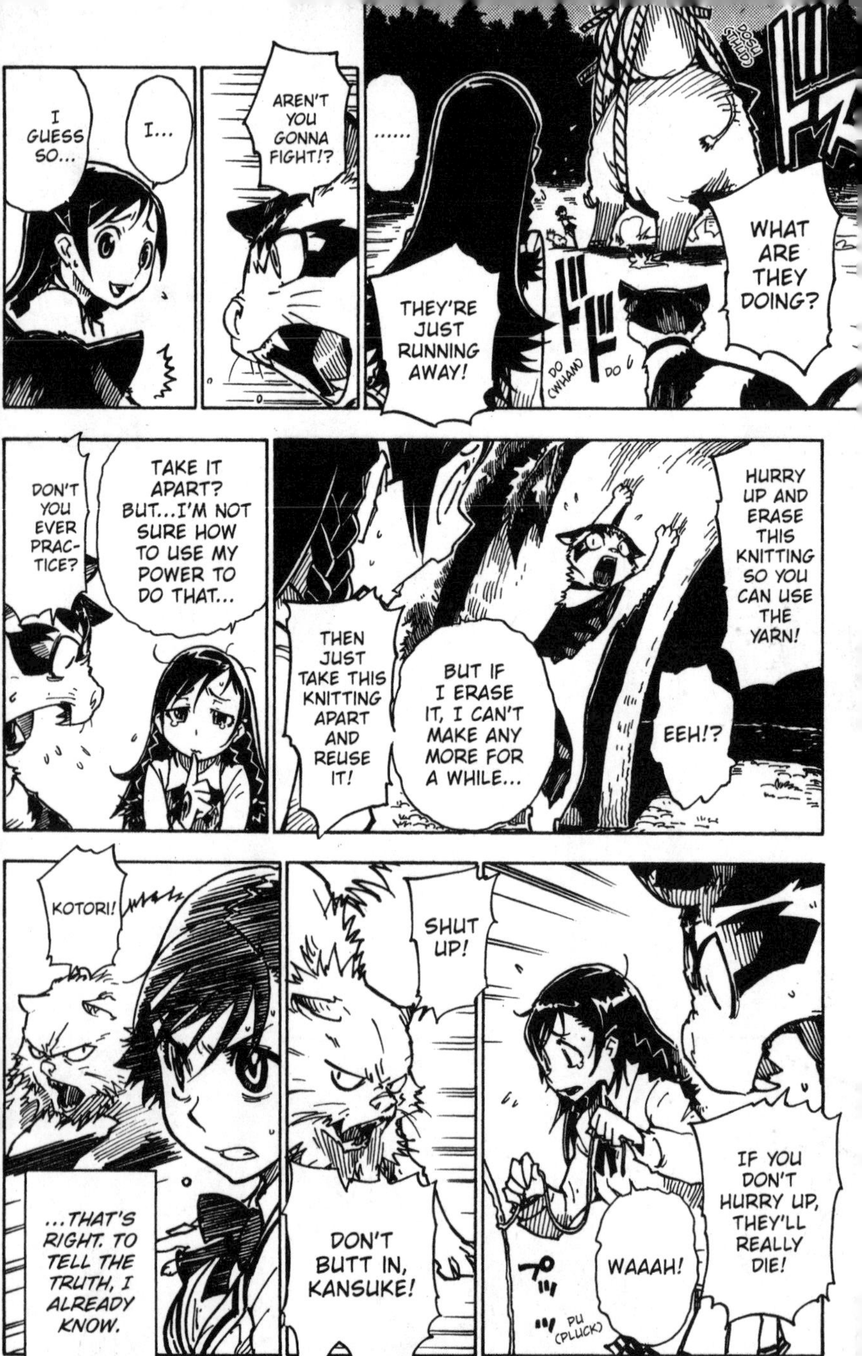
DOSU (THUD)
WHAT ARE THEY DOING?
DO (WHAM) DO
......
THEY'RE JUST RUNNING AWAY!
AREN'T YOU GONNA FIGHT!?
I...
I GUESS SO...
HURRY UP AND ERASE THIS KNITTING SO YOU CAN USE THE YARN!
EEH!?
BUT IF I ERASE IT, I CAN'T MAKE ANY MORE FOR A WHILE...
THEN JUST TAKE THIS KNITTING APART AND REUSE IT!
TAKE IT APART? BUT...I'M NOT SURE HOW TO USE MY POWER TO DO THAT...
DON'T YOU EVER PRAC-TICE?
IF YOU DON'T HURRY UP, THEY'LL REALLY DIE!
WAAAH!
PU (PLUCK)
SHUT UP!
DON'T BUTT IN, KANSUKE!
KOTORI!
...THAT'S RIGHT. TO TELL THE TRUTH, I ALREADY KNOW.

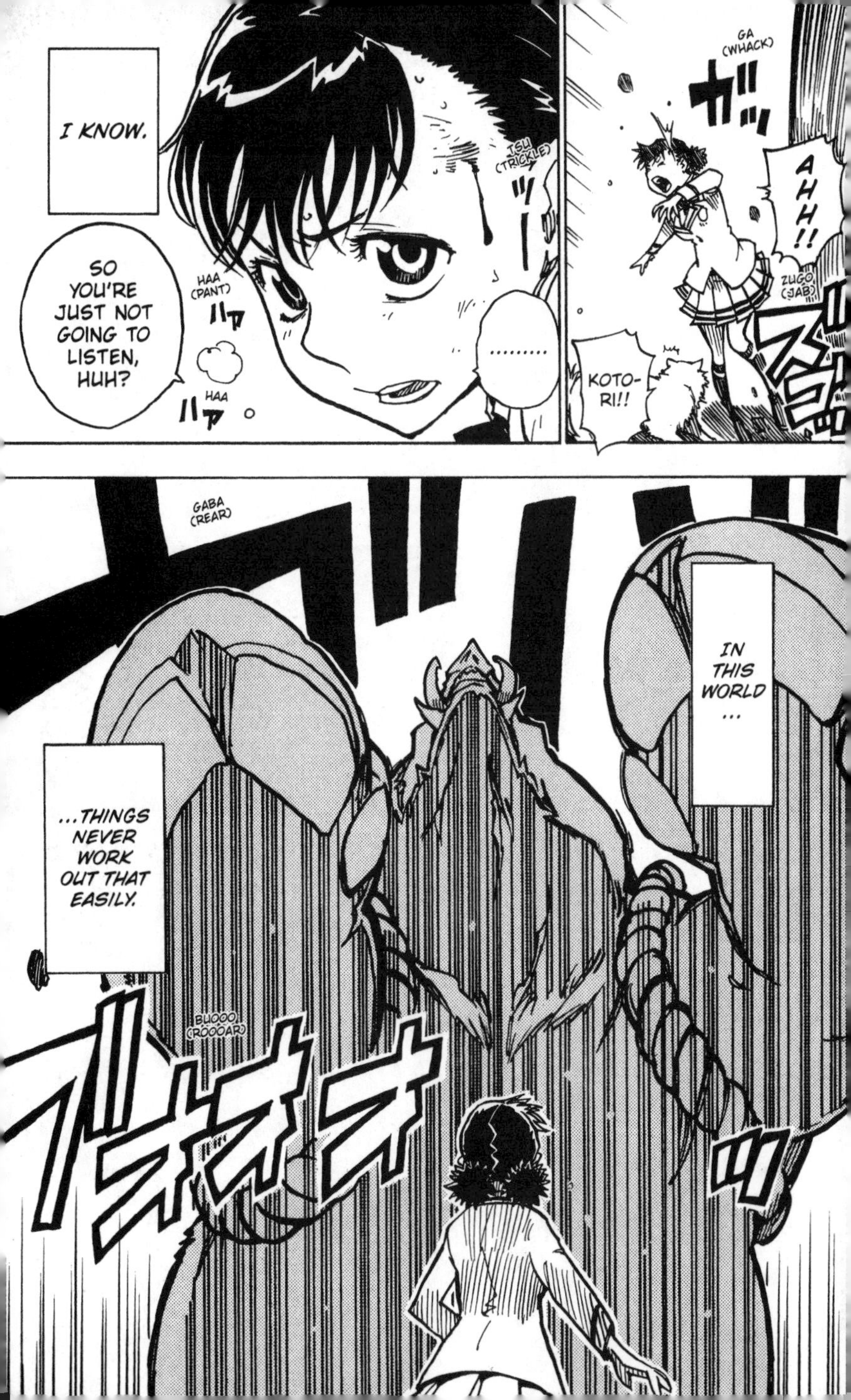
GA (WHACK)
AHH!!
ZUGO (JAB)
KOTO-RI!!
TSU (TRICKLE)
I KNOW.
....
HAA (PANT)
SO YOU'RE JUST NOT GOING TO LISTEN, HUH?
HAA
GABA (REAR)
IN THIS WORLD...
...THINGS NEVER WORK OUT THAT EASILY.
BUOOO (ROOOAR)

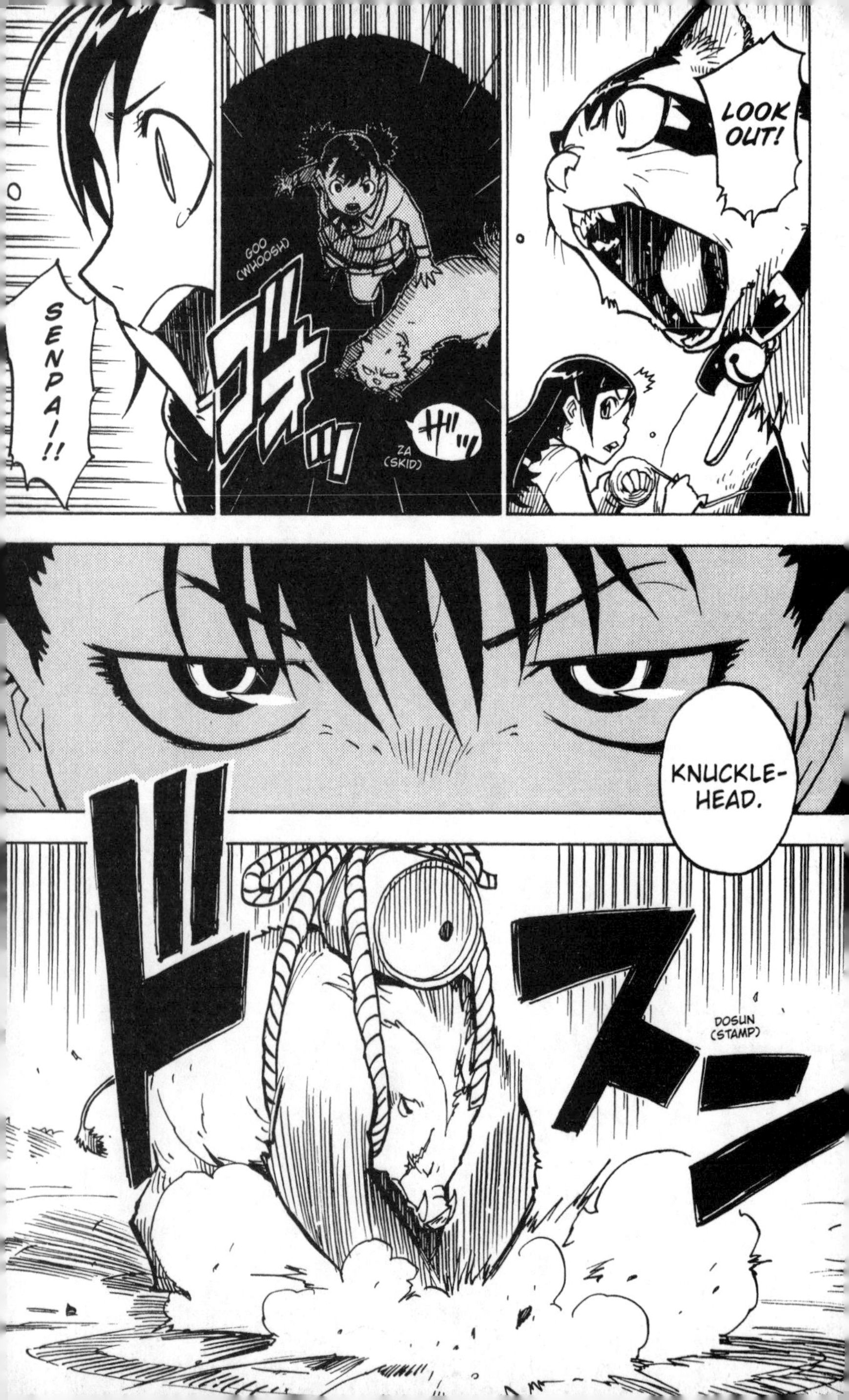
LOOK OUT!
GOO (WHOOSH)
ZA (SKID)
SENPAI!!
KNUCKLE-HEAD.
DOSUN (STAMP)

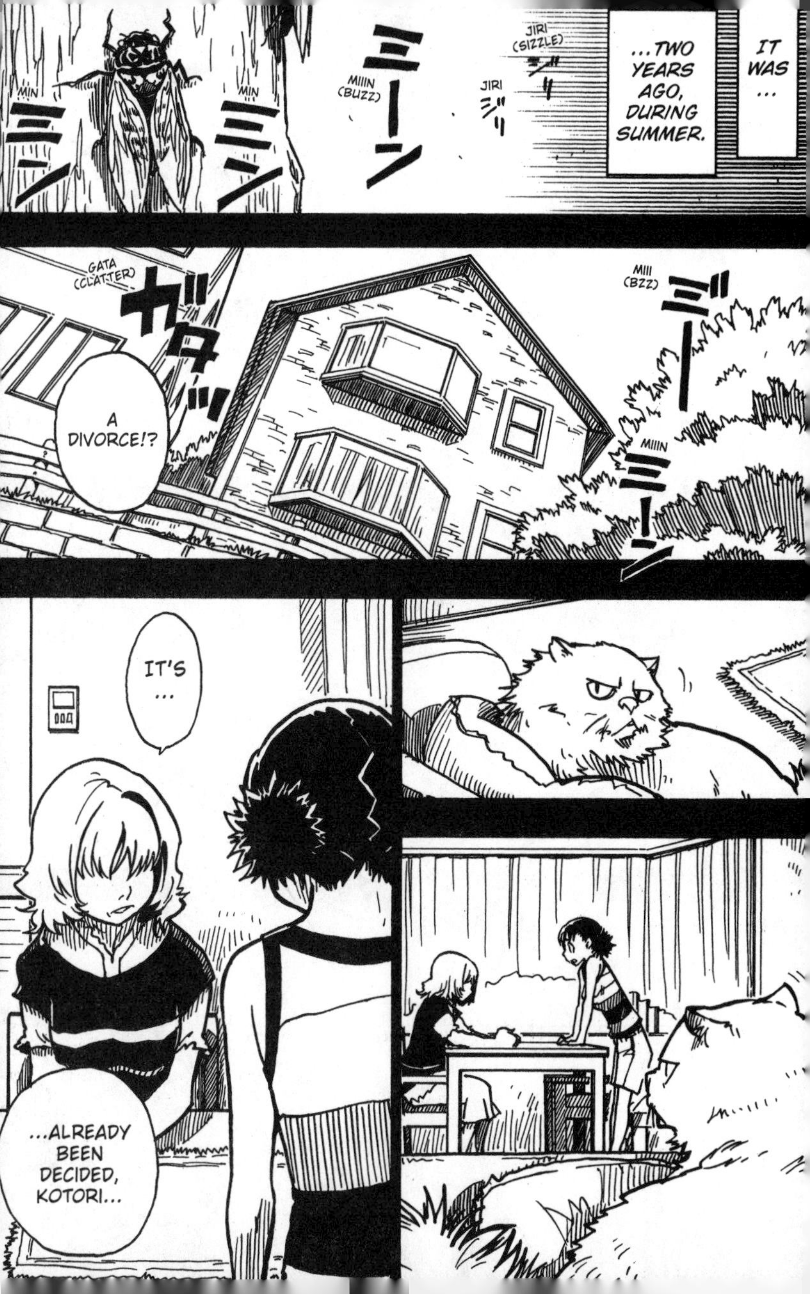
IT WAS...
...TWO YEARS AGO, DURING SUMMER.
JIRI (SIZZLE)
JIRI
MIIIN (BUZZ)
MIN
MIN
MIII (BZZ)
MIIIN
GATA (CLATTER)
A DIVORCE!?
IT'S...
...ALREADY BEEN DECIDED, KOTORI...

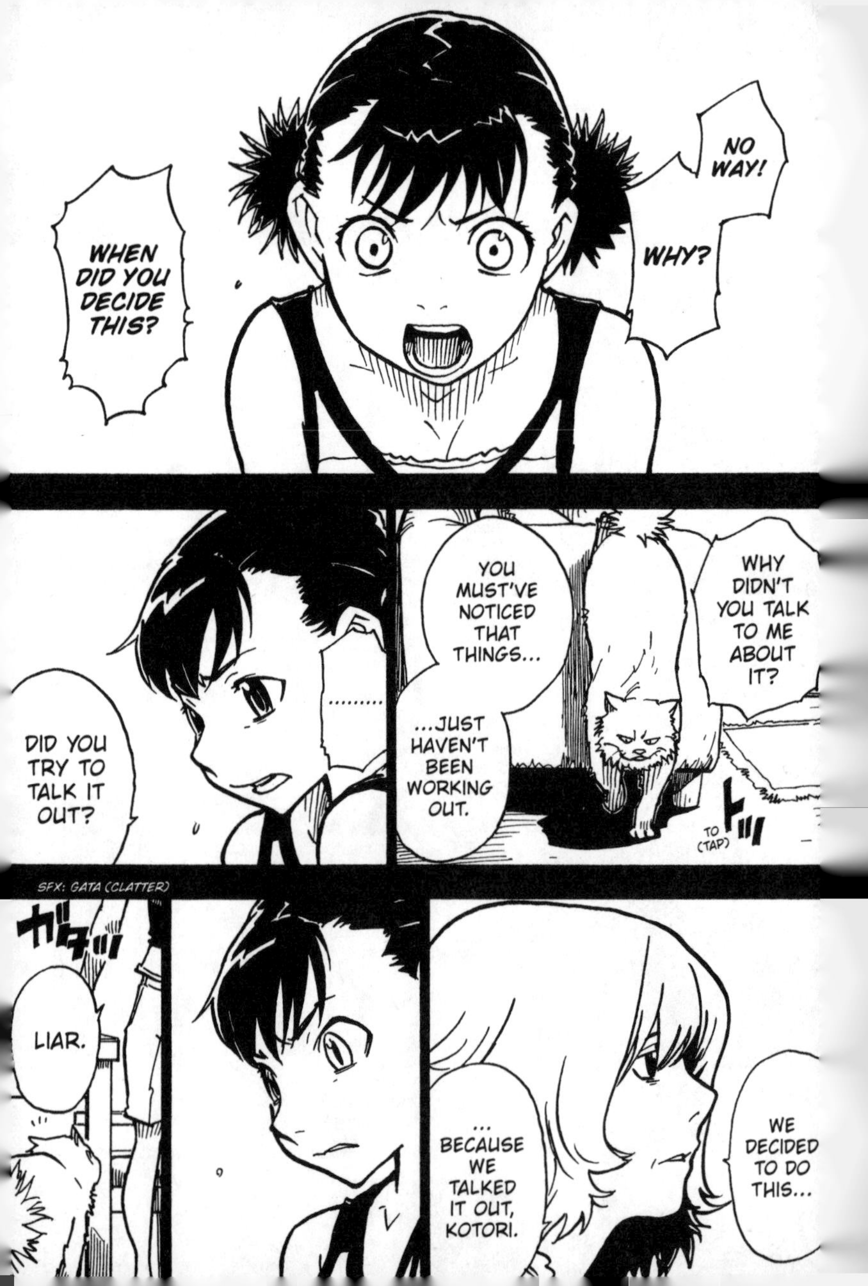
NO WAY!
WHY?
WHEN DID YOU DECIDE THIS?
WHY DIDN'T YOU TALK TO ME ABOUT IT?
YOU MUST'VE NOTICED THAT THINGS...
...JUST HAVEN'T BEEN WORKING OUT.
TO (TAP)
....
DID YOU TRY TO TALK IT OUT?
WE DECIDED TO DO THIS...
...BECAUSE WE TALKED IT OUT, KOTORI.
LIAR.
SFX: GATA (CLATTER)

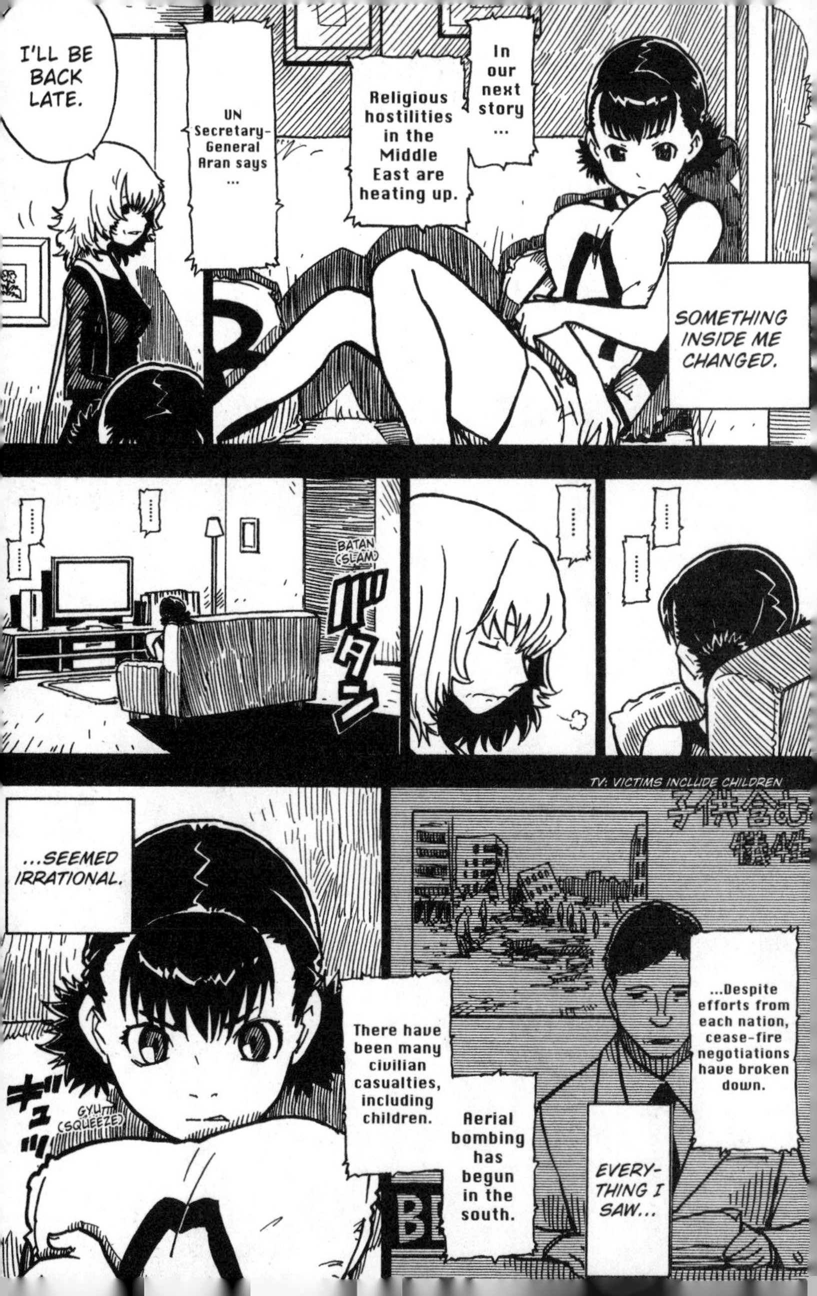

In our next story ...
Religious hostilities in the Middle East are heating up.
UN Secretary-General Aran says ...
I'LL BE BACK LATE.
SOMETHING INSIDE ME CHANGED.
......
......
......
......
......
BATAN (SLAM)
TV: VICTIMS INCLUDE CHILDREN
...Despite efforts from each nation, cease-fire negotiations have broken down.
EVERY-THING I SAW...
Aerial bombing has begun in the south.
There have been many civilian casualties, including children.
...SEEMED IRRATIONAL.
GYU (SQUEEZE)

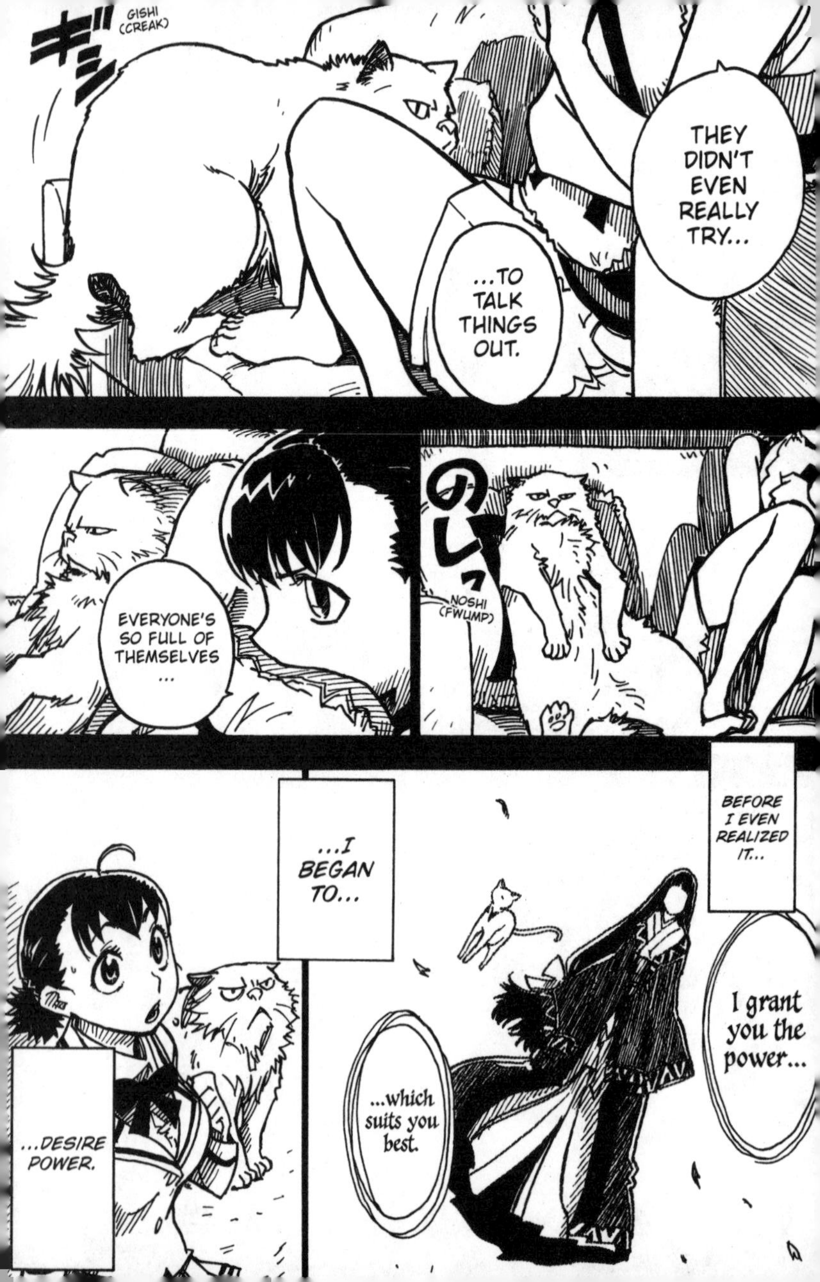
THEY DIDN'T EVEN REALLY TRY...
...TO TALK THINGS OUT.
ギシ
GISHI (CREAK)
のしっ
NOSHI (FWUMP)
EVERYONE'S SO FULL OF THEMSELVES ...
BEFORE I EVEN REALIZED IT...
I grant you the power...
...which suits you best.
...I BEGAN TO...
...DESIRE POWER.

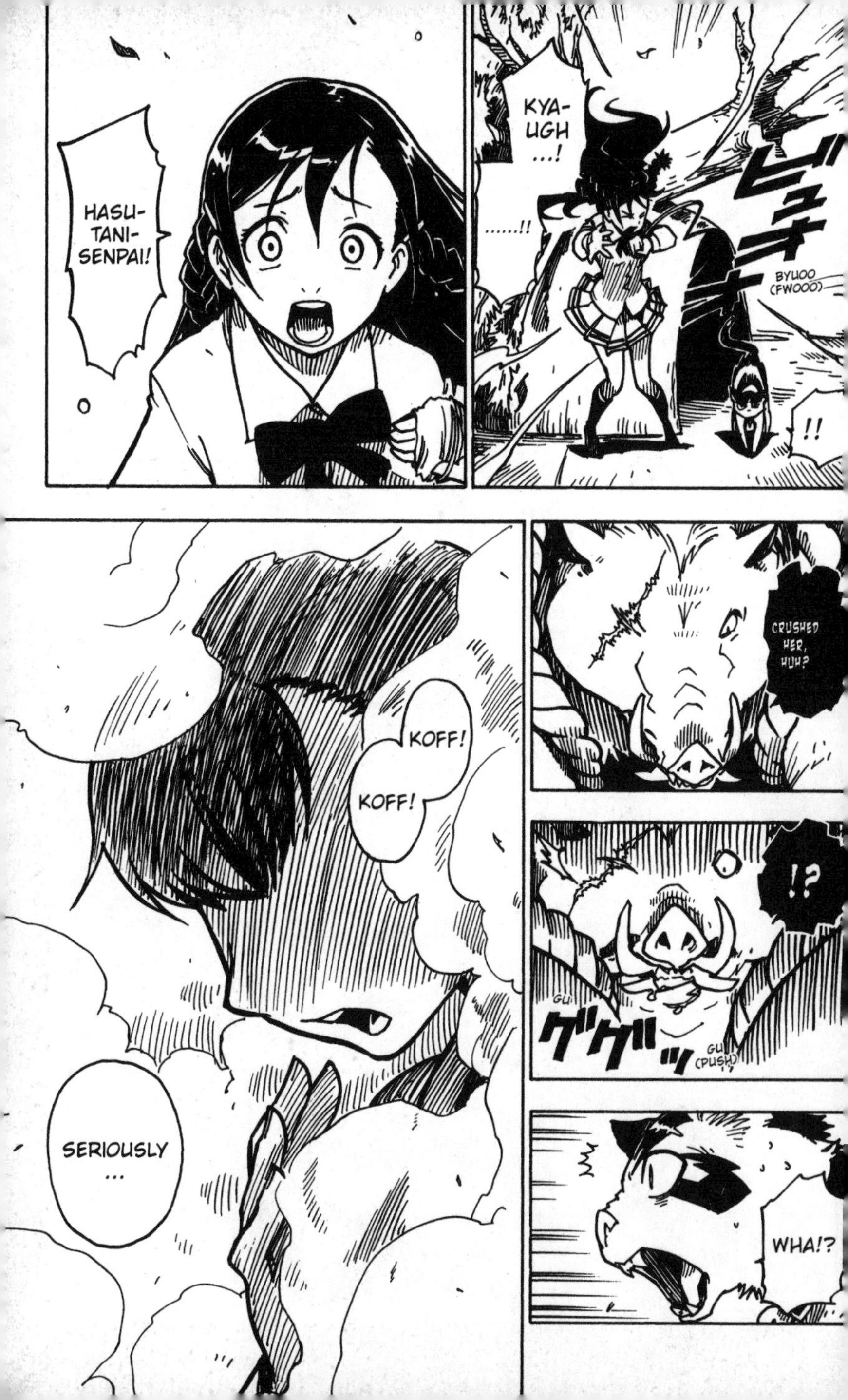
KYA-UGH ...!
......!!
BYUOO (FWOOO)
!!
HASU-TANI-SENPAI!
CRUSHED HER, HUH?
!?
GU
GU (PUSH)
WHA!?
KOFF!
KOFF!
SERIOUSLY ...

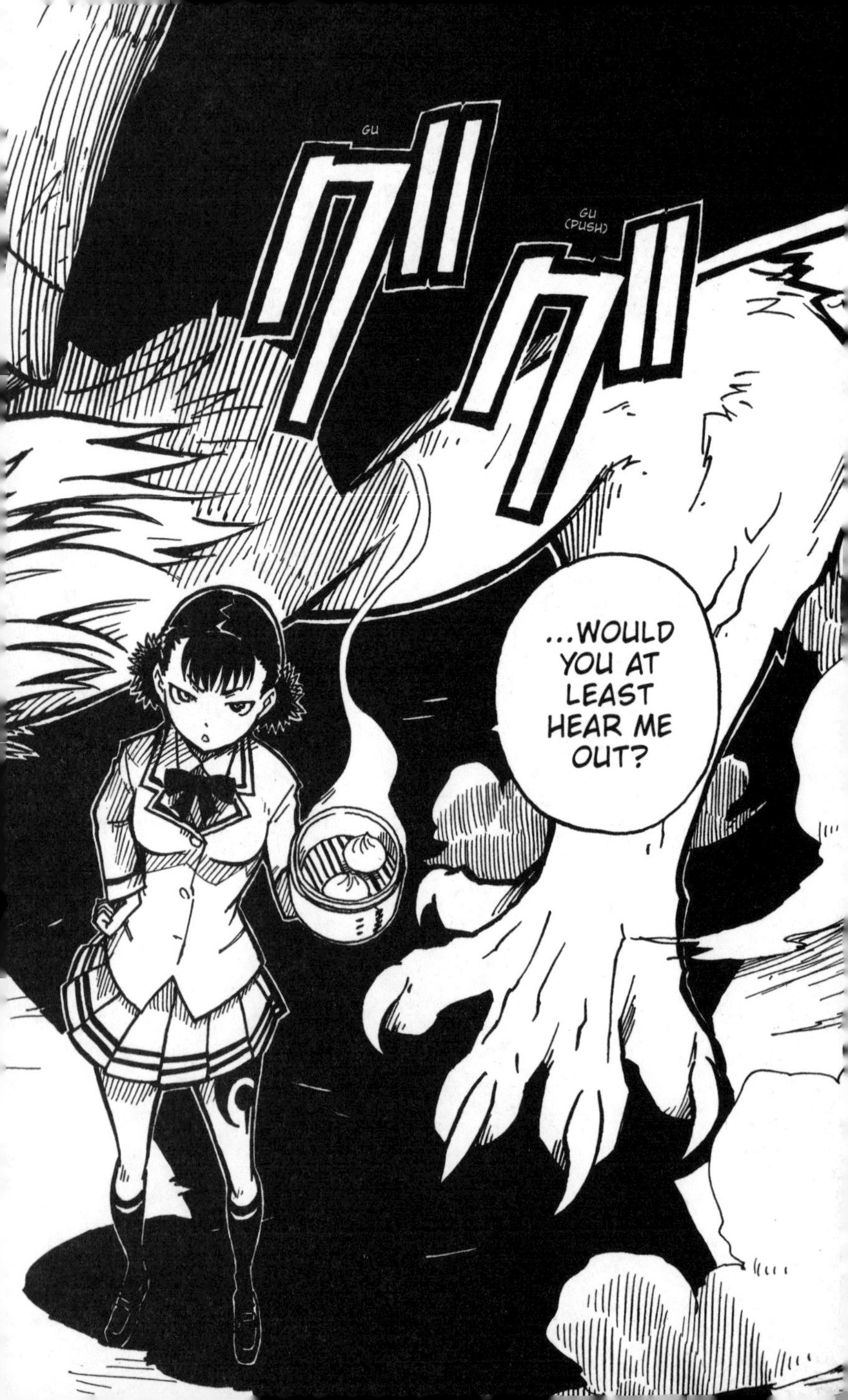
GU
GU (PUSH)
...WOULD YOU AT LEAST HEAR ME OUT?

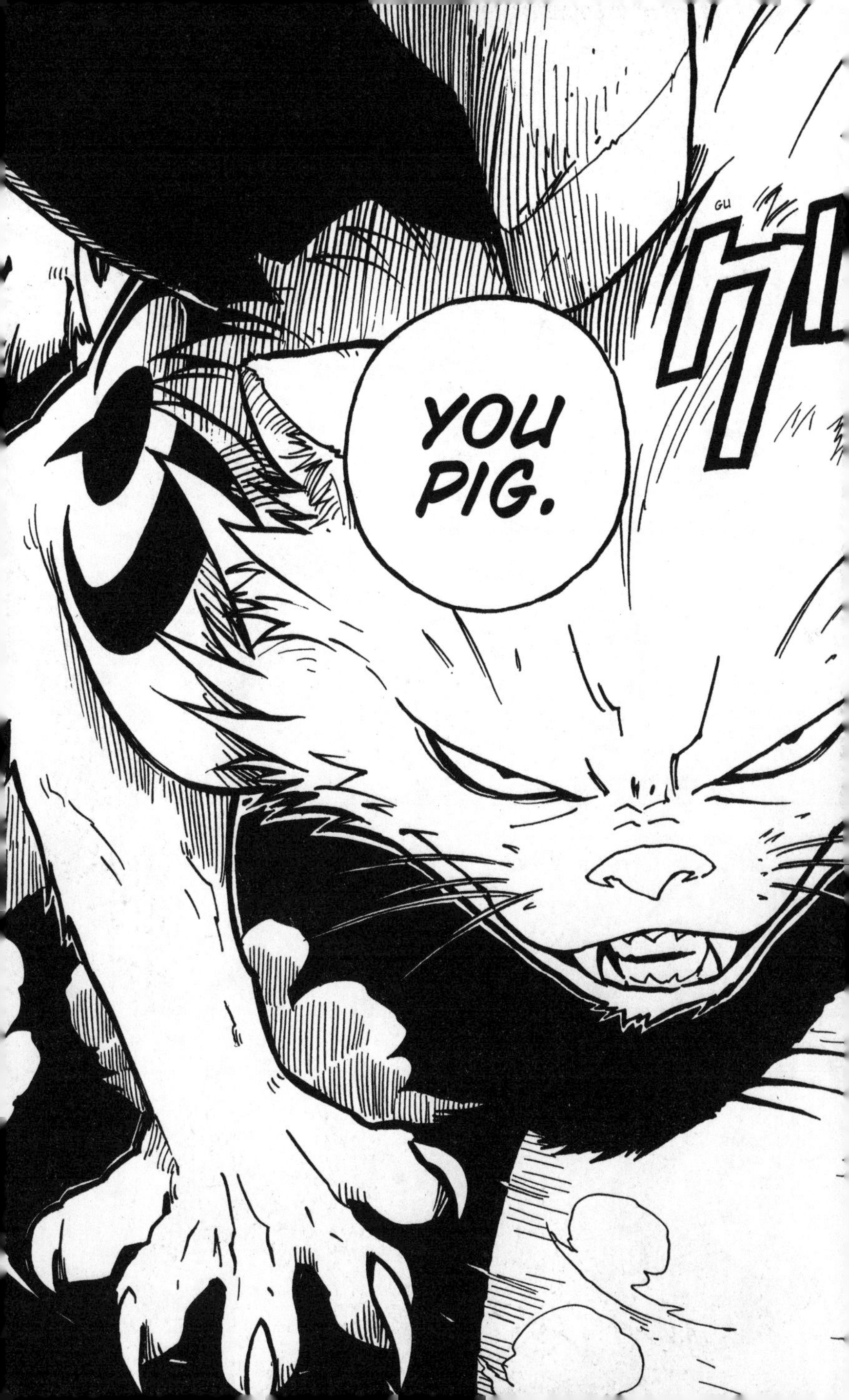
GU
YOU PIG.

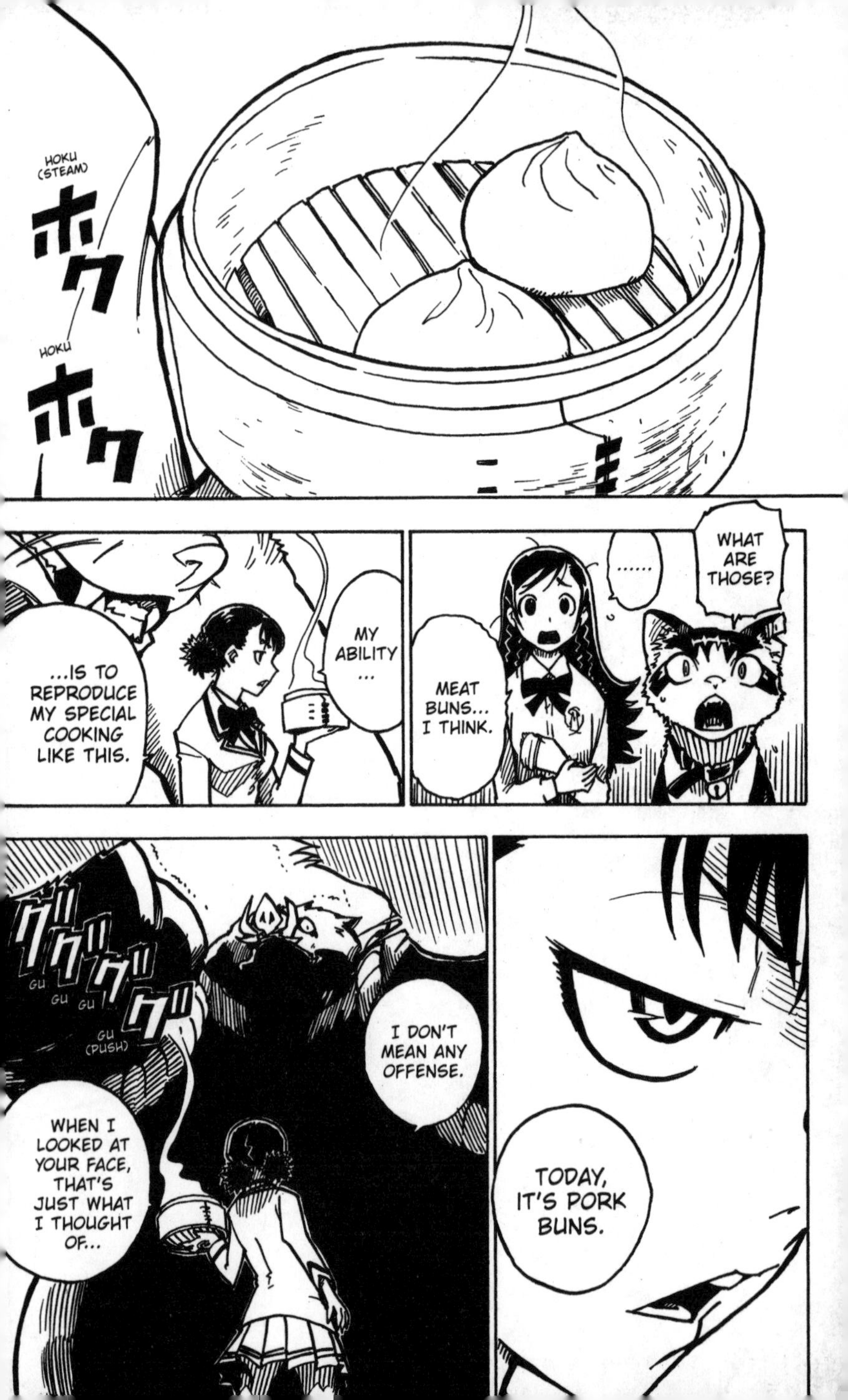
HOKU (STEAM)
ホク
HOKU
ホク
WHAT ARE THOSE?
......
MEAT BUNS... I THINK.
MY ABILITY...
...IS TO REPRODUCE MY SPECIAL COOKING LIKE THIS.
TODAY, IT'S PORK BUNS.
I DON'T MEAN ANY OFFENSE.
ググググ
GU GU GU GU (PUSH)
WHEN I LOOKED AT YOUR FACE, THAT'S JUST WHAT I THOUGHT OF...

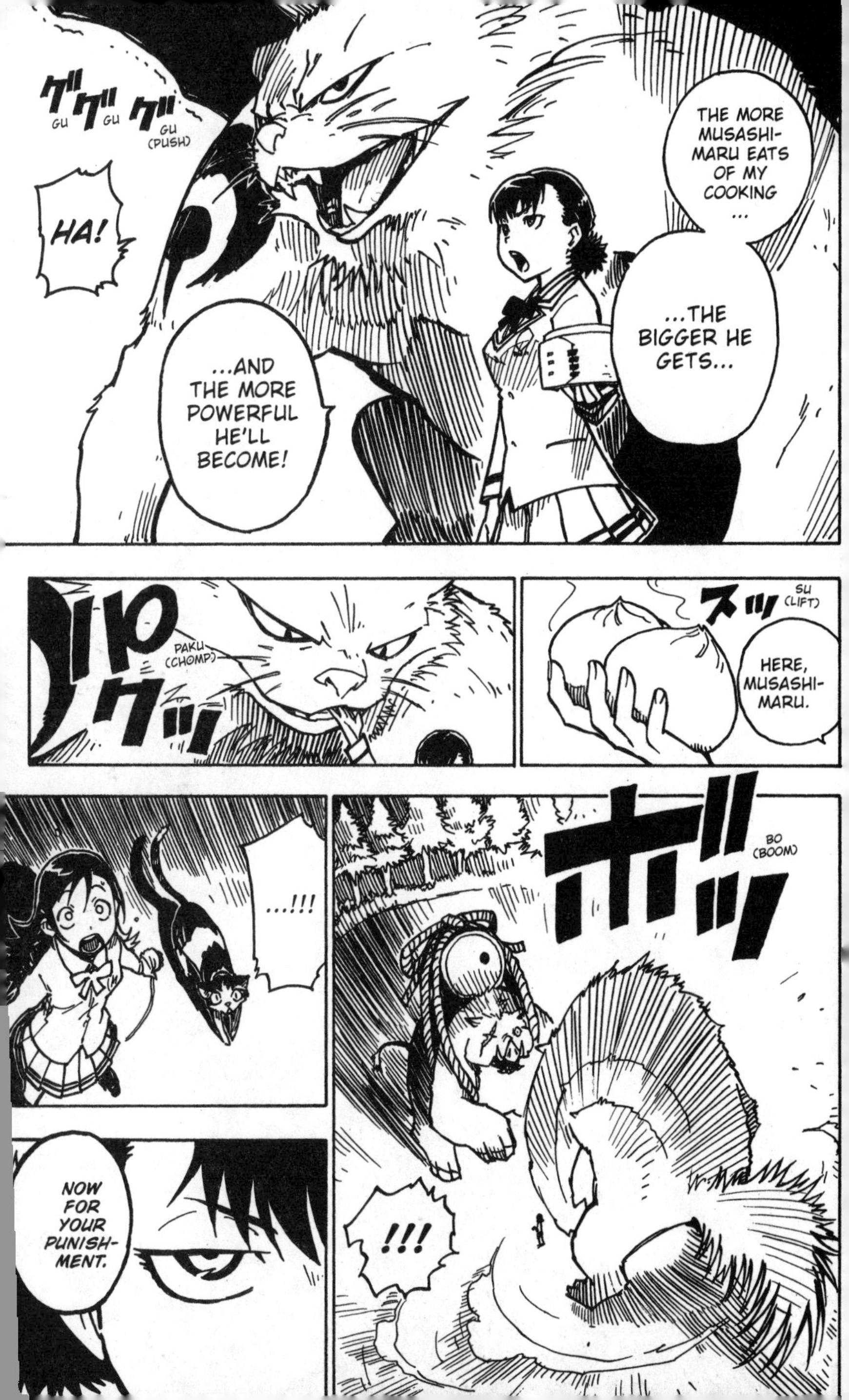
THE MORE MUSASHI-MARU EATS OF MY COOKING ...
...THE BIGGER HE GETS...
GU GU GU (PUSH)
HA!
...AND THE MORE POWERFUL HE'LL BECOME!
SU (LIFT)
HERE, MUSASHI-MARU.
PAKU (CHOMP)
BO (BOOM)
!!!
...!!!
NOW FOR YOUR PUNISHMENT.

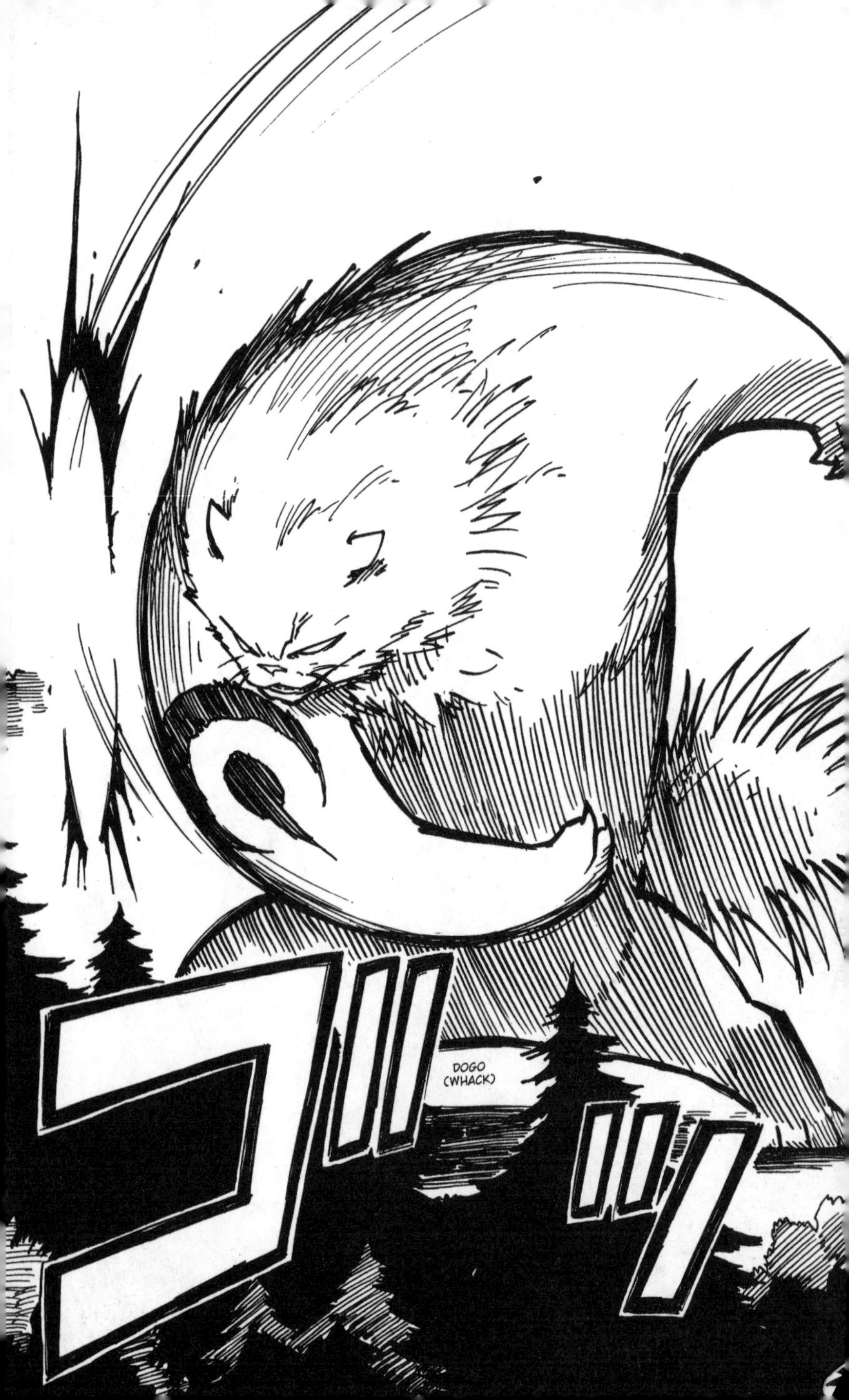
ゴッ
DOGO
(WHACK)

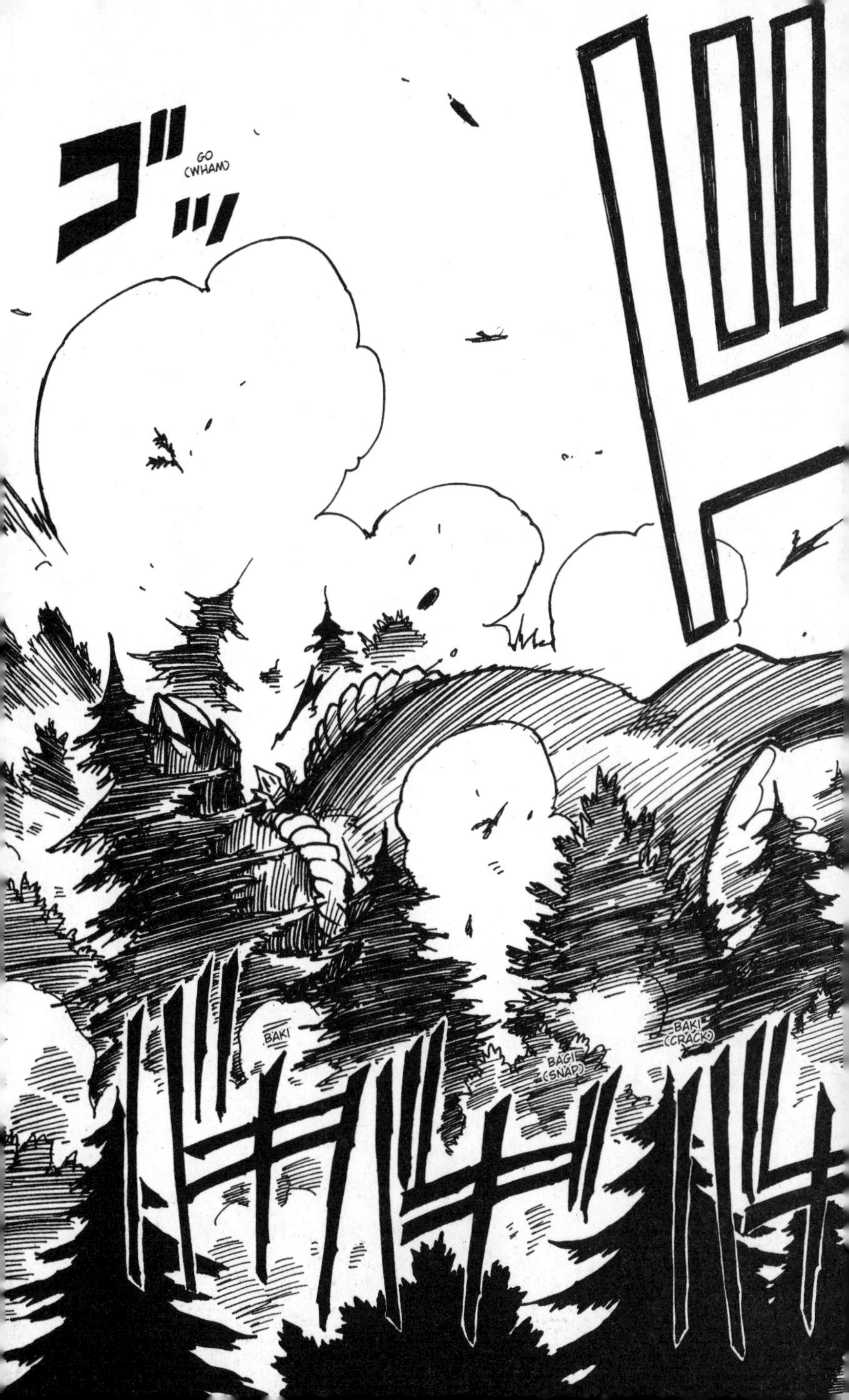
ゴッ
GO
(WHAM)
BAKI
BAKI
(CRACK)
BAGI
(SNAP)

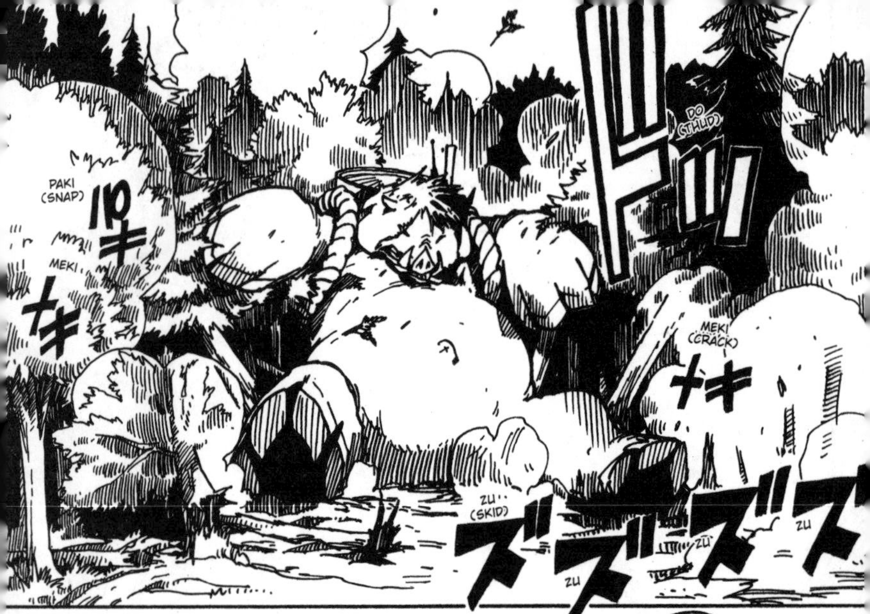
DO (THUD)
ドッ
MEKI (CRACK)
メキ
ZU (SKID)
ZU
ZU
ZU
ズズズズ
PAKI (SNAP)
パキ
MEKI
メキ

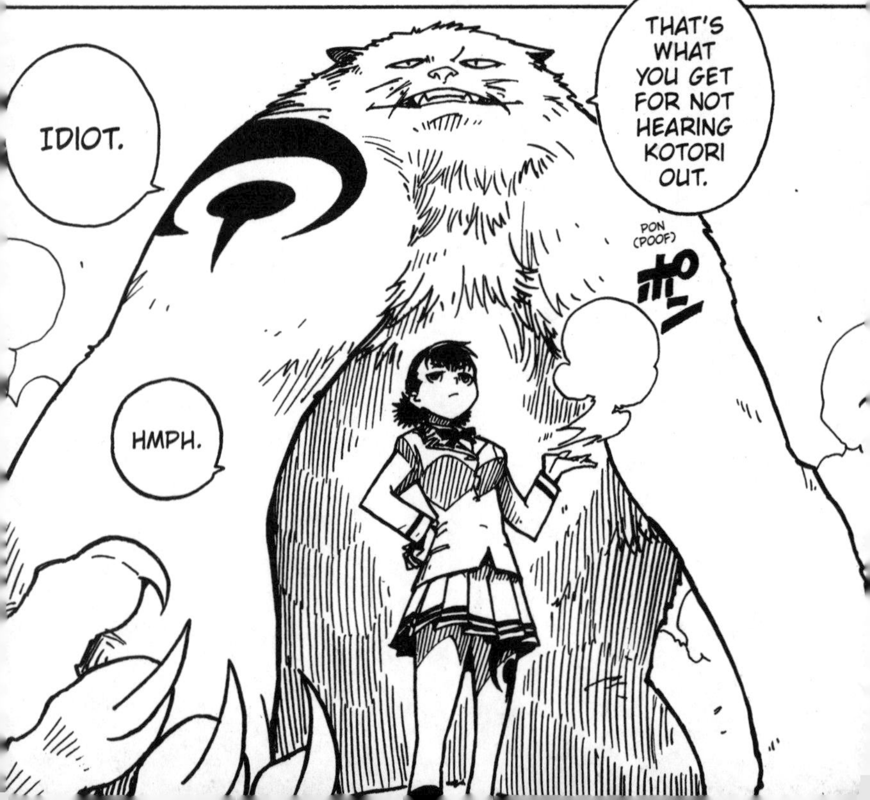
THAT'S WHAT YOU GET FOR NOT HEARING KOTORI OUT.
PON (POOF)
ポン
IDIOT.
HMPH.

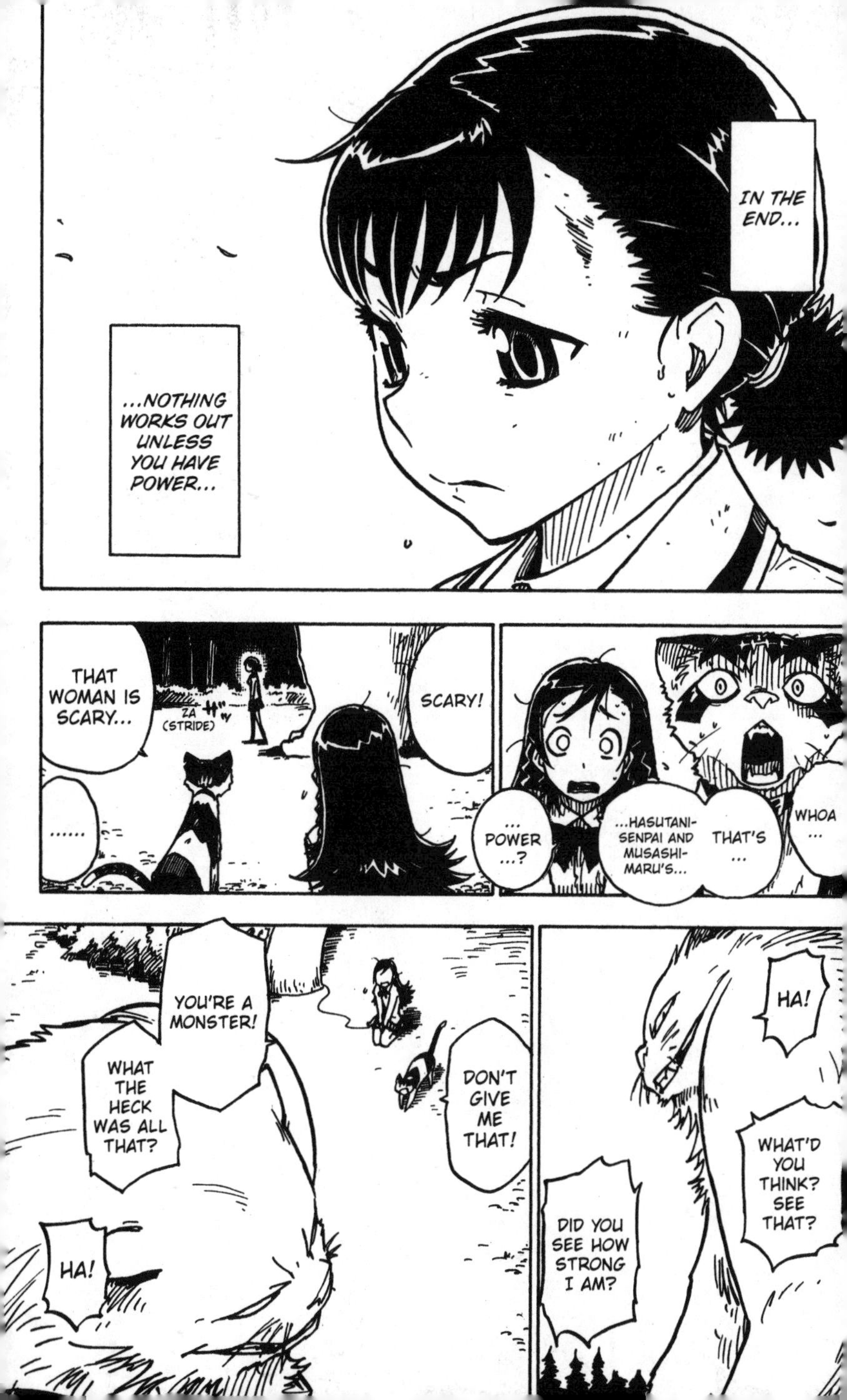
IN THE END...
...NOTHING WORKS OUT UNLESS YOU HAVE POWER...
WHOA...
THAT'S...
...HASUTANI-SENPAI AND MUSASHI-MARU'S...
...POWER...?
SCARY!
THAT WOMAN IS SCARY...
ZA (STRIDE)
......
HA!
WHAT'D YOU THINK? SEE THAT?
DID YOU SEE HOW STRONG I AM?
YOU'RE A MONSTER!
DON'T GIVE ME THAT!
WHAT THE HECK WAS ALL THAT?
HA!

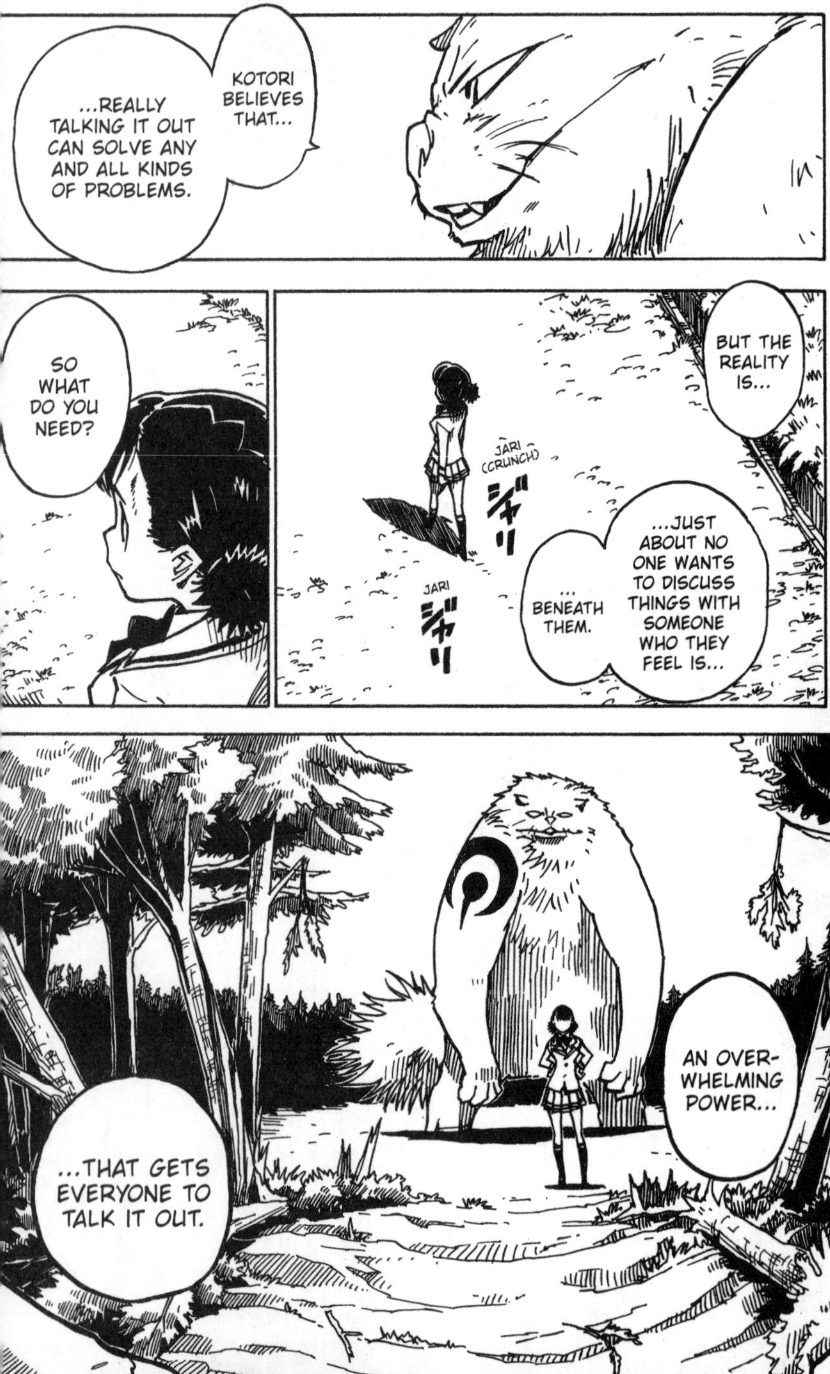
KOTORI BELIEVES THAT...
...REALLY TALKING IT OUT CAN SOLVE ANY AND ALL KINDS OF PROBLEMS.
BUT THE REALITY IS...
JARI (CRUNCH)
ジャリ
...JUST ABOUT NO ONE WANTS TO DISCUSS THINGS WITH SOMEONE WHO THEY FEEL IS...
... BENEATH THEM.
JARI
ジャリ
SO WHAT DO YOU NEED?
AN OVER-WHELMING POWER...
...THAT GETS EVERYONE TO TALK IT OUT.

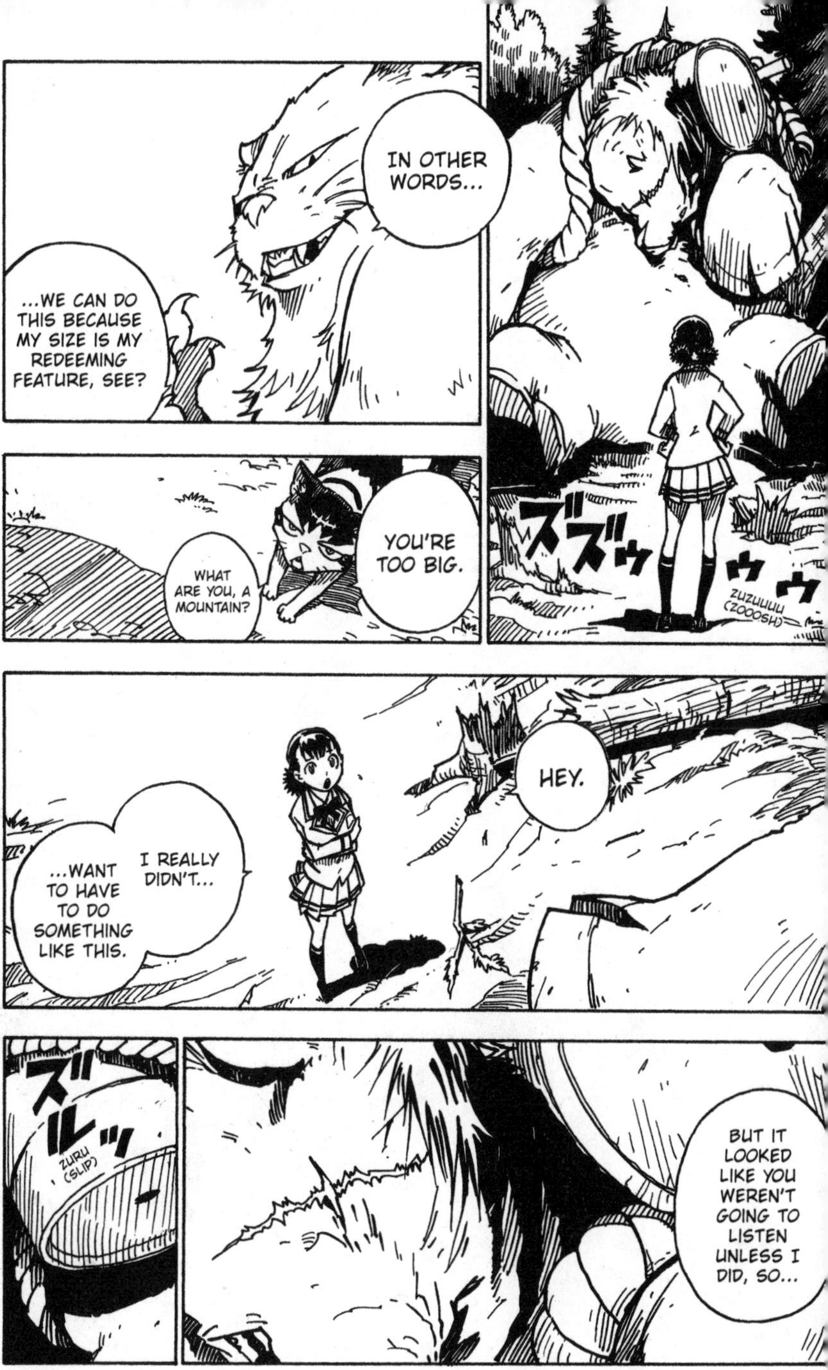
ズズゥゥゥ
ZUZUUUU (ZOOOSH)
IN OTHER WORDS...
...WE CAN DO THIS BECAUSE MY SIZE IS MY REDEEMING FEATURE, SEE?
YOU'RE TOO BIG.
WHAT ARE YOU, A MOUNTAIN?
HEY.
I REALLY DIDN'T...
...WANT TO HAVE TO DO SOMETHING LIKE THIS.
BUT IT LOOKED LIKE YOU WEREN'T GOING TO LISTEN UNLESS I DID, SO...
ズルッ
ZURU (SLIP)

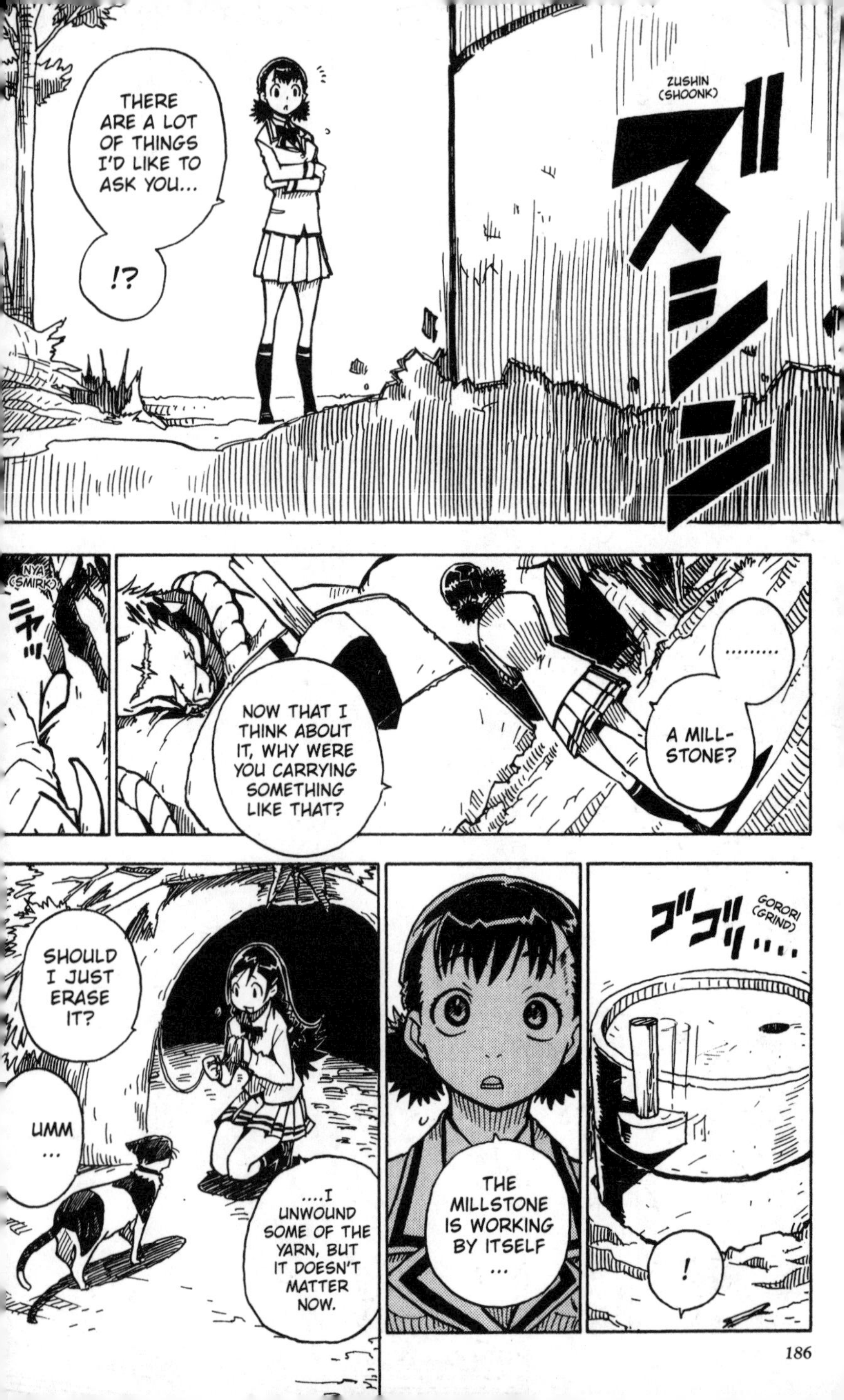
ZUSHIN (SHOONK)
THERE ARE A LOT OF THINGS I'D LIKE TO ASK YOU...
!?
....
A MILL-STONE?
NOW THAT I THINK ABOUT IT, WHY WERE YOU CARRYING SOMETHING LIKE THAT?
NYA (SMIRK)
GORORI (GRIND)
!
THE MILLSTONE IS WORKING BY ITSELF ...
SHOULD I JUST ERASE IT?
UMM ...
....I UNWOUND SOME OF THE YARN, BUT IT DOESN'T MATTER NOW.

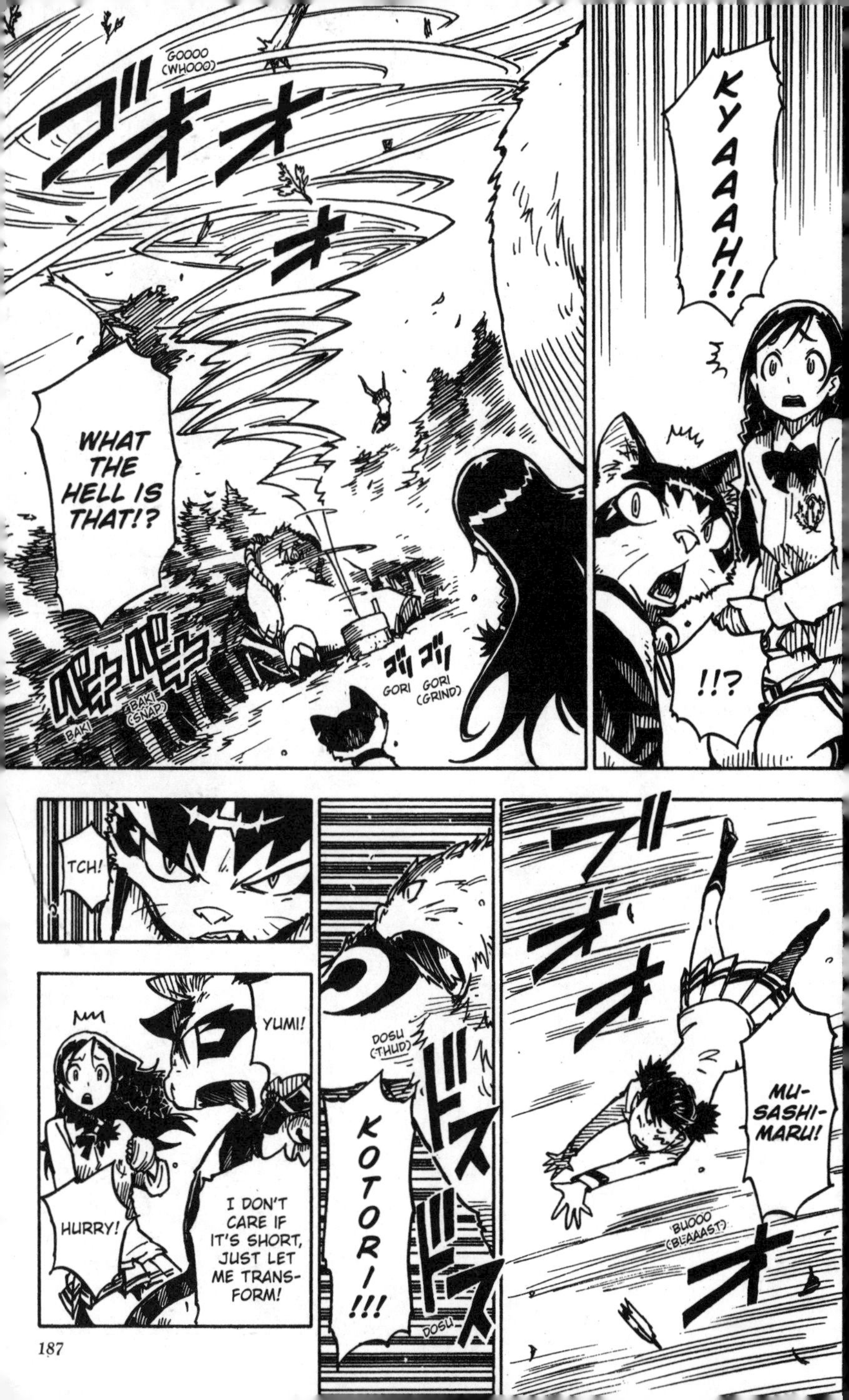
KYAAAAH!!
!!?
ゴオオオ
GOOOO (WHOOO)
WHAT THE HELL IS THAT!?
バキバキ
BAKI BAKI (SNAP)
ゴリゴリ
GORI GORI (GRIND)
ブオオオ
MU-SASHI-MARU!
BUOOO (BLAAAST)
ドスドス
DOSU (THUD)
KOTORI!!!
DOSU
TCH!
YUMI!
I DON'T CARE IF IT'S SHORT, JUST LET ME TRANS-FORM!
HURRY!

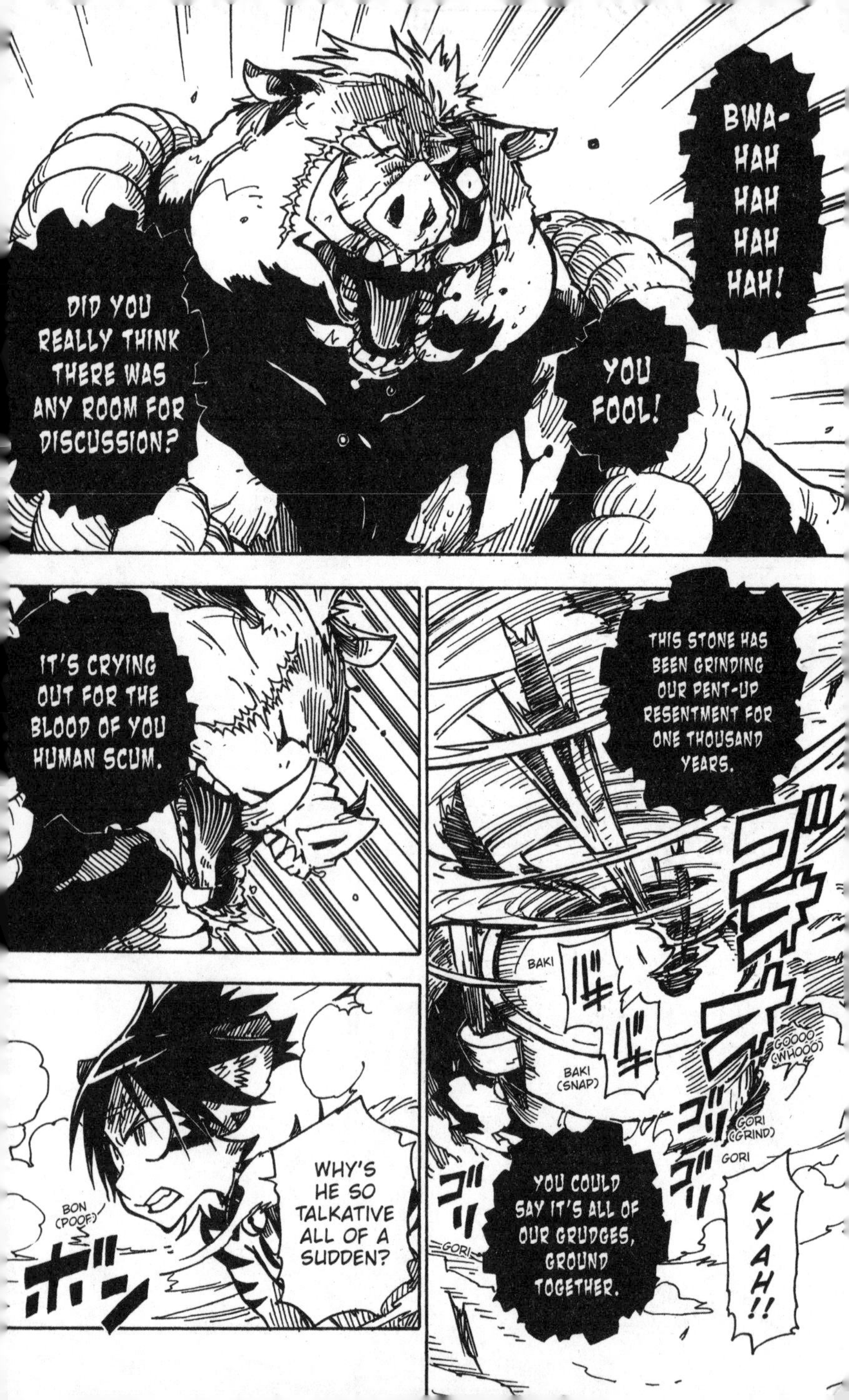
BWA-HAH HAH HAH HAH!
YOU FOOL!
DID YOU REALLY THINK THERE WAS ANY ROOM FOR DISCUSSION?
THIS STONE HAS BEEN GRINDING OUR PENT-UP RESENTMENT FOR ONE THOUSAND YEARS.
GOOOO (WHOOO)
BAKI
バキ
BAKI (SNAP)
バキ
ゴリ
GORI (GRIND)
ゴリ
GORI
KYAH!!
YOU COULD SAY IT'S ALL OF OUR GRUDGES, GROUND TOGETHER.
ゴリ
GORI
IT'S CRYING OUT FOR THE BLOOD OF YOU HUMAN SCUM.
WHY'S HE SO TALKATIVE ALL OF A SUDDEN?
BON (POOF)
ボン

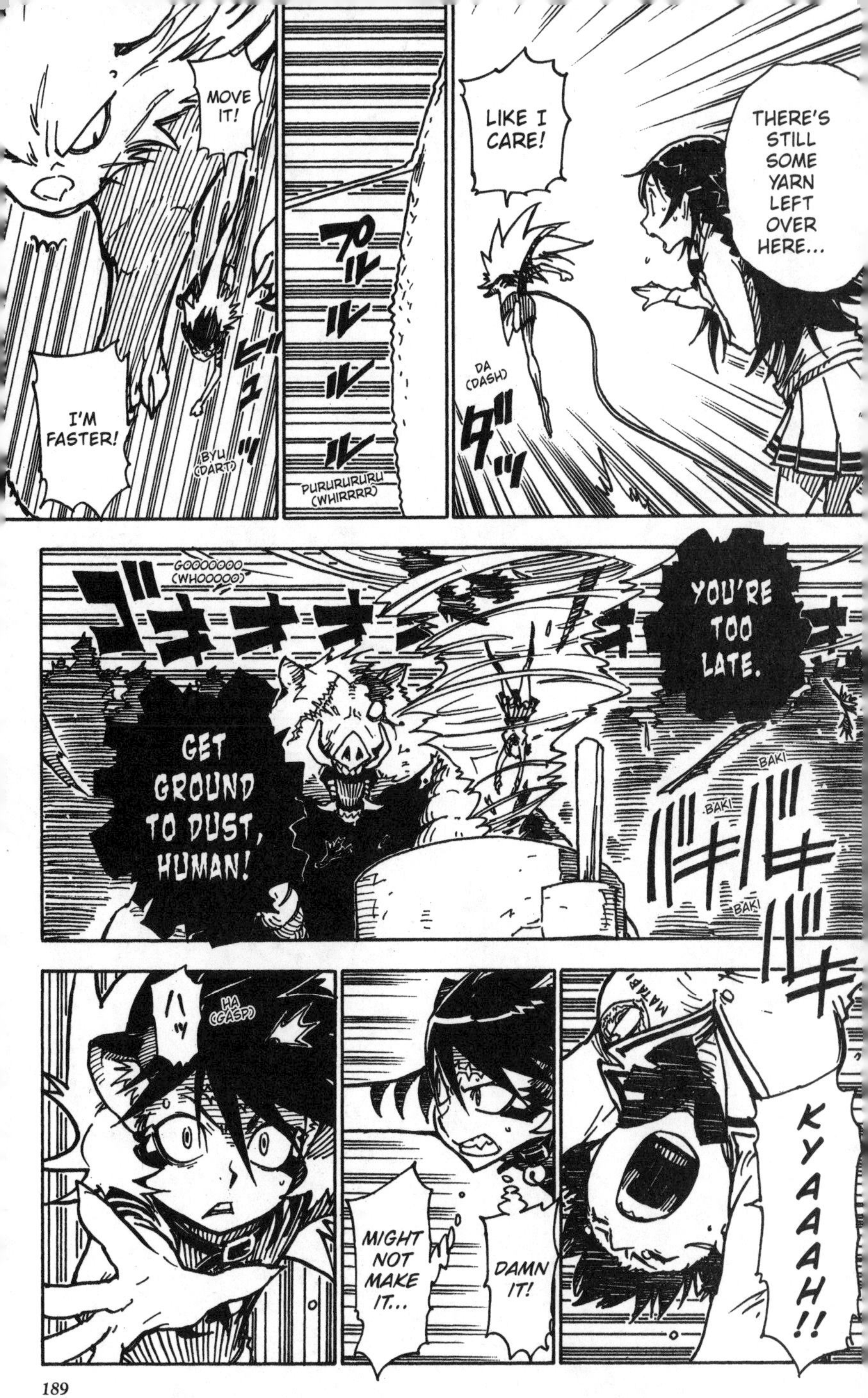
THERE'S STILL SOME YARN LEFT OVER HERE...
LIKE I CARE!
DA (DASH)
PURURURURU (WHIRRRR)
MOVE IT!
BYU (DART)
I'M FASTER!
YOU'RE TOO LATE.
GOOOOOOO (WHOOOOO)
GET GROUND TO DUST, HUMAN!
BAKI
BAKI
BAKI
KYAAAAH!!
DAMN IT!
MIGHT NOT MAKE IT...
HA (GASP)

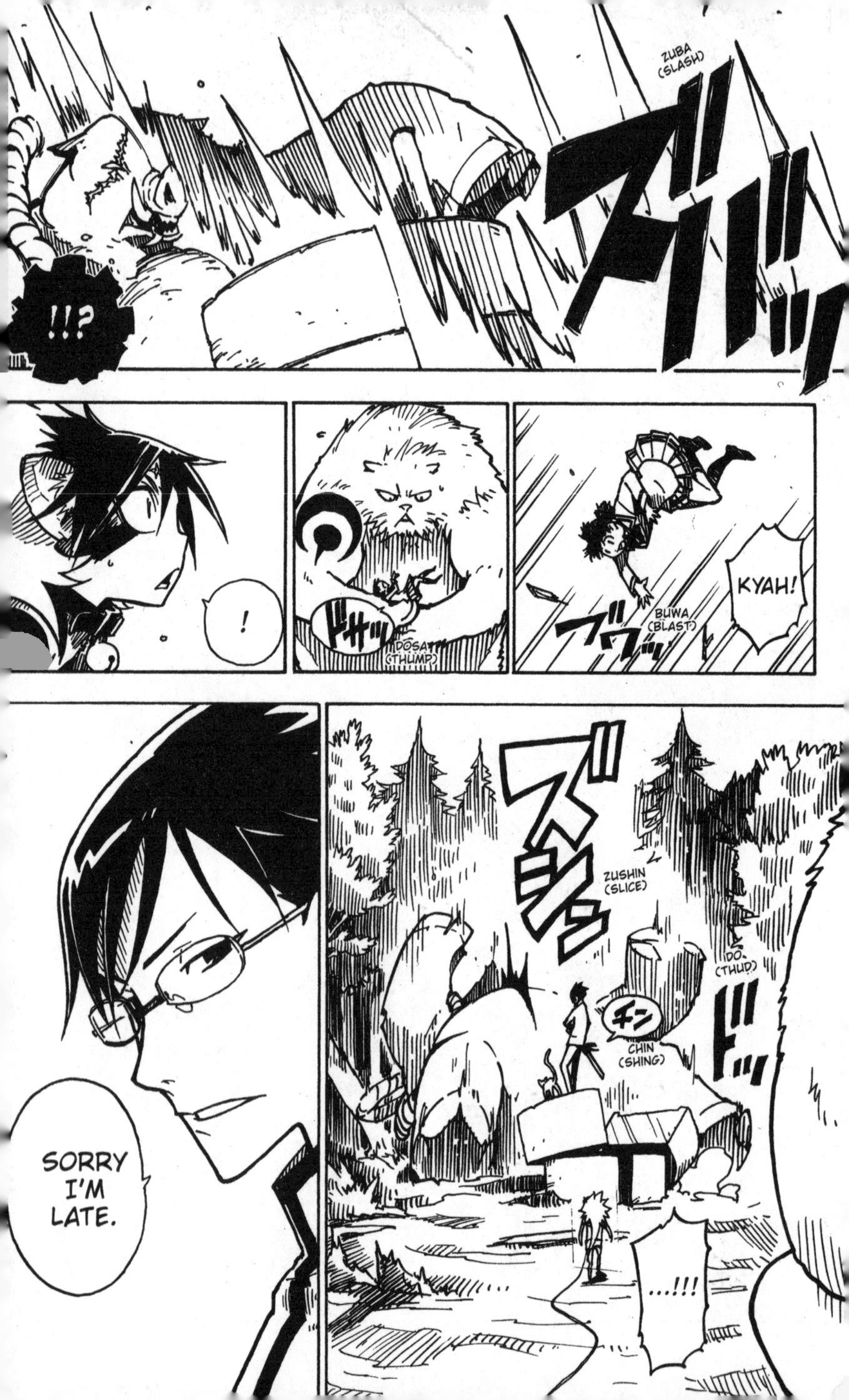
ZUBA (SLASH)
!!?
KYAH!
BUWA (BLAST)
DOSA (THUMP)
!
ZUSHIN (SLICE)
DO (THUD)
CHIN (SHING)
...!!!
SORRY I'M LATE.

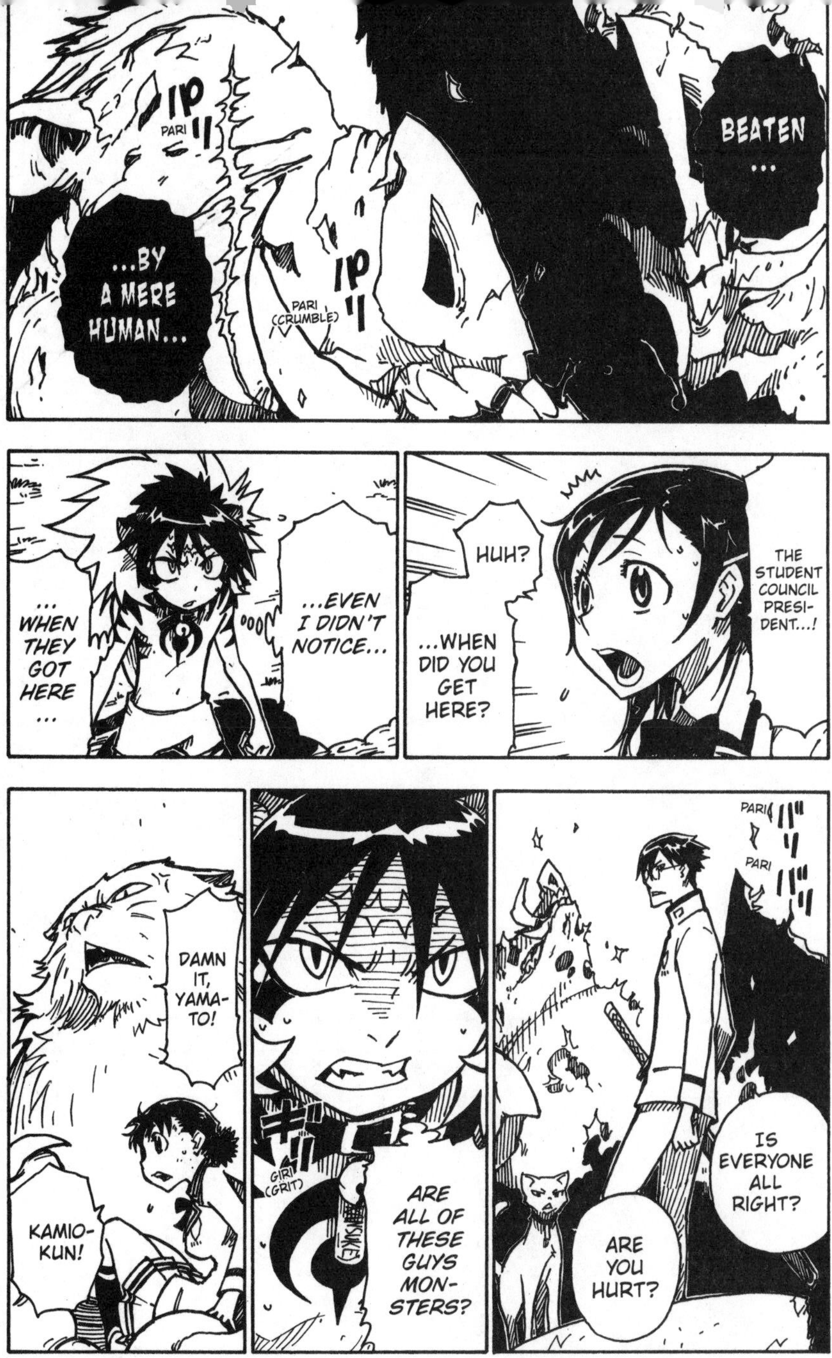
BEATEN...
PARI
...BY A MERE HUMAN...
PARI (CRUMBLE)
THE STUDENT COUNCIL PRESIDENT...!
HUH?
...WHEN DID YOU GET HERE?
...EVEN I DIDN'T NOTICE...
...WHEN THEY GOT HERE...
PARI
PARI
IS EVERYONE ALL RIGHT?
ARE YOU HURT?
GIRI (GRIT)
ARE ALL OF THESE GUYS MONSTERS?
DAMN IT, YAMATO!
KAMIO-KUN!

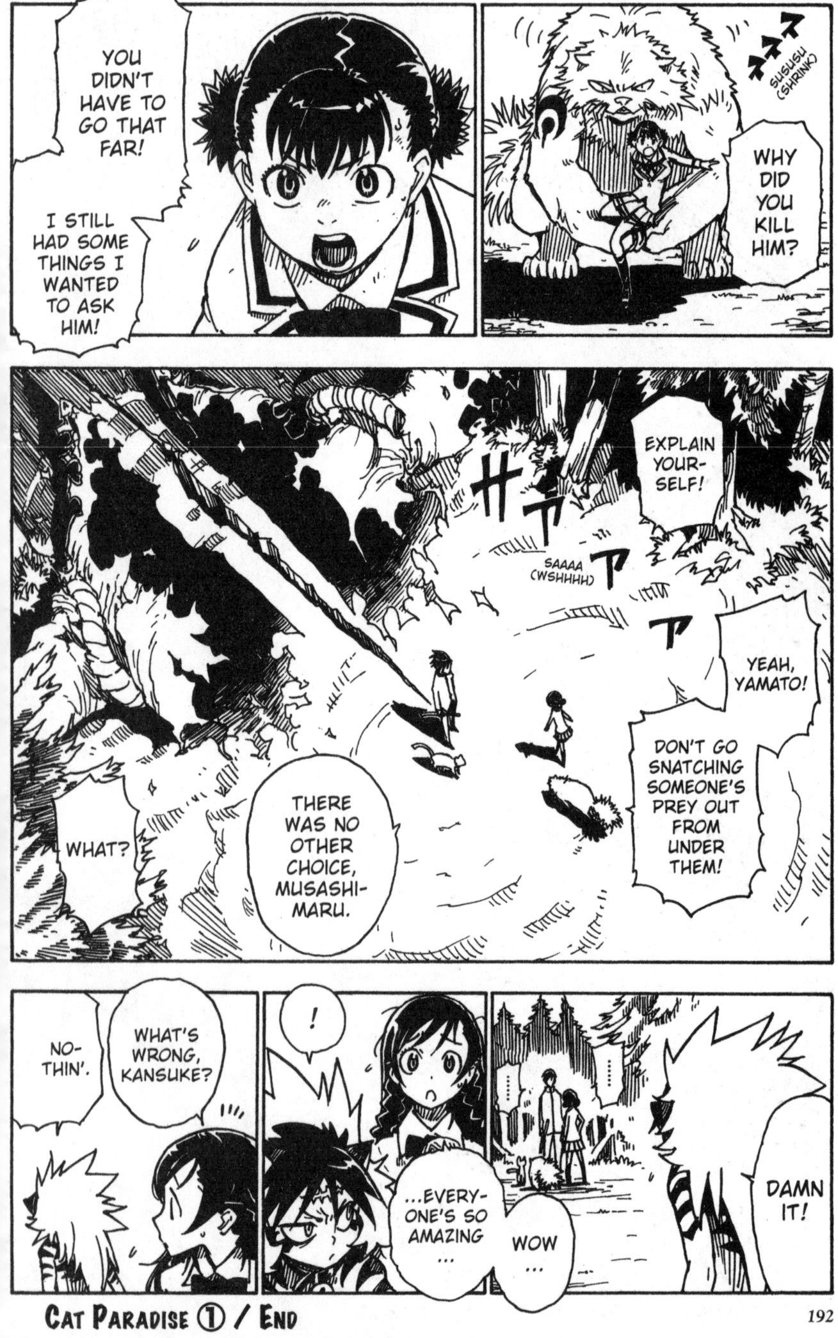
SUSUSU (SHRINK)
WHY DID YOU KILL HIM?
YOU DIDN'T HAVE TO GO THAT FAR!
I STILL HAD SOME THINGS I WANTED TO ASK HIM!
EXPLAIN YOURSELF!
SAAAA (WSHHHH)
YEAH, YAMATO!
DON'T GO SNATCHING SOMEONE'S PREY OUT FROM UNDER THEM!
THERE WAS NO OTHER CHOICE, MUSASHIMARU.
WHAT?
DAMN IT!
!
WOW ...
...EVERYONE'S SO AMAZING ...
WHAT'S WRONG, KANSUKE?
NOTHIN'.

CAT PARADISE ① / END

*APPARENTLY, IN MY PREVIOUS WORK (KING OF THORN), THERE WERE SOME PEOPLE WHO TOOK THE LAST BONUS SECTION TO BE THE REAL ENDING OF THE MAIN STORY. SO JUST TO BE SAFE...

THIS SECTION HAS ABSOLUTELY NOTHING TO DO WITH THE MAIN STORY!

THE CUSTOMARY BONUS PAGE

CAT PARADISE BEHIND THE SCENES!

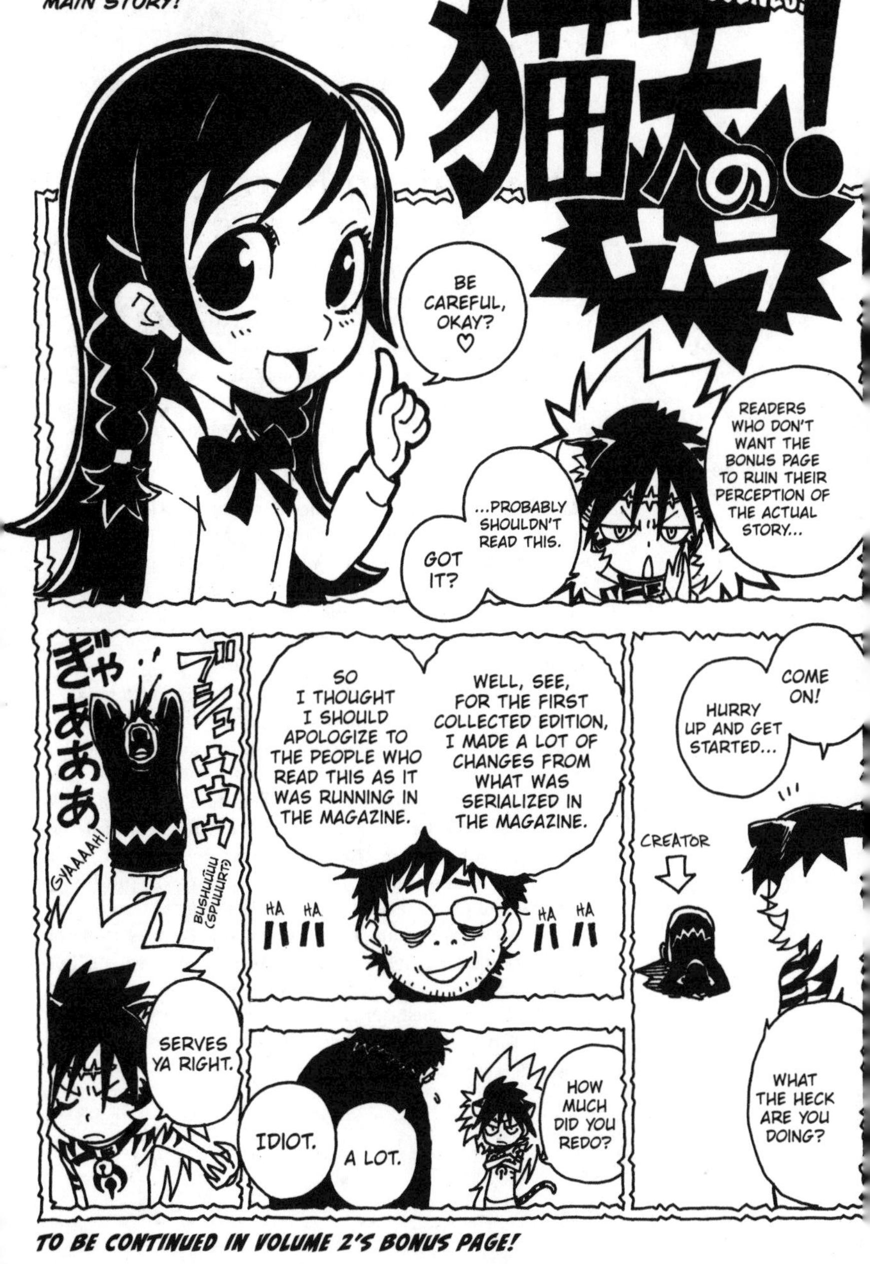
猫天!のウラ
READERS WHO DON'T WANT THE BONUS PAGE TO RUIN THEIR PERCEPTION OF THE ACTUAL STORY...
...PROBABLY SHOULDN'T READ THIS.
GOT IT?
BE CAREFUL, OKAY? ♡
COME ON!
HURRY UP AND GET STARTED...
CREATOR
WHAT THE HECK ARE YOU DOING?
WELL, SEE, FOR THE FIRST COLLECTED EDITION, I MADE A LOT OF CHANGES FROM WHAT WAS SERIALIZED IN THE MAGAZINE.
SO I THOUGHT I SHOULD APOLOGIZE TO THE PEOPLE WHO READ THIS AS IT WAS RUNNING IN THE MAGAZINE.
HA HA
HA HA
HOW MUCH DID YOU REDO?
A LOT.
IDIOT.
ブシュウウウ
BUSHUUUU (SPUUURT)
ぎゃあああ
GYAAAAH!
SERVES YA RIGHT.

TO BE CONTINUED IN VOLUME 2'S BONUS PAGE!

Translation Notes

Pg. 4

Nekomata is a two-tailed demon cat. In Japanese folklore, when a cat reaches a certain age or size, if it is fed in a certain place for a long time, or if the tail reaches a certain length, it will become a *bakeneko*, or "ghost cat." In some cases, the tail may fork in two, making it a *nekomata*. The cat thus gains supernatural powers, such as the ability to shape-shift, reanimate the dead, and create fireballs.

Pg. 7

Matabi is written with the same character used for the *mata* in *nekomata*. The second character, *bi*, means "beauty." However, there is a different character, also pronounced *bi*, which means "tail." Thus, the *Matabi* name itself could be seen as a reference to the two tails of the *nekomata*.

Pg. 164

The Tale of the Bamboo Cutter, called *Taketori Monogatari* in Japanese and sometimes called *The Tale of Princess Kaguya*, is one of the oldest Japanese folktales. It revolves around an old, poor, and childless bamboo cutter who discovers a tiny baby no bigger than his thumb inside a stalk of bamboo. The baby's name is Princess Kaguya, and she comes from the moon. The old man and his wife raise her as their own, and the princess grows into a woman of normal size and great beauty. She attracts the attention of five princes who each want to marry her, but Princess Kaguya is reluctant and assigns them impossible tasks to win her hand. Eventually, the princess reveals that she is not of this world and must return from whence she came. After writing sad letters of apology, she is taken back up to the heavens.

CREATOR
COMMENTARY

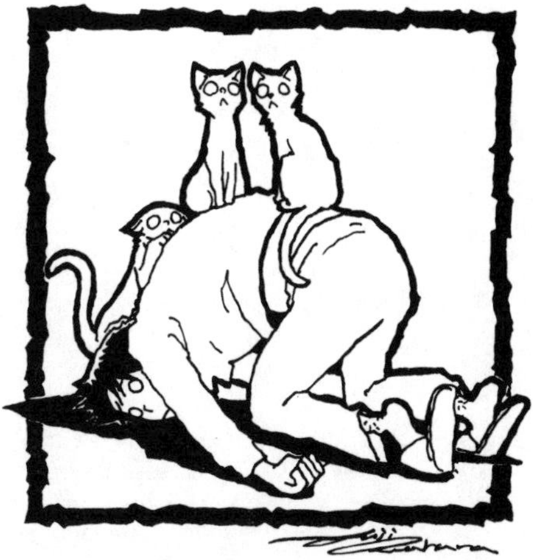

Though I usually go for big, grand themes when I draw manga, this time I went back to the most basic of the basics—a school setting. Then I added another old standard—talking animals (cats)—to turn it into a fantasy-styled story that reads like an anime! I hope you enjoy what I've come up with!

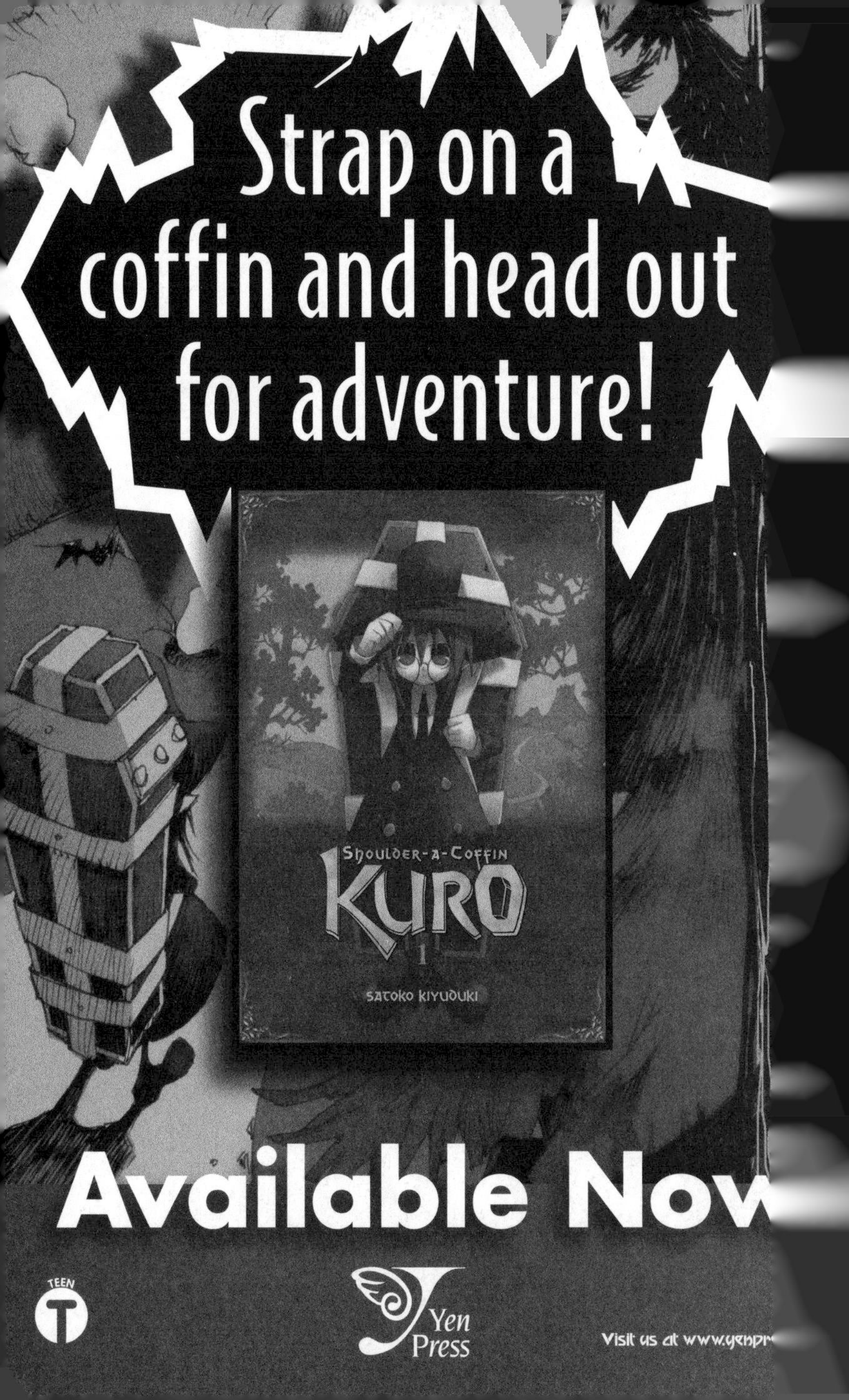

Strap on a coffin and head out for adventure!
Shoulder-a-Coffin
KURO
1
SATOKO KIYUDUKI
Available Now
TEEN
T
Yen Press
Visit us at www.yenpr

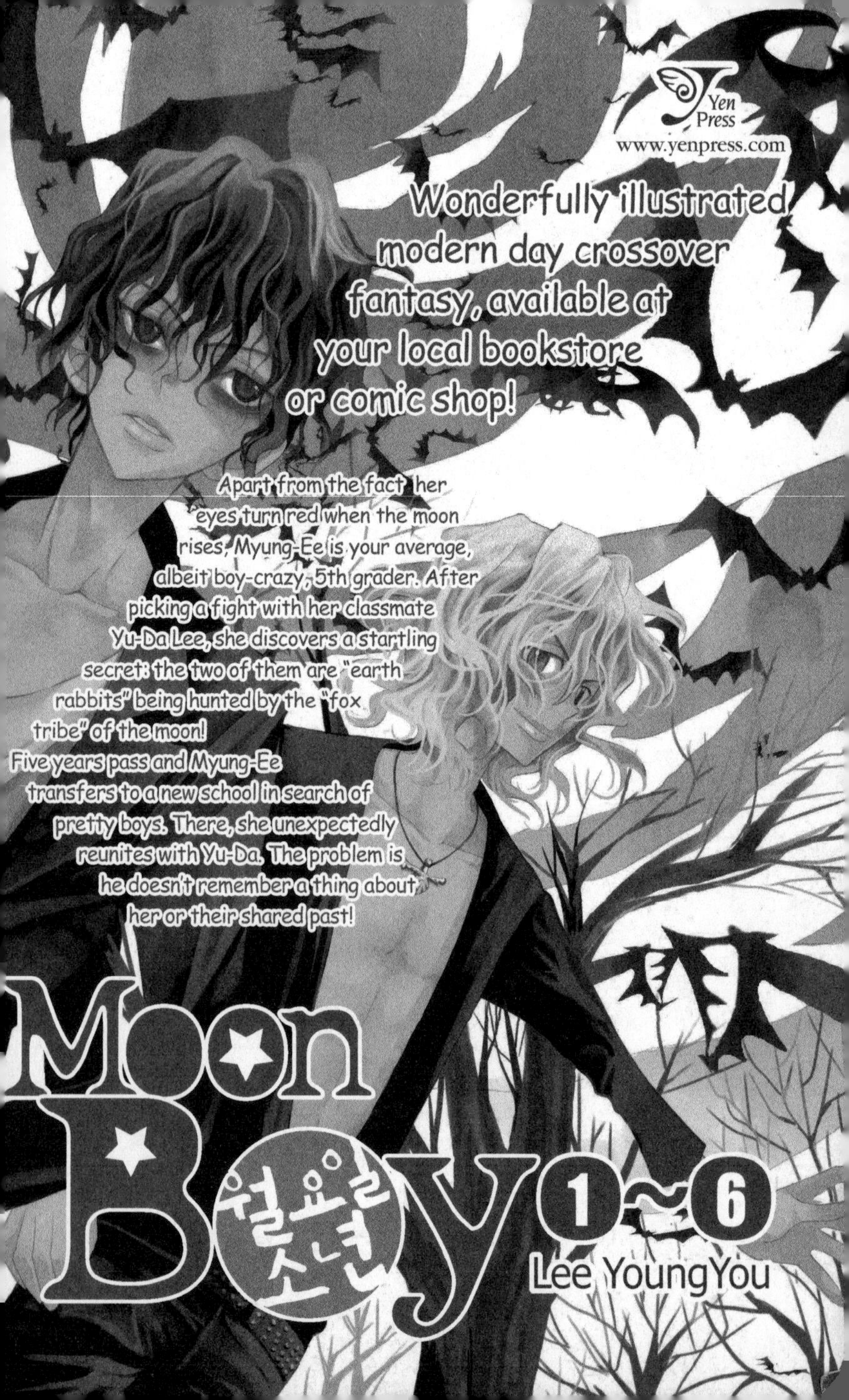
Yen Press
www.yenpress.com
Wonderfully illustrated modern day crossover fantasy, available at your local bookstore or comic shop!
Apart from the fact her eyes turn red when the moon rises, Myung-Ee is your average, albeit boy-crazy, 5th grader. After picking a fight with her classmate Yu-Da Lee, she discovers a startling secret: the two of them are "earth rabbits" being hunted by the "fox tribe" of the moon! Five years pass and Myung-Ee transfers to a new school in search of pretty boys. There, she unexpectedly reunites with Yu-Da. The problem is he doesn't remember a thing about her or their shared past!
Moon Boy
월요일 소년
1~6
Lee YoungYou

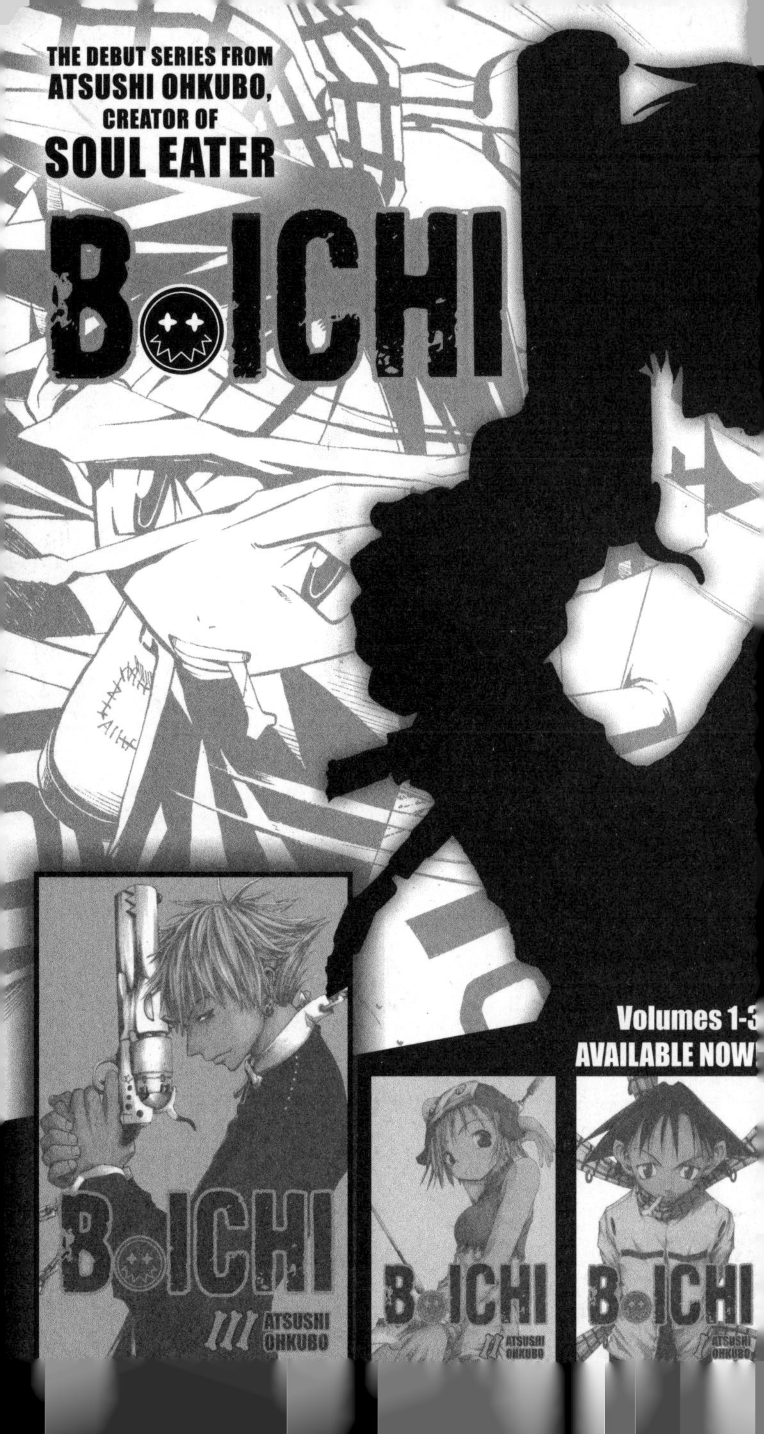
THE DEBUT SERIES FROM
ATSUSHI OHKUBO,
CREATOR OF
SOUL EATER
B ICHI
Volumes 1-3
AVAILABLE NOW!
B ICHI
III
ATSUSHI
OHKUBO
B ICHI
II
ATSUSHI
OHKUBO
B ICHI
ATSUSHI
OHKUBO

The newest title from the creators of <Demon Diary> and <Angel Diary>!

Once upon a time, a selfish king summoned the monstrous Bulkirin into the real world. The monster killed half of all human beings, leaving the rest helpless as to what to do. That is, until one day when a hero appeared and defeated the Bulkirin with the legendary "Seven Blade Sword." But...what does all this have to do with 8th grader Eun-Gyo Sung?! First, she gets suspended from school for fighting. Then, she runs away from home. The last thing she needed was to be kidnapped—and whisked into the past by a mysterious stranger named No-Ah!

Available at bookstores near you!

Legend

1-5

K a r a · W o o S o o J u n g

CAT PARADISE ❶ JAN 2010
Yuji Iwahara

Translation: Amy Forsyth

Lettering: Alexis Eckerman

GAKUEN SOUSEI NEKOTEN! Vol. 1 © 2007 Yuji Iwahara. All rights reserved. First published in Japan in 2007 by Akita Publishing Co., Ltd., Tokyo. English translation rights arranged with Akita Publishing Co., Ltd. through Tuttle-Mori Agency, Inc., Tokyo.

English translation © 2009 by Hachette Book Group, Inc.

Yen Press
Hachette Book Group
237 Park Avenue, New York, NY 10017

Visit our Web sites at www.HachetteBookGroup.com and www.YenPress.com.

Yen Press is an imprint of Hachette Book Group, Inc. The Yen Press name and logo are trademarks of Hachette Book Group, Inc.

First Yen Press Edition: July 2009

ISBN: 978-0-7595-2923-6

10 9 8 7 6 5 4 3 2 1

BVG

Printed in the United States of America